Gertrude Jekyll

GERTRUDE JEKYLL

essays on the life of a working amateur

Edited by
Michael Tooley and Primrose Arnander

Michaelmas Books

Published by Michaelmas Books
The Old Vicarage, Witton-le-Wear,
Co. Durham DL14 0AN, England.

First published 1995

Typeset in Bembo
Designed and Produced by David Jobson Designs
01904 659091

British Library Cataloguing in Publication Data
Tooley, M.J.
Gertrude Jekyll: Essays on the Life of a Working Amateur
I. Title II. Arnander, Primrose
635.092

ISBN 0 946426 06 6

Contents

Illustrations and Tables

Contributors

Heather Angel is a professional, peripatetic photographer of wildlife, plants and gardens. Among her many illustrated books are several on photographic techniques, including *Photographing the Natural World*, one on garden design, *A View From a Window*, and one on plants, *Kew: a World of Plants*. From 1984–6 she was President of the Royal Photographic Society, and in 1994 was appointed Professor in the Life Science Department of Nottingham University.

Primrose Arnander is Gertrude Jekyll's great great niece and the second daughter of David McKenna whose grandfather was Sir Herbert Jekyll. She studied the 'cello at the Royal College of Music. She is married with four children, and lives in London. Whilst living in the Middle East between 1973 and 1985 she co-edited two illustrated books of Arabic Proverbs.

Mavis Batey is the President of the Garden History Society and was Honorary Secretary from 1973 to 1985. She contributed the biography of Gertrude Jekyll in the *Dictionary of National Biography: Missing Persons*. She has been a pioneer in the conservation of historic parks and gardens. She has written books on *Oxford Gardens, The Historic Gardens of Oxford and Cambridge, The English Garden Tour* (with David Lambert) and *Arcadian Thames*.

Richard Bisgrove is Senior Lecturer in the Department of Horticulture and Landscape in the University of Reading. He studied Horticultural Science at Reading and Landscape Architecture at the University of Michigan, then worked briefly as a landscape architect in Florida. His main research interest is the garden designs of Gertrude Jekyll. He was a member of the Council of the Garden History Society and is currently a member of the Gardens Panel of the National Trust of England and Wales. He has written six books, including a seminal volume on *The Gardens of Gertrude Jekyll*.

Joan Edwards was born in Auckland, New Zealand. She studied embroidery at Hammersmith College of Art and from 1968 until 1978 she lectured in embroidery for the Education Department of the Victoria and Albert Museum. She has written books on *Bead Embroidery and Crewel Embroidery in England*. She has written and published a series of *Small Books on the History of Embroidery* which includes *Berlin Work, Black Work, Sample Making* and *Gertrude Jekyll – Embroiderer, Gardener and Craftsman*. In 1993, she was invited to give the Richardson lecture in the Museum of Garden History to mark the 150th anniversary of the birth of Gertrude Jekyll, and published the lecture in the Small Books series with the title *Gertrude Jekyll: Before the Boots, the Gardens and the Portrait*.

Paul Everson is a field archaeologist and the Head of the Keele Office of the Royal Commission on the Historical Monuments of England. He developed an interest in historic gardens through surveying the earthwork remains of early gardens, such as those at Chipping Campden, Gloucesershire (*Garden History* **17**(2), 109-21; *Garden Archaeology* ed. A.E. Brown).

Rudy Favretti is Professor of Landscape Design in the University of Connecticut, Storrs, Connecticut, U.S.A.

Annabel Freyberg is a great great niece of Gertrude Jekyll and eldest daughter of the second Lord Freyberg, whose grandfather was Sir Herbert Jekyll. She is a graduate of the University of Oxford and Kingston Polytechnic, and is the Chief Copy Editor of *World of Interiors*.

Fenja Gunn was trained as an artist and now specialises in watercolour paintings of gardens. She is a contributor to *Country Life* and *The Garden,* and is author and illustrator of *Lost Gardens of Gertrude Jekyll*.

Margaret Hastings is a graduate of the University of Durham. She is music and social work librarian at Kingston University, and is a keen gardener.

David McKenna is a great nephew of Gertrude Jekyll, grandson of Sir Herbert Jekyll, and son of Pamela and Reginald McKenna. He was a member of the British Railways Board, Chairman and General Manager of Southern Railway. He was Chairman of the Bach Choir and of Sadlers Wells and a member of the Council and Honorary Secretary of the Royal College of Music.

Susan Schnare is a graduate of the University of Connecticut, and the University of York, where she graduated with a doctorate from the Institute of Advanced Architectural Studies. Her research interests include Gertrude Jekyll's gardens in the United States of America and rock gardens in England.

June Swann was Keeper of the Boot and Shoe Collection, Northampton Museum from 1950-1988 and is a consultant on the History of Shoes and Shoemaking. She is the author of *Shoes and Shoemaking*.

Michael Tooley is Professor of Geography at the University of St Andrews, and lately of the University of Durham. He is author and editor of several books and articles on Gertrude Jekyll.

Martin Wood was trained as a textile designer. He now specialises in garden design and contributes articles to *The Garden* and chapters in books on garden history and design, with particular reference to Gertrude Jekyll.

Acknowledgments

It is a great pleasure for us to acknowledge with warmth and gratitude the constant help, support, encouragement and forbearance of Christopher Arnander and Rosanna Tooley, without whom this project would not have been successfully completed.

We are most grateful to David Jobson who has designed and produced the book, selected the typeface and integrated the artwork so effectively with the text.

The majority of the text has been word processed by Mrs. Alison Wilkinson at the University of Durham, and at a late stage in the preparation of the text for the printer Mrs. Joan Andrews and Miss Lisa Tempest at Durham and Mrs. Florence McAndie at the University of St. Andrews ensured that all the final adjustments were made. Most of the copy photographs were made by Miss Michele Johnson at Durham, but others were made by Richard Greenly and Rodney Todd-White. We are most grateful to them for their help.

There are many individual acknowledgements, and the mention of a name, in many cases, conceals the debt of gratitude we owe for the unstinted work they have undertaken; but we thank them all most warmly, and hope that this book, in small measure, rewards their effort: Mr. Steven Allan, Miss Katharine Arnander, Mr. Conrad Arnander, Mr. Michael Arnander, Mr. Henry Baker, Mrs. Jane Brown, Mrs. Joan Charman, Sir Robert and Lady Clark, Mr. Arthur Corner, Mr. James Cousins, Mr. Oliver Davies, Mr. William Drummond, Mrs. Elizabeth Gilpin, Sir Andrew Duff Gordon, Mrs. Sally Festing, Lady Freyberg, Mr. Simon Houfe, Mr. Derek Hudspeth, Mr. David Hume, Mrs. Vicky Innes, Miss Michele Johnson, Mrs. Mary Links, Mrs. Martin McLaren, Baron Imre von Maltzahn, Mrs. Hannah Mellor, Mrs. Rosemary Nicholson, Mr. Sebastian Nohl, Dr. Alan Pearson, Lady Peel, The Viscount Ridley, Mrs. Judith Tankard, Mrs. Peggy Tracey, Mrs. Jennifer Vine.

Mr. Paul Everson wishes to make specific acknowledgements: Mr. J F T Albury; members of the Surrey Gardens Trust; members of the Munstead Wood Working Party (Peter Goodchild, Stephen King, Brenda Lewis, Judith Tankard, Michael Tooley and Martin Wood), the owners of Munstead Wood and adjacent properties (Sir Robert and Lady Clark, Mrs. M. Collins, Mr. & Mrs. G. Robinson and Mrs. J. Woodington) who allowed access to the survey team. The RCHME staff responsible for the work were Sid Barker, Mr. Wayne Cockcroft, Mr. Paul Everson, Paul Struth and Paul Sinton.

Illustrations

©Elizabeth Banks, Figure 13.4.

©Country Life Picture Library, Figures p.6, p.83, 7.7, 7.8, 7.9, 7.10, 7.18, 7.19, 7.23, 7.25.

©The Jekyll Estate, Frontispiece, p.1, p.3, p.184, Figures 1.2, 1.3, 1.4, 1.6, 1.8, 1.9, 1.11, 2.1, 2.4, 2.7, 2.8, 2.11, 2.12, 2.14, 2.19, 3.10, 3.11, 4.1, 4.7, 4.2, 4.3, 7.26, 7.27, 13.3, 14.1.

©Royal Commission on the Historical Monuments of England. Crown Copyright, Figures 6.1, 6.3, 6.4, 6.5, 6.6, 6.7, 7.1.

©Museum of Garden History, pp.77–78.

Mrs. Robin Barber, Figure 8.2.

Bridgeman Picture Library, Figure 1.5.

College of Environmental Design, Documents Collection, University of California, Berkeley, California, USA, Figures 3.10, 3.11, 7.4, 7.11, 7.17, 7.24, 7.35, 12.2, 12.3, 12.4, 12.5, 12.6, 12.7, 12.8.

Mr. William Drummond, Figures 2.2, 2.3, 2.5, 2.6, 3.5, 3.6, 3.7, 3.8, 3.9.

Sir Andrew Duff Gordon, Figures 2.15, 3.3.

Mrs. Elizabeth Gilpin, Figure 8.6.

Lt. Col. R.P. Grenfell, Figure 10.2.

Mr. Derek Hudspeth, Figure 13.1.

Baron Imre von Maltzahn, Figure 2.23.

Mr. Sebastian Nohl, Figure 13.3.

Miss Jane Ridley, Figure 10.2.

The Royal Horticultural Society, Lindley Library, Figures 4.1, 4.2, 4.3, 4.4, 4.5, 4.6, 4.7, 4.8, 4.9, 4.10, 4.11, 5.1, 7.20, 9.1, 9.2.

Surrey County Council, The Surrey Local Studies Library, Figures 11.5, 11.6, 11.7, 11.8.

Susan Schnare, Figure 12.1.

Miss June Swann, Figure 13.2.

Tate Gallery, London, Figure 13.4.

Professor Michael Tooley, Figure 12.3.

Mrs. Rosanna Tooley, Figure 7.21.

Mrs. Peggy Tracey, Figure 9.10.

Private Collections, Frontispiece, x, xii, p.1, p.3, p.184, Figures 1.2, 1.3, 1.4, 1.6, 1.7, 1.8, 1.9, 1.10, 1.11, 2.1, 2.4, 2.7, 2.8, 2.11, 2.12, 2.13, 2.14, 2.17, 2.19, 2.20, 3.4, 3.12, 5.2, 5.3, 7.2, 7.3, 7.5, 7.13, 7.28, 7.29, 7.30, 7.31, 7.32, 7.36, 7.37, 14.2.

Foreword

David McKenna

Pastel portrait of David McKenna by Juliet Pannett, 1975.

This book is not another biography. It is, rather, a carefully researched and authoritative account of the background and achievements of Gertrude Jekyll in the form of a series of essays by a number of acknowledged experts in those fields which she herself had explored.

It would never have occurred to her even to contemplate that, some sixty years or so after her death, she might be regarded as a person of some importance and worthy of biographical attention. Yet too often biographers are apt to attribute characteristics and motivations to their subjects of a purely speculative nature which bear little resemblance to the truth and succeed only in creating and sustaining myths.

This book, on the other hand, is by its very nature one after Gertrude's own heart; and as the last surviving member of her family who actually knew her, I am most grateful to Michael Tooley, my daughter Primrose, and their team of contributors for their admirable work in producing the kind of book by which Gertrude would have liked to have been remembered.

Introduction: Gertrude Jekyll, a working amateur

Michael Tooley and Primrose Arnander

Gertrude Jekyll: essays on the life of a working amateur - a curious title to choose and one that might seem to denigrate the memory of a great gardener, artist, craftswoman and author, many of whose books are still in print today more than ninety years after publication. But to describe her as an amateur is to use Gertrude Jekyll's own words from the subtitle of her first book published in 1899 - *Wood and Garden: Notes and Thoughts, Practical and Critical of a Working Amateur.*

The correct definition of an 'amateur' in this context is of one who works at a project for love of the undertaking and desire for excellence without the incentive of financial gain; a positive, exhilarating and exciting approach. The more critical use of the word, as applied to one who cultivates an activity as a pastime and for personal enjoyment, but without the serious training which leads to high standards of performance and expertise does not come under consideration in this volume; the thoroughness and enthusiasm with which Gertrude Jekyll applied herself to her various pursuits was never less than that required of the most dedicated student towards the mastery of her chosen subject. The absence of significant financial reward for much of her work in no way detracts from the excellence of her achievements in many different spheres.

It was for her writing and her work with plants and gardens that Gertrude Jekyll became well known, not only in her native county of Surrey, but also nationally and internationally, and in these fields her great energy and clarity of thought lead to the making of a true professional. Although an artist in horticulture and garden planning she never allowed herself to stray from the realms of the practical. Her ideas, methods and practices transformed the gardens of late Victorian and Edwardian England, and gradually spread to continental Europe, the United States of America, Australia and New Zealand.

In addition to her own garden designs and planting plans she also worked in close collaboration with others. Apart from her celebrated working relationship with Sir Edwin Lutyens, which started almost from the time of their first meeting in 1889 when she was 45 and he 26 years old, she accepted commissions and developed working friendships with architects, designers, and garden experts throughout her life. Across oceans and years, from letters written in 1893 to Sir Herbert Baker giving planting advice for his designs in the Cape to commissioned garden plans for the Early Modern architect Oliver Hill working in the English home counties of the 1920s, her enthusiasm never waned.

The many architects who worked with her appreciated her skills, but it was Sir Edwin who made the most remarkable public expression of gratitude towards her in a review of her book *Old English Household Life,* written in the journal *English Life* in 1925 under the title 'The Genius of Miss Jekyll':

> 'it has been a matter of profound satisfaction to me to have been able her to pay event a passing tribute to this book and to its author; not that I flatter myself I have thus discharged even in the smallest degree any of my great obligations to Miss Jekyll, her wisdom and encouragement, which has accumulated over many years.'

As can be seen in the bibliography at the back of this book her literary output was astonishingly large, and the many books and hundreds of articles

Top: Russell Street, Drury Lane 1865, Gertrude Jekyll's arm being cast by Brucciani, drawn by Mary Newton.
Bottom: The Triumvirate – discussing plans for Egypt; Walter Severn (Mary Newton's brother) Mary Newton and Gertrude Jekyll 1865, drawn by Mary Newton.

she wrote were, in the early years, often illustrated with her own photographs and meticulous designs. The first books she wrote were published by Longmans simultaneously in London and New York. Books published by Country Life Library London, were also published by Charles Scribner's Sons in New York. One of her books, *Wood and Garden,* was translated into German with a foreword by the German landscape gardener Gertrud von Sanden and published by Julius

Baedeker of Leipzig in 1907. The relevance and continuing appeal of her books are such that most of them are still in print today.

The volume of her work in both garden design and practical gardening was equally impressive, Before her death in 1932 more than four hundred garden plans and tens of thousands of plants were sent to commissions throughout Britain and abroad. She kept all the accounts herself.

In her youth Gertrude Jekyll was skilled as a painter, interior decorator, wood carver, silversmith and embroiderer, and had lead an active life in London which brought her into contact with many of the leading artists, musicians and scholars of the day. She and her brother Herbert, two years her junior, who shared her skills and tastes, grew up together under the same powerful intellectual influences. Later the two households, Gertrude Jekyll at Munstead Wood and Herbert Jekyll and his family at Munstead House, were to uphold artistic and musical traditions, allied with creative gardening and home making, in a vital and innovative way. Their intellectual curiosity and sense of humour did not diminish over the years, and for over 50 years a visit to Munstead was an inspiration to guest and visitor alike.

In this book is gathered a collection of essays by fifteen contributors who have aimed to highlight the achievements of Gertrude Jekyll, and to set her in her historical, artistic, gardening and even geographical context. The last category is specifically fulfiled by Paul Everson's technical account in Chapter 6 of the Munstead Wood Survey, which demonstrates how the latest mapping techniques were brought to bear on the lost garden design on Munstead Wood; it is the Royal commission's only example of a twentieth century garden site.

Chapter 1 and 2 are about the background history of the Jekyll family, divided into two parts: Chapter 1 covers the early history with older generations that included Sir Joseph Jekyll, Master of the Rolls, and Joseph Jekyll (Gertrude Jekyll's grandfather), who was a Whig MP from 1787 until his appointment as Master in Chancery in 1815, as well as the period in the first half of the eighteenth century when the Jekyll family lived in Boston, Massachusetts. Chapter 2 focuses on Gertrude Jekyll's parents Edward and Julia Jekyll, their other children and their upbringing in London, Surrey and Berkshire. These chapters have been contributed by two of Gertrude Jekyll's great great nieces, Primrose Arnander and Annabel Freyberg, who have had access to the unpublished papers of the Jekyll Estate.

Joan Edwards describes in Chapter 3 the early training that Gertrude Jekyll received from Richard Redgrave, Christopher Dresser and John Marshall, and their influence on her as an artist, embroiderer and interior designer. Her training, skill and ability as an artist considerably enriched her talent as a garden designer.

Examples of Gertrude Jekyll's rich and varied design work are given in Chapter 4, in which Fenja Gunn analyses the designs in Gertrude Jekyll's Work Book in the Lindley Library. Mavis Batey provides an historical context for her designs work in Chapter 5, which is about the Arts and Crafts Movement. Heather Angel in Chapter 11 writes on the photography of the period, Gertrude Jekyll's work in this field and the use of her own photographs as illustrations in her early books.

There is a word portrait and technical description of the famous gardening boots by June Swann in Chapter 13. And, of course, mention of the gardening boots draws attention to those chapters which dwell on the area of her greatest fame and achievement; Gertrude Jekyll as a gardener, garden designer, plantswoman and garden writer. In Chapter 7 Martin Wood has described in detail her garden at Munstead Wood with the help of a new, comprehensive garden plan by the Royal Commission on the Historical Monuments of England, based on the work of the Munstead Wood Survey; Richard Bisgrove has written in Chapter 10 not only of Gertrude Jekyll's practical skills but also of his perception of her artistic intuitions and philosophy. Susan Schnare and Rudy J. Favretti have researched into the background of three gardens that were designed for clients in the United States of America, and their findings are in Chapter 12. Michael Tooley has written of those aspects of Gertrude Jekyll's gardening career where the original observations of the 'working amateur' had indeed, as a result of long years of hard work, given way to the achievements and rewards of the professional. In Chapter 8 he writes of her successful plant nursery at Munstead Wood, and in Chapter 9 he describes and lists the plants that she herself selected, bred and named.

After the Postscript, written by David McKenna, her great nephew and the last surviving member of the family to have known her well, the book concludes with a Bibliography drawn up by Margaret Hastings and Michael Tooley, and a complete list of her Garden Plans, in England and abroad, compiled by Michael Tooley. Finally there is a Calendar of her life set against a background of

Pencil and Charcoal drawing of Gertrude Jekyll, aged 77 (after William Nicholson).

contemporary events, and including notable dates in music, literature, architecture and gardening.

Taken together these varied essays present a rounded portrait of the life and work of Gertrude Jekyll. Chapters 3, 5 and 10, by Joan Edwards, Mavis Batey and Richard Bisgrove, arose from lectures given in 1982 at St Aidan's College, Durham, and were published in 1984 in Michael Tooley's book *Gertrude Jekyll: artist, gardener, craftswoman*. The essays have been revised and additional artwork has been added. Chapter 12 by Susan Schnare and Rudy J Favretti was first published in 1982 in *Garden History,* the Journal of the Garden History Society and is reproduced here, in revised form, by permission of the editors of *Garden History.*

The other chapters have not appeared in print before and contain much new material. We, the editors, are most grateful to the expert individual contributors for their scholarship and generosity in writing these detailed and illuminating essays. They were attracted to Gertrude Jekyll by the quality of her work within their own fields of interest, and we hope that their enthusiasm will communicate itself to you, the reader. This book does not attempt to give a full or narrative account of Gertrude Jekyll's life; three full biographies by Francis Jekyll, Betty Massingham and Sally Festing and the story of her collaborations with Sir Edwin Lutyens, *Gardens of a Golden Afternoon* by Jane Brown, have already covered this ground in great detail; nor is it a book soley about gardens and gardening as might be supposed from her commanding position in this field. It is a celebration of the rewarding life of Gertrude Jekyll whose name is still alive in the modern, technological world of today, more than one hundred and fifty years after her birth. Personal acclaim was never her ambition, but her standards were the highest and through dedication and hard work, focussed by her belief in God and the wonders of His creation, she used her talents to the utmost and the results were remarkable.

In *Wood and Garden,* where typically she had played a large part in the design and lay-out of the book as well as providing illustrations form her own photography, Gertrude Jekyll wrote the appropriate words in the Introduction to encourage the amateur towards the demanding journey that leads to success in a new passion whatever it may be:

"Let no-one be discouraged by the thought of how much there is to learn... For the first steps are steps into a delightful Unknown, the first successes are victories all the happier for being scarcely expected, and with the growing knowledge comes the widening outlook, and the comforting sense of an ever-increasing gain of critical appreciation. Each new step becomes a little surer, and each new grasp a little firmer, till, little by little, comes the power of intelligent combination, the nearest thing we can know to the mighty force of creation."

May her energy, vision and fulfilment be yours!

The 'exquisite perfection' of the Michaelmas Daisy Borders in the September Garden at Munstead Wood c.1911.

Introduction

It was almost by accident that I came to take an interest in family history. Many years ago wishing to have an armorial book plate engraved, I visited the College of Arms and obtained there a correct drawing from which the book plate was designed and engraved by C. Sherborn. At the same time I was shown the family pedigree the first part of which, beginning early in the 16th Century, is recorded in the Visitation of Essex. This had been continued at a later time in another volume down to my grandfather Joseph Jekyll (1753-1837)

HERBERT JEKYLL.

I furnished the College with further information with a view to bring the pedigree up to date, which was accordingly done, so the College now has a complete record of twelve generations, covering a period of more than 400 years.

Curiosity, aroused by the sight of the pedigree led me to wonder who & what these people were, and I sought to find out, if I could something about them. I examined a number of Wills at Somerset House and consulted County Histories and books of reference such as the printed volumes of the Harleian & British Record Societies the Calendars of State Papers, the proceedings of Archaeological Societies, and many other likely sources of information. I also made frequent visits to the Library and the MSS Department of the British Museum, and occasional visits to the Public Record Office. From each of these something was gathered, and in course of time I collected a mass of information, which, in addition to correspondence and diaries in my own possession, furnished materials for an outline of the histories of my own family and of others with which it was connected. Prompted at first by mere curiosity this kind of research became a sort of game, quite as amusing as cross word or jigsaw puzzles, while it often led me into strange by ways of English History, and afforded faint & elusive glimpses of life in past centuries. To get on the track of an ancestor, to hunt him down, and at last to run him to ground is excellent sport. When, as happens not infrequently we find ourselves on the wrong scent, there is nothing for it but to hark back and try again. The common temptation to jump to conclusions on insufficient evidence is one that must be firmly resisted. We must know where to look for information and much patience is needed, but perseverance is often rewarded, and the chance mention of a name in a Will or a Parish Register may give a clue which points in the right direction.

I am bound to confess that the outcome of my researches is not particularly interesting. My forefathers were respectable gentlefolk - lawyers, clergymen bankers merchants soldiers sailors and servants of the Crown, of whom only one attained to any degree of wealth and distinction. Though fairly well to do they were not rich,

1

Jekyll Family History

Primrose Arnander

The name of Gertrude Jekyll (1843-1932) has not lost its resonance over the years. Although she was undeniably the 'great gardener' and 'true artist with an exquisite sense of colour' described in *The Times* obituary[1] something in her personality and achievement gives her a deeper and more universal appeal. Born in the first half of the nineteenth century, only six years after Queen Victoria had come to the throne, her formative years were spent in the age of repressive Victorian behaviour, the age of bustle and crinoline, when a 'woman's place was in the home'. Gertrude did not conform. Her sphere of activity was relatively small, based upon aesthetics and a trained mind, a wide knowledge of botany and horticulture practically applied, and a talent for creative home-making, but her influence remains wide-spread throughout years that have seen vast social change and the almost complete destruction of the old ways of her upbringing. Her books are still read avidly as much for her practical advice as for her forthright and challenging attitude towards the world and her Maker.

Agnes Jekyll, Gertrude's sister-in-law,[2] and ultimately her close friend, was in a position to know and appreciate her independent, yet fulfilled, life at Munstead Wood better than most. In the introduction to the memoir by her son Francis Jekyll (1882-1965), published in 1934[3], she writes this appraisal: "Gertrude Jekyll was a pioneer spirit. Long before women had claimed their present independence in the arts and professions, in trade, in travel, in sport and in many difficult crafts, she had quietly and firmly established her right to self-expression." What were the family antecedents for her flowering of aesthetic appreciation, intellectual vigour and tireless physical discipline, backed up with such disregard for conventional behaviour and great confidence in the right way forward?

Family History

The Jekylls can be traced back through 13 generations, as can be seen from the family tree (Figure 1.1 overleaf). This chapter sets the scene for Gertrude's branch, the Jekylls of Munstead, whose family name only died out in 1965, with the death of her nephew and biographer, Francis Jekyll, the last male of this line. Fortunately, Herbert Jekyll (1846-1932), Gertrude's adored younger brother and inheritor of Munstead House, spent much time researching the history and genealogy of the family after his retirement from the Civil Service in 1912. Three bound volumes (of which the second volume is now missing) and an appendix, meticulously hand written (Figure 1.2) and illustrated by family trees, armorial bearings and photographs, were the fruit of his work.[4] As a Jekyll family record, they are invaluable and in this chapter have been much referred to, so that Herbert's name becomes the point of reference for his generation of sisters and brothers.

"I am bound to confess," Herbert wrote disarmingly in his introduction, "that the outcome of my researches is not particularly interesting. My forefathers were respectable gentlefolk – lawyers, clergymen, bankers, merchants, soldiers, sailors and servants of the crown, of whom only one attained to any degree of wealth and distinction. Though fairly well to do, they were not rich nor did they own ancestral estates descending from father to son so far as my own family were concerned. My grandfather made a considerable fortune, the bulk of which came eventually to my father, so it is to

Left: Figure 1.2 Facsimile of a page from Herbert Jekyll's 'Studies in Family History' Volume 1.

THE JEKYLL FAMILY

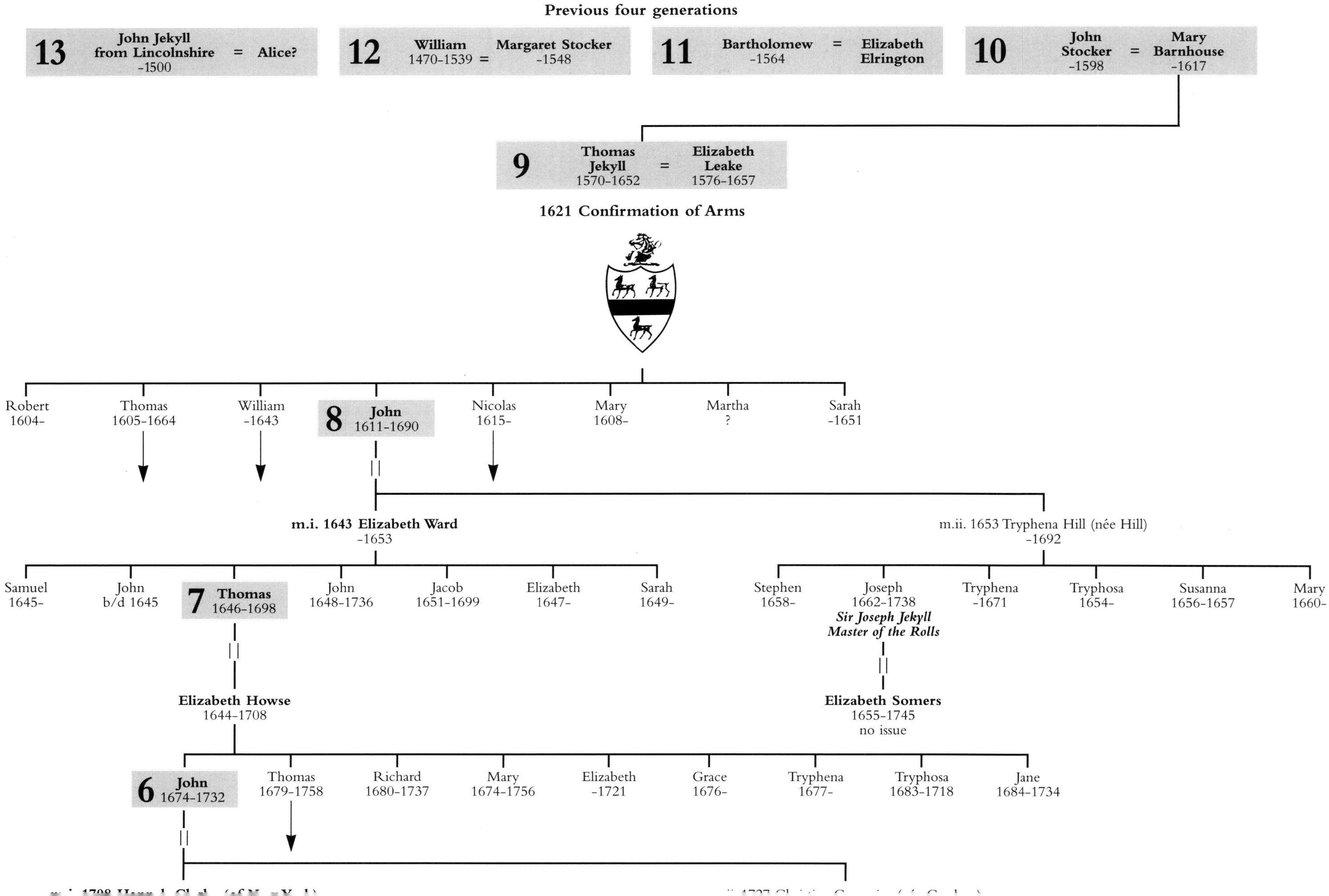

Previous four generations

13 John Jekyll from Lincolnshire -1500 = Alice?

12 William 1470-1539 = Margaret Stocker -1548

11 Bartholomew -1564 = Elizabeth Elrington

10 John Stocker -1598 = Mary Barnhouse -1617

9 Thomas Jekyll 1570-1652 = Elizabeth Leake 1576-1657

1621 Confirmation of Arms

8 John 1611-1690 == m.i. 1643 Elizabeth Ward -1653 / m.ii. 1653 Tryphena Hill (née Hill) -1692

Robert 1604–

Thomas 1605-1664 →

William -1643 →

Nicolas 1615– →

Mary 1608–

Martha ?

Sarah -1651

Stephen 1658–

Joseph 1662-1738 *Sir Joseph Jekyll Master of the Rolls* == Elizabeth Somers 1655-1745 no issue

Tryphena -1671

Tryphena 1654–

Susanna 1656-1657

Mary 1660–

7 Thomas 1646-1698 == Elizabeth Howse 1644-1708

Samuel 1645–

John b/d 1645

John 1648-1736

Jacob 1651-1699

Elizabeth 1647–

Sarah 1649–

6 John 1674-1732 ==

Thomas 1679-1758 →

Richard 1680-1737

Mary 1674-1756

Elizabeth -1721

Grace 1676–

Tryphena 1677–

Tryphosa 1683-1718

Jane 1684-1734

9

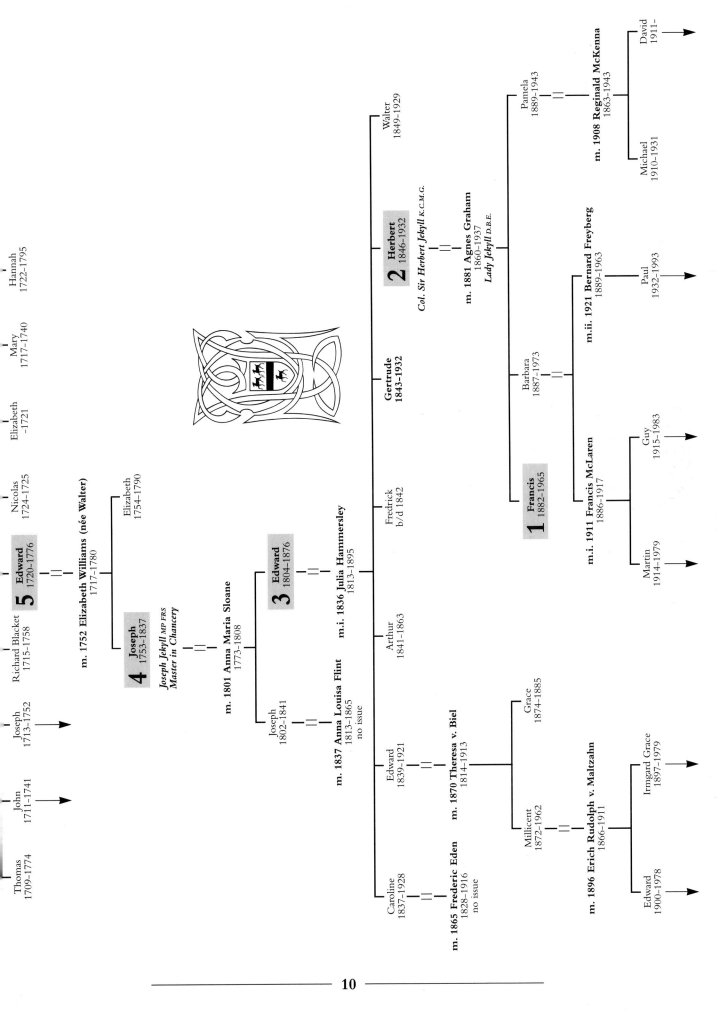

him that we owe such worldly goods as we have. Some of my remote ancestors, particularly those of my two grandmothers,[5] had great estates with centuries of possession behind them, but no Jekyll can claim such distinction."

What the Jekylls of earlier times can claim is exceptional energy and clarity of thought, which, in addition to Herbert's work, has resulted in a collection of hand written material and well-preserved family papers which are fascinating to study. From the late 18th century onwards, letters, diaries and other documents abound. Herbert's grandfather, Joseph Jekyll, (1753-1837) who became a Whig Member of Parliament, was a prolific writer; the diaries of his early youth, the numerous letters that he wrote to his friends and confidantes and his own reminiscences provide a vivid insight into the busy public and private life of a man possessed of great humour and the intelligent detachment of a born observer. These traits, which can be seen as outstanding Jekyll characteristics through the ages, were passed to his son, Edward, (1804-1876), whose own letters and diaries ran to thousands of words, and on down to the next generation, where all six of Edward's children were enthusiastic letter writers and Herbert, Gertrude and Walter (1849-1929), the three youngest, left their own written legacy of published and unpublished work.

"The history of a family cannot be understood properly without some knowledge of others with which it was connected.." Herbert continues in his introduction, and his researches were prodigiously thorough. Wills, parish registers, inscriptions on monuments, marriage licences, court rolls and county histories all came under his scrutiny but, alas, the full scope of his findings is too extensive for this chapter, which must be confined to the Jekyll path that leads to Munstead and must ignore many of the fascinating by-ways.

"It is rarely possible to visualise the lives of people long since dead, or to invest the framework with any degree of vitality. It is only when we come to later times, when information becomes more abundant and personal, that we can picture to ourselves, even faintly, what our forefathers were like or how they lived." Taking heed of Herbert's wise advice, the coverage of the early lives will be brief and extended mention will be made of only some half-dozen Jekylls, whose lives were somewhat out of the ordinary.

From Lincolnshire roots to the City of London

In the fifteenth century, it was known that there

Figure 1.3   The Jekyll Coat of Arms and Crest.

were several families called Jekyll living in Lincolnshire, from one of which came William Jekyll (1470-1539), who married Margaret Stocker and had four children by 1500. He was the Purveyor of Forage for the King's Horse and probably from him stems the Jekyll crest of a horse. His grandson, John Stocker Jekyll (died 1598), married Mary Barnhouse and, by 1570, when their third son, Thomas Jekyll (1570-1652), was born, the family had moved from Lincolnshire and was established in London and at Bocking in Essex. From that time, "information becomes more abundant and personal". Thomas was an attorney at Clifford's Inn, a successful lawyer, like his grandfather, Bartholomew (died 1564), and became Secretary of the King's Bench and one of the Clerks of the Papers. However, it was as an antiquarian that he achieved fame, and there is a modest mention of him as such in the *Dictionary of National Biography.*[6]

His hand-written researches on the counties of Essex, Suffolk and Norfolk alone ran to forty volumes and some of his papers ended up in the Library of All Souls College, Oxford and in the British Museum.   In addition, his local parish researches received high commendation from the great historian of Essex, Morant: "The History of this Parish (Bocking) would be imperfect if I should not take notice of the memory of this Gentleman who though he was no Lord of any Manor in this town, nor in his life time made any great figure in the world, as living a Recluse and Studious life, yet deserves a remembrance amongst the most worthy persons mentioned in this History."[7]

During Thomas' life, in the year 1627, his acquaintance, Sir William Segar, Principal King of Arms, granted him a licence to alter the Jekyll Arms and Crest: an escutcheon of the Jekyll Arms, quartering Stocker, Barnhouse and Britcheston (Britixton), with a horse's head as Crest, was established (Figure 1.3). Many years later, in her philological games and conversations with Logan Pearsall Smith, these were the arms which enabled Gertrude to produce the old word "armigerous", as a challenge, and him, surely, to apply it in his mind and remember her as an *armigerous* 'old Amazon' as she fired her parting, and alas final shot, in their life–long battle about words.[8]

John Jekyll, the fourth son of Thomas (1611-1690), was born in Bocking. Unlike his brothers who remained in the county, he left Essex, married Elizabeth Ward, the daughter of a City Merchant and Clothworker, and became a Citizen of London, as well as a member of both the Fishmongers and Haberdashers Companies. The early Jekylls, with their long and active lives, must have been possessed of iron constitutions, and John was no exception. He died at the age of 79, by which time he had fathered 13 children by two wives. His second wife, Tryphena Hill, as well as bringing a son, Francis Hill,[9] from her first marriage gave birth to six of John's children; her second Jekyll boy, Joseph, was to become the most eminent and successful member of the family in its early history. Although not in the direct line of the Munstead Jekylls, he died childless and his influence and generosity towards the children and grandchildren of his half-brothers through one of whom the line passed, was powerful and far-reaching.

Sir Joseph Jekyll, Master of the Rolls (1662–1738)

Joseph (Figure 1.4) was born in 1662, called to the Bar at the age of 25 and became the Chief Justice to the City Palatinate of Chester in 1697, when he was knighted by William III. He was a Member of Parliament for Eye, Lymington and Reigate in succession and became Master of the Rolls and a Privy Councillor in 1717, remaining in this office for 21 years until his death in 1738.[10] His wife, Elizabeth Somers, was the sister of John Somers (1651-1716), another brilliant lawyer who, at 42 years of age, was made Lord Keeper of the Great Seal, which had been in commission since the accession of William III, and who became Lord High Chancellor in 1697, and was ultimately raised to the peerage as Baron Somers of Evesham.[11] With these powerful connections, Sir Joseph became a rich man and his money and estates were of great benefit to the family for years to come, even though his will was greatly complicated by an eccentric wish to leave his East India and South Sea stock to the Kings and Queens of England after his wife's death, "to be applied to the use of the Sinking Fund as Parliament may direct."[12] As there appeared to be no workable system for the disposal of this gift, which was intended to help reduce the national debt, the nation finally returned most of the money to Sir Joseph's heirs, but such were the legal complexities that only after 36 years and five Acts of Parliament was his estate finally wound up, well into the lifetime of his namesake and great-great-nephew, Herbert's grandfather, Joseph.

It was through Thomas (1646-1698), the third son of John Jekyll, and one of the older half-brothers of Sir Joseph, that the direct line of the Munstead Jekylls continued. He was educated at Merchant

Figure 1.4   Portrait of Sir Joseph Jekyll by Sir Godfrey Kneller.

Taylors School and Trinity College, Oxford and entered the church as Minister of New Chapel in Westminster, where he served for most of his life and instituted a free school. In his later years, he studied at Cambridge and emerged a Doctor of Divinity from Sidney Sussex College in 1694, four years before his death.[13] He had nine children of whom the eldest, John, broke the mould of the London based professional Jekylls, eschewed the Law and the Church and ended up in America.

The "Darling of all Fair Traders" in New England

John Jekyll (1674-1732), after travelling widely in Europe as a young man, was appointed Collector of Customs in the port of Boston in 1707, during the reign of Queen Anne, and continued in that office until his death. He married twice, firstly Hannah Clark of New York[14] who bore him nine children before dying suddenly at the age of 36, and secondly Christian Cummins, who was the widow of Archibald Cummins, another Civil Servant for the Port of Boston, and Agent for the Perquisites of Admiralty, New England. There were no more children. John was a popular man who settled happily in his country of adoption, even though most of his children were to return to England. He died in 1732 and was buried in a vault which he had built in the graveyard of the King's Chapel, Boston. The following notice occurs in the *Annals of King's Chapel:* "On Saturday last in the afternoon

died here John Jekyll Esq. in the 59th year of his age, who for the space of about 27 years was Collector of His Majesty's Customs for the Port of Boston, and one of his Majesty's Justices of the Peace for the counties of Suffolk and Middlesex. He was a very free and hospitable gentleman, and who discharged his trusts to good acceptance, and his death is very much lamented."[15] Later in the *Annals* is quoted an appreciation of John from an issue of the *Boston Weekly Newsletter* which came out shortly after his death. It includes these lines: "He was publicly conspicuous of his office of Collector for the faithfulness and application in his Duty to the Crown; by his courteous Behaviour to the Merchant, he became the Darling of all Fair Traders; he was not of an avaricious sordid Temper, but with much Humanity took pleasure in directing Masters of Vessels how they ought to avoid the Breach of the Acts of Trade." A glowing tribute, but despite his easy assimilation into his country of adoption, he remembered always where his duty lay and, as shown in the following quotation from *The British Colonial Papers* by Palfrey: "Mr. Jekyll's fidelity to the Crown led him to report to the Lords of Trade in 1720 that the Council have their dear Idol the Charter much at heart, and great love for independency."[16] The American Revolution was on its way (Figure 1.5).

John Jekyll had acquired a considerable estate at Pompos-itticut Hill, Stow, 25 miles from Boston,

Figure 1.5 '*A View of the Port of the Town of Boston in New England and British Ships of War Landing their Troops, 1768.*'

*Figure 1.6   Miniature of Captain Edward Jekyll R.N. by an
unknown artist.*

where his widow Christian lived until her death.
His second son, John, the only son who remained
in America, succeeded him in the office of
Collector of Customs in 1732, and married an
heiress from Philadelphia, Margaret Shippen, two
years later. They bought their own land in Boston
and Cambridge but after John died suddenly in
1741, at the early age of 29, Margaret went back to
Philadelphia. She finally sold their New England
properties in 1750, just before her death, and their
son, also called John, went to England never to
return. There is a much later reference to the Stow
Estate, after the death of Christian and the War of
Independence, in documents in the probate
registry of the county of Middlesex, Massachusetts,
dated 4 December 1782: "The above bounden
Joseph Gardner is appointed... to be Agent for the
heirs of John Jekyll late of Stow in the county of
Middesex, Esq. deceased, which heirs are subjects
of Great Britain and have not been inhabitants of
this Commonwealth so as to enjoy the protection
thereof since the present War, and who are the
owners of houses and lands within the
Commonwealth which it is necessary to protect
from damage and trespass."[17] Eventually the land
must have been sold and divided amongst the
descendants in England.   Thus, the estate at
Pompositticut Hill in Stow with 900 acres and
including five Negro slaves vanished into history
and the Jekylls surrendered their American
affiliation.

But in at least one place the name of Jekyll lingers
on in the United States of America, and that is as a
result of a tribute to Sir Joseph and his wife. When
General Oglethorpe, founder of the colony of
Georgia, dispossessed the Uchee and Creek tribes
of what was then known as Whale Island, he re-
christened the new estate 'Jekyll Island' after the
friend who had made a generous contribution to
his pioneering venture. There is a record of the
General visiting the island in 1736, and it
continued to be a military settlement until 5th
April 1768 when it was made over as a Crown
Grant to a civilian, Clement Martin, under the
name of the island or tract of Jekyl.[18] Thereafter the
island and separate building plots changed hands
many times, until in 1886 Du Bignon acquired all
the land and sold it to the specially formed Jekyl
Island Club, which still exists today, with the
second 'l', restored, under the auspices of the State
of Georgia.

Captain Edward Jekyll, RN (1720–1776)

The fifth son of John the Customs Collector,
Edward (Figure 1.6), was the direct ancestor of the
Munstead Jekylls, and Herbert's great grandfather.
He did not receive the direct patronage of his great
uncle, Sir Joseph Jekyll, who had brought three of
his older brothers back to England, and grew up in
Boston until he joined the Royal Navy while still
very young. His early life was spent at sea under the
protection of Sir Peter Warren, who commanded a
squadron in America. By the time that he received
his first commission in 1742, he was already
twenty-two years old and his father had been dead
for 10 years. He was based back in England by then
and in 1744, as a 2nd Lieutenant in HMS Essex, he
took part in the Action of Toulon between the
combined fleets of France and Spain and the
British fleet. His naval life was eventful as it was a
period of war, and by 1746 he was already
appointed Captain, only to be placed on half pay
two years later at the cessation of hostilities.[19] There
was peace until the outbreak of the Seven Years War
in 1756, and it was during those calmer years that
he married a Welsh widow, Elizabeth Williams, and
had two children, Joseph, born in 1753, and
Elizabeth, born a year later. By 1758 he was back at
sea and in command of HMS Rippon (Figure 1.7),
in which ship he took part in the siege of the
Havana, and after the successful culmination,
brought home to England the victorious overall
commander, the Earl of Albemarle.[20] His career
then faltered, and he was on half pay for nearly
eight years, which ended with a three year spell in
command of HMS Egmont, a guardship based at
Portsmouth. In 1775, when relations with the

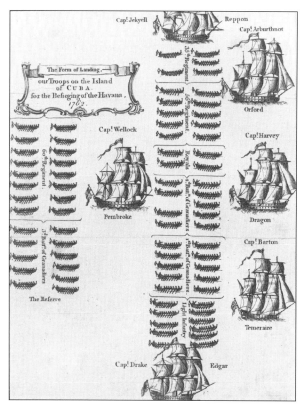

Figure 1.7   The Siege of the Havana, 1762.

American colonies were strained, his son Joseph Jekyll recorded that, "Giving free scope to his opinions as a native American, he incurred the wrath of Lord Sandwich."[21] The memories and sympathies of his childhood in Boston had doubtless proved a bar to promotion and, despite his long and distinguished service, at the time of his death in 1776, he was one of the oldest Captains in the navy, although it was said that he would have been promoted to Admiral had he lived a few weeks longer and not succumbed to the dropsy which killed him.[22]

Joseph Jekyll, MP FRS (1753–1837)

Notwithstanding his many years at sea and the vagaries of his career, Edward Jekyll had managed to give his children a secure upbringing. For 11 years from 1765, the family lived in a house in the Broad Sanctuary, Westminster and his son Joseph, Herbert's grandfather, went to Westminster School, where he excelled himself before going on to Christ Church, Oxford in 1771. Joseph proved to be a boy well worth his education. After taking his BA degree, he spent some months in Blois and became fluent in French, before his father was taken ill and he was recalled from France to be at the Captain's death bed. In 1778, he was called to the Bar and began the long career in the Law and in Parliament that established him among his peers

and shaped his life as that of a confirmed Londoner, wit and man about town.[23]

Joseph Jekyll (Figure 1.8) bursts upon the family within the manners and conventions of his age but with the attitudes and awareness of modern man. The strong impact of his personality on his descendants is reflected in the length and detail of Herbert's writings about his grandfather. Although he died just before the birth of Caroline (Carry), his oldest grandchild, the enormous quantity of his hand-written papers, letters, poems, epigrams, and his personal diaries and reminiscences must have made him appear almost as close to his grandchildren as if they had known him personally. Herbert could write about him with confidence and familiarity: "Joseph Jekyll started life with few advantages. The son of a naval officer who had little to bestow upon him beyond a good home, a few influential acquaintances, and the priceless gift of the best education that was to be had, he owed his success in life entirely to his own personality and exertions. Endowed with a good constitution and a brilliant intellect, he added to these natural gifts energy, industry and quickness in seizing such opportunities as came his way. He was universally popular, and from school and college days onwards made friends wherever he went. The secret of his

Figure 1.8   Portrait of Joseph Jekyll painted in 1815 by his friend Thomas Lawrence. P.R.A.

popularity lay in his good breeding and engaging manners coupled with unfailing gaiety and humour. High spirits were habitual in him."

In 1787, when he was 33 years old, Joseph combined his profitable legal practice, established on the western circuit, with the life of a Member of Parliament; he was elected to represent the pocket borough of Calne, which was in the gift of his friend, the Earl of Shelburne, who had recently been created Marquis of Lansdowne.[24] 1790 was an equally important year for Joseph: he was presented at Court, the Prince of Wales being already a close acquaintance, was elected a Fellow of the Royal Society and of the Society of Antiquaries and, during one of his frequent visits to France, met the French revolutionary, Mirabeau, in Paris[25]. In a letter written to his friend Nathanial Bond on September 10th, 1790, Joseph says "The National Assembly is my chief occupation in the mornings… I receive great Civility from the Bishop of Chârtres, the Bishop of Rodez, and the Duke de la Rochefoucault. M. de Mirabeau has introduced me very much to the Members of the Assembly, and when I don't dine at the Houses I have mentioned he carries me to the Political Clubs. Paris is by no means quiet. Three nights ago the Mob demanded the Heads of the Ministers and the National Guards patrolled the whole night."[26] The French visits came to an end three years later when England declared war on France, but affairs at home kept him fully occupied. In the course of 1794 Joseph, who had changed chambers and become a member of the Inner Temple, rode 2,300 miles on horseback on circuit business and spoke frequently for the opposition in Parliament. His physical energy in those early years must have been enormous, but the vigour of youth fades swiftly and he was soon to be attacked by the gout that plagued him for the rest of his life; from 1796 onwards, his journeys were undertaken by chaise. Those bachelor days of intense activity were also drawing to a close. In 1801, when he was 48, he married Anna Maria Sloane, who was twenty years his junior, and the daughter of Colonel Hans Sloane of Paultons, near Romsey in Hampshire.[27] The young couple took a house in the heart of London in New Street, Spring Gardens[28], which remained his permanent home until his death 36 years later.

This comfortable home was to prove of great importance, for his adored young wife, Anna Maria (Figure 1.9), was not strong and, after giving birth to two boys, yet another Joseph in 1802 and Edward in 1804, she only lived for another four

Figure 1.9   Miniature of Anna Maria Jekyll by an unknown artist.

years. Her early death was devastating for her husband; it was the tragedy of his life. His diary entry for that time reflects his state of desolation and is in marked contrast to his usual ebullient style. She was buried in late November 1808 in the vault of St Martins-in-the-Fields, on what is described as a "Christmas Day of grief and wretchedness." The little boys lived with him in London under the care of their mother's governess, with long annual visits to Paultons in the summer. Joseph combined his position as Solicitor General to the Prince of Wales, a King's Counsel and a Bencher of the Inner Temple, with the duties of a devoted and loving father whose involvement in and appreciation of his boys increased the older they became. Nicknamed by him 'Il Penseroso' (Figure 1.10) and 'L'Allegro', a reflection of their contrasting personalities, a marvellously spontaneous relationship grew up between the sophisticated father and his sons, which lasted all their lives. Nor did these years of paternal responsibility seriously affect his career. He remained on very good terms with the Prince Regent and, on his personal insistence, Joseph was made a Master in Chancery in 1815; the following year he finally gave up his seat in Parliament, became Treasurer of the Temple and confined his activities to London and the law courts.

From January 1818 until shortly before his death, Joseph's confidante was his sister-in-law, Lady Gertrude Sloane Stanley, the wife of Anna Maria's

Figure 1.10   Popular print of Joseph Jekyll, the elder of Joseph Jekyll's sons.

"You know I was never much encouraged by my purchase at Wargrave and I began to think if I had thrown the money into the Thames instead of laying it out on the Banks it would have been equally productive and less troublesome."[31] In the light of Gertrude's gardening future, one more quotation from a letter written to Mrs. Hill in November 1820 by Joseph Jekyll, an avowed urban dweller, proves irresistible: "Today I send by the Reading waggon from the White Bear Piccadilly a hamper containing some Rhododendron Plants. Mr. Sloane directs their Roots should be put into Peat or Bog Earth on planting – a Species of Soil his Vicinity abounds with, and which I believe yours fortunately does not." Mrs. Hill finally died in 1824, but there was no question of a change of heart; Joseph cleared Wargrave Hill, effected a few small repairs and rented out the property, while he and the boys, who were by now grown up, remained based in London.

Joseph and Edward grow up

After attending Westminster School, Joseph and Edward had gone up to Christ Church, Oxford, still following in paternal footsteps, in 1821 and 1822 respectively. But then their ways parted; after only one year at Oxford, Edward expressed a wish to go into the army. Influence was brought to bear and an interview with the Duke of York proved rewarding. In July 1823 Edward was gazetted, and at the age of 19 joined the 86th regiment as an Ensign. "On the 30th (of October) my dear Ensign departed from home," wrote Joseph to Mrs. Hill, "for a journey of 300 miles to Holyhead, where with his immense Baggage he arrived last Saturday, and I apprehend crossed the sea to Dublin on Monday... He went away in all the High Spirits of Youth entering on the active Pursuits of life, and I must say that his splendid Regimentals became him. From the Tip of the Feathers in his Cap to his Heel measured nearly 8 feet. No Leave of Absence, I believe, is granted during the first year of service, so in our State of Existence, God knows if I may ever see him again." These fears were unfounded, and just over two years later, in February 1826, Edward's apprenticeship was over and he returned to duties in London and promotion to Lieutenant in the Grenadier Guards, with whom he served until his marriage to Julia Hammersley in 1836.[32]

Joseph graduated from Oxford in May 1824, but his ideas for a career were far less clear cut than those of his brother. He made a brief attempt to settle in chambers in the Temple and study law, but fell ill and moved back to stay with his father in Spring Gardens. He was, to quote Herbert, "neither

brother, William.[29] He wrote countless letters to her between 1818 and 1836, which were later published as a book in 1894.[30] They give a lively picture of his role in the society of the day and the emergence of Joseph and Edward as their father's pride and joy.

Further letters closely involved with the childhood and upbringing of the boys were written to Mrs. Hill, the widow of Joseph Hill, the erstwhile lawyer and friend of the poet William Cowper, whose great-grandmother Tryphena had married John Jekyll in 1653 and was the mother of both Francis Hill and Sir Joseph Jekyll. It was in the will of the childless Joseph Hill that, after the death of his wife, Wargrave Hill, the house which he had built in the 1780s, and the land that went with it, should pass to his kinsman, Joseph Jekyll. Mrs. Hill had always taken a special interest in the two boys, and even persuaded their father to purchase more land nearby and thus increase the size of the estate. Grumbling somewhat at this unwanted excursion into rural matters, the unregenerate Joseph complied, although he was later to write Mrs. Hill:

physically robust nor strong in character", and soon settled into a quiet pattern of reading and the study of scientific matters, his special interests being chemistry, medicine and homeopathy. Although not very out-going by temperament, he was well mannered and personable and did not lack for invitations. Nor was his life wholly sedentary; he loved water activities, and was a keen oarsman on the Thames; whenever possible, he and his father indulged their love of sailing, which led eventually to the young Joseph's purchase of a yacht, Louisa, and membership of the Royal Yacht Squadron.

Joseph remained very close to his father and was his companion both in London and on their annual country visits to Paultons, until the old man's death in March 1837. Eight months later, he married Anna Louisa Flint, the daughter of an old friend[33]; the couple planned to give notice to the tenants and take up residence at Wargrave Hill, but alas it was not to be. Joseph's health finally gave out and he died aged 39, only four years after his marriage and before they were fully established on the estate. Once again, the house became the property of a widow for her lifetime, and Anna Louisa lived there with her second husband, Spencer Dudley Montagu.[34] The Montagu and Jekyll families were not close, and it was not until her death in 1865, that Edward finally came into his inheritance, whereupon he and Julia abandoned their long established, but rented, family home at Bramley and moved from Surrey to Berkshire, to the dismay of Gertrude, Herbert and Walter, the three younger children who were still based at home.

Family influences

The intellectual ability of Gertrude and her brothers can be traced readily to their paternal grandfather, Joseph, but the source of their love of plants and artistic talent must be sought elsewhere. Edward was very musical and played the flute to virtuoso standard, but his father treated this accomplishment with his customary amused tolerance and with no deep appreciation. Herbert in his history sheds further light on the music making of his grandfather's generation. "The Duke of Wellington, when he came to Paultons in 1832 was entertained with music by the family; Gertrude (Lady Gertrude's daughter) played the Pianoforte, my father (Edward Jekyll) the flute, and Mr. Stanley the Violoncello. He was said to have had 10,000 lessons on this instrument, and was never in tune within an octave. He used to ring for the footman to tune it."

A passage in one of Joseph's letters, to his friend, Hugh Leycester, expresses his attitude towards

natural scenery: "Whenever I praise Hills, Valleys, and Waterfalls, I suspect myself of affectation and jargon. For I really believe my mind is so unfortunately moulded into Abstraction that a Grove and Brick Kiln seem to me little more than different modifications of Matter."[35] The pleasure he took in fine art was equally perfunctory and Herbert wrote: "While abroad he made a point of visiting picture galleries, but such comments as he made indicate no more that a faint interest in their contents, and still less critical faculty. He had no works of Art of his own except a few family portraits and a number of Greek, or as they were then called, Etruscan vases. Of these he made a collection, which at a time when such things were comparatively rare, was one of considerable importance. The collection passed to his son Edward, and was a notable feature in the houses which he successively occupied."

Joseph's talents undoubtedly lay in communication and the use of language (Figure 1.11). With the tastes of an intellectual and a scholar, he had nonetheless performed his public duties, if not with the distinction that leads to fame, with the ability and liberal-minded tolerance that characterised the whole of his long and, but for the disaster of his wife's premature death, happy life. He wrote to Lady Gertrude in appraisal of his years as a Member of Parliament, as a stalwart Whig always in opposition: "For 33 long years, I gave hopeless votes for Reform, Catholics, Dissenters and black men, but all has been accomplished and I may now sing the song of Simeon and be let depart in peace."[36]

Verbal wit requires a keen ear for the use of language and awareness of the social nuances of the day, both of which the shrewdly observant Joseph had to a high degree. Some of his epigrams, pamphlets and verses seem somewhat contrived nowadays without their topical immediacy, but his skill was undeniable and it was no wonder that his presence in the salons of London was eagerly sought after and his letters treasured by their recipients. The infirmity of old age finally caught up with him and with an all too familiar dig at the medical profession, Joseph wrote, in the heroic couplets typical of his time:

"One skilled physician like a sculler plies
The patient lingers and by inches dies.
But two physicians like a pair of oars
Waft him more swiftly to the Stygian shores."

In 1837, in his 84th year, Joseph was finally wafted across the Styx; Herbert shall have the last word about his fascinating, genial grandfather: "His long life covered an eventful period. Born in the reign of George II, he lived through the reigns of three

Figure 1.11 Contemporary drawing of Joseph Jekyll by an unknown artist.

succeeding Sovereigns, and died two months before the accession of Queen Victoria. In his time occurred the Seven Years' War, the American War of Independence, the French Revolution, the rise and fall of Napoleon, and the series of wars that closed at Waterloo. He saw changes – political, social and economic – greater than had occurred since the time of the Stuarts – the transition in fact from ancient to modern history. He himself was what would now be called 'a link with the past'. As a boy, he saw human heads on Temple Bar, and at the age

of 22 he saw, in France, a man broken on the wheel for the crime of house-breaking. Much later, he declined to purchase an area of some extent, which now includes the site of Belgrave Square, because he thought £400 an acre at which it was offered to him an extravagant price for land so far from London. Brighton, when he first knew it, was little more than a fishing village with one Inn. It would be easy to multiply examples of things within his recollection which to us seem scarcely credible."

Edward and Julia Jekyll, the parents of Gertrude

Despite the great difference in their upbringing, the marriage of Edward and Julia was long and successful; it lasted from 1836 until Edward's death in 1876, forty years later. Julia was the third eldest of eleven Hammersley children in a family of seven girls and four boys, whereas Edward, with an elderly father and one delicate brother had a loving but masculine dominated childhood and was soon to be the only surviving member of his immediate family. Edward, high spirited and volatile, was balanced by Julia's quiet, practical efficiency, and a uniting bond was their mutual love of music, both as keen listeners and able performers. Julia's piano playing and contralto singing and the high standard of Edward's flute playing gave rise to much favourable comment, and demonstrated not only talent but also the dedication and discipline necessary to produce a high enough standard of technique for successful performance regardless of temperament. They also complemented one another admirably as parents and created a stable and stimulating environment for their six children which is elaborated in the next chapter.

The Jekyll characteristics already described in this chapter can be found to a greater or lesser extent in all Edward and Julia's children, who in their turn developed personalities which, allied to application and a strong sense of duty, resulted in intellectual and practical achievement. But it is Gertrude who built on the foundations of the past and employed her many talents to such creative effect throughout her long life that the fame and example of her achievements have lived on with enduring relevance to the present day, more than one hundred and fifty years after her birth.

Logan Pearsall Smith, a man of literature, and an intellectual sparring partner of Gertrude's in his youth and years later in his maturity and her extreme old age, used words to describe his appreciation of his old friend and her successful elevation of the gardening art to the level of the art of music. In an article written in 1933, a year after her death, he speculates on her background and antecedents, of which he was largely ignorant, and finally, without denying their importance, puts them in their place. "The background may have been there; I feel sure that it was there, and Miss Jekyll was, I dare say, proud of its existence. It gave a certain distinction to her staunch old figure; but her much more real and rare distinction was her talent, and her long life assiduously devoted to its cultivation. She had made herself the mistress of a beautiful art, a beautiful humane profession; she had carried her craft, her 'mystery' to a more exquisite perfection, and had enriched in her own way the world with a new ideal of beauty. She was an old, erudite, accomplished and famous expert (figure 1.12); the world had acknowledged her pre-eminence, and applauded her achievement. And what distinction, armorial or other, is comparable to that?"[37] Quite so, but plant breeder herself Gertrude would have been the first to acknowledge the value of the stock; it is on the history of her stock, its vigour and its characteristics that this chapter has dwelt.

Figure 1.12   Gertrude Jekyll, aged 80, in the Spring Garden, Munstead Wood.

2

Edward and Julia Jekyll and their family

Annabel Freyberg

In the summer of 1848, Captain Edward Jekyll 'thinking it undesirable to keep so large a family of children in London' sold his London home and took a lease on Bramley House in Surrey. He can little have imagined the effect the place would have on his brood of six children, and in particular on the whole course of his younger daughter Gertrude's life.

The family became 'rooted' in the area, and the character and customs of rural Surrey in the mid-19th century associated with all that was pleasing and good. When, some 60 or 70 years later Gertrude's younger brothers Herbert (1846-1932) and Walter (1849-1929) came to write of their Bramley childhood, they were able to recall with clarity and in detail the day–to–day rituals, local characters, family friends, special celebrations, and the lay–out of house and garden.

Edward's own upbringing had been largely in London. "You know my detestation of the country, and my opinion that every day spent there is a day given to the grave before one's decease," wrote his father Joseph in December 1824 from Wargrave Hill[1]. He had recently inherited the house from Joseph Hill (Edward's godfather, hence his full name Edward Joseph Hill Jekyll), and was quickly arranging its leasing out.

A barrister, wit, Whig MP for Calne 1787-1816 and Master in Chancery, Joseph Jekyll's milieu was a highly sophisticated one embracing the worlds of law, politics and literature, and included friendship with the Prince Regent (with whom Joseph was dining when he received news of the Battle of Waterloo), Gibbon, Fox, Sheridan, Sir Joseph Banks, Boswell, Byron, Mrs. Siddons and Talleyrand. Edward and Joseph (1802-41), had lost their mother, Anna Maria, when they were only four and six years old and seem to have been unusually close to their comparatively elderly but irrepressible father (he was over 50 when Edward was born), as is shown by references to them in the lively and irreverent letters he wrote to his sister-in-law Lady Gertrude Sloane Stanley[2], wife of Anna Maria's brother William.

Moreover, in spite of Joseph's relish of London and his fear of stultifying in the countryside, as children Edward and his elder brother Joseph went often to Wargrave (as well as to Paultons, the Sloane Stanley family home near Romsey in Hampshire, and to Bowood, the Wiltshire estate of Lord Lansdowne, Joseph's political patron), and it had happy childhood associations.

Unlike his elder brother Joseph, Edward was a sturdy boy. From Herbert's family memoir he emerges as a spirited and engaging character much given to practical jokes and playing the flute. His father had intended him for the Church, but when in 1823, after a year at Christ Church, Oxford, he declared his interest in joining the army, Joseph managed through the Duke of York to secure him a commission within ten days.

Edward (Figure 2.1) was straightway posted to Ireland, where he enjoyed a busy two years engaged in social and military matters: "going on a Cruize in a yacht to the Giant's Causeway... quelling an Orange Riot at Newry by opposing Bayonets to Brickbats... [He] seems as happy as fighting and fluting can make a Man."[3]

In February 1826 Edward was promoted to Lieutenant in the Grenadier Guards, and returned to England and duty at the Tower of London.

Left: *Figure 2.1 Edward Jekyll by John Hayter after Maria Cosway.*

Soldiering in peacetime was not onerous, but Edward took his duties seriously, and seems to have inherited his father's ability to get on with people, being befriended by both the Duke of Cumberland and the Duke of Cambridge (two of George IV's younger brothers) when he was sent to protect them at Kew. In a rare reference to things horticultural, Joseph Jekyll reports to Lady Gertrude in 1829: "My Lieutenant speaks with Wonder of the Botanical Gardens, four hundred Acres, with glazed Conservatories lofty enough for Palms and other gigantic exotic Trees".[4] Joseph also describes with amusement the dandyish decor of Edward's cottage in Kew, and the extravagance of the army's elaborate uniforms – not to mention a tigerskin waistcoat given to Edward.

When Joseph's old friend King George IV[5] died on 26 June 1830, Edward took part in the funeral at Windsor, while that November he was among the 10,000 soldiers drafted into London to control public unrest. Joseph Jekyll describes their unusual barracks: "Three nights did they bivouac under arms in the new Palace [Buckingham Palace]. How my poor George IV would have stared to see Lancers and Guards eating Oysters and drinking Punch among his Scagliola Columns! On the second night Edward sent home for a Mattress to rest his bones upon. Some slept on the inlaid Floors, which had been newly oiled and arose with the Patterns inflicted on their new embroidered Regimentals... Such are the Horrors of War the Guards encounter after all their perilous Campaigns in Pall Mall and St James's."[6] In December, Edward was promoted to Captain.

Over the next few years Joseph's letters contain many references to Edward as he travelled to and from Ireland, Brighton, Windsor and went on frequent shooting trips (for two months or so almost every year from 1830 till 1845) which his father treated with mock bemusement. An illustrated table of who caught what during a shooting party in November 1833 at Norman Court, home of Baring Wall MP, shows that Edward was a good shot and bagged more birds than the other three guns.

After 13 hugely enjoyable years, Edward's army career came to an end in 1836 when he decided to embrace married life instead. Believing that the continual travelling soldiering entailed was unsuitable for a married man, he left the Guards with regret. Herbert commented: "He often spoke of them [his brother officers] and recalled incidents of his military life. When he joined the Army the men wore powdered hair, and were armed with flint and steel muskets with an effective range of 200 yards... Flogging of appalling severity was of almost daily occurrence, and a man rarely survived the infliction of 500 lashes...."[7]

Edward and Julia Jekyll's early married life

On 25 July 1836 Edward and Julia Hammersley were married at Mary Le Bone Church. Julia was the daughter of Charles Hammersley (of the Army Agency, later Cox's Bank) and Emily Thomson, third daughter of John Poulett Thomson of Waverley. The last mention of Edward in his father's correspondence comes in a letter written a few months before his death: "As no one can form a better Judgment on such a point, I am glad to hear your Approval of Edward's choice of a Wife, whom with Mrs Hammersley he brought to me for an hour a day or two before their Marriage."[8]

Comparatively little is known about Julia, but she appears to have been capable and likeable. She was certainly extremely musical and a talented needleworker, while Francis Jekyll describes her as an accomplished amateur artist.[9] Edward may have given up the peripatetic life of the army, but he showed no desire to settle in one place, and his and Julia's early married life was an extraordinary sequence of travel interspersed by the births of their children. His diaries of these tours start with their 14-week honeymoon round the Isle of Wight (by sea, which Edward loved) and through Dorset, Devon and Cornwall, looking for a place to live. They finally settled on Holne Park near Ashburton, which they rented for the next two years. Their first child, Caroline, was born here on 16 March 1837, a week after Joseph Jekyll's death.

While at Holne Park the first mention is made of Edward's interest in explosives, in a letter dated 21 June 1837 from Edward Bigge, Fellow of Magdalen, to his brother Charles:

"I have stayed with Jekyll without being blown up with gunpowder or any of the combustions which abound... On my arrival a large flag was run up on a staff on a steep hill behind the house and the Mortar 'wizzed off' by the chief gunner and factotum in honour of my arrival. The quantity of powder consumed is great as we had since I came the anniversary of Waterloo, Magna Charter [sic], and a birthday, and today is Lord Howe's victory, and Ned is at this moment in the 'Justice Room' making blue light for a grand display after dinner... Mrs J is a very good match for him, a capital musician and a quiet sensible person. She likes to see him playing his pranks and has rather a good

notion of joining in them. There is a little Miss J –
the image of Ned – a beauty of course."[10]

Towards the end of 1838 Edward and Julia set out
on a two-month tour of Belgium (including the
battlefield at Waterloo) and Paris, which Edward
found in every way inferior to London. In the
summer of 1839 they settled at Grantham House,
West Cowes, where on 18 August the second child,
Edward, was born, and where they remained until,
early in 1841, Edward bought a house in London.
No. 2 Grafton Street (demolished in the 1890s)

became the family's home for the next seven years,
and was the birthplace of Arthur (b. 5 April 1841),
Frederick (b. July 1842), who only lived a few
weeks, Gertrude (b. 29 November 1843) and
Herbert (b. 22 November 1846).

The children were all baptised at St George's Hanover
Square. Gertrude's godparents were Lady Gertrude
Sloane Stanley – proxy Caroline Hammersley –
Catherine Hammersley, and Frederick Calvert –
proxy Hugh Hammersley. (The three Hammersleys
were Julia's siblings). Edward Bigge, Vicar of

Figure 2.2   Pencil sketch of 'The Idle Club', Seaview, Isle of Wight by Gertrude Jekyll.

Figure 2.3   Water colour painting of 'The Needles from H. Hammersley's house at Lymington' by Gertrude Jekyll.

Eglingham and Archdeacon of Lindisfarne, came from Northumberland to baptise her. Gertrude was named after Lady Gertrude Sloane Stanley, as Walter explained in a letter to Mrs Charles Hammond from Lucea, Jamaica on 22 November 1917: "My grandmother's (Mrs Jekyll's) brother, William Sloane Stanley, of Paultons, near Romsey, married Lady Gertrude Howard, a daughter of the then Lord Carlisle. My sister was named after her. I can just remember her as a stately old lady of whom I was rather in awe. We were très liés with them all, as they were my father's only near relations."[11]

No. 2 Grafton Street had previously been part of a larger house owned by the Earl of Pembroke, and contained a fine staircase and good rooms with handsome chimneypieces. "I often heard my parents talk about the house and their life in London," Herbert wrote.[12] "They went much into Society, were devoted to music, and frequented the Opera in the days of Malibran, Grisi, Mario, Tamburini and Lablache. Mendelssohn was a frequent visitor, and used to accompany my mother who had a charming contralto voice, which she retained till well advanced in years. He promised to write songs for her, but died before fulfilling his intention. My mother often recalled his singular charm. It was his habit on entering the room to go to the piano and improvise for hours, while my mother watched his curious technique. His fingers tumbled over each other in such a singular way that she asked him how he contrived to avoid mistakes. 'I cannot make mistakes' he replied and continued his playing, talking all the time. She often heard Chopin play – the last time at a party given by Lady Antrobus when he was so feeble that he had to be carried into the room."

In 1847 Edward and some of his musical friends founded an orchestra, The Amateur Musical Society, which flourished for a number of years (Prince Albert and the Duke of Cambridge were amongst its members). At first it met at Grafton Street, and was conducted by Lord Gerald Fitzgerald. Edward continued to be an active participant after the move to Bramley until the Crimean War when so many members were lost that the Society shortly afterwards disbanded. Also close to Grafton Street was The Royal Institution in Albemarle Street, which Edward, who was intimate with the physicist and chemist Michael Faraday, often visited.

In September 1841 Edward's brother Joseph died, and Edward received some accession to his fortune, though Joseph's widow remained at Wargrave Hill[13]. In the summer of 1843 Edward and Julia set out on a tour of Switzerland and Italy which lasted 3 months, taking with them Caroline, their eldest child, then aged 6, a maid and a courier. Edward studied fortification wherever they went, "and took every opportunity of hearing military bands and seeing soldiers' artillery practice and military exercise which he criticised with the exacting eye of an ex-adjutant of the Guards; while with his innate love of water in all forms he revelled in Rivers, Lakes, Waterfalls, and fountains." Their diaries reveal that Edward was far from well, though "frequent complaints of suffering...[are] relieved... by whimsical remarks which reflect his habitual gaiety."

In the summer of 1844 the family went for the first time to Seaview, a small fishing village in the Isle of Wight, where for many years afterwards they spent several months annually and later Gertrude drew caricatures of fishermen (Figure 2.2) and painted watercolours of the island (Figure 2.3). Edward built a house there called Vectis House – the largest in the village at the time – but later on they sold it and stayed instead at Arctic Cottage, "a very small abode. The fitting of us all into it was a triumph of my mother's domestic management." It was one of the westernmost houses on Nettlestone Point and in 1856 the family watched the ships that had taken part in the Crimean War sail into Spithead, and Walter Jekyll recorded this "notable sight: frigates, two-deckers, three-deckers."

The first year there Edward hired the yacht Ariel to sail in the Solent, and then bought the Alarm – a cutter of 42 tons – in which in 1845, accompanied by Charles and Hugh Hammersley, and Dr Finch as their medical attendant, he and Julia made a two-month voyage through the inland waters of Holland and up to Denmark and Sweden. In later years at Seaview Edward engaged a wherry, the Oakapple, for the season.

Bramley House

In the summer of 1848 the family moved to the country. Attracted by its ponds and streams, Edward took a 21-year lease of Bramley House and about 60 acres of land from Colonel Wyndham – afterwards created Lord Leconfield – at the 'absurdly' low rent of £200 per annum. This was to be the Jekylls' happy home for the next 20 years. With the birth of the 7th and last child Walter on 27 November 1849, the family was complete.

Rural, unpopulated Surrey, as it then was, was an idyllic place for children, who were free to play in the grounds, fish in the ponds and roam in the surrounding fields, lanes and footpaths. "We were

Figure 2.4   Bramley House from the south-east.

all fond of flowers," remembers Walter, "and knew the names of them all, both under glass and out-of-doors." Gertrude, who came between two elder and two younger brothers, naturally spent more time following their boyish pursuits than with her much older sister Caroline.

For Edward, Bramley House was the most permanent and settled of all his homes, and in spite of becoming more of an invalid he was able to indulge his scientific interests to the full. Julia ensured that order reigned domestically: "She hated disorder and unpunctuality. Breakfast and dinner were to the moment, and the household was perfectly regulated. As she used to say of herself: 'I should have made a good housemaid'." The children, ranging from 12 year old Carrie to the baby Walter, enjoyed each other's company, and indeed remained good friends into old age when they were separated by great distances. They were taught by a succession of tutors and governesses before, in the boys' cases, being sent to school or into the services. The family also played an active role in the village, and had friends and relations to stay.

Bramley House (Figure 2.4) was a small farmhouse, rebuilt and enlarged by Lord Egremont who bought it as a rest house between London and Petworth, and "to secure the use of the water to feed the Wey and Arun Canal in which he was interested...The House itself, built about 1830, was substantial and roomy. It stood on slightly rising ground, and though partly surrounded with water, was remarkably dry. The two principal sides were furnished with Ionic colonnades, which gave the house a certain degree of dignity." (HJ)

There were good rooms on the ground floor, with unremarkable bedrooms upstairs. On the south–east side, "a large dining room with a black marble chimneypiece at each end, and two small rooms, one the school room, afterwards converted into a bedroom for my father, and the other the workshop. On the NW side, the drawing room 60 ft long, divided by partitions into three with arched openings," the last of which was fitted with shelves upon which were arranged Joseph Jekyll's collection of Greek vases. Between the two principal rooms was a long stone paved hall along whose sides "were ranged casts of antique statues, which my father bought at the sale of his friend Colonel Needham, interspersed with some of the larger Greek vases on stands, and smaller casts such as a horse's head from the Parthenon and various bas reliefs. Among these was the head of a lion with open mouth, which we used to feed with pieces of toast." (HJ)

In the dining room, the furnishings were more

eccentric. There was an orrery (a mechanical model of the solar system), a windmill and a full-rigged brig – both very large. "The ship was the model of a brig such as was used for training lads for the Royal Navy. At one time there was an Erard grand pianoforte in the room too. The brig, the windmill, the pianoforte and a marble slab table of considerable size completely filled that end of the room. On that table towards the end of November reposed three cakes, our birthday cakes. Gertrude, Herbert and I were born within one week at a distance apart each of 3 years: Gertrude 29 November 1843; Herbert 22 November 1846; Walter 27 November 1849." (WJ)

The orrery, windmill and brig came from the sales Edward attended, especially at Stevens auction rooms in Covent Garden. So too did a model of Drury Lane Theatre fitted with trap doors and scenery, which also resided in the dining room. "The theatre, windmill and brig were incredibly dusty, but were never allowed to be cleaned."

The workshop, known as 'the shop', was Edward's domain. "Here were made the models of steam engines which were my father's chief amusement.

He kept a mechanic named Hill – engaged for a fortnight and stayed 14 years – who made all the parts. When a new engine was completed, steam was got up and it was made to go. From time to time several engines were connected with the boiler and there was a grand display." (HJ) Edward also made clockwork models of steamboats, which cruised on the upper pond.

In the garden, the first thing to arrest attention was the fortification close to the front door. It was a model, "laid out by my father and Colonel Hamilton, of part of the enceinte of a fortified town on the modern French system, with bastions, curtains, ravelins, and covered way complete, and was about 40 yards long from end to end... the whole affair, smothered with coarse and uncut grass, became an untidy jumble of shapeless mounds. But it enjoyed a peculiar sanctity, and survived as long as we remained at Bramley." (HJ)

In other respects, the gardens were more typical of their period: "On each of the two principal sides of the house was a parterre of flower beds, the one facing the dining room consisting of concentric rings, the outer of which was always filled with

Figure 2.5   Watercolour painting of Bramley House and Garden by Gertrude Jekyll.

Tom Thumb geraniums, and the others with lobelia, calceolaria and other common bedding plants. The centre of the circle was marked by a large stone vase containing an aloe. On the drawing-room side the parterre was semicircular with a fountain in the middle (Figure 1.5), and beyond it a large bush of sweet briar. The beds on either side displayed more variety than the others, and even varied from year to year. The planning of next year's arrangement was a matter demanding long and anxious thought. Under the colonnade were wooden stands in stages between the windows filled with flowering plants in pots. The water for the fountain was pumped up by a waterwheel from the stream to a cistern on the roof of the house."

"A short distance from the house on the south side was a circular enclosure surrounded with shrubs, called the Verbena garden[14]. It had a shallow circular pond in the middle filled with watercress and fed by a trickle of water from the adjacent swamp. Beyond this again was a shrubbery, mostly rhododendrons, with a few trees among which Arbor-Vitae [*Thuya*. Northern White Cedar], a cut leaved beech and a Pinus Excelsa were prominent. In the extreme corner of the shrubbery were the children's gardens bounded by a muddy ditch with a bank beyond. On the west side of the Verbena garden was a no man's land of swamp and bog with a tangle of brambles, rushes, reeds and water plants."

"The walled kitchen garden, an acre in extent, was a quarter of a mile from the house, contained a long range of glass houses and a separate one for stove plants. Over the entrance gate was a small antique lion in low relief sculptured in Pentelic marble probably from the Egremont collection. The walls were well furnished with fruit trees and we had an abundancy of peaches, nectarines, plums, cherries and pears... A mulberry tree, which in its young state we nearly killed by stripping it of leaves to feed our silkworms, grew to a large size and fruited well." (HJ)

"It was an understood thing that we children were not to touch peaches on the wall, but that we might pick up those that dropped," Walter relates. "I rather think that dropping was sometimes, though not often, artificially aided. Gooseberries, currants, strawberries, raspberries we could pick to our hearts' content and the sweet-water pears and Quarenden apples in the orchard. On either side of the path that divided the larger walled space in the kitchen garden into two equal parts was a mixed border of old-fashioned plants flanked by a sweet-pea hedge. In the middle was a tank. At one time we had a tame sea-gull, brought back from the Isle of Wight, and fish were put into the tank for him to eat." (WJ)

Beyond the gardens were the ponds: "The lower or mill pond was four acres in extent. In summer we fished in it and boated, and in winter we skated upon it. It was the skating-ground of the village and the whole neighbourhood. The smaller upper pond we reserved to ourselves... Beside the boat, on the waters of the big pond floated a relic of ancient home-brewing, a beer-cooler, a square thing in which we punted about by help of a pole. The ponds abounded in fish: perch, gudgeon, carp (which could never be caught), roach, bream. In after years we added pike, which throve well. The stream which supplied the ponds held trout in its upper reaches, and I used to fish it ...

"At the end [of the upper pond] nearest the house was a little stage from which the gardeners dipped for water. A rustic bridge crossed a small trickle that ran into the head of it. Hops grew there, and caterpillars called hop-dogs, pretty furry things, were objects of interest. The thicket through which the trickle ran was penetrable only for children. There were nests of black–caps and whitethroats and even nightingales to be found there.

"Crossing the rustic bridge, one came to the fernery, never a successful affair; a box-bush close to it once contained a bottle-tit's nest, a great find. We extracted one egg with a salt-spoon and left the rest. The path skirted the pond and met the carriage-drive by the Austrian pines, leaving it again at the bridge over the outflow. Passing the hatch, which to my knowledge was never opened, one came to a quince tree overhanging the water. Some of its boughs dipped in and moorhens nested in them. The damp ground also suited a medlar. In late autumn excellent medlars, that had dropped, rewarded a careful searcher.

"By the catalpa tree, on which missel-thrushes nested, was a short bridge to the island, on which were trees, shrubs and a summerhouse. There were other islands. The next one had a very shaky longish bridge, which finally collapsed. As long as it was available we crossed it in order to set sight-lines for eels." (WJ)

There was also a dairy which adjoined the orchard, "and we had a plentiful supply of milk, cream, and butter from a herd of 6 or 7 Alderney Cows. One year, during a visitation of Foot and mouth disease, then called Rinderpest, the entire herd had to be slaughtered." (HJ)

"A yew hedge of great height and thickness protected the garden on the East side. The gardener, Elsley and his family, occupied a cottage inside the walls. My father took in additional land on the West side, and planted a hornbeam hedge to separate the garden ground from the adjoining field. He took great pride in this hedge which reminded him of a Battalion on parade... We had a head gardener and 4 labourers. In 1851 labour cost £183.19.2½, seeds £11.13.6, and sundries £11.9.10½. Total £207.2.7." (HJ)

At one end of the farmyard was a large barn, where the canary-coloured chariot with C springs and silver mountings which the Jekylls had used in London was kept for a time, in a sadly dilapidated condition. Julia drove herself in a pony carriage drawn by a black mare, and the younger Jekylls used to drive about in a queer little cart drawn by one of the two ponies, Toby or Peggy. "Gertrude was generally the charioteer. Crim [the family dog, a mongrel] ran on ahead, his ears flopping, and we used to sing to a tune from Nicolai's Merry Wives of Windsor... Sometimes we had a spill, but never got hurt. When Gertrude saw that an accident was inevitable, she would sing out cheerily 'Sit loose', the notion being that we might fly clear of the danger of wheels and hoofs. Eva Weguelin [a Hammersley cousin], I remember, once took it as a personal affront when she was capsized into a ditch. We others never thought ill of such happenings." (WJ)

In the early years at Bramley Edward travelled up to London several times a week unable to reconcile himself to a country life, and spent the evenings at home copying out music, which he wrote with great facility. He also pursued his interest in explosives, giving occasional displays of "squibs, crackers, Catherine Wheels, Roman Candles and Rockets – not all of home manufacture. Home-made squibs were used to destroy wasps' nests, which were dug out the next day and the grubs used as bait for fishing. We had a 5in brass mortar, from which Mangel Wurzel projectiles were sent hurtling through the air," Herbert relates. "We also made Montgolfier fire balloons of tissue paper, the lifting power supplied by cotton wool soaked in spirit. On calm days they went up well, but the least wind caused them to burst into flames." The building of bonfires was another accomplishment, the largest of which was one supervised by Edward at Aldershot (for Julia's brother Fred Hammersley), in honour of the marriage of the Prince of Wales and Princess Alexandra. It was mainly composed of furze bushes and tar barrels and took days to collect and pile up. "All the King's horses and all the King's men were

engaged in the work. We went over on the night, my father provided with a Staff Officer's Cap for the occasion, and saw the grand blaze, which fully justified his temporary appointment." (HJ)

Although he had left the army years before, Edward still took an interest in matters military, and kept in touch with his former associates. When the Crimean War broke out, he followed it closely through friends who were still serving. He decided to give a lecture on the subject to the villagers, and threw himself wholeheartedly into its preparation, as he described to Lady Duff Gordon (a great friend of the family, to whom he often wrote), sticking up handbills, making drawings and models of guns, mortars, and sandbags. "Now do not think me a vain Ass, but my labours were wonderfully rewarded. The room was filled to suffocation, 240 were squeezed in... and the crowd outside reached far down the road." Edward announced that he would talk again in two nights time, "and the disappointed multitude retired. I discoursed my audience for one hour and a half, and never did I hear a more breathless silence. I explained the attack and defence of a Citadel; my enlarged plan of Sevastopol explained our position and the defences of that place..."[15]

Such was the appetite for information, the second night was more crowded than the first, and Edward found himself embarking on a lecture tour at Godalming, Guildford (twice), Dorking, Reading, Cranley [whose name was later changed to Cranleigh to avoid confusion with Crawley in Sussex], the London Polytechnic, Maidenhead, Eton, amongst others, charging entrance at a shilling a head to raise money for the Patriotic Fund. "...my mind is so much harassed by all the late hours I hardly know what I am about... I cried like a child when I heard the fatal news respecting the Battle of the 5th (Inkerman). Old comrades of 30 years standing, and others near and dear to me, all numbered with the dead," he wrote to Lady Duff Gordon[16]. And later, "I took Faraday for my model, who never allows one word to pass unexplained. I heard him say, if you mention a pin, describe it if you think there are those among your hearers who do not know what it means."[17]

In February, Edward lectured at the Royal Institution, "before a host of bigwigs, and have been complimented by being asked to print my lecture. Faraday was most kind, as well as all the other great Philosophers. They all said my performance was 'wonderful'... as I made no boggling or hitch, and when my hour was up, and I told them I had more matter if they liked to hear it, a round of applause greeted me..."[18] More engagements followed at

Harrow and Oxford, while at Westminster School, "my old place of learning, I had a most enthusiastic reception"[19]. By his second visit to Oxford – his 22nd appearance – he had had 5028 listeners and raised £200 for Patriotic Fund.

The high point of Edward's lecture-giving came in April, when he travelled with Carry to Cambridge. At dinner he sat next to Dr Challis, the Custode of the Observatory, who invited him to come and see the telescopes the following day.. "I gladly responded yes, and for 5 hours did we discuss scientific matters..."[20]

In addition to such pursuits, Edward was a devoted family man. In the summer of 1855 he looked after Herbert and Walter, both of whom were suffering from whooping cough, while Julia, who had been ill with ague, travelled to Bavaria to take the waters with 18-year-old Carry, 11-year-old Gertrude, and their cousin Sophy Weguelin. He wrote emotionally and at length about the condition of the two boys to Lady Duff Gordon: "Pardon this long account, but I think of nothing else all the long day...."[21]

He suffered much from ill health himself, and "as time went on became more and more of an invalid. He went about in a wheeled chair drawn by one of the servants, and in this he visited the garden and village daily. It was his habit to go the round of the cottages with parcels of tea, sugar and tobacco, which he distributed among the occupants, with whom he sat talking and smoking. He was a real friend to them and they enjoyed his visits. The only light they had was the rush lights which they made themselves. My father slept so badly that he did not get up till the afternoon, and almost turned day into night. He spent most of the night in writing letters. When at school I had a letter from him every day." (HJ) Again, when Herbert was fighting in the Ashanti War in 1874, Edward wrote him daily.

The younger Jekylls seldom left Bramley except for their summer sojourn on the Isle of Wight and occasional trips to their Hammersley grandparents at 25 Park Crescent in London. Edward took them to the British Museum, the Zoological Gardens, the Great Exhibition in 1851, Wellington's funeral in 1852, and the Royal Institution to hear Faraday's children's lectures.

Visitors often came to Bramley – "usually uncles and aunts, Littledales, Stuarts, Barings and Weguelins, who came in couples for 3 weeks at a time, accompanied by some of their children...Other regular visitors were Lady Duff Gordon and her two daughters, the William Sloane Stanleys, the George Sloane Stanleys, Col Hamilton, my father's old brother guardsman, Colonel Bigge and his nephew Arthur, Mr., afterwards Sir Charles, Newton of the British Museum and his wife, who painted a spray of Passiflora racemosa on the wardrobe in Julia's bedroom, Walter Broadwood, Mr. afterwards Sir, Gilbert Lewis, William Brougham (afterwards Lord Brougham), Mr. afterwards Sir, Henry Layard."

"When visitors were staying we used to come in to dessert, waiting ready dressed in the hall, until the moment arrived to be ushered in and seated at intervals among the Company. The dinner hour was 7. The most constant of our visitors was Georgie Duff Gordon. We called her Duffy, and her great pleasure was to sing. 'Now let us run through an Opera,' she would say whereupon a volume was brought out, Donizetti or Rossini as a rule, and with my mother playing the accompaniment and taking the contralto part, while Duffy took the soprano, they would plod solidly through the whole work."[22](HJ)

The children's favourite game was archery. They also enjoyed bowls, quoits and cricket. "But when, with the peace that followed the Crimean War croquet came in, a ground was made in the meadow and all other games abandoned. So keen were we that we often played after dark with lanterns." (HJ) Another devotee of the new game was one of the weekend visitors, Mr Layard of Nineveh fame "He flew to the ground on his arrival and bade me (the Imp, as he called me) to a contest. Those were the days of the 'tight' croquet. You put your foot on your own ball, placed against your adversary's and then gave a whack which sometimes hit your foot as well as the ball. Now, said Mr Bull (our name for him after the Assyrian bulls of his discovery), I'll send you to kickerybobus, and down came the mallet and off went my ball towards the pond. Sunday with us was rather rigidly observed, and Mr Bull's proposal that we should play croquet and call it Pilgrim's Progress was not favourably entertained."[23](WJ)

The children were taught the alphabet (and bible lessons) by Julia Jekyll and could read by the age of 4. Every year they gathered wild violets for her birthday, the 18th March: "we knew all the habitats, and our favourite places were Bramley Hill, Snowdenham, Tangley, and a small spinney leading up to Wonersh Church... We could look into the window of the Grantley family vault there and see the rows of coffins." They had a Swiss bonne, called Marie and all chatted French when quite small." The big boys – Teddy and Arthur – had a German tutor, Mr Camera, till they went to school

Figure 2.6   Watercolour painting, 'From Wargrave Hill' by Gertrude Jekyll.

in 1853. Carry and Gertrude had governesses... while Mr Burnside was engaged for Walter and me...".[24] Walter also went to Elstree for a few terms. In 1863 Arthur died when HMS Orpheus, in which he was midshipman, was wrecked in Manakau Harbour in New Zealand. The family were deeply distressed; Walter described his state of misery and shock when he was shortly afterwards sent to Harrow, where he remained for two years, 1864-6, afterwards returning home to be tutored for entry to Cambridge.

By now the Jekylls' time at Bramley was drawing to a close. On the death in 1865 of Mrs Spencer Montagu, the widow of his brother Joseph, Edward had succeeded to the Wargrave estate. Although the younger Jekylls resisted, Edward decided to live at Wargrave Hill, the house he had known in his childhood, and which he had been waiting to inherit for 24 years. Having obtained permission from Colonel Wyndham to cancel the last year of his lease, Edward made arrangements to give up Bramley House in 1868. Colonel Wyndham was willing to sell him the place, but he declined the offer.

Wargrave Hill

Wargrave Hill was an estate of some 300 or 400 acres and a small park, with a magnificent view of the river (Figure 2.6). "The house itself, built in the 18th century, was old fashioned and much too small for our requirements," wrote Herbert, "so my father commissioned our neighbour Mr Woodyer of Graffham... to make plans for its enlargement. A new wing was built on to each end of the old house, new offices were added on the north side and a colonnade on the South, while the interior was entirely remodelled." The house was more than doubled in size (Figure 2.7), while at the same time a terrace garden was increased and additions made to the kitchen garden glass houses. These works took two years, and the house was ready for occupation in the summer of 1868. A stream of vans drove from Bramley to Wargrave: "The cast of

Figure 2.7   The rebuilding of Wargrave Hill.

the Venus de Milo strapped onto the tailboard of the last van presented a strange appearance. One van was filled with garden tools, vases and plants including an assortment of border plants which my sister Gertrude had begun to collect."

The grandeur of Wargrave (Figure 2.8) in no way

Figure 2.8   Wargrave Hill from the south-west.

made up for the sadness of moving from Bramley, and in spite of the beauty of the river, none of the family ever became reconciled to the place. "There is little to record in the next few years," Herbert reports flatly, though from Gertrude, who lived there much of the time, came a constant stream of

work: woodcarving, metalwork, embroidery, painting and other skills (See Chapter 3). Edward, who was 64 at the time of the move, was by now a confirmed invalid. On 26 March 1876, he died, and was buried in Wargrave churchyard.

Munstead

There was nothing to keep the family in Berkshire, so Gertrude and her mother Julia returned to Surrey, buying land from the Fisher Rowes of Thorncombe Park on unpopulated Munstead Heath – a great concession as they were reluctant to sell any of the land they owned. Just a few miles from Bramley, Munstead was a favourite childhood resort on account of its lizards. Herbert made the original design for a symmetrical, classical house, but when this proved too expensive to carry out the architect John James Stevenson[25] was commissioned to build a house in the local Bargate stone.

It was at Munstead [House], where she lived from 1878-1895, that Gertrude created her first garden (Figure 2.9) from scratch. She turned the untouched, gently sloping heathland into a formal garden merging into woodland – a combination of borders, terraces and lawn interspersed with cut grass walks and informal woodland planting so uncontrived it might always have been there. She

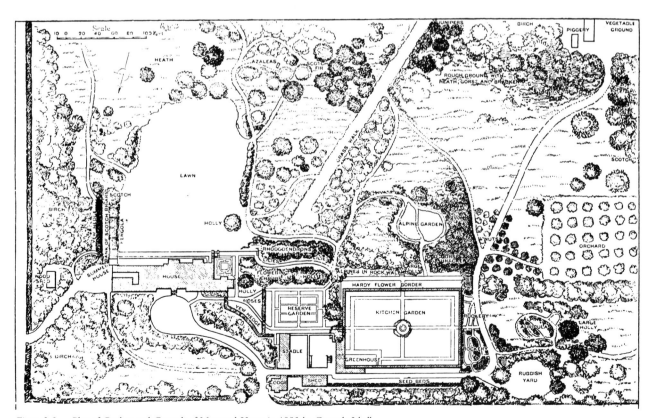

Figure 2.9   Plan of Gardens and Grounds of Munstead House in 1883 by Gertrude Jekyll.

Figure 2.10   The Hardy Flower Border, Munstead.

incorporated steps and raised beds at different levels, put in inlaid paths, a nut walk, a rock garden and a large walled kitchen garden, along the back of one of whose walls ran the long South Border (Figure 2.10). She had a workshop in the main house where she continued to turn out metalwork, carve wood, and also supervised all aspects of the garden and maintenance work. In the mid-1960s a pair of her spectacles was discovered high up on a beam of the old fire engine shed, where she had presumably been inspecting the roof.

Julia and Gertrude's life at Munstead was far from reclusive as the visitor's book shows, with numerous visits from siblings, relations and friends. Charles Newton of the British Museum, a friend of Edward Jekyll and excavator of Halicarnassus came, while the painter Hercules Brabazon, a friend of Gertrude and Herbert, was a frequent visitor, as were Barbara Bodichon, the Blumenthals, William Robinson and many other gardening contacts such as the Rev. Canon Reynolds Hole and the botanical illustrator Marianne North. Edwin Lutyens' name first appears in Jan 1892.

Across the road from Munstead [House] was a plot of 15 or so acres of land which the family were spurred into buying when it was proposed that a school be built there – schoolchildren would have meant disruption and noise. This was where Gertrude later built Munstead Wood. She wrote in 1932 that the site "came into my hands a little before the year 1882 when my mother gave me the land with the intention that I should make a home here after her death." In the 1880s she began to garden there, and in 1894, under her directions, a house known as the 'Hut' was built, as a place where she could work and entertain guests. Julia Jekyll's death the following year resulted in a family rearrangement, with Munstead [House] left to Herbert. Gertrude moved into the Hut and set about organising the building of Munstead Wood.

THE BROTHERS AND SISTERS
Caroline (1837–1928)

During a visit to Ireland in 1849, Edward wrote[26] about his daughter, "Carry I cannot praise too highly, she is so good, so well bred, so lively, so intelligent, it is indeed a pleasure to have her with me, her punctuality, precision, cleanliness alike good and praiseworthy, and tho' her father, I cannot help lauding her method, and the way she keeps, packs and takes care of her various things. She is a great darling."

Caroline, who was always known as 'Carry' (Figure 2.11), continued to be regarded with great affection when she grew up. Her brother Walter called her: "the greatest dear, beloved by everybody... she had no gifts that make a name, but she had a genius for that small talk which makes people popular."[27]

In 1865 Carry married Frederick Eden (1828-1916), a Commissioner in Fishery, and a semi-invalid. Agnes Jekyll (Herbert's wife) claimed in a short memoir, that marriage only 'partially' emancipated Caroline. Walter explained that their father was reluctant to consent to the match: "Yet there could never had been a happier one. They were devoted to each other."

Figure 2.11   Caroline (Carry) Jekyll.

In 1870 the Edens settled in Venice "as the place in which life could be lived with the least walking. His [Frederick Eden's] electric launch – almost unique in those days – took him over from Palazzo Barbarigo [where they had an apartment] to their great garden." This was the large garden on the neighbouring Giudecca that became known as 'The Garden of Eden' which, with its farm, they acquired in 1884. The Edens spent their summers at a villa near Belluno, where Frederick painted watercolours of the mountains of Cadore. Mrs Eden became a well–loved hostess and supported the English Hospital in Venice and the Sailors' Home.

In an article in *Country Life* in 1903, Frederick Eden described[28] how the six-acre garden evolved from being a ruin when they bought it to a formal garden of willow-wood pergolas growing with vines, rose arbours, crushed seashell paths and borders edged with brick or box. They decided to "make changes only as were needed to utilise and beautify it.... Our individual taste loves vegetation as Nature grows it rather than as man clips it." Gertrude was already established as a garden designer and, according to her niece Barbara Freyberg (née Jekyll), advised on planting and layout.

After Frederick Eden's death in 1916 Carry remained in Venice till the mid 1920s, when she returned to England, and lived in a house in Alexander Square in London. Eventually, in the late 1920s she sold the garden, still tended by Angelo the trusted gardener, to Princess Aspasia[29], morganatic wife of the King of Greece who died of a monkey's bite.

Edward (1839–1921)

After just under two years at Harrow, in April 1855 'Teddy' was removed from school by his father and sent to a tutorial establishment near Lubeck "to learn German and useful things".[30] Nearby lived the Baron and Baroness Biel, dairy farmers on an enormous scale. "Fancy 1178 gallons of milk per diem, making 180lbs of butter in a Brobdignag churn, turned by two horses," wrote Teddy's father Edward to Lady Duff Gordon.[31] The Baron's first wife was Julia Jekyll's aunt Sophia, who had died in 1826 soon after her marriage. Teddy became a frequent visitor to the Biels and their eight children, and was described as the 'perfect gentleman' with an "open handsome English face... with all the ladies of the place somewhat in love with him already."[32]

As a boy Edward had been a volunteer in the local company at Bramley, and he duly followed his

Figure 2.12   Edward (Teddy) Jekyll.

father into the Grenadiers (Figure 2.12); his service included a tour of duty in India and he rose to become a Captain. In 1870, Teddy returned to Germany and married the Biels' sixth child, Theresa. After the death of his father in 1876, Teddy and Theresa bought the Higham Bury estate at Pulloxhill, near Ampthill, Bedfordshire, and lived there in a house that Teddy built and partially designed, with a garden around it (Figure 13.3). They had two daughters, Millicent and Grace, who died when she was only eleven. Apparently Theresa was the first person to introduce rubber tyres to her carriage in Bedfordshire[33]. Teddy led the life of a local squire, much interested in the affairs of the village and the county. He was a Justice of the Peace and for a time Deputy Lieutenant of Bedfordshire. On his mother's death in 1895 he inherited his father's Etruscan vases, but sold them in July 1914 when they fetched only £900, which was less their original cost[34]. In 1920 at the age of 80, he moved to Kew, where Gertrude designed a garden for him, but he died the following year.

In the late 1920s, after the death of her own husband, Baron Erich von Maltzahn, Edward's daughter Millicent went out to to Jamaica to look after her uncle Walter Jekyll, and built him a house.

Figure 2.13   Arthur Jekyll.

Arthur 1841–63

Arthur (Figure 2.13), like Edward, went to Harrow in 1853, but seems to have left even earlier than his brother, for in a letter of October 1854, his father Edward informs Lady Duff Gordon that Arthur's ship was about to sail. Thirteen-year-old Arthur had become a midshipman in HMS Cossack[35]. The ship's captain, Captain Fanshawe, described him as an "ever zealous intelligent youth". Arthur's father wrote to Lady Duff Gordon: "Arthur says she [HMS Cossack] is only half manned, and her present crew are the scrappings of every Prison in the country, and the men openly say they intend to run away as soon as they can, and only entered the Navy to get their clothes and advance pay."[36]

The Cossack finally sailed in 1855 in the Baltic fleet of 101 British ships. In April she got stuck in the ice at Sansorana in Sweden, and Arthur ended up in hospital for 5 weeks with frost-bitten feet. After recovering he wrote that "The Swedish ladies are capital fun, they took me out riding, and my French was of great use, for I could talk to and make love to them." Edward commented, "Pretty well for a child not 13½ years old."[37]

Arthur's activities for the next few years are unknown, but he progressed to Lieutenant, and never came home again for any length of time. He was drowned in February 1863 when his ship HMS Orpheus was wrecked on the bar of Manakau harbour in Auckland, New Zealand; 189 men died.

Figure 2.14   An example of wood carving by Herbert Jekyll.

Figure 2.15   Herbert and Walter Jekyll, 1868.

When Herbert's elder daughter Barbara lived in New Zealand, from 1946-52, as wife of the Governor General, The Lord Freyberg VC, she presented a piece of Julia Jekyll's needlework to Government House, Wellington in memory of Arthur.

Herbert 1846–1932

For almost 40 years after the death of their mother Julia in 1895, Herbert and Gertrude lived in neighbouring properties at Munstead, and saw each other continually. They had much in common. Both had inherited their father's desire to make things and see how they worked, Gertrude in gardening and crafts, Herbert in woodcarving – at which he was extremely skilled (Figure 2.14) – and in engineering projects. Moreover both preferred pursuing their interests to social life. In addition, Herbert was a talented watercolourist, an organist and a founder member of the Bach Choir, which was formed to give the first complete performance of JS Bach's Mass in B Minor in England in 1876.

Herbert had originally wanted to train as an architect, but was persuaded by his father to join the army instead. By going into the Royal Engineers (Figure 2.15) he got as near to building things as he could, and carried on his father's interest in fortifications. In July 1863, aged 16½, he

entered the Royal Military Academy at Woolwich, and passed out with the Sword of Honour, the highest distinction available to RE cadets. He was gazetted as Lieutenant in 1866, and spent the next two years at Chatham.

In the early 1870s he became involved in building telegraphs (Figure 2.16)[38]. The Government had purchased the country's private telegraph systems in 1870 and placed them under the Post Office. Work on them had fallen behind, so Royal Engineers were brought in, which resulted in a body of thoroughly trained military telegraphists.

This proved useful in the Ashanti War. Herbert was amongst the first of Sir Garnet Wolseley's expeditionary force to arrive on 12 December 1873, and he was responsible for erecting a telegraph line into the interior. When he returned to London, he remained in special employment under the Postmaster-General. He lived in Morpeth Terrace, where Gertrude often stayed. In 1876, he received the first of many secondments to the Civil Service as secretary to Lord Carnarvon, then Secretary of State for the Colonies, who became a close friend. Three years later Carnarvon became chairman of the Royal Commission on the Defence of British Possessions and Commerce Abroad, and Herbert, by now a captain, followed him there at his request, staying until 1882.

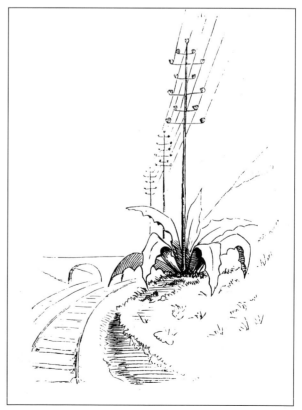

Figure 2.16   'Agave telegraphica' by Herbert Jekyll, 1871.

Figure 2.17 Francis (Timmy) Jekyll by Edward Burne-Jones.

Meanwhile, on 29 December 1881 Herbert had married Agnes (known as 'Aggie') Graham[40], youngest daughter of William Graham, Liberal MP for Glasgow, and an exceptional businessman, art collector and patron of the Pre-Raphaelites. They went to Munstead and to Paris for a short honeymoon, after which Herbert returned to work on Lord Carnarvon's Commission on the Defence of Coaling Stations.

The couple lived at 7 Seville Street (it belonged to the Edens and is now pulled down). Their first dinner party of eight there included Ruskin, Burne Jones, Robert Browning, Laura Tennant, afterwards wife of Alfred Lyttelton, and Frances Graham (Aggie's sister and a member of the Souls).[39] They used to go to Munstead for weekends, "greatly welcomed by Granny Jekyll and more tepidly by Gertrude, to whom we were, I fear, a sad interruption," wrote Aggie, in a Golden Wedding account of her and Herbert's life together.

They had three children, Francis (1882-1965 Figure 2.17), Barbara (1887-1973) and Pamela (1889-1943) – the two girls appear in a number of Gertrude's photographs (Figure 2.18); she also describes them sifting roses at Munstead Wood for

Figure 2.18 'The little nieces', Pamela and Barbara Jekyll, at Munstead Wood 1899.

Figure 2.19   Detail of a wall paper designed by Gertrude Jekyll for Oakdene, Surrey.

pot-pourri, and holding 'tank-parties' whenever her stone tank was freshly filled with water. When Francis was a year old, Herbert and Aggie left him at Grosvenor Place with Aggie's parents and travelled out to Singapore and Ceylon to report on coastal fortifications and design new ones. In 1886 they travelled to Gibraltar on the same task, and soon afterwards moved to Ireland where Herbert was again wanted as private secretary by Lord Carnarvon, the Lord Lieutenant, till he retired the following year. Herbert then worked for Lord Rosebery as Secretary to the Royal Commission on the Melbourne Centenary Exhibition and spent five years on the Royal Artillery and Engineering Works Committee, checking the detailed designs of defence works.

From Christmas 1884 for seven years, barring several leasings (for example to Lord Wolseley), Herbert and Aggie rented Oakdene near Guildford (it later became Mount Brown, the Surrey police force headquarters). An entry in Herbert's accounts book indicates that Gertrude contributed to its decoration: '18 February 1885. Wallpapers. Miss Jekyll – £17.11.6.' (Figure 2.19) Rake in Milford was the family's next home for 5 months from May 1892, before they returned to Ireland, where Herbert served under Lord Crewe (then Lord Houghton) for the next three years, and they lived at the Private Secretary's Lodge in Dublin. Sir John Colville, whose mother was Lord Crewe's daughter, recalled the family dictum that during Lord Crewe's long absences from Ireland the entire day-to-day responsibility for Irish affairs fell on Herbert's shoulders.

Ireland in the early 1890s was full of drama, with "sentries and passwords, with shadowing detectives, and murders and bombs and crime everywhere".

But there were compensations in the brilliant society "composed of the Irish Bar headed by Lord Justice FitzGibbon, the military world with Lord and Lady Wolseley... the intellectual society of Trinity College... the Gaelic group, with Yeats, A.E. Russell, Sarah Purser, and many another gifted and unquiet spirit", while Irving, Ellen Terry, Paderewski and Thomas Hardy all visited.

Having reached the rank of colonel, Herbert returned to military duties and took over the command of the Royal Engineers in the Cork District until 1897. Later he was appointed to the prestigious position of Secretary of the Royal Commission for the Paris Exhibition of 1900 and sent to Paris for a year in charge of the British section. Aggie described the British Pavilion (Figure 2.20 overleaf), which was evolved by Edwin Lutyens and Herbert, as "full of beautiful pictures and furniture... with an English atmosphere of bowls of roses, tea and music. It was a touch and go affair at first, for the French had been bitterly against us throughout the Boer War. The Dreyfus and Fashoda episodes had evoked passionate resentments, but champagne flowed continually, Barbara and Pamela (Figure 2.21), giving long-stemmed La France roses with a smile to suspicious pressmen, gradually sweetened the

Figure 2.21   Pamela and Barbara Jekyll at Munstead House, 1902.

Figure 2.20   The British Pavilion at the Paris Exhibition designed by Edwin Lutyens and Herbert Jekyll.

atmosphere, and perhaps the greatest compliment I ever had was when M Cambon, the French Ambassador, attributed the ultimate success of 'L'Entente Cordiale' to its birth and infancy in the Pavillon Grande Bretagne in the Rue des Nations in 1900.''

In 1895 Herbert had inherited Munstead House from his mother, and it became his and Aggie's base till they died. For the first two years Herbert was stationed in Ireland, and letters to Aggie at Munstead touch on such subjects as curtains and chair covers. Unlike Herbert and Gertrude, Aggie was passionate about the company of friends, in particular artists, writers, politicians, musicians, and was an inspired and attentive hostess. But this difference between husband and wife in no way cast any shadow over one of the happiest marriages conceivable. David McKenna remembered that Herbert would join the company not more than ten minutes before entry to the dining room: "He was an attentive and amusing host throughout the meal; but he would retire shortly after to his book-room to pursue his researches."

Herbert carried on the garden Gertrude had created at Munstead House and was a subscriber to the plant expeditions of Frank Kingdon Ward. Every so often, years after the initial subscription had been made, small, unidentified shrubs and small trees would turn up at Godalming station. What they were would only become clear after they had been planted and grew and flowered.

In the house Herbert installed an organ, which he played daily, and set up a work-bench for his wood carving in the style of Grinling Gibbons, which he practised until his death at the age of 85.

Herbert and Aggie were also great friends with 'Ned' Lutyens, who used to stay with them at Munstead House when he came to see Gertrude, and it was through the Jekylls and their circle that he received many commissions. Both Barbara and Pamela became clients of his after marriage. Barbara commissioned him to design interiors of her houses at 8 Little College Street, and later in Clarendon Place, where the fireplaces and woodwork were carved by Herbert. For Reginald and Pamela McKenna he designed 3 houses; 36 Smith Square, Mells Park in Somerset and Halnaker Park within the Goodwood Estate in Sussex. He also supervised the design of a house in Hampstead Garden suburb that was built for David McKenna on his marriage to Cecilia Keppel in 1932.

After Paris, Herbert was appointed KCMG. He retired from the army in July 1901 and passed almost immediately into the Civil Service at the Board of Trade as Assistant Secretary in the Railway Department. It was now that he began to woodcarve in earnest, keeping meticulous records of each piece of work completed. As well as working at Munstead where he designed and made the staircase, he carved much of the woodwork for their London home at 3 Green Street (which today houses a members club and a bridge club) from 1904-5. In 1907 he was made chief of the London Traffic Branch in the Board of Trade..

During this period "London vehicular traffic, from being almost entirely horse-drawn, became largely motor transport." He was responsible for laying down plans for new trunk roads (dual carriageways) out of London such as the Great West Road and he remained at this post till he retired in December 1911 on reaching the age limit.

The first three months of 1912 Herbert spent on holiday with Aggie in Jamaica, visiting his brother Walter, and staying with Sir Alexander and Lady Swettenham at the foot of the Blue Mountains. Retirement gave him the opportunity to carry out research on family genealogy, and write 'Studies in Family History' which has been heavily drawn on in chapters 1 & 2. From 1911 until 1921 he also served as Secretary-General to the Order of the Hospital of St John of Jerusalem, and as their Chancellor from 1911 until 1918.

From the mid-1890s Herbert and Gertrude lived in neighbouring houses and saw each other continually. Two gates were put in facing each other between the two gardens − with just a road in between − to facilitate visiting and carrying messages. The gates are still there. Bernard and Barbara Freyberg's son Paul always remembered crossing the road from his grandparents' house to visit his great aunt Gertrude and her cats. For Gertrude, Herbert was the person with whom she had the greatest affinity, and when he died on 29 September 1932, aged 85, she was devastated. In response to a letter of commiseration from Ellen Willmott she wrote, "6 October [1932] My dear Ellen, My love and thanks for your kind letter. Life seems very empty without my dear Herbert who was everything to me. Your affectionate Gertrude". She herself died some two months later on 8 December 1932. She left her whole estate to Herbert's widow Aggie, who died in 1937, and it was Timmy, Herbert and Aggie's son, who moved into Munstead Wood and continued the nursery business for the next five years.

Gertrude, Herbert and Aggie are all buried in the same enclosed grave at Busbridge Church, which was designed for them by Sir Edwin Lutyens.

Walter 1849–1929

The youngest child, Walter, was educated at Harrow and Trinity College, Cambridge. After leaving Cambridge he was ordained, and became the Curate of Heydon. Later he was appointed to a minor Canonry of Worcester, an appropriate post for his musical talents. After a few years he left for Malta as Chaplain, but soon afterwards renounced his Orders, having found that he had no vocation for the church.[41]

He then spent some time in Milan studying singing under the famous master Lamperti.[42] He returned to London, and moved to Birmingham, where he taught music and "gave penny singing lessons to poor people." From Birmingham he went to Bournemouth where he made friends with Robert Louis Stevenson, who may have named his famous character Dr. Jekyll after Walter.[43] Walter then moved to Newton Abbott in Devon where he lived for several years.

To an even greater extent than Herbert and Gertrude, Walter (Figure 2.22) eschewed the company of other people in favour of pursuing his own interests unmolested. He had always suffered

Figure 2.22   Walter Jekyll, c. 1885.

from asthma, and in 1894 decided to winter in Jamaica ("24 Oct, 1894 Sailed for Jamaica from Southampton in Para SS" reads an entry beside his name in Munstead's Visitors' Book). After his mother died in 1895 Walter moved there

permanently, living on his own (except for the last few months) for the rest of his life – another 34 years.

In Jamaica he continued to study music, and in 1907 published through the Folklore Society *Jamaica Song and Story*[44], the local stories and tunes of men and boys in his employ which he had carefully taken down. It was the only work on the subject for many years. He also took a great interest in Claude Mackay, the poet of the Jamaica Constabulary, and wrote an introduction to his 'Songs of Jamaica' in 1912. For a time he devoted himself to studying the works of Schopenhauer, and this resulted in 1911 in the publication of *The Wisdom of Schopenhauer as Revealed in some of his principal writings, selected and translated by Walter Jekyll, MA*. On its completion, he presented all the works he had consulted for it to the Institute of Jamaica.

Walter led a solitary, almost ascetic life, and was vegetarian. One of the few close friends he made in Jamaica was William Fawcett, Director of Public Gardens and Plantations, for whom he wrote the *Guide to the Hope Gardens,* the country's main botanical gardens (though it is said that "he was sometimes pained by their colour schemes"). He also wrote articles on the Jamaican flora and gardens both for local newspapers and for *The Garden* in London[45], and corresponded with William Robinson right up to the late 1920s. On 26 April 1928, he wrote, "Robinson sends me a new book, *Laughter and Health*, by an American doctor. He says that hearty laughter is one of the most potent agencies for the keeping of good health..." Like the other Jekylls he was a conscientious and articulate letter writer, and he kept in touch with his brothers and sisters – sending Gertrude shells for her shell pictures – to the end, though with the exception of Herbert, he never saw any of them again.

In 1907 Walter's house was damaged in an earthquake, after which he gave the property to his headman and moved to a hired house at Mavis Bank, nearer Kingston. Some time later, unable to continue with his extensive walks, he moved to Hanover and lived in a rented house near Lucea, where much of his time was spent giving lessons, teaching music and singing, French, Latin, Greek History, Geography, and Arithmetic. His last house was built by Millicent von Maltzahn, his niece, who latterly lived with him at Bower Hill near Riverside (Figure 2.23). By the time he died "he had divested himself of all his possessions," Herbert wrote. "My niece sent me a faded photograph, a two-foot rule and 3 or 4 books of little or no value. He had given away everything else."[46] [HJ 16 March 1929]

Walter was a highly intelligent, restless, complex character out of step with the modern world – in 1916 he wrote to a friend that he was using a fountain pen for the first time, and that he had never been in a motorcar or an aeroplane or seen a cinema – as, to a different degree were both Gertrude and Herbert. Living puritanically in the Jamaican countryside, sharing his scholarship with the local people, he seemed to have found fulfilment.

Without doubt, Gertrude and her siblings enjoyed an extraordinarily carefree, happy and fulfilling childhood at Bramley, at a time when village life in Surrey was untouched by electricity, tarred roads or any other modern intrusion. They were free to enjoy country pursuits, to watch the local tradesmen going about their work in much the same way as they had for hundreds of years, and above all to wander unfettered in extensive gardens and countryside. Something of the peaceful, wooded landscape seems to have entered their souls and lodged there permanently. It certainly engendered a love of gardens and growing things, for Carry, Edward, Herbert, Walter and above all Gertrude all tended gardens.

The influence of their lively, cultured parents is also apparent: their musical mother Julia's sense of order and creation of a comfortable, welcoming home; their father Edward's inquisitive pursuit of what interested him – explosives, electricity and military fortifications in particular – setting up a workshop and taking pleasure in explaining what he discovered in public; all seem to have rubbed off on their children, though in rather different combinations. They also had a great sense of family solidarity and as adults kept in close touch, visiting each other and writing.

Their father Edward Jekyll was a product of the Regency period. He was both unconventional and yet conservative, resenting change. That mixture was echoed in his children, and nowhere more clearly than in Herbert and Gertrude's misery at the disappearance of rural West Surrey.

Herbert ascribed the creeping suburbanisation to the growth of the population – by the 1920s it was four times that of the 1850s – and the extension of the railway. "The change was so slow as to be hardly perceptible in our time and had not made much way as late as 1876 when we returned to the neighbourhood," he wrote. "It was not till about 1890 that a marked difference in the appearance of the countryside began to make itself felt. Since then it has advanced with such ever increasing speed as

Figure 2.23   Walter Jekyll and Millicent von Maltzahn in Jamaica.

grievously to impair the rural character of the district... Nowhere is the change more marked than in the roads, which though greatly improved for transport, have lost the charm which they had when they were neither blacked with tar nor edged with hard cement kerbs, nor disfigured by unsightly telegraph poles and still uglier advertisement hoardings. It is no longer a pleasure to walk on a country road as it used to be meeting nothing but an occasional farm cart or timber wagon with its team of horses decked out in all their finery of brass ornaments, instead of, as now, a procession of motor cars, charabancs, omnibuses and bicycles."

For Gertrude, being back in Surrey was what mattered. The Old West Surrey of her childhood might be receding, but it lived on unextinguished in her mind.

3

Gertrude Jekyll: prelude and fugue

Joan Edwards

Of all the decorative arts few have more in common than gardening and embroidery: why else did gardeners call their parterres *broderies,* and Thomas Cromwell describe his garden as "a robe of embroidered works"? Although it would be absurd to suggest that all gardeners are *ipso facto* interested in embroidery, it is a proven fact that given the opportunity most embroiderers will make a garden, and that throughout the ages flowers have always been by far and away their favourite motifs.

I am neither a gardener nor a garden historian but an embroiderer, and my interest in Gertrude Jekyll began a number of years ago with the discovery of two designs by her in a charming little *Handbook of Embroidery* that was published in 1880 by the highly prestigious Royal School of Art–Needlework.[1] It was compiled by Miss L. Higgin and edited by the chairman of the Council, Lady Marian Alford.[2] The literature of embroidery was then in its infancy and it was forty years since the last handbook had been issued. It was their intention to provide practical instruction for those unable to attend classes at the School, and "to remind past students of the many important details that are easily forgotten once lessons are over." Ever mindful of the need to promote the School's other facilities, they printed a supplement of designs available in its showroom at the end of the book, from which readers could order "prepared or finished work," that is, a pattern traced out onto the textile for them to work at home (the School never dealt in transfers), or one to be embroidered for them by a member of the highly trained staff in the workroom. Nos 9 and 10 are by Gertrude Jekyll and are recommended for chair seats and cushions

(Figure 3.1 and Figure 3.2). Predictably the subjects were floral, one being based on periwinkles and the other on irises.[3] The designs told me several things I had not previously known about her. *First,* that she drew well; *second,* that she had some practical experience of embroidery, because she had so simplified and adapted the flowers without losing any of their natural characteristics that even a beginner would not be frightened to attempt them, and an accomplished embroiderer still find plenty for imaginative invention in the choice of stitches, threads and colours; and *third,* that because many of the other designs in the supplement were by men of such eminence as William Morris, Edward Burne-Jones, Walter Crane, Selwyn Image and Fairfax Wade (architect of the palatial new building in Exhibition Road into which the school had moved in 1875) it must follow, I thought, that she was regarded by her contemporaries as one of the foremost embroiderers of her day.

The periwinkle and iris patterns belonged originally to a set of six cushion covers she designed in November 1870, the others being based on the dandelion, pomegranate, strawberry and mistletoe, that is, on three flowers and three fruit.[4] A search in the design room at the Royal School revealed no trace of these or any other patterns by her. Later, Mavis Batey told me about the small designs of mixed flowers, chiefly roses, tulips and lilies in identical containers, that were found amongst her garden designs in the Reef Point Garden Collection, University of California. These are all beautifully observed and sensitively drawn, and closely resemble the motifs on the title pages of her books, but it struck me as curious that they are in no way like botanical drawings but are, on the contrary, purely decorative, and I wondered why.

Gertrude Jekyll's fame as a garden designer is so great it is all too easy for us to forget that in the beginning she wanted to be a painter and that when, in a tragically short space of time, she was forced to abandon this because of what she herself described as her "painful and inadequate sight", she immediately set about developing her very considerable talent for design and handcrafts and, with astonishing courage and fortitude, made a successful career for herself as an embroiderer, craftsman and interior decorator. The depth of her disappointment was unfathomable and even in old age still haunted her. "When I was young I was hoping to be a painter", she wrote, "but to my life–long regret I was obliged to give up all hope of this after a certain amount of art school work."[5] All the same, there can be little doubt that the training of the eye, the hand and the mind she received in Sir Henry Cole's art school in South Kensington, founded in the aftermath of the 1851 Exhibition, was fundamental to the success of everything she subsequently created, including her gardens.[6]

The 1851 Exhibition revealed the unpalatable fact that although Britain might be the richest nation on earth, in matters of taste, design and colour, her manufactured goods (particularly in the field of textiles, carpets, lace and wallpapers) fell far below the standard of the Continental exhibitors. Enquiries into the reason for this disturbing state of affairs, disclosed a profound difference between the European and British attitudes to industrial design, and the consequent effect of this upon the methods of teaching in the design schools. In Europe design was of prime importance and the teachers were themselves professional designers who taught their students to follow their designs through every stage of manufacture, adapting them to the machines, and supervising the mixing and matching of the colours. In Britain, where the nowadays archaic sounding terms *pattern-drawer* and *pattern drawing* were still used, the majority of students in the government schools of design enjoyed few of these advantages. The teachers who were artists were not necessarily interested in design and many considered it vastly inferior to art. Was it, they sometimes wondered, really art at all? Furthermore, they thought it demeaning to have anything to do with the men on the factory floor, with the result that comparatively few of the designs sent down to the factory managers were any use until they had been redrawn and this task they either performed themselves or left to the untutored hands of their

workmen, who also chose the colours.

But if the exhibition made people aware of the problem it also provided the men and money to remedy it. A Department of Practical Art was set up under the Board of Trade, the design schools became "art schools" and an entirely new system of art education was introduced, the object of which was to raise the standard of industrial design by attracting better teachers and students, and to produce competent designers who would be not only artists, but also scholars and men of scientific knowledge.

In 1853 the Central School of Design at Somerset House was moved to Marlborough House in Pall Mall, where a small museum consisting of purchases from the Exhibition and objects loaned by private individuals, including some lace and a great deal of Sèvres porcelain from the Queen, was already established. The objects were displayed in such a way that visitors would learn to discriminate between "good" and "bad" art. In the entrance hall, which later became known as the Chamber of Horrors, they were presented with examples of Bad Art based upon False Principles: scissors formed like birds, candlesticks as human beings, egg cups as birds' nests, and plaid checks so large it needed two people to wear them; while beyond in the galleries was Good Art – Paradise in Pall Mall – that is, objects it was thought desirable for students, designers and manufacturers to study and copy.

By 1857 the museum, enlarged by annual state grants, had outgrown Marlborough House, which had in any case been designated as the town house for the Prince of Wales. This combination of factors led to the erection of temporary premises at South Kensington for both the museum, now named the Victoria and Albert Museum, and the art school, and in 1861 Gertrude Jekyll and her cousin Susan Muir Mackenzie enrolled as students. That her parents agreed to her doing this is, I think, the measure of their understanding of her character and appreciation of the unusual nature of her talents. They were, in a sense, conceding her right to be modern, to move away from the past and begin to live fully in her own generation.

She was fortunate, too, that the practice of admitting women to the design schools had been carried over into the art schools, though the sexes were always taught separately and women were never allowed in the life room. The school year consisted of a Spring and Autumn term. There were full-time classes for men from 10.00-12.30 and for women from 1.00-3.30, the subjects including drawing, geometry, perspective, modelling, design and painting in monochrome, oils and watercolours. Naturally the students had access to the museum collections and to the museum library (now the National Art Library) for the use of which they paid 6d a week, ls 6d a month or l0s 6d a year; fees were also payable for a variety of additional courses that were open to both full- and part-time students. During the Spring term women students attended the lectures on anatomy given by Dr John Marshall, a surgeon at University College Hospital Medical School,[7] reported by Francis Jekyll to have been so impressed by the excellence of his new student Gertrude Jekyll's anatomical drawings that he asked if he might use them to illustrate one of his textbooks, though if anything came of it he failed to make acknowledgement to her.[8]

Another lecturer was the distinguished botanist and designer, Dr Christopher Dresser, credited by his contemporaries with being the man who did more than anyone to raise the standard of industrial design and improve the status of designers. He was a Fellow of the Linnean Society and Professor of Botany at South Kensington where he taught botanical drawing, botany as applied to ornament and the history of ornament, a subject on which he was also an expert.[9]

Dresser's teaching was based upon the theory that through a knowledge of botany, i.e. the principles on which Nature works, students would cease to draw flowers and plants with the excessive naturalism associated with Bad Art, and through looking at them from a more scientific angle, would discover new patterns in them. In 1859 he wrote two little paper covered books for his students: *Unity in Variety as Deduced from the Vegetable Kingdom* and *The Rudiments of Botany, Structural and Physiological* and in 1862, coinciding with the International Exhibition, published a study of *The Development of Ornamental Art* through which he hoped "a wholesome stimulus would be given to the progress of art as applied to manufactures". The copies he presented to the museum library, are still there with his inscription in the front. How much, we may wonder, was the way in which Gertrude Jekyll drew the periwinkles and irises just eight years later due to the influence of Christopher Dresser?

The Principal or Art Superintendent of the school was Richard Redgrave, R.A., who had held the same post at Somerset House where Dresser himself had been a student.[10] He was interested in colour and the scientific principles underlying the harmony in the combination of colours, and particularly in the discoveries of M. E. Chevreul,

head of the dyeing department at the Royal Gobelins tapestry works in Paris. Chevreul's book *The Law of Simultaneous Contrast of Colours,* published in France in 1837[11], had identified two different types of colour harmony: the harmonies of analogous colours and the harmonies of contrast. In 1853 Redgrave himself published *An Elementary Manual of Colour* for his students in which he advised them to read not only M. Chevreul's famous book but also R. Field's *Chromotology* (1835), a treatise on colours and pigments, D. R. Hay's *Law of Harmonious Colours* (1838), Sir David Brewster's study of sight and light in relation to each other entitled *Optics* (1838), and a recent work by his friend and colleague Owen Jones, *An Attempt to Define the Principles which regulate the employment of Colour in the Decorative Arts* (1852). This list gives a fair indication of the intellectual toughness of the training Gertrude Jekyll received at South Kensington. She also started her systematic study of Turner's use of colour, based upon Ruskin's *Modern Painters,* the first volume of which containing "The True, the Beautiful and the Intellectual" appeared in 1845, and the last "Of Leaf Beauty; of Cloud Beauty; of Ideas of Relation; of Invention Formal and Invention Informal" in 1856. It is perhaps not surprising that Francis Jekyll should have remembered that his aunt's copy, as well as her copies of *The Stones of Venice* and *The Seven Lamps of Architecture,* was heavily annotated.

In 1857 Ruskin issued a catalogue of the Turner paintings at Marlborough House (the intractable problem of the housing of the Turner Bequest was then in its infancy), and another of the drawings and watercolours at the National Gallery. By arranging the paintings in chronological order he provided students with a view of the development of Turner's style commencing with the period between 1800 and 1820 when he was a student, through the years when, as Ruskin put it, "he was working out the principles he discovered during his studentship", and when, between 1835 and 1845 "his strong instincts conquered the theories of art altogether", to the ill-health which made his later work of inferior value. Presumably when Gertrude Jekyll wanted to copy one of the paintings she spread a cloth on the gallery floor and set up her easel upon it as students have done since time immemorial.

But the student who wishes to study an artist's drawings and watercolours must be able to handle them, and to facilitate this Ruskin selected a hundred from those in the National Gallery, had them glazed, and then arranged them in sequence, regardless of chronology, to illustrate a supposed trip up the Rhine, through Switzerland to Venice and back again. He next divided them into groups of five to ten sketches which the student could take "one by one in his hands into a good light, arrange them in order as he chose, and thus describe or copy them at his ease" without doing any damage to them. They were, he told them, to observe "the excessive thinness and tenderness of the tints" on which their chief effects depended; to remember that "every touch in them represents something complete and definite"; and that for the most part "as much is done with the given number of touches and quantity of colour as is possible to be done by the human hand".

Gertrude Jekyll must have been very familiar with this system and so also must her brother, Herbert, who shared her pleasure in the academic study of Turner's colours, and was himself a talented painter. Gertrude Jekyll (Figure 3.3) made a good copy of a painting by J. M. W. Turner entitled 'Clapham Common', painted between 1800 and 1805.[12] The painting was given by Gertrude Jekyll to Sir Gilbert Frankland Lewis of Harpton Court, Radnorshire. Two of Sir Herbert's paintings, presented by Lady Jekyll after his death in 1932 to the Department of Prints and Drawings, are entitled 'Lausanne looking over the lake of Geneva'

and 'Venice: the Giudecca looking out to Fusina' and these also are copies of two watercolours in the Turner Bequest.[13]

Having pieced together this account of the direction her mind was given at South Kensington, I venture to suggest that if her draughtsmanship was recognisably superior to that of most students, her theoretical knowledge of colour, acquired from Redgrave and Ruskin, and developed over a lifetime of study and practical experience of devising colour schemes for rooms and gardens, was at least as great if not greater than that of any other gardener before or since, and was incomparably more extensive than the easy journalistic catch phrase about her "unusually sensitive eye for colour" either conveys or is intended to convey. Her own modest rating of her knowledge was that she had perhaps "given more thought to arranging growing flowers, especially in the ways of colour-combination, than amateurs in general."

Following the Autumn Term in 1863 she spent three happy months travelling with Charles and Mary Newton in the Levant.[14] Charles Newton, discoverer of the Mausoleum of Halicarnassus in Asia Minor, had just been appointed Keeper of the Department of Greek and Roman Antiquities in the British Museum and the object of the trip was

Figure 3.3   Painting by Gertrude Jekyll of 'Clapham Common' by J M W Turner.

Figure 3.4   *Gertrude Jekyll in 1863 by Mary Newton.*

to enable him to visit recent excavations in the area prior to finshing his book *Travels and Discoveries in the Levant*.[15] Although Mary Newton[16] was considerably younger than her husband she was already an established painter. Being an exceptionally fine draughtsman, she drew some of the illustrations for this book (though they lose much of their original distinction through being reduced in size), and made large-scale drawings of classical sculpture for Newton to use when lecturing. The watercolour sketch she made of Gertrude Jekyll working in her cabin on one of the ships they travelled in is beautifully observed (Figure 3.4). She has seen her as a competent, serious and quietly determined artist, her mind concentrated upon her work, her eye watching the colours change as she lays one wash over another until the desired effect is obtained. The profile is charming, the mouth pretty. But here already are the ingredients of the portrait Sir William Nicholson would paint over half a century later; the plain, workmanlike dress, austere as a nun's habit, the pushed back sleeve and the crisp white collar and cuffs, the smooth hair with its centre parting and those terribly disfiguring spectacles with the thick lenses and uncompromisingly severe steel frames. She will work and work and one day she

will be a great gardener, but never the painter which, at this very moment, she still believed she would become.

Between 1865 and 1870 Gertrude Jekyll exhibited nine pictures and all were of animal subjects. The first, a study of her brother's dog Cheeky with the fashionably fancy title 'A Native of Cawnpore, 64th Regiment' was hung in the North Room of the Royal Academy, together with J. A. Whistler's 'Little White Girl' and G. D. Leslie's 'The defence of Lathom House.' The report of the exhibition in *The Times* (24 May 1865) referred to the "unusually large proportion of pictures [in The North Room] that attract and reward attention", amongst which 'Cheeky' was described as "a capitally painted small pug". Two years later she sold one called 'Toby in the Snow' privately, and exhibited with the Society of Female Artists[17] 'Quiet to Ride and Drive, has carried a Lady' and 'Jehu Driving Furiously' (Figure 3.5) which, when Ruskin saw it he described as "very wonderful and interesting" though this may or may not have been high praise. In 1868 came 'Neptune's Horses' and 'Donkey Foal – Life Size,' and in 1870 'Roman Cattle' (Figure 3.6), followed by three pictures whose titles suggest she was perhaps flirting with the idea of becoming a book illustrator: 'Froggy would a-wooing go' (Figure 3.7), 'Mr Punch's Dog Toby' and 'Portrait of Thomas, a Favourite Cat, in the Character of Puss-in-Boots, Puss carrying a present of rabbits to the king' (Figure 3.8). But although she continued to paint for many years there were no more major works to exhibit. The career that seemed so promising was over.

Gertrude Jekyll and her father shared the same

Figure 3.5   *Sketch for the painting by Gertrude Jekyll, 'Ahab pursued by Jehu'.*

Figure 3.6   Sketches for 'Roman Cattle' by Gertrude Jekyll.

Figure 3.7   Sketch for the painting by Gertrude Jekyll, 'Froggy would a wooing go'.

Figure 3.8   Sketch for the painting by Gertrude Jekyll, 'Portrait of Thomas in the Character of Puss-in Boots.'

tastes and interests. Both had a natural aptitude for handling tools and materials, both were practical and inventive and both were collectors.

Captain Jekyll's father was a member of Parliament, a Fellow of the Royal Society and the Royal Society of Arts, and was one of the founders of the Athenaeum Club in Pall Mall;[17] it is not surprising, therefore, that his son should take an active interest in the advancement of science and technology, electricity, engineering and archaeology (to which his friendship with Michael Faraday and Charles Newton bears witness), maintain a well equipped workshop and encourage his children to use it, make model steam trains and collect Etruscan vases (See chapters 1 and 2). When an attempt to send Gertrude to boarding school ended in disaster she could have had no better or more stimulating a teacher. Thinking back to this period many years later she gave two instances of his influence upon her:"I must have been instilled with a reverence for

Greek art from childhood, as my father had a large collection of life-size casts of the Milo Venus, the Venus of the Capitol, and other fine examples" and "I think a shred of my father's mantle must have fallen upon his daughter, for I have always taken pleasure in working and seeing things grow under my hand". After this we must, I think, believe that he took her to the British Museum to study the Elgin Marbles, the first original Greek sculptures of the Classical Age to become accessible to the public, and that the first casts she ever drew from were those she saw daily in his collection.

Her own study collection of textiles, embroideries, costume, vestments, lace and ribbons which she started during her holiday in the Levant, and added to on future visits to France, Italy and North Africa, survives now only in the specimens she gave in 1916, 1917 and 1924 to the Victoria and Albert Museum, and which were chosen by the Keeper of Textiles, A. F. Kendrick. Examination of them suggests she was less interested in the quality of her acquisitions than in their intrinisic value – their patterns and colours – and an occasional quotation from her diary indicates that from an early age she had a strong instinct to save anything she thought was in danger of being lost or damaged. This is entirely consistent with her habit when, years later, she started to collect agricultural tools and household utensils in Surrey. That her attitude to collecting was essentially romantic is spelt out in the letter she wrote to Kendrick in which she tells him not to expect to see a great collection of textiles, but one consisting of "the pretty things such as are almost unconsciously picked up by a person of accumulative proclivity."

Her reason for making the collection is set out in a letter from A. J. Wace who succeeded Kendrick as Keeper, in reply to an enquiry from Francis Jekyll. He told him that Miss Jekyll had allowed the selection to be made "because she felt the purpose for which she had brought the collection together, could be better furthered in a museum, where the specimens would serve as a constant source of inspiration, and as models of fine craftsmanship to successive generations of students and designers."[18] In 1981, several items were shown in the Lutyens exhibition at the Hayward Gallery, London.[19]

As a young man Captain Jekyll inherited a house, on the banks of the Thames at Wargrave in Berkshire, called Wargrave Hill (see Chapter 2). Because it was subject to a life tenancy agreement he did not obtain possession of it until 1865, and before the family could move there from Surrey (a prospect they viewed with considerable dismay), it

naturally had to be completely redecorated. The planning and supervision of this major undertaking he entrusted to his younger daughter with absolute confidence in her ability to carry it out. It was a challenge, an opportunity for invention and experiment, for the practical application of her theoretical knowledge of design and colour, and for making things with her hands.

The whole thing may have been purely coincidental, but appreciating the close relationship existing between father and daughter and the fact that already the strain imposed on her sight by continuous drawing and painting was probably beginning to manifest itself, it seems possible he took advantage of the death of the tenant to create for her the really big job that would engage all her skills and faculties, in the hope it might give her mind a new direction.

Be this as it may, it was her work at Wargrave Hill that caused the painter, George Leslie, who visited her there when collecting material for his book on the Thames and its riverside inhabitants,[20] to draw up that catalogue of her accomplishments: "there is hardly any useful handicraft the mysteries of which she has not mastered – carving, modelling, house-painting, carpentry, smith's work, *repoussé* work,[21] gilding, wood-inlaying, embroidery . . . everything being carried on with perfect method and completeness", and which the author of her obituary notice in *The Times* was only one of the innumerable writers who may be assumed to have quoted and adapted it. He amended it to read: "There was little her skilful fingers could not bring to perfection, from a finely wrought piece of silver to the making of her gardening boots, . . . all achieved with equal skill and enjoyment".

Gertrude Jekyll's dauntless courage in the face of adversity is never more in evidence than when, in 1870, at the very moment when she must have known she was showing her paintings for what was almost certainly the last time, she started to exhibit embroideries with the London International Exhibition Society in New Bond Street. They caught the quick and discerning eye of Frederic Leighton then settling into his newly built residence in Holland Park (now the Leighton House Art Gallery) and, not liking to approach her directly, wrote to her cousin, Georgina Duff Gordon, to ask whether there was any chance of her embroidering a cover in the same style for his dining room table. The piece he particularly admired had a design based upon scrolls and fish and seemed to him "of such remarkable merit in point of colour and arrangement" that he hesitated to attribute it to an amateur and presumed it was not of her own devising. Did Miss Jekyll, he asked, do these things solely for her own delight? or were they accessible to outside admirers, and if so, was the cost very ruinous? Upon receiving a favourable reply, he wrote again to Georgina Duff Gordon, with exceedingly polite and more specific suggestions. The cover was to be between 6ft. 6ins. and 7ft. square, "of some good design and rich tone, executed on serge wool or wool and silk" and, once again, he asked what she would charge for it. Presumably they met to discuss her sketches and proposed colour scheme and in the winter there was a note in her diary saying "Began Mr Leighton's tablecloth."[22]

So Sir Frederic Leighton joins John Marshall and George Leslie in recognising *at first sight* some special quality in Gertrude Jekyll's work which set it apart from other people's. We call this impact of the personality of artists, designers and craftsmen upon their work *style*. For Leighton, the artist, her style had to do with the nature of her design, her choice of colours, and the manner in which she combined them; for Marshall, the scientist, with the accuracy of her observation and mastery of drawing, that is, of representing three dimensional form on a two dimensional surface, one of the most intellectually difficult of all skills to attain; and for Leslie who himself used two media, paint and words, with equal facility, with her sure and confident touch in handling a variety of media from paint, plaster and iron to wood, gold leaf, threads and textiles.

Leslie discovered the same combination of artistic experience, scientific knowledge and craftsmanship in the garden she made at Wargrave Hill, but of which he found little or no evidence in the other Thames-side gardens he visited. He described it as "a perfect wilderness of sweets", and noted that "old-fashioned flowers bloomed there in the greatest profusion". This is probably the earliest published description of the new style of garden design she would develop fully at Munstead House and Munstead Wood and which, over sixty years after her death, still influences our own gardens.

Leslie made another perceptive remark about her. He noticed the generosity of her nature, declaring he would long remember with grateful admiration the *generous way* she reaped him an armful of lavender "with a lavender sickle of her own construction", as a home-going present. According to Francis Jekyll this pleasant habit, common to most gardeners, of speeding the parting guest with a bunch of freshly cut flowers, she practised also

with her craftwork and constantly occupied herself designing and making things for her friends' houses, well knowing that the present we all appreciate most, no matter how small, is the one made specially for us by the giver and which, even when worn out and broken, we are still reluctant to throw away.

Much as we may regret the things Francis Jekyll did *not* tell us about his aunt, we may be grateful to him for his choice of quotations from her diary referring to her work up to 1880 during which

Figure 3.9   Model at Gigi's Academy, Rome.

time she spent increasingly longer periods in London.

Here she is in Paris in 1866 with Georgina Duff Gordon copying paintings in the Louvre and taking singing lessons, and in 1867 attending classes at a studio in Grosvenor Square, making copies (chiefly of Turner) in the National Gallery, visiting G. F. Watts at Holland House, and copying his painting of white oxen ploughing, and, Mary Newton having died in the previous year, making drawings to illustrate a course of lectures by Charles Newton. In February 1868 she is in Rome with Susan Muir Mackenzie, studying at Gigi's *atelier* (Figure 3.9) and taking lessons from a frame-maker named Placide in carving, gesso and gilding and, before the year is out, applying these newly acquired techniques to making pear wood frames for the pictures she hung on the walls at Wargrave Hill, gilding stands for porcelain plates and ornaments, and arranging the pots she herself had collected in Rhodes. There are also references to her having taken lessons from Legros,[23] making masks and painting scenery for private theatricals.

The fact that in March 1869 she recorded a visit to William Morris suggests it had some special significance for her. Was she seeking his opinion on her chances of selling her craftwork and getting commissions for decorating rooms in the style she had devised for Wargrave Hill? Was it he who suggested she should offer some of her embroidery designs to the Royal School? and did she on this occasion meet his younger daughter May, then only seven years old, but who would in 1893 publish *Decorative Needlework,* the first book by a professional designer who was also an embroiderer? There is no doubt in my mind that Gertrude Jekyll owned a copy of it if only because May Morris was also a gardener and her thoughts on gardening and embroidery were as inseparable as her own. Take this, for example, and decide if you can which of them wrote it : "There is some quality about blue that invites contrast as an alternative to harmony"; or this : "After a little observation and experiment you will find out that besides their positive values, colours have a relative value of which you have never dreamt hitherto"; and is it about gardening or embroidery one of them wrote that it is "nothing if not pursued with due method and soberness and carried out in a womanlike way"?

In 1870, as well as designing and embroidering the cushion covers, she was again copying the Turners and the Dutch and Italian paintings in the National Gallery, painting some rush seated chairs she had made in High Wycombe, making spoons with ornamental heads, riveting up a large tobacco jar, and making iron stands to hold the glass in the frames with which she covered the cucumbers she was growing at Wargrave.[24]

The writer of the obituary in *The Times* made special mention of her enduring friendship with Jacques and Leonie Blumenthal,[25] whom she met for the first time in 1871, and whose house in Hyde Park Gate, overlooking Kensington Gardens, became a second home to her during the increasingly long periods she spent in London as her new career took shape. He wrote: "Their famous hospitality in London and at their lovely chalet above Montreux, brought Gertrude Jekyll happy relations with many artists and musicians and social notabilities."[26] These included the painter Hercules Brabazon,[27] whom Ruskin described as the only painter since Turner at whose feet he could sit and worship and learn about colour, and for whose music room she painted some furniture in 1872, and his neighbour in Sussex, Madame Bodichon, the celebrated pioneer of women's education who was a founder of Girton and Bedford Colleges, the Society of Female Artists and the first classes at which women could draw from the nude model; she knew Rossetti, Morris and the other leading figures in the Arts and Crafts Movement, and was used by her friend George Eliot as the model for the heroine of *Romola*.[28] During the winter of 1873/74 Gertrude Jekyll, Hercules Brabazon and two other friends, Frederick Walker[29] and George Cayley, spent three months with her and her husband at their home in Algiers. There was plenty of time for drawing, painting and music, for plant collecting expeditions led by the local professor of botany, and a course of intensive study of Islamic art directed by Cayley.

Gertrude Jekyll's work became known to many people through a reception given in her honour by the Blumenthal's, to mark the completion of her redecoration of rooms at Hyde Park Gate, and by 1875 she had so much work on hand that it was necessary for her to have a permanent address in London where she could receive clients. It was decided, therefore, that she and her brother Herbert should set up house together in Morpeth Terrace, a quiet street of terraced houses within easy walking distance of Whitehall, a happy arrangement which lasted until Herbert's marriage in 1881.

The trust people imposed in her good sense and sound judgement, and in her ability to handle workmen, is well illustrated by the request of the Duke of Westminster that she act as what he called 'umpire-in-chief' over the arrangement of the furniture and furnishings at Eaton Hall. Work on the enlargement and modernisation of this vast mansion in Cheshire started in 1870 to plans drawn by Alfred Waterhouse, architect of the Natural History Museum in South Kensington, with no expense spared, especially over the interior decoration. There were stained glass windows, marble mosaics, and a library curtain made from 200 yards of Utrecht velvet so heavy that it had to be hung on a beam and drawn and opened with special pulleys; the material for the upholstery in the state apartments was woven at Spitalfields, the chimneypiece in the dining room came from a palace in Genoa and the dinner service was Minton's showpiece from the 1851 Exhibition. But nobody could agree how best to display these magnificent trappings and all the suppliers quarrelled; it looked as though the place would not be finished in time for the official opening. There is a note of near panic in the Duke's note to Gertrude Jekyll in which he wrote: "I don't know how, without your advice, it will ever be satisfactorily accomplished."

Waterhouse's plan provided for what amounted to a second mansion for the family, attached to the first and in default of any other evidence, I think it may be for these rooms that the Duke commissioned designs for curtains and furnishings from her, as well as five embroidered panels which she called "Turret Stairs", and had had worked at the Royal School under her supervision. In *The Guide to Eaton Hall* by Rupert Morris (c. 1888), it is noted that the tapestry in the Drawing Room was designed by Miss Jekyll and worked by the

Royal School of Art Needlework, in 1882. It would be interesting to know whether the three quilts mentioned in her diary, one for Frederic Leighton, another for Edward Burne-Jones, and one simply described as "blue", were also made there, but the records, like those at Eaton Hall, have long since disappeared. Even though the writer of *The Times* obituary mentions her having made patchworks *(sic)* and done quilting, these three quilts have always puzzled me. It was impossible to believe they were to be used on beds. Eventually, when Michael Tooley showed me two photographs from the Reef Point Collection, taken by Gertrude Jekyll herself in the Blumenthal's drawing room, I got the answer (Figures 3.10 and 3.11). They were quilted curtains, beautifully soft, voluminous and opulent, drawn up into great swags and folds that swung halfway across the room and back again: theatrical as befitting to a salon, but which, by the loosening of a cord, will transform it into a small, intimate private place where two or three close

Figure 3.10   The Blumenthals' Drawing Room at 43 Hyde Park Gate, London, decorated by Gertrude Jekyll in 1886.

Figure 3.11   The Blumenthals' Music Room at 43 Hyde Park Gate, London, with a curtain and door, designed and partly worked by Gertrude Jekyll in 1886.

friends can talk for their own pleasure.

Recently I was shown a pair of doors identical with those in the photograph of the drawing room (Figure 3.12), in a house in the village of Copdock near Ipswich, formerly occupied by the Misses T. M. and A. Bernard, nieces of Leonie Blumenthal, and their brother, a retired naval officer. It is not known when or under what circumstances the doors were removed from Hyde Park Gate and re-hung in Copdock, but it can hardly have been before Leonie Blumenthal's death in 1927. Local information suggests that the inlaid work on the doors was not, as I had assumed, executed by Gertrude Jekyll herself, but by Leonie Blumenthal with her help. This makes one wonder how many other objects in the room were, in fact, the result of what was doubtless very pleasurable collaboration between the two ladies.

It is clear from every word Gertrude Jekyll wrote in her books on gardening and in her great celebration of rural craftsmanship – *Old West Surrey* – that she was a perfectionist, that for her there was always a margin, an horizon, beyond her present achievement, an unattainable goal, towards which she strove with dedication and sincerity. But she was stimulated rather than discouraged by the thought that with every season there was something new to be learnt about gardening, and always fresh problems in craft work to be mastered, for experience had taught her that "with growing knowledge comes the widening outlook, and the comforting sense of an ever increasing gain of critical appreciation." She was saying the same thing but more succinctly when she wrote: "The lesson I have learnt most thoroughly is never to say

In whatever material she worked she respected its limitations, what craftsmen call its breaking point, beyond which in either direction the object being made is out of scale with the tool in the craftsman's hand, ceases to please the eye, and develops defects that prevent it performing its function properly. It was precisely this ability "to combine beauty of form with utilitarian purpose" that she so greatly admired in the work of the Surrey craftsmen and sought to emulate in her own. But her appreciation of their farm implements, iron pots and simple wooden stools was neither uncritical nor sentimental, and she knew at a glance the difference between the work of a man whose rush light holders, candlesticks and snuffers were functional but commonplace, and that of the master craftsman whose work, besides being technically sound, was also aesthetically pleasing. Reflecting on one of the chimney cranes in her own collection which she gave in 1907 to the Castle Museum, Guildford, she wrote this: "What a true artist he was, the grand blacksmith who did this admirable piece of work in his village forge. How well he *felt* where his material should go for simple strength and use, and *when* and *where*, having served this purpose, it might be drawn out into pure ornament, to gratify the eyes of those who would see it for hundreds of years to come, and to satisfy his own pride and delight in doing beautiful work". I would defy anyone who has not themselves experienced the craftsman's pride and delight in doing beautiful work and the sense of satisfaction and fulfilment deriving from it, to have composed that phrase.

From time to time the old debate, professional *versus* amateur, breaks out again. As we have seen, Gertrude Jekyll leaves us in no doubt about her own status, and even when she was devising colour schemes for gardens, calls herself an amateur, *i.e.* the person who is always learning from the professionals, the masters of the mysteries of one particular craft, and whose expertise is only very rarely achieved by the amateur. She found it surprising, therefore, but immensely encouraging, that Surrey craftsmen were sometimes reluctant to teach her, fearing she might set up in competition with them. "They who show this spirit," she wrote, "can hardly know how hugely the compliment – evident though unintended – flatters the vanity of the amateur." Nevertheless, her attitude towards her work, and towards the clients who sought her advice and commissioned work from her, was always completely professional.

Like all craftsmen, both professional and amateur, what she so greatly enjoyed was the creative process; the putting forth of effort, the involvement of the hand, the eye and the mind in the resolution of the problems that inevitably arise between the conception of the idea – the thing seen in the mind's eye – and its realisation in terms of the chosen material, in a way that is both technically and aesthetically satisfying. It is difficult, I know, for the layman to understand that with the creative artist, the designer/craftsman, fame is never the spur and that the sheer fun of seeing an idea through from start to finish, no matter how many the problems and how great the frustrations, is more interesting by far than the object when finished. Fun in this context is compounded of

Figure 3.12   Inlaid door designed and worked by Gertrude Jekyll and Leonie Blumenthal, formerly at 43 Hyde Park Gate, London.

enjoyment, satisfaction, fulfilment and completeness, leading to the composure, self-possession and equanimity which so struck Edwin Lutyens on the occasion of their first meeting.

In *Wood and Garden* she described the attributes of a good gardener as "a combination of common sense and sincerity of purpose, allied to a sense of beauty and artistic knowledge," which we may interpret as practical wisdom derived from long experience of handling tools and materials: a mind devoid of pretence and affectation; an appreciation of form, line, proportion, balance, harmony, contrast, colour, tones and textures; and a sound knowledge of the principles of drawing, design and painting. They are also, of course, the hallmarks of all 'grand' craftsmen.

I have said elsewhere that I believe the quality for which Gertrude Jekyll would best like to be remembered is her integrity. I think she would also like us to think of her as a grand craftsman.

But first, last and all the time she was a painter. She thought like a painter and she observed her surroundings with the eye of a painter. For who but a painter would look in a garden for "the quality artists call drawing" and go on to define this as "a right movement of line and form and group"; or compare soil to "a canvas on which the gardener paints or embroiders a picture, already more or less complete in his mind, using for his pigments the plants that best suit his purpose"; or, when lifting up long stems of old fashioned roses in order to loop them over the branches of a tree, be reminded of "painting with an immensely long-handled brush"? By the same token there can be precious few laymen, whether gardeners or not, who notice that "on a clear day the gardener's eye is distracted by seeing into too many picture planes" or know that these occur at the point at which the eye of the spectator meets the world of the picture. It was just this ability to express herself in the language of painting, allied to her garden knowledge and the honest craftsmanship with which she handled words, that gave her prose style the distinction William Robinson immediately recognised and made him welcome her as a regular contributor to *The Garden*. It is what still makes her gardening books such sheer delight to read.

I suggest, therefore, that in the final analysis it was her experience at the art school under Redgrave and Dresser, her study of Turner, and her brief career as a professional painter which ultimately enriched beyond measure her garden designs and colour schemes.

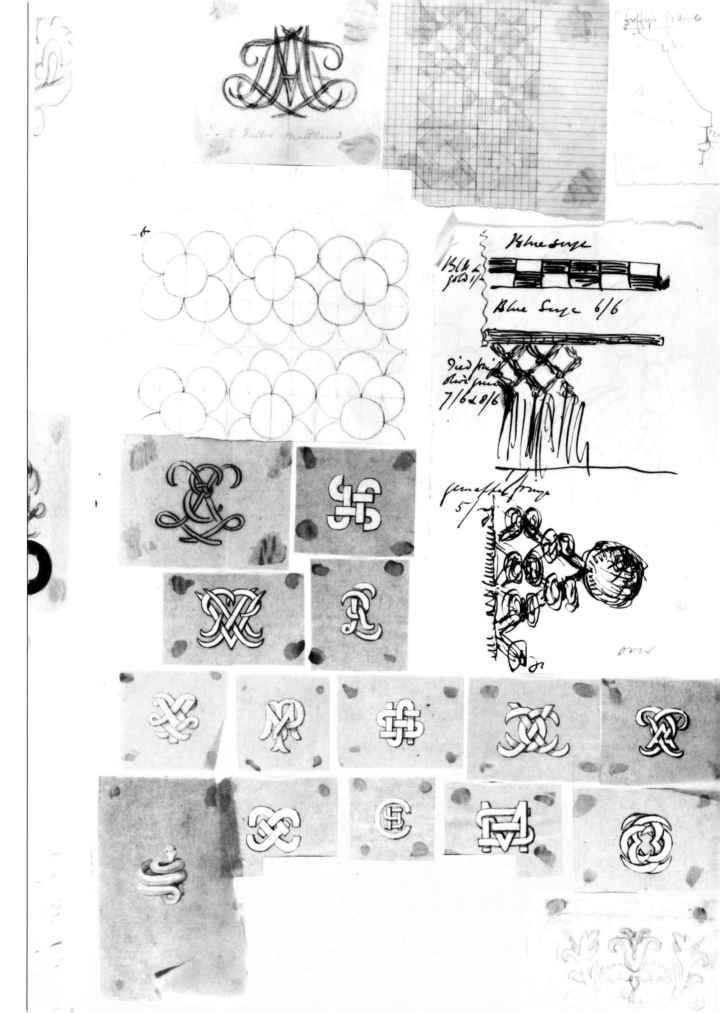

4

Gertrude Jekyll's workbook

Fenja Gunn

Gertrude Jekyll's creative energy and fertile imagination as an artist and craftswoman are evident in the pages of a workbook[1], acquired at auction in 1993 by the Royal Horticultural Society's Lindley Library. This varied collection of sketches and designs covers a period of Miss Jekyll's life between 1866 and the early 1900s. The work follows no chronological order and was pasted into the pages of the book in an apparently random fashion. The fact that these drawings were saved at all suggests that Miss Jekyll considered them of value for both aesthetic and personal reasons, for there are many items in the book which connect her with family and friends.

After Miss Jekyll's death, the workbook was acquired by the office of J.G. Crace, the firm of architects and decorators who worked closely with the designer and architect, A.W.N. Pugin. Later the book was owned by a private collector of Arts and Crafts artifacts. Turning its pages, one can see why this collection of material would have inspired anyone working in the field of design and craftsmanship. The extraordinary mixture of ornament and objects is instantly striking: intricate friezes from the Vatican drawn in delicate pen and ink, elegant carved mirror and picture frames, lace patterns and embroidery designs[2], jewellery, artifacts from museums, all these examples of a sophisticated, cultured taste are combined with a choice of homely objects. Miss Jekyll's love of practical implements is shown in her drawings of tools and evidence of her rural life in Surrey is provided by examples of country crafts. From the pages of the book we also learn of her absorption with the design of heraldic devices and monograms of interwoven lettering (Figure 4.1).

Miss Jekyll's own designs share space with material sketched to provide inspiration. The earliest drawings in the book were produced when she was in her twenties, during a period when she still travelled and studied abroad. In this respect, the workbook provides a link with the chronology of her life as well as giving us an insight into her development as an artist.

The appeal of the workbook lies in the essentially personal choice of material. This allows one to appreciate her restless, inquisitive spirit as an artist. She appeared always anxious to find fresh sources of inspiration and to experiment with new ideas. Yet once she had settled on some new craft, she studied it with penetration. Although she often referred to herself as an amateur[3], her approach was thorough and professional.

If there is a thread of continuity running through the workbook, it is her love of plants (Figure 4.2).

Figure 4.2   Stem, leaf and fruit design by Gertrude Jekyll.

Flowers, fruit and foliage featured prominently as a design element in any craft she tackled. Her own designs were confidently drawn with a spare economy of line. She eliminated any superfluous detail which interrupted the flow of shape and

Left: Figure 4.1 Monograms designed by Gertrude Jekyll.

form while still preserving the botanical integrity of each plant. Here one can appreciate the tuition she received from Dr. Christopher Dresser at the South Kensington School of Art.[4]

The style of drawing which she used for her original designs illustrates her appreciation of the individual qualities of her craft materials and their limitations. Thus carved woodwork was drawn in bold unfussy curves of line, often in soft lead pencil; whereas for jewellery or precious metals which were capable of being fashioned into precise and delicate objects, she produced drawings in pen and sepia or black ink on tracing paper. Coloured designs for wallpaper or fabric were painted in translucent or opaque watercolour (gouache). Some colour schemes were simply indicated by written instructions. For example, a design for Russian embroidery, fashionable towards the end of the nineteenth century, was noted thus: "Ribbon amber silk and red velvet ground. Centres of flowers sulphur satin with light red soft silk inside with gold cord."

Her ideas for wallpapers and ceramics shared themes and patterns in common with her embroidery. A wallpaper (Figure 4.3. Another example is given in figure 2.19) in soft powder blue was patterned with winding leafy tendrils reminiscent of the periwinkle design[5] she planned for a set of chair covers (See Figure 3.1). In the undulating lines of these patterns, one can observe a principle of design advocated by Owen Jones in his definitive *Grammar of Ornament* (1856).[6] His

Figure 4.4   Tile design by Gertrude Jekyll (left), inspired by an early Egyptian tile (right).

influence on Miss Jekyll can also be seen in the number of decorative patterns she traced from this source and pasted into the pages of the workbook. One of the most arresting items in the book is a double page spread which shows, on the right hand page, a sixteenth century tile from Cairo (Figure 4.4) sketched at the South Kensington Museum (later to become the Victoria and Albert Museum). This design proved the inspiration for her own tile design, on the left hand page, of thorn branches and blossom in two shades of blue matching the colours of the antique tile. It is one of the clearest examples in the book of the way she used an item from a museum as the foundation of one of her own ideas. Yet her design is not a pastiche of the Egyptian tile, but something entirely original and contemporary. Her interest in Middle Eastern decoration is clearly seen through the pages of the workbook. She had first come into contact with Oriental design during her travels with Charles and Mary Newton in the Levant in 1863[7] but later, in 1873, she made a memorable excursion to Algeria to stay with her friends Eugene and Barbara Bodichon in their villa on the outskirts of Algiers. During her visit, she was introduced to Arab decorative design by the painter, George Cayley.[8] The lasting impression which richly coloured ceramics, intricate patterns and exotic jewellery made on her is evident.

The drawings of jewellery are among the most intriguing, particularly as they represent a craft not generally associated with Miss Jekyll. The Oriental character of many of these pieces is undeniable. She would have seen jewellers at work in Istanbul or Algiers and later copied their style of design which she much admired: "The work of the simplest Oriental jeweller has that precious quality of rightness of purpose and distinct human interest".[9]

Figure 4.3   Wallpaper design, 'G.J. Nov. 29th/75'.

Yet there is also a strong Arts and Crafts influence apparent in her jewellery designs: this creates an unusual blend of styles resulting in some highly individual pieces. Among the most distinctive, are her designs for four necklaces, drawn in meticulous pen and ink line. The motifs she used for each necklace give each piece its originality: cloves, nutmeg and pepper; thistles, fish and waves; flowers, fruit and leaves of myrtle. The fish and wave and myrtle necklaces were repeated in watercolour (Figure 4.5), and each given a wash of colour to indicate that one was to be made up in a pink shade of gold, the other in a yellow gold.[10]

The other pieces of jewellery in the book were drawn with the same careful attention given to details of beading, fastening clasps and the construction of chain links. Such precision indicates that these were working drawings of objects that were to be manufactured. A fine chain design with a repeated motif of roses was captioned with this specification: "Chain of gold & silver 17" long, 29 links. Each single link takes $^1/_2$" wire, 29 links = 43$^1/_2$" = 3'7$^1/_2$". Wire of each metal. Thickness of wire between gauges nos. 2 & 3. Stuff for roses about 13 gauge."

There is little doubt that Miss Jekyll was capable of making up some of her own jewellery designs. A line drawing of a necklace of Egyptian mummy beads provides a reminder of days spent in her workshop. Stringing this necklace had proved "quite one of the most fidgety and difficult pieces of work I ever undertook."[11] Gold beads for this necklace were manufactured in her workshop where the small household god, "the tutelary divinity of the workshop," Pigot, presided. There is a pencil sketch in the workbook of his own diminutive silver and coral beaded necklace.

Miss Jekyll designed other objects in precious metals in her workshop and made her own chasing tools. Files for her metalwork were acquired from Paris. The workbook contains a number of examples of delightful designs in silver including a silver watch stand, chased with a decoration of twining honeysuckle and the initials "C.L.," and a

Figure 4.6   Badge for the 22nd Surrey Volunteers by Gertrude Jekyll.

Figure 4.5   Design for a gold necklace by Gertrude Jekyll.

Figure 4.7   GJ Monogram.

silver knife design signed and dated "G.J. March 11th 1890."

Her travels in Italy also introduced her to decorative work in precious metals. A map in the work book indicated where the best silver and gold workshops could be found in an – unfortunately unspecified – Italian city. But her numerous sketches of ornament in the Palazzo Borghese might indicate that this street of shops was in Rome. She visited Rome in 1868 where she developed a profound admiration for the artistic skills of the Italian master craftsman with whom she studied carving and gilding.[12]

The workbook contains a number of ideas for mirror and picture frames with carved flowers and leaves which may have been gilded at a later stage. On one page there is a pair of tiny colour tinted photographs of gilded frames. A plain design of frame dated July 1908 was produced to set off her elaborate shell pictures. Inlay patterns were used to decorate frames as well as the panels of furniture. These inlay designs based on flower and foliage shapes were typical of her ornamental style.

Miss Jekyll produced many designs especially for her friends and drawings in the book also recall old friendships: lace patterns for a woman friend; a sketch of a simple cross for the grave of the painter, George Cayley; numerous designs for personal monograms; intertwined initials for a fob watch; a design for silver cutlery with initialled handles; pieces of fine cotton or linen pasted on one page of the book delicately embroidered with initials on each sample of fabric. She designed a badge with ingeniously combined letters for the 22nd Surrey Volunteers (Figure 4.6) and experimented with her own initials G.J. (Figure 4.7), devising a variety of alternatives which she incorporated into carving. The last drawing in the book is an elaborate design dated 1906, with her initials as a centrepiece (Figure 4.8).

There may be a link between Miss Jekyll's interest

in monograms and her fascination for heraldry. Both establish identity by means of formalised design. In the case of heraldry, there was the added romantic appeal of its history and the established conventions of its special language which, to judge from the caption for the Goldsmiths Company coat of arms, she had assimilated with her customary thoroughness. Mottos incorporated in coats of arms, like monogrammed initials, also involved designing with lettering; heraldic emblems were used both for badges and to identify personal possessions. There are many drawings of coats of arms in the book including one of the Jekyll family, discovered in 1881 at the College of Arms in *Prince Arthur's Book,* a fifteenth century work commissioned by Henry VII for his son.

Through the pages of the workbook one is made aware of Miss Jekyll's wide range of tastes. Together with elegant ornament sketched in Italy of fine objects drawn in museums, there are sketches of plainer English pieces of furniture and decoration. Visits to English country houses are also recorded. She drew details of carving and furniture and a number of interiors at Berkeley Castle in Gloucestershire in April 1869. The borders and terraces at Berkeley were later described in *Some English Gardens* (1904) on which she collaborated with the artist, George S., Elgood. Sketches of Jacobean chairs and a heavy carved fireplace, "drawn from recollection", at Audley End, the fine Jacobean house in Essex, were indications of her fondness for the robust style of this period.

Functional pieces of furniture appealed to her. The design for the range of drawers in her workshop is preserved in the workbook. A practical looking umbrella stand was sketched in pencil. Another sketch showed a stylish but simple design for a glass display case mounted on a wooden stand. Early in the workbook, there appears a precise pen and ink drawing of glass display cases at the British Museum captioned as follows: "I went to the British Museum, and looked up the Etruscan vase cases. The sketch below shows the dimensions as estimated, for I had no measure, but I can guarantee their being tolerably accurate." Her father, Captain Edward Jekyll, owned a collection of Etruscan vases (see Chapter 2), so one can speculate that this drawing and possibly her own design for a display case were commissioned by him or produced with him in mind.

If this is so, it is one of several items in the workbook which link Miss Jekyll to her family. She produced three wrought iron weathervane designs for her younger brother Herbert's house at High

Figure 4.8   GJ Monogram on a keystone of a decorated lintel by Gertrude Jekyll.

Wycombe. Herbert, was an accomplished artist himself; his beautifully controlled watercolour of the marble pavement of the Duomo in Milan is preserved in the book with a pencil identification by his sister, "Drawn by Herbert." Her youngest brother, Walter, contributed a jewel-like painting of a mosaic at Pompeii which was dated April 3rd 1872, and included a note to:

"My Dear Gug, this is from a mosaic at Pompeii and would make a good subject for your clothwork, I think– the original is quite delicious– it is about 18ft. long."

Changes in the fortunes of the Jekyll family and in Miss Jekyll's own domestic life can be traced through the pages of the workbook. In 1868, following her visit to Rome, the Jekyll family moved from Bramley, Surrey to a house inherited by Edward Jekyll by the Thames at Wargrave in Berkshire.[13] Here Miss Jekyll became involved with a local project – the construction of a roofed shelter to protect a well at Crazies Hill, known as Phillimore's Spring, named after a former curate, the Rev. Grenville Phillimore. Her pencil sketches of the well, with notes on its drainage and construction, the drawing of the roofed shelter and alternative patterns of brick paving painted in

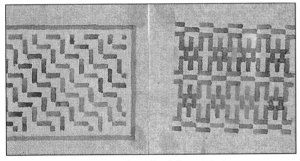

Figure 4.9   Brick pavement design for Phillimore's Spring
by Gertrude Jekyll.

terracotta red watercolour (Figure 4.9) all feature in the workbook. The pavement pattern finally selected, Miss Jekyll noted, was "laid at the spring, 1870." She designed a two-handled drinking cup to be used at the well, inscribed with the same date.

The move back to her beloved Surrey took place in 1876. The workbook is full of reminders of Surrey, her participation in local life and, one senses, her enjoyment of it. A flower-festooned banner was designed for Busbridge School in June 1902 and she painted a floral inn sign for T. Hester, the landlord of The Jolly Farmer. Evidence of her interest in rural life can be seen in the design for a serviceable looking riding cape, a sketch of bullock shoes and details of rush seated chairs. The rubbings

Figure 4.10   Sketch of a stone garden seat by Gertrude Jekyll.

taken of smock stitch patterns used in rural smocks recall her photographs of local countrymen in *Old West Surrey* (1904).

Memories of her home life at Munstead Wood also feature in the workbook: a design for a chimney breast which combined oak, plasterwork and stone, and a pencil drawing of a topiary cat for the garden. A few designs for garden seats (Figure 4.10) and sketches of tanks for the centre of a walled garden proved a link with Miss Jekyll in her capacity as a garden designer and her original delightful line decorations remind us of her well-known books – the title page and spine drawings, dated 1899, for *Home and Garden* and a drawing of ears of corn intertwined with vines for *Old West Surrey* (Figure 4.11).

The wide range of crafts represented and the discernable links with Miss Jekyll's life give this book a unique value. Above all it reveals the depth of her experience as a craftswoman and the richness of her education as an artist. It was this background which gave such creativity to her work designing gardens.

Figure 4.11 Design for the spine illustration of Old West Surrey by Gertrude Jekyll.

5

Gertrude Jekyll and the Arts and Crafts Movement

Mavis Batey

Garden making is always in the mainstream of cultural history, and when we look at garden design in relation to one particular movement, Arts and Crafts, we see all the same ideas and influences that affected social history, architecture and the decorative arts.

The Industrial Revolution was born in England and gathered incredible momentum in a short time, dealing heavy blows to the traditional hand-made crafts. The Great Exhibition of 1851 was the rallying point for the new technological age, symbolising the country's pride in its achievements and its boundless hopes for the future. The catalogue[1] highlighted the mass products available even for modest homes and the Victorian age of bric-a-brac was ushered in. Craftsmanship needed powerful bolstering if it was to survive 'art and industry' backed by Prince Albert, capitalism and the empire builders. The two great crusaders against the shoddy materialism of the Victorian age were John Ruskin and William Morris, who left an indelible mark on Gertrude Jekyll and her age.

John Ruskin's influence on education, morals and art was enormous, but it was William Morris, painter, designer, printer, weaver, dyer, wood engraver and poet who turned craft ideology into realities, and inspired the Arts and Crafts Movement. In 1861 he was instrumental in founding the firm of Morris, Marshall, Faulkner & Co., in which Dante Gabriel Rossetti, Ford Maddox Brown, Philip Webb and Edward Burne-Jones were partners, which brought about a revolution in decorative taste. Even before the self-conscious return to designer craftsmanship as a reaction to mass production, Ruskin and Morris

had studied and eulogized the mediaeval age of crafts and guilds in a Pre-Raphaelite revolt against academic theory. It was the Pre-Raphaelites' sympathy with mediaeval workmanship that drew attention to the beauty of colour in the accessories of daily life, which penetrated the Arts and Crafts Movement. The Morris-inspired movement, which did not actually take the name Arts and Crafts until after the Arts and Crafts Exhibition of 1888 (the first exhibition of decorative arts) believed that a designer should not just be an artist but combine his visual skill with a knowledge of the craft. The Art Workers' Guild had been formed in 1884 to promote "the Unity of all the aesthetic Arts", and was backed by Morris who was their Master in 1892. Mediaeval guilds had represented the interests of individual craft skills, but in the Art Workers' Guild weavers, silversmiths, wood engravers, printers, illuminators, architects and others all joined forces to give a new impetus to the idea of craftsmanship through the maintenance of high standards of design and the understanding of craft materials.

Gertrude Jekyll, herself a designer craftsman (Figures 5.1, 5.2, 5.3 and 5.4) in the Morris mould, brought gardening into the Arts and Crafts Movement. Not that the Art Workers' Guild recognised gardening as a craft skill qualifying for membership, nor had they any provision for women members, but Gertrude Jekyll who had attended the school of art attached to the South Kensington Museum, heard Ruskin lecture. She was imbued with Morris's ideas and, as for him, Arts and Crafts became a lifestyle and not just a hobby. Perhaps she did not envisage an earthly paradise of designer-craftsmen working for love of their art rather than for a profit-orientated society in the Morris manner, but she shared his love of country life idealised by the Arts and Crafts Movement. The magazine *Country Life,* which came into being in 1897 eulogized country values and was read by people rich enough to buy Arts and Crafts handmade products. Gardening played no small part in the cult of the countryside and Gertrude Jekyll, a devotee of the country life she knew so well in her beloved West Surrey, became gardens adviser to *Country Life.* Gardening, if seen

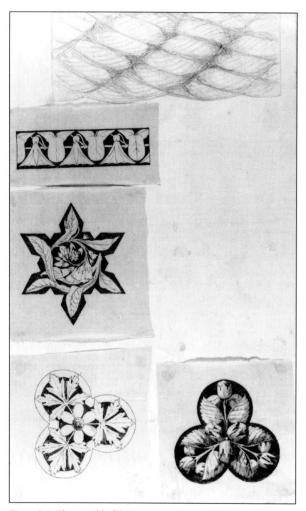

Figure 5.1 Flower and leaf designs.

as the setting of a building, presented a problem in the concept of designer-craftsmanship. Should the garden be designed by the gardener, who had nothing to do with the house, or the architect, who was unlikely to know anything about planting? Reginald Blomfield, author of *The Formal Garden in England* (1892) felt strongly that it was the architect and not the gardener who should be responsible for the design of the garden, which should harmonise with the house by echoing

architectural themes. William Robinson, the authorative editor of *The Garden,* and author of *The Flower Garden* and *The Wild Garden* immediately took up the cudgels in *Garden Design and Architects' Gardens* and thundered in Ruskinian prose that it was "barbarous, needless and inartistic" to make gardens harmonise with architecture. John Dando Sedding, a member of the Art Workers' Guild and an architect who did understand gardening, had tried to bring the two points of view together in his *Gardencraft Old and New* (1891) in which he advocated a garden that "curtseys to the house" in the decorative picturesque Queen Anne style. It was left to Edwin Lutyens, architect, and Gertrude Jekyll, gardener, to give the new century a new style which would reconcile architects, gardeners, craftsmen and the rival merits of formal design and natural planting.

For Gertrude Jekyll, the Arts and Crafts creed of the unity of the arts was not just an artistic concept but fundamental to her special art and skills in home-making. Sir Herbert Baker said of her that her "outstanding possession was the power to see, as a poet, the art and creation of home-making as a whole in relation to life – the best simple English country life of her day."[2] It was this ideal of the artistic unity of the house, its contents and gardens, which she, the woman, passed on to Edwin Lutyens inspiring him to build not just houses but homes. Writing in *Country Life* in 1901, Gertrude Jekyll commented approvingly on Orchards in Surrey: "It is a house that has the true home feeling – good to live and die in. The architect is Mr E. L. Lutyens".[3]

Herbert Baker, who knew both Edwin Lutyens and Gertrude Jekyll well, felt that she was the most formative influence in his life. Lutyens, who was largely self-taught, was also a native of West Surrey and had learned much about its architectural traditions from a Godalming builder. When he met Miss Jekyll he was only twenty years old and she twenty-five years his senior. Lutyens learned from her the Arts and Crafts understanding of materials and to design not so much for style in building but for comfort and sympathy with surroundings. After her contact with the Arts and Crafts Movement she had looked at Surrey's vernacular traditions in a new light and it was observation of West Surrey vernacular buildings which was the starting point of Lutyens' brilliant and original career. As soon as they met in 1889 they shared their enthusiasm for Surrey cottages (Figure 5.5), barns, farmsteads and countryside.

Day after day they drove around the narrow lanes together in Miss Jekyll's dog-cart, sketching and photographing details that appealed to them; a

Figure 5.3   Shell picture by Gertrude Jekyll.

buttressed wall, a patterned chimney, the angle of a building which although the result of chance was pleasing in design. The Surrey domestic architecture is particularly rich in vernacular detail, especially in the weavers' cottages in the Godalming, Bramley and Guildford area, where generations of craftsmen, some of whom traced their origins back to the Flemish weavers, had built their tilehung cottages with a feel for material and design which was absent from the homes of agricultural workers. A special feature duly noted by Edwin Lutyens and Gertrude Jekyll was the galleting made with tiny chips of ironstone picked up from the greensand which ran, like a string of beads, through the mortar courses which bound the rough local Bargate stones together.

"Eye and brain must be alert to receive the impression and studious to store it to add to the hoard of experience" counselled Miss Jekyll.[4] For her it was the accompaniment of planting with the domestic buildings which was especially noted and assimilated into her garden designing; lavender and hollyhocks by an old weather-boarded barn, snapdragons along a brick wall, cottage porches wreathed with roses, ferns in dipping wells, reflections, patterns of brick and ironstone or millstones set in garden paths. Helen Allingham of Witley has made familiar to us the Surrey scenes which inspired her friend Gertrude Jekyll's woodland cottage gardening, where sunken lanes, sandy paths and cottage gardens blended with heath and woodland.[5]

Miss Jekyll knew the local cottagers well and later published her study of Surrey crafts and her childhood memories of cottage life in *Old West Surrey* (1904). She rescued from destruction all kinds of household objects that were becoming obsolete including some fine examples of Wealden ironwork, which now form the Jekyll collection in Guildford Museum. Like Morris she abhorred the collecting of bric–a–brac and echoed his views given in an address on 'The Beauty of Life' at the Town Hall in Birmingham: "Have nothing in your houses that you do not know to be useful, or believe to be beautiful".[6] In *Old West Surrey* Miss Jekyll was distressed to find that "cottages, whose furniture and excellent daily appointments have come through several generations are now furnished with cheap, pretentious articles, got up with veneer and varnish and shoddy material. The floor is covered with oilcloth, the walls have a paper of a shocking design and are hung with cheap oleographs and tradesmen's illustrated almanacs".[7]

The Surrey cottages themselves were endangered. There was an increasing demand for commuter houses in Surrey after the arrival of the railway and she made a passionate plea for the protection of the old domestic buildings which were being destroyed to make way for them. The listing and protection of buildings was far off when she said, "to retain them untouched, to preserve them from decay or demolition should be felt our duty. I feel sure that in another hundred years this will be known more widely and felt more strongly even than now".[8] Like Morris, who had founded the Society for the Protection of Ancient Buildings in 1877, she was deeply aware that the harmony between domestic buildings and their landscape sprang from the intimate relationship between the soil and the local building materials; a harmony which she saw was being disrupted by the easy rail transport of mass-produced bricks and slates.

In 1894 Gertrude Jekyll was in a position to plan for a home of her own at Munstead Wood and it was Edwin Lutyens, sharing her feelings for the Surrey vernacular and the Arts and Crafts lifestyle, who designed it for her. Lutyens came to excel in sharing his clients' aspirations for dream homes. He built Goddards amidst the Surrey pinewoods for a philanthropist who wished to provide a rest home for tired lady social workers from London. A skittle alley was built as an integral part of the house, and an enchanting garden court, like a mediaeval lady's pleasaunce, with a dipping well in the middle which had a band of the local galleting decoration that he and Gertrude Jekyll had noted on their sketch pads. He entered into the romantic dreams of newly rich business giving them a Castle Drogo or a Marsh Court hunting lodge. For Miss Jekyll, from whom he had learned so much, he was especially anxious to design a house to fit her garden and her personality. It was to be an Arts and Crafts home to reflect the needs and contain the work of a true designer-craftsman: honest workmanship and everything beautiful and useful. It should have her repose and serenity and, as she wished, "a little of the feeling of a convent".[9] Above all, Munstead Wood was to belong to West Surrey.

Edwin Lutyens and Gertrude Jekyll had William Morris' capacity for looking at the traditions of the past with a fresh eye. Munstead Wood was not to be a mere picturesque imitation of old forms but to be built in the spirit of the Surrey craft workmanship which allowed for fresh development to meet changing needs. Built in the local Bargate stone, it was described by its owner as "designed in the thorough honest spirit of the good work of old days, and the body of it so fashioned and reared has, as it were, taken to itself the soul of a more ancient dwelling place. The house is not in any way a copy of an old building, though it embodies the general character of old structures in this district"[10]. Miss Jekyll's garden led it back naturally into the Surrey countryside from which its fabric had been taken in the way that Morris' ideal homestead partook of the continuous life of the earth.

Morris' own Oxfordshire Kelmscott Manor, which had "grown up out of the soil and the lives of those that lived on it"[11] had been eulogized in his novel *News from Nowhere*, published in 1891, a few years before the building of Munstead Wood. It is the shrine of the Arts and Crafts Movement. In the alterations for the old 17th century house every nail was made by the village smith, the stone for the windows came from local quarries and the roof and dado were made from Kelmscott elms. It was Morris' "earthly paradise" in which to pursue his arts and crafts ideology. In the nearby lanes he

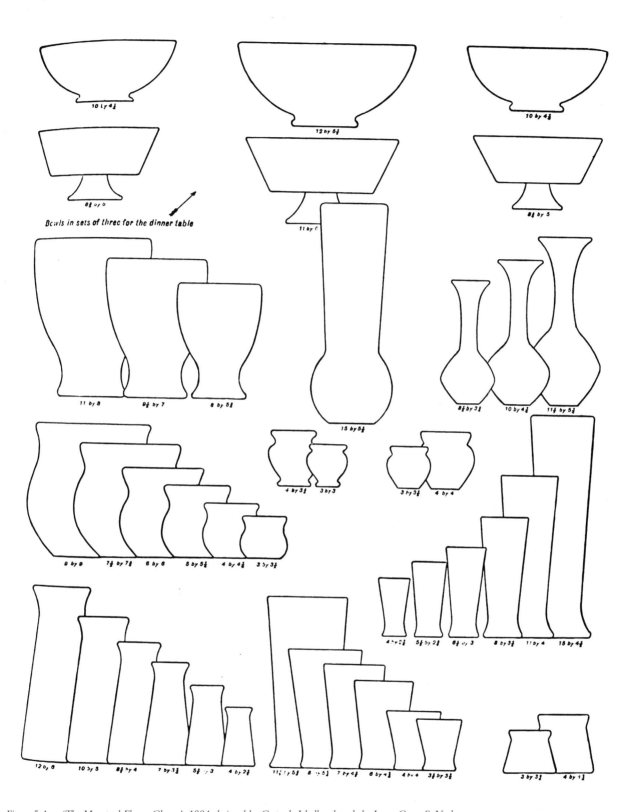

Figure 5.4   'The Munstead Flower Glasses', 1884, designed by Gertrude Jekyll and made by James Green & Nephew.

collected reeds, roots, flowers and willow twigs for making dyes, and studied the plants and birds which were favourite designs for his textiles. The materials of the landscape were spun back into the "old house by the Thames".

Munstead Wood has the same sense of harmony with its surroundings. Every detail has a West Surrey precedent worked by local craftsmanship, and it was to make a deep impression on Vernacular Revival architecture. One Arts and Crafts architect, the Scot, Robert Lorimer, wrote lyrically about it: "It looks so reasonable, so kindly, so perfectly beautiful, that you feel that people might have been making love, and living and dying there and dear little children running about for – the last – I was going to say 1,000 years – anyway 600. They've used old tiles which of course helps – but the proportion, the way the thing's built (very low coursed rubble with thick joints, and no corners) – in fact it has been built by the old people of the old materials in the old unhurrying way, but at the same time 'sweet to all modern uses' . . . and who do you think did this for her – a young chap called Lutyens, 27 he is....."[12] Miss Jekyll delighted in watching Munstead take shape under her young architect:"How I enjoy seeing the whole operation of the building from its very beginning. I could watch any clever workman for hours. Even the shovelling and the shaping of ground is pleasant to see, but when it comes to a craftsman of long experience using the tool that seems to have become part of himself, the attraction is so great that I can hardly tear myself away."[13] Gertrude Jekyll's admiration for traditional crafts was the basis of her own Arts and Crafts creed of the understanding of materials; not only in her craft skills in embroidery, silverwork and carpentry but also in gardening, the art that made her famous.

William Robinson, who had branded Reginald Blomfield as a garden designer who knew nothing about plants, the materials with which he needed to work, held that a garden artist had to "choose from ten thousand beautiful living things; to study their nature and adapt them to his soil and climate; to get the full expression of their beauty; to grow and place them well and in right relation to other things, which is a life-study in itself".[14] Like Robinson, Morris and Ruskin, Gertrude admired plants for their individual beauty and abhorred carpet-bedding. Planting should be suited to the land and to the natural growth, and plants should look as though they had a right to be there. She maintained that a garden designer should see what form of garden would suit a place and its environment and that "except in rare cases there is no need to keep rigidly to any one style: it is, in fact, almost impossible actually to define a style for whether a garden is called Italian, French, Dutch or English, each one of these merges into and overlaps the other, for they all have features in common that vary only in detail or treatment."[15] In Arts and Crafts philosophy good craftsmanship was always to be preferred to mere styles. Morris had called for

the same armistice in the battle of styles in interior decoration. At Wightwick Manor, a house of strong Morris influences, a Roman marble fireplace is surrounded by de Morgan Arts and Crafts tiles and Persian rugs. Miss Jekyll produced gardens with different themes and colour schemes side by side, which influenced the Hidcote and Sissinghurst type of compartmented garden or the "nookiness" of the Alfred Parsons gardens, so suited to the Kate Greenaway child.

In the second edition of *Garden Ornament,* published in 1927, when she was assisted by Christopher Hussey, Miss Jekyll wrote a new preface in which she considered the relation of a garden to an historic house: "A picturesque old house may be surrounded by a formless riot of colour but where the house is obviously, in its way, a work of art and appeals to the historical sense, unassisted originality needs to be wary." She approved of the fleur de lys knot garden which had been created at Broughton Castle in Oxfordshire to offset the old building. She felt that "literal reproduction is not the proper object of the historical sense in gardening. Rather it is the directing of the visual sense by means of a frame composed of justifiable features of a design akin to that of the house." A Georgian house should not have random paving and in general the nature of the house should suggest the main lines which frame the garden.

The Arts and Crafts Movement proclaimed the unity of the arts, the need for understanding craft materials in design and the superiority of craft to style. It also stimulated an interest in a studied use of colour. The boiling of dyes for weaving, the staining of glass and the glazing of tiles taught William Morris, Edward Burne-Jones and the Arts and Crafts designers a great deal about colour. There were also new and exciting ideas about impressionism and the realising of sensations through colour, particularly in painting. Ruskin referred to Turner's colour painting as "Turner picturesque."[16] Hitherto picturesque had implied what painters had come to paint in traditional composition. Now painters were obsessed by colour which blended in the eye and mind to make an impression. Gertrude Jekyll was a friend of Hercules Brabazon, of whom Ruskin had once said that he was "the only person since Turner at whose feet I can sit and worship and learn about colour."[17] She acknowledged her debt in learning "colour beauty" from Brabazon and used to copy Turner's paintings as a student (see Figure 3.3).

The preoccupation with the "Turner picturesque"

Figure 5.5   'The Clothes Basket' by Helen Allingham.

gave Gertrude Jekyll her feeling for the arrangement of borders in colour harmonies. The new range of exotic plants had produced the strong colours, which when combined in garish carpet-bedding brought down the wrath of Ruskin and Robinson. "No artist has so wide a palette as the garden designer and no artist has need of both discretion and reserve", warned Lutyens.[18] It was Michel Chevreul's work *The Principles of Harmony and Contrast of Colours, and their Application to the Arts* translated into English in 1854 and studied by Gertrude Jekyll as an art student, which influenced colour ideas in arts and crafts; it also greatly influenced the Impressionist painters. Michel Chevreul was Director of Tints at the Paris Gobelin's tapestry factory and observed in his work what the eye actually perceived in colour. In experimenting with woollen threads he found that two of a different dye appear as a single colour at a distance. He went on to produce a theory of optic mixtures and colour harmonies and contrasts, based on his experience of tapestry tints, and in the last chapter of his book suggested that there were horticultural implications for his theory.[19] Here are to be found many of Miss Jekyll's planting ideas – no one colour is seen alone, colour is affected by colours around it, white flowers are the only ones that possess the advantage of heightening the tone of flowers which have only a light tint of colour, grey helps all colours gain in purity and brilliance. Gertrude Jekyll in *Colour Schemes for the Flower Garden* emphasises that colours in proximity influence and modify one another: "any experienced colourist knows that the blues will be more telling – more purely blue – by the juxtaposition of rightly placed complementary colour."[20] Gardeners, she laments, are not helped by seedsmen in the forward planning of their colour harmonies. Their wording on seed-lists does not describe the colour accurately but "appears to be intended as a complimentary euphemism". Thus Messrs Sutton had been guilty of giving the seed list name "azure-blue" when the flower was in fact a tender pale lavender-lilac, a "blue" aster turned out to be light purple and a "dark blue" aster a rich dark purple[21].

Gertrude Jekyll's books on colour and planting design were widely read and when the Glynde School for Lady Gardeners was founded the teaching was based on her methods. She was asked to design gardens in Europe and America and corresponded with enthusiastic American lady gardeners; one who was particularly influenced by Jekyll ideas was Mrs. Francis King, herself an horticultural writer and a Founder of the Garden Club of America: "I am so glad you are taking up the colour question and trying to show what you mean by colour words," Miss Jekyll wrote to her in reply to her request to write the Preface to her new book.[22] In the Preface to *The Well Considered Garden* Gertrude Jekyll wrote: "What is needed for doing the best gardening is something of an artist's training, or at any rate the possession of such a degree of aptitude – the God-given artist's gift – as with due training may make an artist; for gardening, in its best expression, may well rank as one of the fine arts. But without the many years of labour needed for any hope of success in architecture, sculpture, or painting, there are certain simple rules, whose observance, carried out in horticulture, will make all the difference between a garden that is utterly commonplace and one that is full of beauty and absorbing interest. Of these one of the chief is a careful consideration of colour arrangement."[23]

Gertrude Jekyll's influence was far-reaching and led to a new vision of the English Garden. Mrs. King dedicated a later book, *Chronicles of the Garden,* 1925, to Miss Jekyll "who, more than any other has made the planting of gardens in the English-speaking countries one of the Fine Arts."[24] She was the perfect craftsman painter-gardener, who understood the living materials of her craft, where and how to grow her plants, and when they would flower in her colour planting schemes. Gertrude Jekyll inherited a number of gardening traditions, but it was her special contribution to garden art that through her Arts and Crafts leanings she could reconcile some styles which had come to be seen at variance with another, picturesque and gardenesque, Ruskinian truth to Nature and traditional gardencraft.

6

The Munstead Wood survey, 1991

The methodology of recording historic gardens by the Royal Commission
on the Historical Monuments of England

Paul Everson

Introduction

In the autumn of 1991 archaeological field staff from the Keele office of the Royal Commission on the Historical Monuments of England (RCHME) carried out a topographical survey of the garden laid out by Gertrude Jekyll at Munstead Wood near Godalming in Surrey. The survey highlighted the development of RCHME methodology in recording gardens and proved its flexibility in dealing with an archaeologically unusual landscape. Just as importantly it afforded a test of the contribution that archaeological survey can make in studying a landscape of quite recent creation, where in particular the presumption might be made that adequate records exist already in the form of plans and designs, photographs and documentary accounts.

The survey by the RCHME was undertaken at the request and instigation of Mr. Peter Goodchild of the Centre for the Conservation of Historic Parks and Gardens at the Institute of Advanced Architectural Studies, University of York, and of a scholarly group established in 1990 and convening as the Munstead Wood Working Group (see Acknowledgements). Short-term considerations lent weight to the request. There had been considerable storm damage in the wooded southern sector of the site in 1987 and 1989, with consequent potential pressure for replanting. This replanting needed to be informed by a clear understanding of losses and survivals and of what might remain of Miss Jekyll's planting and management of the woodland. There was, furthermore, the prospect of an exhibition on Gertrude Jekyll and her work at the Museum of Garden History in 1993 together with the possibility of a complementary publication, which has come to fruition in the present volume.

The RCHME had reasons itself to be interested in this particular garden by virtue of its core duties under its Royal Warrant, of record creation and archive curation relating to the country's ancient and historical monuments. One aspect of this concern related to the buildings on the site. Munstead Wood Hut (1894-5), Munstead Wood (1896-7 Figure 6.1), Munstead Orchard (the former head gardener's house, 1894), and the Thunder House (1895), all designed by (Sir) Edwin Lutyens, are individually listed buildings of grades I or II.[1,2] As a group and with The Quadrangle, greenhouses, potting shed and workshop, curtilage and garden walls, they have an enhanced interest. Without a good understanding of the garden layout within which they formed constituent parts and in which the buildings were in siting, orientation, and detailing in a designed and dynamic relationship with the landscape, appreciation of the buildings themselves is necessarily impoverished. This relationship of buildings to landscape, so essential to the understanding of both, is especially obvious at Munstead Wood because of the well-documented mutual cooperation between Miss Jekyll and Edwin Lutyens and justifies an architectural interest in a record of the garden remains. Wider application of this philosophy, a commonplace as it is to landscape archaeologists,[3] is something that the RCHME is becoming more concerned to promote through its own work on sites such as Munstead Wood.

A second area of interest for the RCHME was related to historic photography of the garden at Munstead Wood. This exists in some quantity, has

Left: Figure 6.1 South-west view of Munstead Wood in 1992.

its origins in photographs Miss Jekyll herself took, and extends through both private and commercial photography including the *Country Life* collections now deposited in the RCHME's care in the National Monuments Record (NMR).[4,5] While many of the views in these photographs are readily identifiable, others are not. The task of producing a consolidated catalogue and identifications has proved to be difficult enough within a single collection like the Jekyll albums held at the University of California at Berkeley and on microfilm by NMR.[6] When extended across a wider range of material that has been estimated at a minimum of 2500 relevant photographs, the task required the production of a large-scale, high quality site plan to act as the agreed focus of concordance. With that available it becomes possible to plan a systematic programme of work gathering and cataloguing historic photographs, and that is a task that the Working Party and the Institute of Advanced Architectural Studies, York (IoAAS) has set itself to do.

A third and perhaps most obvious reason for the RCHME's concern is its well-established and considerable role in pursuing the systematic recording of the physical remains of historic garden sites, principally as earthworks, within its archaeological survey programmes.[7,8] Such detailed recording cannot extend to every 19th and 20th century garden as perhaps it might to the much rarer and more vulnerable remains of formal gardens of the Renaissance and early post-mediaeval eras. Here in Munstead Wood, though, is a garden of acknowledged national and international importance. It was Gertrude Jekyll's own home, garden and plant nursery, through which ideas and techniques were developed which permeated her influential writings and contributed significantly to late 19th and 20th century garden design internationally. The surviving physical remains of this garden, now fragmented into five modern properties and eroded by continuing piecemeal land-use changes, were worthy of systematic recording for their own sake. Surprisingly, too, there was no accurately surveyed plan of the whole garden available other than the Ordnance Survey basic scale sheets in successive editions at 25" to the mile and 1:2500, with the limited level of detail inherent at that scale and prescribed by Ordnance Survey practice. Published detailed plans and designs by Miss Jekyll herself were confined to the central part of the garden around the main house and The Hut, concentrating on such features as the Nut Walk, the Spring Garden and the Rockeries[9,10] and limited therefore to a small fraction of the total garden, to the exclusion most obviously of the extensive woodland area in the south and the orchard gardens in the north.

RCHME surveys of gardens

The work at Munstead Wood involved the recording of hard details such as paths, walls, beds and planting, and very limited earthwork features. It therefore offered an opportunity to test whether the methodological approach typically deployed by the RCHME on large-scale archaeological surveys for sites of all periods would accommodate the particular specifications inherent in this garden. It might be seen as an attempt to link in recording practice the two traditional faces of garden history; structural design and planting.

The RCHME methodology of recording gardens has evolved, with changing equipment and product requirements, in the same way as the understanding of garden remains has evolved. In general the RCHME's awareness of the monument type arose simply through encountering the earthworks of early gardens as morphologically distinctive and more or less obvious features in the landscape, which needed to be planned and understood for what they were, like any other archaeological remains. This was further promoted by the progressive extension of the terminal date for the RCHME's recording obligations since the Second World War from 1714 to the present guideline date of 1945, and by increasing use of historical maps in elucidating field monuments. Important garden remains were nevertheless sometimes overlooked or masked in conventional monument categories, for example, at Cerne Abbey[11] and Bindon Abbey,[12] and plan-making as a record tended to be confined to the limited needs of book illustration. Largely through the insights of Christopher Taylor in the published Cambridgeshire and Northamptonshire inventories and in scholarly publications[13] recognition of earthwork early garden remains became a routine part of the English Royal Commission's fieldwork, as in the selective inventory of West Lindsey[14] and in subsequent individual site surveys. Field recording did not exclude an awareness of the possible significance of planted materials in the context of gardens, and has certainly extended to selective plan-positioning and identification of obvious residual planting for example at Harrington[15] and Stanfield.[16] However, the RCHME has not normally dealt with extensive planted material in so systematic and thorough a way as to have treated it as physical evidence on a par with built and earthwork features.

A major step in the increasing emphasis on recording planted material is to be seen in a RCHME survey at Wanstead in NE London, formerly Essex, undertaken in 1989-90 (NMR, TQ 48 NW 13). Here the site of a 16th-century and later house, demolished in 1824, with elaborate formal terraces and parterres, a pleasure ground with mounts and an amphitheatre, and water features was complemented by planting which survived principally from the redesign of the parkland in the 18th and 19th-centuries. Relevant standard trees, hollies, yews and thorns were duly plan-positioned. This positioning of planted material assisted in the historical assessment and formulation of management options by consultants who took on and enhanced the RCHME's survey product and fed back their results into the archive record of the site. Technically this presented no special problems for the RCHME's fieldwork process. Like all similar large scale RCHME surveys involving original plan-making, the metrical and angular authenticity of the task was underpinned by a survey traverse scheme – in that case extending to 38 stations – observed with a modern electronic theodolite with an EDM facility

('total stations'). The resultant data, automatically logged in the field, were computed and adjusted by standard procedures within strict tolerances and fed to a drum plotter for automatic output on standard plastic field sheets. Completion in the field was effected by routine graphical methods. These processes allowed tree centres, for example, to be routinely and accurately positioned on plan as with any other topographical detail.

The site

At Munstead Wood knowledge of the circumstances of the garden's creation helped to define the survey task. In 1768, Munstead Heath (Figure 6.2a) was unreclaimed, but three tracks crossed it. In about 1882 Miss Jekyll acquired a large elongated triangle of land bounded by the track on the opposite side of the road from her mother's home 'Munstead', latterly 'Munstead House'. This land, which consisted of two closes, extended to nearly 15 acres (6 ha). These two closes appear on the Godalming tithe award map of 1844. At that date the northern close was unnamed but was reckoned to lie in arable cultivation; the larger southern one was depicted with scattered coniferous tree symbols and was named like many

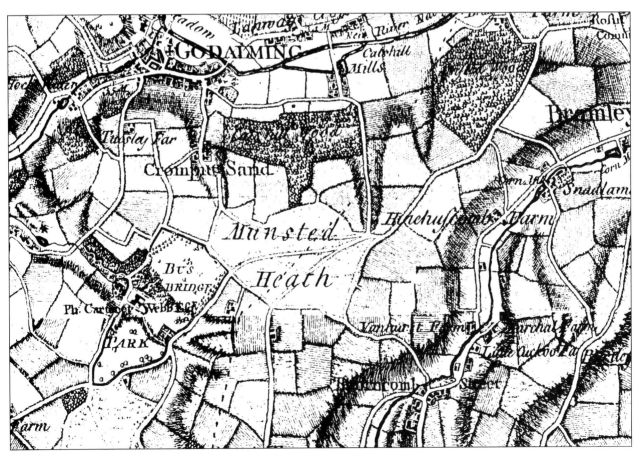

Figure 6.2   (a) Munstead Heath in about 1768.

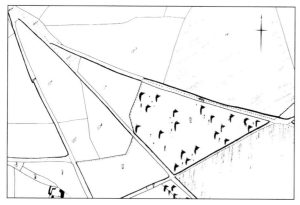

Figure 6.2   (b) Site of Munstead Wood on Munstead Heath in 1844.

adjacent parcels as 'Munstead Heath' and described as "firs and rough"[16] (Figure 6.2b). The first large scale Ordnance Survey planning carried out in 1871 and published as the first edition 25" maps in 1873, shows a zone of deciduous trees intermixed with the conifers along the NW fringe of the southern close: by the date of the second edition, revised by fieldwork in 1895 and published in 1897, the main garden divisions had been superimposed on the two plots, buildings including The Hut, 'The Quadrangle' (the post 1948 name for the stables) and the potting shed had been erected but not the main house, and small rides are shown cut from the W or NW into the woodland, now shown as mixed deciduous and coniferous throughout. She described it as a "self-sown wood" in 1915, with detailed observations that illustrate her approach:

"A small wood of ten acres adjoins my garden. Formerly it was a wood of Scotch Pine of some seventy year's growth. Under the close-growing trees the ground was bare but for a scant sprinkling of Whortleberry, Heath and Bracken at the lighter edges. Thirty-five years ago the Pines were cut and the ground left bare. Soon it became covered with Heath, Ling and short Bracken, and, on one side especially, a stronger growth of Whortleberry. Then, year by year, tree seedlings of many kinds came up in considerable quantity so that there is not a yard of ground without one or more. This went on for some nine or ten years before the land came into my hands, and by then the seedlings were in many places so thick that it was impossible to get between them. From that time onwards the problem was how best to thin them, and to cut out a few paths on the easiest lines to serve the future laying out of the ground where house and garden were to be."[17]

Until her death in 1932, Munstead Wood was Miss Jekyll's home and its garden was under her direct

control (see Chapter 7). It remained in the ownership of the Jekyll family until 1948. Miss Jekyll's unitary property has latterly been subdivided into five privately owned properties. The garden is nevertheless assessed at grade 1 on the English Heritage non-statutory register of historic parks and gardens.[18]

The Survey

The same methodology that was used at Wanstead was deployed at Munstead Wood in 1991 with adjustments to suit the particular circumstances. The agreed survey scale was 1:500. Since Ordnance Survey basic-scale mapping for the site is 1:2500 this meant that all plan details were originated by the survey and not derived from earlier mapping. The approach was archaeological, that is making an accurate well-observed record of the physical remains of the site as found. This provided a worthwhile permanent record of evidence that might in future be altered or completely obliterated and in addition offered a basis for interpretation and better understanding. Such a record could also serve as a basis for management decisions and specifications, typically by agencies other than the RCHME, including the owners. The area encompassed by the survey was the whole large triangle of land that Gertrude Jekyll acquired in about 1882 running to 15 acres, including the defining road pattern. This area plus the level of originality of survey made it necessary to encompass the site in a ring traverse, from which were run a series of subsidiary traverses and links, with braces to the enclosing ring, to enter and control each of the several modern properties. This finally entailed 44 traverse stations and 3000 points of detail. Where possible locations for the traverse stations were chosen that could be permanently marked or accurately relocated. This process should in principle allow the scheme to be reoccupied in the future, for any relevant land-use changes, excavation, geophysical or any other form of subsidiary survey to be added to the site record to the same specifications. In 1991 only the property known as The Quadrangle was not surveyed and a need therefore exists for future enhancement of the survey in this area. Should access become available at any time in the future the relevant part of the ring traverse could be re-occupied, a link carried into the property and tied out, and the additional data added to the overall data-set to complete the survey to the same specifications. At present if depiction of detail is required within The Quadrangle the solution can be to enlarge the most reliable historic mapping, for example an early

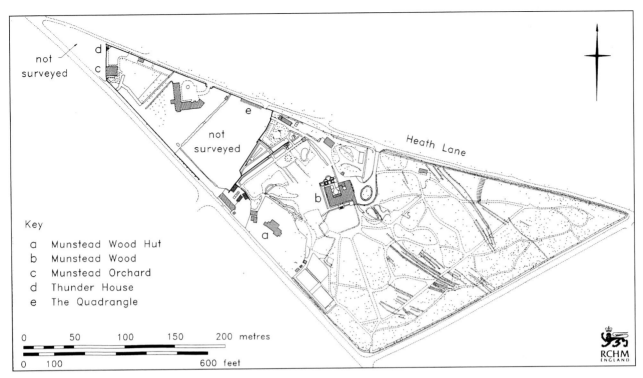

Figure 6.3   CAD – generated diagram of the former Munstead Wood property as surveyed in 1991.

series OS 25" to the mile sheet, and to make a best fit with the control provided by the surveyed property perimeter, or to draw an aerial photographic image. The RCHME would normally differentiate graphically that part of a presented survey plan, for example by screening and/or annotation, to indicate its different source and reliability, or simply that it is not a record of the landscape as found in 1991.

A further technical survey facility was used at Munstead Wood. The machine-based data-capture automatically logs a third dimension (height) for each point of detail recorded. If altitudinal regimes are systematically observed in the field the total data-set can be manipulated through standard software to produce a simplified model of the land-surface to the site. This was a prespecified desideratum of the Working Party since it was intended that a physical model of Munstead Wood be produced for the exhibition at the Museum of Garden History in London in 1993. The software allows modelling at any chosen height interval and the actual site coverage was certainly adequate for such modelling at 1m height interval and without misrepresentation. The result is illustrated in Figure 6.3. As digital information, it is capable of specified rotation and vertical exaggeration and its impact is enhanced if colour is deployed. The model certainly indicates clearly both the overall lie of the site on ground falling something like 15 to 20

metres from its SE corner to its N end near Busbridge church, and the very marked hollowed form of Heath Lane in its southern section. For traditional model-making any number of sections can be generated from the data and can be translated into physical sections that underpin the model (see pp. 77-8, overleaf).

Unlike most of the RCHME's traditional archaeological survey tasks, the range and level of detail of field remains to be depicted had to be a matter of discussion with the Working Party. Surprisingly, on their advice it was deemed desirable to vary between the present-day tenurial properties. The gardens now belonging to Munstead Wood Hut, Heath Lane House and Munstead Orchard were reckoned to have little or no surviving planted material. In contrast everything within the curtilage of the southern property, Munstead Wood itself, was thought relevant. In general the principal component of the task was to plan-position trees. Planned trees were tagged with numbers and a provisional identification listed by the field team. The Working Party undertook to arrange validation of tree identifications. Any further niceties such as recording girth, canopy or ring counts lay at their own discretion as part of continuing work. Azaleas and rhododendrons occurring generally in close-planted beds were not individually mapped, not least because of the need to have the azaleas and

Model of Munstead Wood designed by David Jobson and commissioned in 1993 by the Museum of Garden History for the exhibition to celebrate the 150th anniversary of the birth of Gertrude Jekyll.

The model (scale 1 to 150) measures 153cm x 166cm with a viewing height of 104cm and stands on a trestle support made of limed oak and designed in a style sympathetic to the period. The object of the model is to create a 'surreal' experience for the viewer, in developing an established garden as originally planned by Gertrude Jekyll, indicating mature tree and shrub heights in relationship to flower borders and lawns in the formal areas of garden to the less formal areas of the woodland. The buildings on the site have been modelled with minimal detail, so as not to detract from the main object of the model which is the garden.

In the garden areas the ground, lawns and paths have been produced using veneers of various thicknesses and patterns of fine woods to indicate ground cover of differing levels. The paths are raised or sunk where a formal pathway peters out into a woodland path. The trees, which include Scots pine, oak, sweet chestnut, silver birch, beech, yew and holly of various heights (totalling 200 trees) are made from a brass armature and then sprayed with various coloured materials to give a good impression of the trunk, body and foliage of the species occurring on the site.

The model was developed through consultation with Professor Michael Tooley of the University of St Andrews and formerly the University of Durham; Martin Wood, Consultant Garden Designer; and staff, students and co-opted members of the University of Sunderland Visual Information Design Course. The model was based on the completed computer survey documentation and photographs produced by the Royal Commission on the Historical Monuments of England Survey Unit based at the University of Keele and other contemporary publications and journal articles.

rhododendrons identified to a species or cultivar level. As with the details of the stonework of rockeries this was agreed to be an option for a larger scale local survey within the framework that the RCHME's work provided.

The result of the RCHME survey work was an accurate survey plan at 1:500 as specified, with the provision for re-use and open-ended enhancement. Something in excess of 1300 trees were plan positioned, including a swathe of new planting after the storm of 1987 that may in time alter the balance of distribution of the woodland in the southern third of the site. During the survey, guidance about ignoring as irrelevant fruit trees in the adjacent gardens of Heath Lane House and Munstead Orchard was set aside on the survey team's own initiative in favour of recording the landscape as found in that respect too. On plan (Figure 6.4) the fruit trees emerged as ragged rows

and plausibly the survival of Miss Jekyll's orchard. Subsequent field identification of the fruit by Jim Albury of the RHS Wisley caused him to comment, 'It is an interesting Edwardian collection of fruit trees, almost all of them planted during Miss Jekyll's time there I should think.' Mr Albury identified culinary apples 'Lord Grosvenor', Belle de Boskoop', 'Lane's Prince Albert', 'Northern Greening', 'Beauty of Stoke', 'Bismark', 'Loddington' and 'Herring's Pippin': dessert apples 'Egremont Russet', 'King of the Pippins', 'Adam's Pearmain', 'St Edmund's Pippin', 'Mother (American)' and 'Margil'; pears 'Beurre Hardy', 'Glou Morceau', 'Doyenne du Comice', 'Josephine de Malines' and 'Winter Nelis' with the old French stewing pear 'Catillac', together with some quince trees probably 'Portugal'. This discovery which resulted from the fieldwork was a considerable and unexpected bonus.

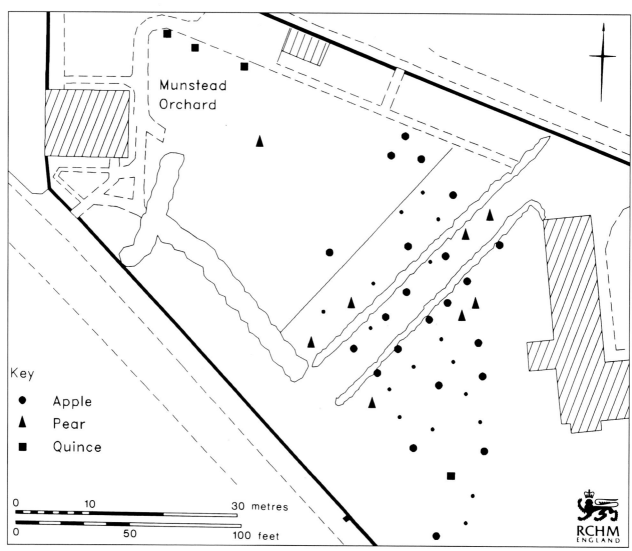

Figure 6.4   CAD – generated extract of the 1:500 scale survey showing the arrangement and types of fruit trees in the orchard.

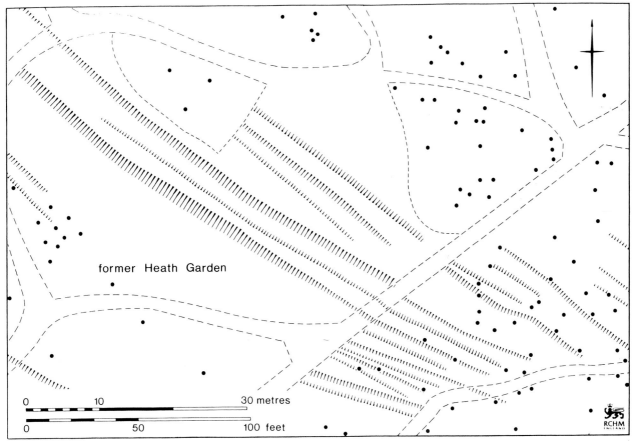

former Heath Garden

| 0 | | 10 | | 30 metres |
| 0 | | 50 | | 100 feet |

Figure 6.5   CAD – generated extract of the 1:500 scale survey showing part of the woodland with packhorse trails as surveyed earthworks.

The principal earthworks of the site, located in the southern area of the garden of Munstead Wood, are a complex network of linear hollows generally lying up and down the slope (Figure 6.5). They are intersecting and overlapping hollow-ways or 'packhorse trails', and are characteristic features of open moorlands and commons in all parts of England, usually of medieval and post-medieval date. Their interest here is two-fold. On the one hand they document archaeologically the 'prehistory', so to speak, of Miss Jekyll's garden. The RCHME's site account sets them in their correct context by establishing from early cartographic sources the former open common of Munstead Heath and elucidating its encroachment through the early and mid-19th century to create the enclosed parcels that Miss Jekyll acquired. On the other hand, Miss Jekyll's cultivation did not obliterate these features, and probably deliberately not. Rather, she both recognised their origin and exploited their water-retentive qualities and different soil structure relative to the surrounding podsolised sandy subsoil by planting up the most prominent of them to form her "waving rivers of bloom":

"Through this wood run shallow, parallel hollows, the lowest part of each depression some nine paces apart. Local tradition says they are the remains of old pack-horse roads; they occur frequently in the forest-like heathery uplands of our poor-soiled, sandy land, running for the most part three or four together, almost evenly side by side. The old people account for this by saying that when one track became too much worn another was taken by its side. Where these pass through the birch copse the Daffodils have been planted in the shallow hollows of the old ways, in spaces of some three yards broad by thirty or forty yards long – one kind at a time. Two of such tracks, planted with *Narcissus princeps* and *N. horsfieldii,* are now waving rivers of bloom, in many lights and accidents of cloud and sunshine full of pictorial effect. The planting of Daffodils in this part of the copse is much better than in many other portions where there were no guiding track-ways, and where they were planted in haphazard sprinklings."[20]

Since the earthworks can be identified, this conceit can more readily be understood and might quite easily be recreated.

In addition to the site survey the RCHME has put in hand a programme of ground photography repeating many of the viewpoints of the earlier historic photography by Miss Jekyll and others. Records of this fieldwork are, of course, keyed in and cross-referenced to the site plan.

As a further step to exploit the potential of the data-gathering exercise that the ground survey represents, the completed plan of Munstead Wood has been taken into a computer-aided drafting (CAD) system. This has opened up a number of possibilities both in interpretation and informative communication of results. They include practical facilities such as being able graphically to distinguish hard surfaces, lawns and beds, with the potential of quantifying these categories to aid site management. When the tree identification is validated, it will be possible to tag the tree locations by species and thereby generate a depiction of their distribution. Since four species only predominate in the southern woodland part of the garden; oak, scots pine, sweet chestnut and birch; it should be possible to give a striking visual impression of their zoning and interplay (Figure 6.6). This can still be perceived in moving around the garden and it was undoubtedly an effect that Miss Jekyll cultivated by her evolutionary management of the mixed tree cover that she inherited on the site. The same information can be used to build up, in an interactive way, the surveyed content of the current site, selecting or omitting at will for example the post 1987 storm plantings. Historic maps, even designs, can be taken in as a layer of information to the system. They can be related to the real topographical base in a best-fit exercise. The result will not be accurate metrically or in fineness of orientation and plan relationships because of the relatively poor basis of the original drawing, but its superimposition on the surveyed landscape can give an insight into intentions and ideas or can illuminate details that survive now only in the most fragmentary way. An example is 'The Nut Walk' lying at an angle to the NW facade of the main house. The area it occupied is now (1991) a combination of lawn, beds and a swimming pool, and its alignment and associated details are represented archaeologically by a few linear earthwork scarps (Figure 6.7).

The flexibility for holding and for manipulating such information, particularly for presentation and communication in both formal and informal ways,

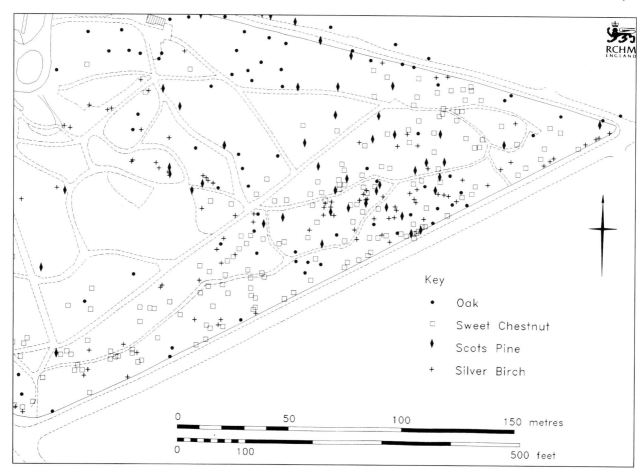

Key
- • Oak
- ▫ Sweet Chestnut
- ◆ Scots Pine
- + Silver Birch

Figure 6.6   CAD – generated extract of the 1:500 scale survey showing the distribution of four tree taxa in the south-east part of Munstead Wood.

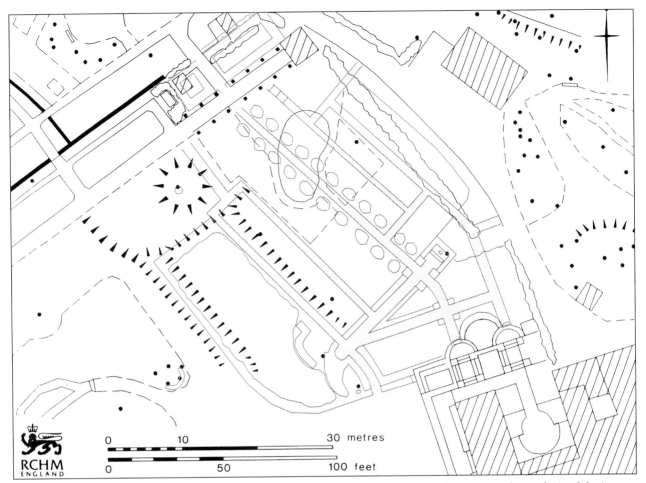

*Figure 6.7   CAD – generated image of The Nut Walk, Shrub Borders, Michaelmas Daisy Borders and Kalmia bed in 1924, with an overlay in red showing a
CAD – generated extract of the 1:500 scale survey, showing the features in 1991.*

is very considerable in a CAD environment. In the
wider professional world use for such facilities is
quite routine. The potential for comparable
applications to record historic gardens has been
demonstrated, for example, in Travers Morgan's
survey and report on Hampton Court,[21] work
sponsored by English Heritage in Victoria Park in
London and elsewhere. The RCHME's
applications at Munstead Wood are at best
exploratory. They nevertheless form part of the
RCHME's development of integrated methods of
storage and retrieval of spatially–based
archaeological information, that is a proposed
future component of the National Monuments
Record in England.

Conclusion

The involvement of the RCHME at Munstead
Wood is necessarily and rightly limited in time and
purpose. It does not extend now to detailed
research into the work of Gertrude Jekyll at
Munstead Wood, about which others are already
expert (see Chapter 7) and it does not extend to

future research which the Working Party and
others may wish to pursue. What it has provided is
an accurate, archaeologically-minded and topo-
graphically–based survey of the site in 1991. This is
an essential preliminary in promoting advances or
enabling action in three spheres:

1. better understanding of the design and
    development of the site and of the survival of
    historically important elements,
2. keying of documentary and photographic
    data; and
3. future management, and public presentation
    of information.

Though alluded to above by way of illustration,
none of these lies directly or exclusively in the
RCHME's hands. As a deposit in the National
Monuments Record[22] the survey serves both as a
record and as a platform or focus to which other
information can confidently be attached. If it is
taken up and referred to by current and future
scholars for that purpose it will stand as a
permanent benefit both to scholarship and to
public information.

7

Gertrude Jekyll's Munstead Wood

Martin Wood

Christopher Hussey, writing in 1950, thought Miss Jekyll was "perhaps the greatest artist in horticulture and garden-planting that England has produced – whose influence on garden design has been as widespread as Capability Brown's in the eighteenth century."[1]

Despite the numerous books and articles written about her, she remains a greatly misunderstood and misrepresented figure whose influence on contemporary garden design remains nevertheless undiminished. To have some idea of her work, the very apotheosis of that long-vanished golden age which was Edwardian England, one must have some appreciation of her own home and garden, Munstead Wood.

The Jekyll family had moved in 1868 from Bramley House, a large Regency mansion in Surrey not far from Munstead Heath, to a house in Wargrave, Berkshire which Captain Jekyll had inherited some years earlier.[2] Captain Jekyll died in March 1876 and his widow, Julia Jekyll, decided to return to Surrey and purchased about 20 acres of land on Munstead Heath on which a house designed by J. J. Stevenson (a member of the Queen Anne Movement) was built. In 1883 or possibly a year earlier, a plot of land opposite Munstead House extending to a little over fifteen acres came on the market and, to stop the possibility of a school being built there, Miss Jekyll bought it.[3] Just who the vendor was is not known but it may have formed part of the Thorncombe Park estate then owned by Edward Rowe Fisher Rowe, an old family friend. It was Fisher Rowe who sold Mrs Jekyll the land for Munstead House and later sold her another small parcel of land across the Hascombe Road on which she built some cottages for her servants.[4]

The word Munstead is thought to be derived from two Anglo-Saxon words, meaning "elevated situation", which indeed it is. However the heath was formerly part of Windsor Great Park, into which it was incorporated by King Henry II shortly after he came to the throne in 1154, and it is possible that the name meant 'protected or guarded place', an allusion to the King's prerogative.[5] To peasants or serfs of the time hunting on the land would have meant certain death. It is well known that all the Plantagenet Kings frequently hunted both from Guildford Castle and the moated Manor House later built just across the river Wey. Surrey was for centuries a playground for the Kings and Queens of England. Indeed, that most magnificent of sovereigns, Queen Elizabeth I, came so often both to Guildford and Farnham, that the county remonstrated to the Privy Council about the bill they were expected to pay for the Queen's horse and carriage![6]

The site of Munstead Wood was triangular in shape, of very poor quality land, sloping down to the north and west, bounded by Heath Lane, Hascombe Road and Bramley Road which are old, well established thoroughfares that can be seen clearly on the 1806-10 survey map published in 1816. The pattern of fields, some of which were later incorporated to form Munstead Wood, is shown on the Godalming and Eashing Tithe Maps of 1844 (see Figure 6.2b), which also show the ownership of land and the rents due in lieu of tithes following the passing of the Tithe Commutation Act in 1836.[7] The southern portion of the property was formerly a plantation of Scots pine which had been felled in the early 1870s, after some seventy

Left: A border of Salvias in the Grey Garden, Munstead Wood, c. 1911.

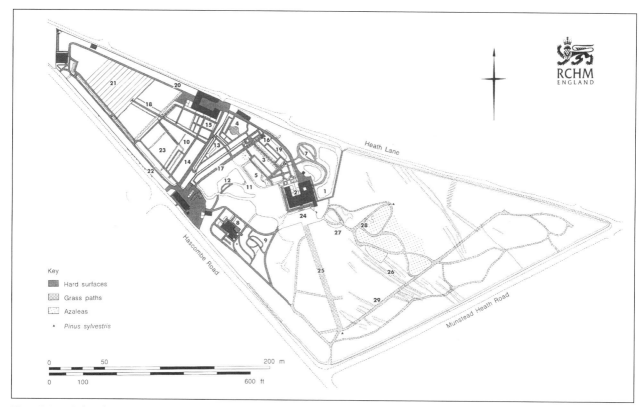

Figure 7.1   A plan of Munstead Wood in Miss Jekyll's day.

years growth, and for the next nine or ten years the ground had been left to its own devices allowing a dense self-sown wood to spring up. The central portion, where ultimately the house would be built, was a chestnut copse and the remaining northern portion, which is the lowest ground, was an arable field with a hard plough bed some eight inches down.[8] The northernmost tip of the triangle was not part of the parcel and is shown on the tithe map as a separate and distinct plot.

In the autumn of 1883 Miss Jekyll engaged the Guildford surveyors Messrs Peak, Lunn & Peak to provide a detailed survey of the estate which they submitted in the November and this clearly shows two woodland paths, a convenient seat for contemplation, and the hand gate across the road from Munstead House.[9] It is this survey which leads to the assumption that the land had been purchased in that year but it would seem most unlikely that she had done so much work on the site in so short a time. Miss Jekyll developed the site on an ad hoc basis, which can be seen from the survey, with no overall plan; each area was taken in hand and treated on its own merits and the whole reconciled in whatever way she was able to contrive after the house was built. This seems an unconventional and rather peculiar way to proceed, in light of the advice to her clients but it would have been quite familiar to any eighteenth

century gentleman.[10] The plan of Munstead Wood (Figure 7.1) was drawn by the Royal Commission for the Historical Monuments of England and is based on many sources. The numbers shown on the plan refer to the descriptions of the various areas of the garden in the following sections.

The Entrance and the House
(1 on Figure 7.1)

The house was built in 1896 and is one of the finest examples of Lutyens' Surrey Vernacular style and its evident success helped launch his career. It is hard to imagine a house more in tune with its setting and so perfectly expressing the character and personality of its owner that even today there remains a feeling of Miss Jekyll's continued presence. Not only did she supervise its building while living in the small cottage called 'the Hut', but also she had a large hand in its design with the result that the house we see today is a perfect blend of the characteristics of the youthful Lutyens and the more restrained and simple style of Miss Jekyll.

Munstead Wood was deliberately designed to give the impression of a modest house set in a wood, which is precisely what was achieved. This impression was carefully fostered by having no carriage drive sweeping up to the front door but merely a simple hand gate and footpath leading from a sunken lane (Heath Lane) with the planting kept as simple as possible. To the right of the gate was a fine multi-stemmed beech, its cool elephant-grey trunk enhanced by a generous background of holly, while the ground beneath was covered with masses of whortleberry *(Vaccinium myrtillu),* male and lady ferns and polypody, and drifts of woodrush *(Luzula sylvatica).* From the house the path turned quite abruptly to the left (Figure 7.2)

Figure 7.2   View from the porch of Munstead Wood looking north-east through the holly tunnel along the entrance path from Heath Lane.

having passed through a tunnel of hollies with the bankings beneath still generously covered with hardy ferns and *Leucothoë axillaris.*[11]

The porch was an extension built out from the main block of the house forming a covered passage, with the front door at one end and entrance to the south terrace at the other. In Miss Jekyll's day the caller would ring the bell, which made no audible sound, yet suddenly the door would be opened and the guest would, as Harold Falkner recalled, be ushered into a large hall which remains to this day the principal sitting room of the house.[12] Miss Jekyll would normally be working either in the garden or in her workroom, which opened off the hall just beyond the staircase, but she would soon appear. At tea there might be some unusual treat, such as crab apple or quince jelly, or even a delicacy

such as radishes grown in leaf mould, a technique which produces an exquisite flavour. All this trouble was taken (as one would expect) for the guest, Miss Jekyll herself being restricted to the more spartan "saccharined tea and one biscuit."[13]

The house was basically 'E' shaped, although more often referred to as 'U' shaped, the principle rooms being arranged along the south front. A beautifully proportioned staircase, comfortable to ascend, led directly from the sitting room, by way of a half landing and the entrance to the book room, to a broad gallery, some ten feet wide, which was cantilevered out for half its width – an example of Lutyens' genius for creating and manipulating space. Between the two wings of the house on the north side, formed by the workshop and garden room on the west and pantry on the east and linked by the hall and long gallery, was the most formal part of the whole garden, the North Court which led to the Tank garden.

The North Court & Tank Garden
(2 on Figure 7.1)

A semi-circle of paving three yards deep, created from some very fine ripple-marked stone slabs (Figure 7.3), was given an edge of dwarf box with the small beds thus formed against the two wings of the house thickly planted with a background of male fern and red and white hardy fuchsias. A vine covered the pantry wall while a *Clematis montana* grew round the workshop window and was trained

Figure 7.3   The North Court.

as swagged garlands from the gallery linking the two wings of the house. Pots of hostas and ferns were used to provide a green background for more pots and troughs filled with lilies, hydrangeas, the beautiful 'Bridal Wreath' *(Francoa sonchifolia)* and even *Campanula persicifolia,* all arranged to add seasonal interest.[14]

Figure 7.4   The Lion Mask by G.D. Leslie RA and view into the North Court.

Figure 7.5   View north-west along the Nut Walk to the Pergola.

A path led from the North Court towards the Tank garden which was set between two broad flights of steps, punctuated by eight clipped balls of box. The tank's cool north-facing wall was covered with ferns which almost concealed a beautiful Lion's mask (Figure 7.4), the work of the Royal Academician G.D. Leslie, set into the retaining wall. From the lion's mouth spouted a jet of water into the pool below.[15] Along the top of the retaining wall small Italian orange pots filled with more 'Bridal Wreath', a great favourite, would be lined out in the summer months.

The Nut Walk
(3 on Figure 7.1)

From the garden room door a broad flight of steps led past the tank and the Cenotaph of Sigismunda, about which more later, to the Nut Walk which Miss Jekyll planted in about 1887 long before the house was built.[16] Two double rows of hazels *(Corylus avellana)* were planted zig-zag fashion ten feet apart, on either side of a five foot path which led to the Pergola (Figure 7.5), and Main Flower Border.

The deep bays created by this arrangement were filled with a collection of Lent hellebores *(Helleborus orientalis)* which had originally come from the noted collector Mr. Archer-Hind of Devon and ranged in colour from dusky red-purple through paler shades to whites. To these were added groups of *Corydalis bulbosa,* early purple dog-tooth violets, which were followed by tall cream erythroniums. The season was extended by the addition of yellow primroses, forget-me-nots (she thought *Myosotis dissitiflora* the prettiest of them all), dentaria, *Tiarella cordifolia* and to continue the season still further, columbines, a fine white form of *Campanula macrantha* and a background of Alexandrian laurel *(Danaë racemosa).*[17]

Eventually the nuts arched overhead to provide, just as Miss Jekyll had hoped, a shady way most welcome in the summer heat. Whether she ever collected any nuts is another matter; the resident squirrel population regarded it as fine sport to swing from branch to branch and strip the bushes bare, all of which was taken in good part[18]. The nuts themselves were off-sets from some bushes that had originally come from a cob–nut nursery at Calcot near Reading. Miss Jekyll later recalled visiting the nursery in 1873 and vividly remembered the forewoman who ran the nursery with only three men, although Miss Jekyll thought the woman could have done "the work of 'all two men' herself."[19]

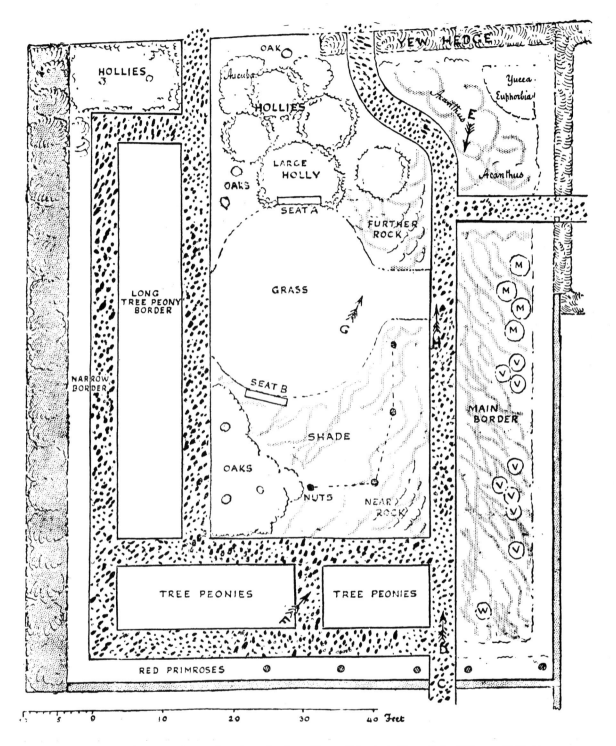

Figure 7.6   Plan of the Spring Garden c. 1908. Arrows refer to photograhs taken to illustrate Colour in the Flower Garden. V. Veratrum, M. Myrrhis, W. Euphorbia Wulfenii.

The Spring Garden (4 on Figure 7.1)

The Nut Walk path continued through the Pergola, past beds of the beautiful shrub *Kalmia latifolia,* to the Spring Garden which is one of the most well documented areas of the garden. The planting, which changed slightly each year, is described in great detail in Miss Jekyll's book *Colour in the Flower Garden* (Figure 7.6). It was also extensively photographed, both in black and white and in autochrome (Figures 7.7, 7.8, 7.9 and 7.10) which shows the garden before the Great War.

The Garden had one large border backed on the

Figure 7.7 & Figure 7.8 The Spring Garden in c. 1911.

south side by the high wall which sheltered the Main Flower Border from cold north-westerly winds and by a yew hedge which formed the continuation of the wall and partially enclosed the Garden, hiding it from the drive and some sheds. At the centre of the Garden a rough circle of grass, providing a restful place to sit, was surrounded by some oaks, hazel and a broad planting of holly. Two pieces of rock work, known as 'Near Rock' and 'Further Rock', were used as decorative features in the central section of the Garden and 'Near Rock' can be clearly seen on one of the autochrome photographs from the period. Three smaller beds ran along the western and northern edges of the Garden and were filled with a collection of tree paeonies. A narrow edging bed at the foot of the western and northern boundary walls was used to grow red primroses of which Miss Jekyll had her own strain, selected over more than twenty years.

To add weight and solidity to the delicate forms of most spring flowers, Miss Jekyll planted a backbone of *Veratrum nigrum,* sweet cicely *(Myrrhis odorata)* and a plant of *Euphorbia wulfenii* (Figure 7.9) at the eastern end of the Main Border, where its bold form was shown up well against the dark yew hedge. Further along on the wall which backed the Main Border were some morello cherries grown as espaliers. For the first few yards the front and centre of the border was filled with pale primroses *(Tiarella cordiflora),* pale yellow daffodils, pale yellow early iris, lemon coloured wallflowers, double white arabis and white anemones. To these were added a pale lilac aubrietia, a pale lilac iris and long drifts of white and pale yellow tulips. At the back of the border deeper colours were used, such as a purple wallflower and a double purple tulip called 'Bleu Celeste'. In the centre the colours deepened with strong yellow tulips, wallflowers and several patches of yellow crown imperial, although paler and lighter colours were still used towards the edge to lead the eye. At the far end of the border (Figure 7.10), where it was backed by the yew hedge, the colours became much stronger with orange tulips, brown wallflowers, orange crown imperials and a taller scarlet tulip.[20]

The Shrub Walk and Cenotaph
(5 & 6 on Figure 7.1)

From the west lawn a path led down towards the south-west end of the Pergola through a double bank of shrubs, some six yards long, which were planted in the late 1890s. Down the centre of the bed, the highest ground, were magnolias and junipers; *Magnolia soulangeana, M. purpurea, M. stellata* and, most beautiful of all, the yulan or 'lily tree' *(Magnolia denudata)* which was considered, at the court of Kubla Khan, a handsome gift even from the Governor of a Province. In front of the *Magnolia denudata* some bushes of *Forsythia suspensa* over ten feet tall would cast out long branches covered in clear yellow flowers which, on a favoured day, would be set clear against the blue sky with the great white cups of the magnolia above. As the flowers of the *Magnolia denudata* drew to a close, a later flowering bush of *Magnolia stellata,*

Figure 7.9   The Spring Garden in c. 1911.

Figure 7.10   The Spring Garden in c. 1911.
Figure 7.11   The shrub borders with Magnolia stellata *looking east towards the house.*

some twelve feet tall and as wide, set among the forsythia, would take their place (Figure 7.11).

A small bush of *Styrax japonica* grew towards one end with some low bushes of *Cistus florentinus* at its feet and the yellow-green leaved bamboo *Sasa tessellata* (then known as *Bambusa ragamowski*). Further on again grew a large bush of Jerusalem sage *(Phlomis fruticosa)* and a fine *Aesculus parviflora,* the bush horse chestnut, followed by some *Olearia haastii* and the blue *Caryopteris incana,* which smells of turpentine. Near the Pergola the ground was worked with large amounts of peat for the benefit of andromedas, skimmias and gale or bog myrtle *(Myrica gale).*[21]

A second path ran parallel to the first between it and the Nut Walk. It was lined on the north-east side by a broad bank of briar roses, some twenty five yards long and six feet wide, backed by nut trees, while on the other side were the Shrub Borders just described. Over the years Miss Jekyll collected many different single and double varieties

of burnet rose *(Rosa spinosissima)* from cottage gardens in the neighbourhood. The first to flower, in late May or early June, was a pale single pink with a low, half trailing habit which would be followed by the bold mass of a burnet rose, covered in creamy–ivory flowers. Miss Jekyll obtained a number of different variations of the same rose, notably a fine semi–double rose coloured form, of which she retained only those of the best colour and with the most pleasing habit. Most of these roses had a very short flowering season with the exception of 'Stanwell Perpetual' which was in flower almost continually throughout the season.[22]

Near the house the two paths emerged onto a wide cross path which, turning left, ran north-east towards and across the end of the Nut Walk. The path was terminated by a fine silver birch, backed by a yew hedge, and with a large seat in front of it made from a single piece of elm of "monumental mass" resting on a wide step of stone pitching. The path was once lined with tall yellow mulliens *(Verbascum sp.),* which combined with the weeping form of the birch beyond to give the whole area a "funereal environment", as Miss Jekyll noted. Edwin Lutyens showed the seat to Charles Liddell who remarked that it looked like the "Cenotaph of Sigismunda",[23] (Figure 7.12), a name too good to lose.

After the end of the Great War in 1919 the Prime Minister, David Lloyd George, summoned Sir Edwin and told him that the Cabinet had decided to erect a "catafalque" (a structure on which a coffin rests during a funeral service) in Whitehall for the Peace Celebrations to be held at the end of July. Sir Edwin, remembering the seat at Munstead Wood and Liddell's remark some twenty five years before, told Lloyd George that they required "not a catafalque but a Cenotaph." After a brief explanation Lutyens designed the whole thing on a sheet of notepaper in a matter of a few minutes and a full set of drawings was in the hands of the Office of Works before ten o'clock the following morning.[24]

The Primrose Garden (7 on Figure 7.1)

North-east of the Cenotaph of Sigismunda was the back drive which led up to the Kitchen Court and beyond which lay the Primrose Garden. It was set in a clearing of oaks and chestnuts with a sprinkling of hazel in the long narrow beds (Figure 7.13) and was virtually encircled by holly and Portugal laurel. There are few people alive today who can remember what a magical picture was so skilfully painted in this wooded oasis. It showed its greatest effect at eventide when the light, which in

Figure 7.12 The Cenotaph of Sigismunda.

England is normally tinged with blue, is warmed and tinted with gold by the embers of a setting sun. On a favoured evening the clearing would glow with a wonderful primrose light, the whole area becoming almost incandescent.

Over many years Miss Jekyll developed her strain of white and yellow bunch flowered primroses, or polyanthus, by careful breeding and selection (See Chapter 9). It all began when she saw a white flowered bunch primrose in a cottage garden in the early 1870s. The cottager gave her the plant and she began to cross it with a "cultivated sort called Golden Plover". Over the years the strain was

Figure 7.13 The Primrose Garden in 1928.

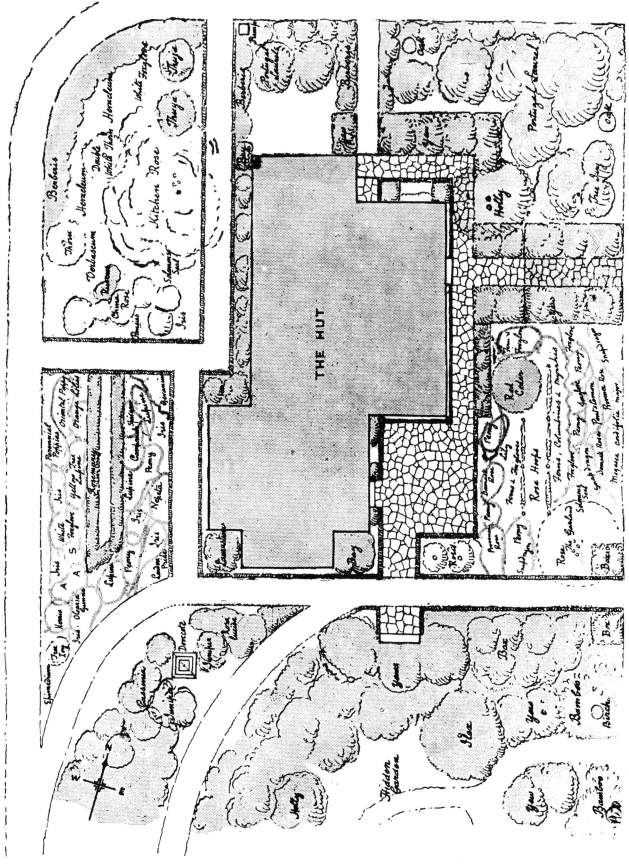

Figure 7.14 Plan of the garden around the Hut – the June garden in c. 1908.

improved and refined to such an extent that one day Miss Jekyll decided to classify the plants, but gave up after writing out more than sixty descriptions! To some she did give names and these formed the backbone of the strain. A very deep yellow, almost orange, she called 'Sultan'; a pure primrose colour, with six wide, wavy edged petals was called 'Lemon Rose' (a great favourite) and a large white, with an eye of citron, she called 'Virginie.'[25]

The Hut Garden & Hidden Garden
(8 & 9 on Figure 7.1)

In 1894 Lutyens designed a small cottage for Miss Jekyll, which she called the 'Hut'. Built across the lawn from the site where the main house was intended to stand it was completed in November of 1894 and she lent it temporarily to an old Surrey lady, Mrs Cannon. Mrs Jekyll died the following year and as Munstead House was bequeathed to Miss Jekyll's younger brother, Herbert, who was married with a young family of three children, Miss Jekyll left her former home and moved to the Hut while Munstead Wood was being built.[26]

The garden around the Hut (Figure 7.14) was in many ways an archetypical cottage garden, complete with dovecote and water pump. It was built with its back to the Hascombe Road, on the south-west side of the ground, and was approached through a tunnel of yews, passing a large holly with *Clematis montana* tumbling out of the top, along a path lined with ferns and rhododendrons. Around the cottage the beds were edged with dwarf box and at one point, where the bed proved far too wide for easy maintenance, a hedge of rosemary was used to edge an access path. At the other side of the cottage, a Garland Rose (Figure 7.15) cascaded onto the path and in the border to the north there was a 'dividing backbone,' created from a double row of rose hoops or arches, set amongst male ferns and sweet cicely.

Designed to be at its best in June and early July, from the published plans one can see that the beds were filled with iris, lupins, peonies and many old roses, with any spaces being planted up with pentstemons and snapdragons to extend the season. Behind a large bush of an old rambling rose ran an equally large planting of the giant hogweed (*Heracleum mantegazzianum*), the foliage and giant flowers of which she so much admired.[27]

A hedge bank planted with pines and hollies shielded the property from the Hascombe Road and at its foot, where the space allowed, Miss Jekyll created a bulb border. Filled with puschkinia, muscari, crocus and scillas, the border, some seventy feet long, was designed to be enjoyed for only a short period, and to cover the bulb foliage as it died back, in any garden always something of a challenge, she planted drifts of male fern which almost totally covered the ground later in the season. At the back of the border, at intervals of ten feet, stout posts with ropes between carried climbing roses, which looped in front of the dark background of pines and hollies, and whose myriad

Figure 7.15 The Garland Rose and the Hut.

flowers were used in the pot-pourri which was made to Miss Jekyll's recipe on the floor of the studio in The Hut.[28]

The southern boundary of the Hut Garden was heavily planted with yews, hollies, box and bamboos beyond which was the Hidden Garden (Figure 7.16). Although two important paths passed a few yards from it, on either side, no major path led to this little sunken garden. One small entrance path ran through a tunnel of bamboos which arched overhead while another ran through a curving tunnel of yews and hollies. Even on the published plan one could see that the surrounding trees would soon grow up and cast too heavy a shade to grow most of the alpine plants successfully.

One bed beneath the shade of a young beech was filled with lilies and ferns and two clumps of tree paeonies were used to add bulk and substance.

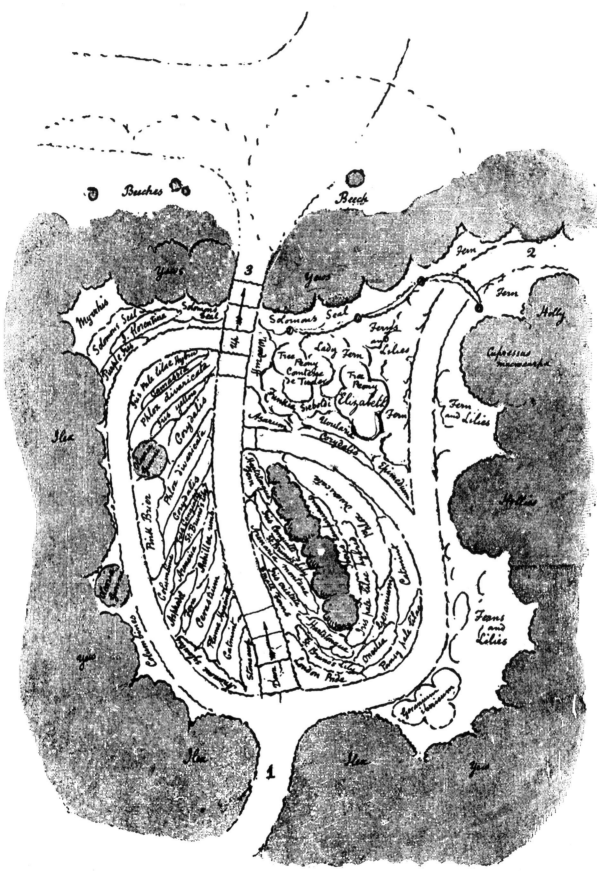

Figure 7.16 Plan of the Hidden Garden in c. 1908.

Drifts of Solomon's Seal grew in the deeper shade at the margins and woodruff, asarum, corydalis and epimediums lined the edge of the path. On the other side of the path grew more ferns and lilies with a *Cupressus macrocarpa* and the hollies and yews of the surrounding planting as a foil. In the central beds, which benefitted from more light, drifts of the blue-lilac *Phlox divaricata* mingled with lilac iris, drifts of corydalis and even catmint. St. Bruno's lilies *(Anthericum liliago)* were planted to shoot up amongst swathes of London Pride *(Saxifraga umbrosa)* and the lilies were repeated across the path, but this time with a backing of blue Iris cengialti and the pale yellow of more corydalis. A pale pink Scotch briar rose was planted in a group with pale yellow corydalis and the white *Arenaria montana* (Figure 7.17) which ran into a bold drift of *Phlox divaricata* speared with deep coloured *Camassia esculenta.*[29]

Across the path from the briar rose the border was filled with pale coloured long spur columbines while a *Rosa brunonis* and Rose 'Paul's Carmine Pillar', which flowered less freely than in the open garden, tumbled from the surrounding trees.

Figure 7.17   View of the Hidden Garden.

Eventually the surrounding yews and hollies grew so large and the trees cast so much shade that the carefully varied planting just described had to be abandoned and this small garden was given over to ferns.

Figure 7.18   Iris and Lupin Borders in c. 1911.

Figure 7.19   Iris and Lupin Borders in c. 1911.

Iris and Lupin Borders (10 on Figure 7.1)

In *Colour in the Flower Garden,* published in 1908, Miss Jekyll expressed a wish to have further June borders, in addition to those around the Hut, where better use could be made of flag iris and lupins. After the book's publication some Iris and

Lupin Borders were created in the Kitchen Gardens, north-west of the Spring Garden, and although retouched for publication, wonderful autochromes of these Borders were used as the frontispiece and the dustjacket to *Gardens for Small Country Houses*, 1912 and in E.H. Jenkins' *The Hardy Flower Book* (1913) (Figures 7.18 and 7.19). Looking towards the stables as in the illustration, the borders were enclosed by yew hedges to the left and at the end, and a hedge of flowering shrubs on the right which backed the July Borders, and led on to the Grey Garden. Although the shrub hedge was formed from flowering currants *(Ribes sanguineum),* guelder rose *(Viburnum opulus),* tamarisk, lilac, snowberry *(Symphoricarpos albus),* *Chaenomeles speciosa* and *Rhodotypos scandens*, she later regretted that she had not used just flowering currants and guelder rose.

The Munstead lupins, long before the advent of Russell lupins, were of three distinct colourings; a pure white, the spikes of which were said to be extremely large, purple-blue, pale purple shading to white, and pink to a red-purple.[30] The border began with a bold patch of the blue flowered *Anchusa* 'Opal' with the white flowered *Olearia gunniana* at its feet. Blue and white lupins followed, in separate patches, to be themselves succeeded by pink China roses, blue-purple iris together with a blue cranes-bill mingled with catmint and an edging of white pinks and pansies. Tall yellow iris were grouped with lupin 'Somerset', a pure yellow with long spikes which had been raised by Kelways, and a bush of golden privet with the colour moving on through deeper yellows to irises and lupins of purple-red colouring, to which were added groups of *Incarvillea delavayi* and *Heuchera americana*. At the far end of the border, backed by the yew hedge, a group of *Asphodelus albus,* white tree lupins and pink China roses were mingled with the rosy lilac flowers of *Iris pallida* 'Queen of the May.'

The Yew Cat and Rock Garden

(11 & 12 on Figure 7.1)

From the south front of the house the lawn swept round to the west and formed a broad grass ride running down to the Main Flower Border. To the north-east were the Shrub Borders, already mentioned, and on this side grew a fine example of the pearl bush *(Exochorda grandiflora).* To the south-west across the ride purple rhododendrons lined a path leading to The Hut and past a large snowdrop tree *(Halesia monticola).* A little further down at the end of a promontory of planting, sat a large topiary cat shaped from two yews planted originally as a bold full stop to the planting of shrubs that

Figure 7.20   Drawing of 'Cat in Yew' by Gertrude Jekyll.

surrounded the sunken Rock Garden. When the yews gradually grew into a large dense mass and seemed to take on a rough animal shape, Miss Jekyll had them cut into the form of a very large cat (Figure 7.20 and 7.21) resting on its paws with a round face and deep set eyes.[31]

To the left of the Yew Cat a path led down a few rough steps to a sunken Rock Garden similar in shape and design to the Hidden Garden. At the foot of the steps the path divided, creating an island bed raised about a foot from the path by a dry stone wall which was generously planted with small ferns, ramondia and the then rare *Haberlea rhodopensis*, while on the sunnier south side grew stonecrops. On the cool shady bankings broad drifts of *Dryas octopetala* and *Cardamine trifolia* were grouped with what Miss Jekyll called "little meadows" of *Linnaea borealis, Campanula pulla* and *Veronica prostrata.*

Figure 7.21   Drawing of the Yew Cat by Rosanna Tooley from photographs taken in 1927.

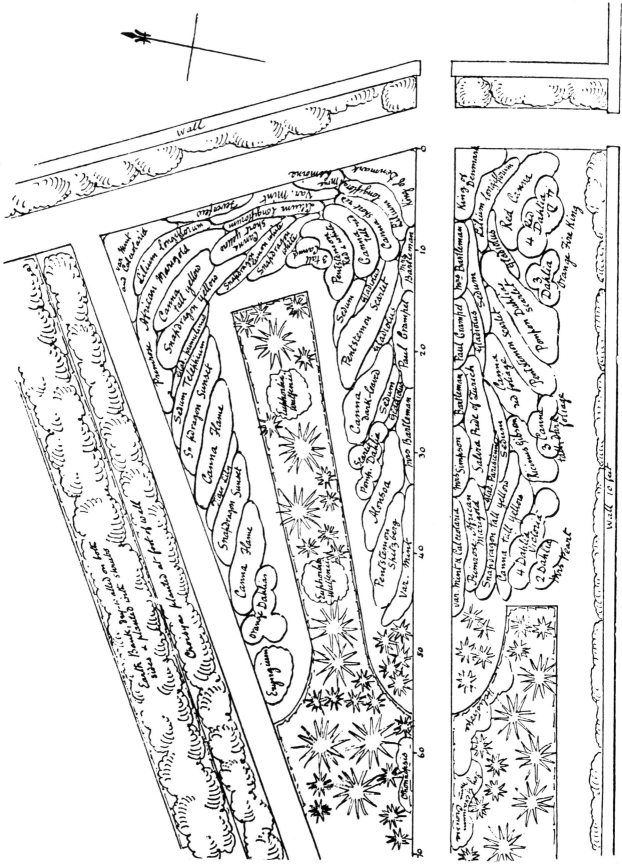

Figure 7.22   Plan of the Garden of Summer Flowers (Annual Garden) c. 1908.

The Annual Garden (13 on Figure 7.1)

Beyond the wall which backed the Main Flower Border lay the Spring Garden to the right of the path and to the left a small triangular shaped plot, known to the garden staff as "three corner garden" (Figure 7.22). The main body of this garden was some thirty feet wide, so the garden was given an "elevated backbone" a few feet wide and some eighteen inches high, using dry stone walls and planted up with yuccas and euphorbias. Elsewhere the beds were planted almost entirely with dahlias, cannas, geraniums, variegated maize and bedding plants, including that delight of park superintendents everywhere, the African marigold. The colour scheme consisted of graduations of red, white and yellow and in many ways it was a forerunner of the July Borders. The space was formerly devoted to paeonies which were the best kinds available and mostly imported from France. (They were described in some detail in *Wood & Garden*, 1899, pp.72–76).

The northern boundary of this rather odd shaped garden was formed by a planted wall which ran north-east to south-west across the property. It was in effect a filled dry stone wall six feet wide at its base, four feet wide at the top and four and a half feet high which was created in 1892 from an old hedge bank. Miss Jekyll planted it with jasmine, barberry and ferns on the shady northern side and on the warm southern side in the narrow border at the foot she planted choisyas, sweet verbenas, some escallonias and groups of pentstemons. Today the most notable feature of the entire garden is an old Judas tree *(Cercis siliquastrum)* which was "old" even in Miss Jekyll's day.

The July Borders and Grey Garden
(14 & 15 on Figure 7.1)

From the Annual Garden a path led to a broad arterial way which cut across the whole property, from the garden yard beside the Hascombe Road on one side to the stables beside Heath Lane on the other. A few yards from the garden yard and potting shed a path parallel to the Hascombe Road led off to the north-west down the side of a large cypress hedge towards the Head Gardener's Cottage. At the foot of the hedge for some years Miss Jekyll had a large bed of pansies; although she never mentioned it in any of her many writings its existence was recorded in a watercolour painting.[32] The bed was probably used to supply flowers for the house, the Edwardians being very fond of both the pansy and the violet. Indeed, Queen Alexandra had a large formal pansy garden at Sandringham House and at Windsor Castle 5000 violet plants were grown to provide flowers the year round.

The July Borders lined another path, which ran parallel to the arterial way described above, and led back to the stable block. They were backed on the left by a hedge of flowering shrubs, which bounded the Iris and Lupin Borders. Looking along these Borders from the cypress hedge the colours were rich; yellows, whites, some orange, which faded to paler shades, and some purple, with a ground of silvery foliage used to lead the eye round a bend in the path into the Grey Garden. Like the Iris and Lupin Borders the July Borders were established after 1908 and are not mentioned in *Colour in the Flower Garden*, although they were described in a long article published during the Great War, leading one to assume that they were still maintained, unlike the Main Flower Border which had been given over to growing potatoes.[33]

From this article it can be seen that a large number of annuals were used in these summer borders, more than in the Main Flower Border. Masses of Sweet Alyssum *(Lobularia maritima)*, the golden Feverfew *(Chrysanthemum Parthenium var. aureum)*, the striped grass *(Glyceria aquatica)* and the variegated mint *(Mentha x rotundifolia 'Variegata')* were used with tall pale yellow snapdragons, Miss Jekyll's own selection of *Chrysanthemum maximum* and a white annual balsam *(Impatiens roylei)*. The colours became deeper with groups of purple clary *(Salvia sclarea)* and erigerons, followed by a long drift of *Salvia nemorosa virgata* as the path approached the Grey garden.

A box hedge and rose arches, with their garlands of rambler roses, enclosed a small Grey Garden known to the staff as "square garden", which was devoted to grey and silver foliage with flowers of purple, pink and white colourings (Figure 7.23). As the years passed, Miss Jekyll became more interested in the use of grey foliage and in these colour combinations, which she wrote about extensively. Again, in the published plans it can be seen that many annuals were used in the form of godetia, China asters and tall snapdragons *(Anthirrhinum majus)*, but with some shrubs and climbing plants, such as clematis, as well. The globe thistle *(Echinops ruthenicus)* was grown in quite large groups in front of *Clematis x jackmanii* which would be trained up into the thistle. Some large *Ceanothus* 'Gloire de Versailles', sea buckthorn *(Hippophaë rhamnoides)* and the rose *(Rosa rubrifolia)* grew towards the back with clumps of Miss Jekyll's own pink hollyhock, 'Pink Beauty' and a few *Lavatera olbia* which, in one form or another, is now so ubiquitous.[34]

The Pergola and Main Flower Border
(16 & 17 on Figure 7.1)

One of the chief glories of Munstead Wood was

Figure 7.23   The Grey Garden in c. 1911.

without question the Main Flower Border. It measured just over two hundred feet in length, fourteen feet in depth, and was backed by a wall of Bargate stone (a type of sandstone) eleven feet high. It is not known exactly when this wall was constructed but it is thought, by dating from the photographic evidence, that it was built in 1890 or 1891.[35] The Border was broken about a third of the way along its length by a cross path which led off, through the famous garden door, to the Annual and Spring Gardens, across the July Borders and thence down to the September Borders in the Kitchen Garden.

At the north-eastern end of the Main Border the path, which ran along its length between the border and lawn, passed beneath the Pergola to a small open summer house. Miss Jekyll loved the pleasant feeling of passing from bright sunlight to the cool, dark and wonderfully gloomy shade. The small open-sided summer-house, seen from afar, appeared to be a black cavern, but as the eye adjusted to the subdued light within it proved a

pleasant place to sit and read. The Pergola itself was a substantial affair constructed from brick piers "seven feet two inches tall" placed in pairs on either side of the path with eight feet between each pair. Miss Jekyll thought that pergolas were often too flimsy and so here she used large rough oak beams which had not been shaped in any way. In less than six years the structure was well covered by jasmine, Dutchman's pipe *(Aristolochia macrophylla)*, a Virginia creeper, vines *(Vitis coignettiae)*, one of which grew so well that it covered the top of a nearby strawberry tree *(Arbutus unedo)*, and probably most beautiful of all, a wisteria.[36]

The high Bargate stone wall was used to provide a background to the careful colour scheme of the border at its feet. By the door grew a *Magnolia denudata*, the lily or yulan tree of ancient China together with Mexican orange blossoms *(Choysia ternata)*. A little further on a Japan privet *(Ligustrum japonicum)* grew next to a pomegranate *(Punica granatum)* which was protected from the worse excesses of the English winter by boughs of fir and bracken. Between two bay trees *(Laurus nobilis)* Miss Jekyll planted the Chinese sacred bamboo *(Nandina domestica)* which, again, was only half hardy as was also the loquat *(Eriobotrya japonica)*, planted on the other side of the bay beside an *Abutilon vitifolium.*[37]

The Main Flower Border was by any standards a masterpiece of artistry with a carefully worked out colour scheme which has never been equalled. Both ends began with a ground of grey and glaucous foliage (Figure 7.24), but at the eastern end the colours were kept to pure blue, grey-blue, white, palest yellow and pale pink. The colours then advanced by way of stronger yellows to orange and red in the centre of the border where the colours were strong and "gorgeous". The colour scheme then began to recede from orange to deep yellow, fading to pale yellow, white and pale pink to blue, and again, grey and glaucous foliage but this time with purple and lilac tones.

In her youth Miss Jekyll spent many hours at the Tate copying the pictures of one of the greatest English artists, J.M.W. Turner. She also learnt a great

Figure 7.24   The grey end of the South Border looking west.

deal about colour and its uses from Hercules Brabazon who was himself a great admirer of Turner and also of Velasquez. If one looks at one of Turner's finest pictures, 'The Fighting Temeraire',

Figure 7.25   The red section of the Main Flower Border.

the ship that followed Nelson's 'Victory' into battle at Trafalgar, and a picture that Miss Jekyll is known to have copied, one can see, there in the sunset, the harmonies and combinations of colour which were planned in the Main Flower Border at Munstead.[38]

Unfortunately there are no known autochromes of the entire border, only of the central red section which shows annual red salvias and red Geraniums followed by scarlet Cannas and a white Gypsophila (Figure 7.25). Beyond the Gypsophila a bold drift of (almost) crimson Dahlias, possibly 'Bishop of Landaff', ran into a group of scarlet red Dahlias which may be the variety 'Fire King' noted on the published plan from 1908, while tall spikes of red Hollyhocks rose up at the back. Again the comparison with Turner's 'Temeraire' is striking, for Turner uses a spot of white to represent his setting sun.

Many people believe that Miss Jekyll 'invented' the herbaceous border, but it is incorrect. The Main Flower Border was a mixed border in which shrubs, herbaceous perennials and annual plants all played a part. Miss Jekyll would use any plant that gave her the effect she sought and thought nothing of resorting to all manner of tricks and devices to keep the Border in good order for as long as possible throughout the season.

A plant of the common golden privet, pruned quite hard each year to produce new growth, of nearly pure yellow would be planted with *Rudbeckia* 'Golden Glow' which would be trained into a bush of golden cut leaved elder *(Sambucus nigra 'Aurea')*. This was done with such skill that one almost believed the *Rudbeckia* flowers belonged to the elder.[39] In another section of the border, where the colouring was mostly white and pink with some stronger purple, a *Ceanothus* 'Gloire de Versailles' would, as with the golden privet, be hard pruned each year to encourage greater flowering. Behind, *Clematis jackmanii* would be trained to cascade out from the *Ceanothus* onto groups of gypsophila, phloxes and heliotrope. This technique of planting in layers can extend the flowering period of a border, or an area of ground, by many months. Another well-known combination used was to plant an everlasting pea behind delphiniums, which would be cut down after flowering, and the pea trained into the space. When the pea finished flowering, in mid-August a *Clematis jackmanii* would be trained to provide flower then and, to extend the season still further a fourth plant *Clematis flammula* was added. By using such devices the Main Flower Border was kept in flower from mid-July well into September.[39]

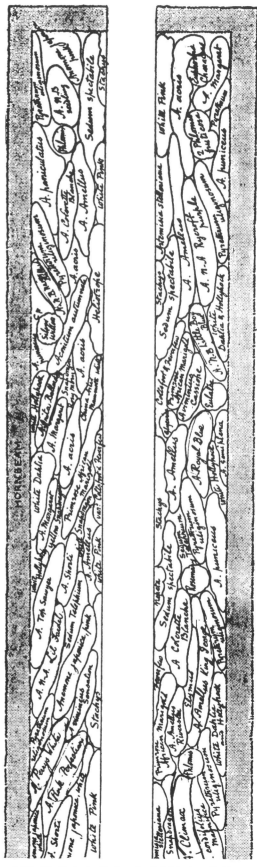

Figure 7.26   The September Borders of early Michaelmas Daisies.

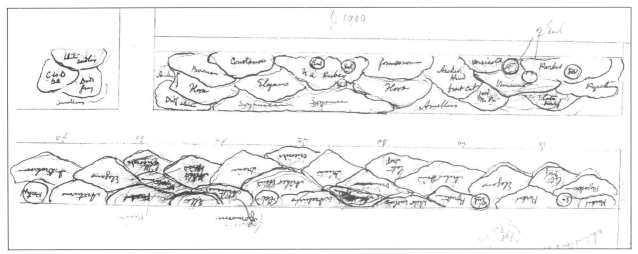

Figure 7.27   The October Borders of late Michaelmas Daisies for 1900.

Autumn and the Feast of Michaelmas
(18 & 19 on Figure 7.1)

With the advent of September, the 'season of mists and mellow fruitfulness', the main focus of attention in the flower garden turned to the Michaelmas Daisy Borders. Before the Second World War, the Michaelmas Daisy was an extremely popular flower but has fallen from favour nowadays due to its susceptibility to mildew. Miss Jekyll had two sets of borders devoted to these delightful flowers; one set designed to be at its best in September and a second set much nearer the house for the October or later flowering types.

The September Borders (Figure 7.26) ran into the Kitchen Gardens and were backed by a hornbeam hedge some five and a half feet tall which had been planted before 1900. The colour scheme, as ever carefully worked out, consisted of the white, lilac, purple and pale pink shades of the asters, to which she added in two or three distinct places some pale yellow and yellowish white flowers "with suitable accompanying leafage" and a ground work of grey foliage (See page 5). An arch of laburnum marked the entrance while a seat was thoughtfully placed from where the view could be contemplated and the vista terminated. Although a number of the aster varieties that she used are no longer available remarkably a few can still be found, including one of the tallest called 'Climax'. Pale primrose African marigolds and feverfew were used to give the tinge of yellow, whilst white snapdragons, dahlias and hollyhocks were planted with *Chrysanthemum uliginosum,* the Moon Daisy whose great white daisy flowers follow the sun.

As September gave way to October and the surrounding trees and shrubs took on their autumn tints another set of Michaelmas Daisy Borders

came into their own (Figure 7.27). These were not as far from the house; they ran parallel to the Nut Walk and bounded it on one side. Towards the end of Miss Jekyll's life a gale helped to make a gap in

Figure 7.28   October Asters and a distant view beyond Heath Lane in 1930.

the surrounding shrubs and trees, affording a view of the distant landscape beyond (Figure 7.28); one of only two views beyond this very private world.[40] The colours were arranged so that blues and solid whites such as 'Blue Gem' and 'Amellus' were followed by stronger purples and a small starry white. Warmer shades followed such as 'Coombe Fishacre', a pale lilac ageing to cream tinged with rose, which was in turn succeeded by stronger pinks offset with white, notably *Chrysanthemum uliginosum*, and then returning to deeper purples like 'Ryecroft Purple' as the border drew to a close, an often repeated Jekyll formula. To this was added an edge of *Stachys lanata*, a yard or two of bergenia and *Ophiopogon jaburan*, although in earlier days the whole edging was a White Pink *(Dianthus)*, possibly 'Mrs Simkins.'[41]

Figure 7.29   From the stable yard, north-west to the Thunder House in 1927.

The Kitchen and Working Gardens
(20 on Figure 7.1)

It is easy to forget that Munstead Wood had a large and profitable Kitchen Garden. From the Stables barn doors opened (Figure 7.29) onto a broad garden yard; the pig sties were against the stable walls to the left[42] and a cart path led down towards the Thunder House built at the north–western tip of the estate. This rather curious belvedere gave a good vantage point from which to watch the lightening that accompanied thunder storms rolling along the Wey valley, a sight which fascinated Miss Jekyll. The bed to the right of the cart path, which ran for almost four hundred feet, was the early vegetable plot. On the backing wall were trained pears, plums[43] and gages, together with, most precious of all, figs. Miss Jekyll was a generous person, her kindness and charity were

Figure 7.30   The long cypress hedge and the Hascombe Road Border in 1926.

abundant and she would share almost anything with the exception of her figs![44] At the bottom of the path on the left were the soft fruit beds, where grew currants, raspberries, a large bed of strawberries and gooseberries trained on wires and grown "espalier fashion" to save hands and wrists from too much scratching.[45]

Miss Jekyll had quite an extensive orchard (21 on Figure 7.1 and Figure 6.4) comprising more than fifty trees. From the surviving trees we know that at least eight varieties of cooking apple were grown which would have provided fruit well into the new year. The same is true of the dessert apples of which there remain six varieties including 'Egremont Russet' and an American variety called 'Mother'. At least six varieties of both dessert and cooking pears were grown. These included the finest of all pears 'Doyenne Du Comice' which has a wonderful flavour and an old French variety of cooking pear called 'Catillac', which would remain firm and useable until early April. Quinces were also grown and still flourish there; indeed, there are no fewer than three trees of the old variety 'Portugal'. Quinces were a more popular fruit in those days than now.[46]

The Kitchen Garden, in common with thousands of other similar establishments, would have been expected to provide enough fresh vegetables for the house for most of the year. Although Miss Jekyll did not write about this side of the garden very often in *Home & Garden* she included a chapter on the subject. It is no surprise to discover that she was a connoisseur of unusual and fine vegetables. Kohl-Rabi, for example, when cooked young she found to have an excellent and delicate flavour. A French form of common dandelion, the seed being obtained from Vilmorins, was grown to provide winter salad. Miss Jekyll dealt extensively with Vilmorins, the Paris seed merchants, for many years even selling them seed of a Lamb's Lettuce which surely is the gardening equivalent of "coals to Newcastle"![47]

The Head Gardener's Cottage, designed by Lutyens in 1893, was on the north-western edge of the property opposite the Thunder House with the hen run between the two. During the Great War, in 1917, Miss Jekyll began to keep six hens to which were added one hen and eleven chicks acquired from Lady Chance of Orchards in 1918. In the Godalming Museum collection is a notebook which records from 1917 until 1928 the number of eggs collected each day, the price obtained for each dozen, and the costs not only of the feed but also the birds themselves. Even the cost of the coop from Lady Chance was recorded.[48]

Figure 7.31   The South Terrace.

On the western side of the property, bounded by the Hascombe Road, a cypress hedge of *Chamaecyparis lawsoniana* (Figure 7.30 and 22 on Figure 7.1) was planted in 1887, not only to screen the path used for church-going on Sundays from the plant nursery but also to provide much needed shelter from the cold north-westerly winds which swept across the property. The young trees were three feet high when planted, three feet apart, and cost fifteen shillings each which was a great deal of money at the time.[49] Between the hedge and boundary wall lay the Hascombe Border which was not only a stock border, filled with herbaceous plants to be lifted, divided and sold, but also used as a source of material to fill gaps in the borders of the main pleasure gardens.

Beyond the cypress hedge lay some of the nursery beds which were dotted around the kitchen gardens. Running at right angles to the Iris and Lupin Borders were three long beds of daffodils and two beds of lily of the valley used for cut flowers (23 on Figure 7.1), the blooms going to the florists in Godalming. Garden pinks *(Dianthus)* were also grown for sale, particularly the soft pink with a fine scent called 'Inchmery' a bed of which lined a cross path.[50] There were also three beds of

roses grown for pot-pourri which was made in large quantities and to obtain a better crop of bloom they were pegged down, encouraging them to flower along their stems, a technique practised in many gardens today.[51]

The South Terrace (24 on Figure 7.1)

From the spacious sitting room a garden door led to the South Terrace flanked by borders filled with that pretty pink China rose *(Rosa chinensis)* 'Old Blush', bushes of rosemary, *Olearia gunniana* and hydrangeas (Figure 7.31). The walls of the house were generously covered with the royal muscadine vine *(Vitis rotundifolia)*, a myrtle and a white jasmine, while narrow borders at the base of the south lawn were filled with *Leucothoë axillaris* and clumps of *Lilium candidum* grown in pots made from lengths of drain pipe![52] Three broad steps led up to the lawn, flanked on either side by scotch briar roses, mostly white but with a few yellow and rosy pink (Figure 7.32). From the lawn which was about fifty feet wide and ran up to the edge of the woodland, five paths each with a different character led up into the woodland.

Many people think that the lawns at Munstead were like bowling greens, which they were not. Miss Jekyll thought that an informal lawn should be a tapestry of colour and texture. The south lawn had been made from planting tufts of the sheep's fescue *(Festuca ovina)* and the crested dog's-tail grass *(Cynosurus cristatus)* which soon knitted together to form a lawn of a low toned green which she much preferred to the bright green of a more standard lawn.[53] These two grasses, together with mosses and heaths which were allowed and encouraged, had the advantage in Munstead's dry sandy soil of requiring cutting only every three weeks. Miss Jekyll paid much attention to the 'selvedge' between lawn and woodland and an example is given of her effective plantings at the selvedge (Figure 7.33)

Figure 7.32   Scotch Briar Roses and a view of the Wood from the porch.

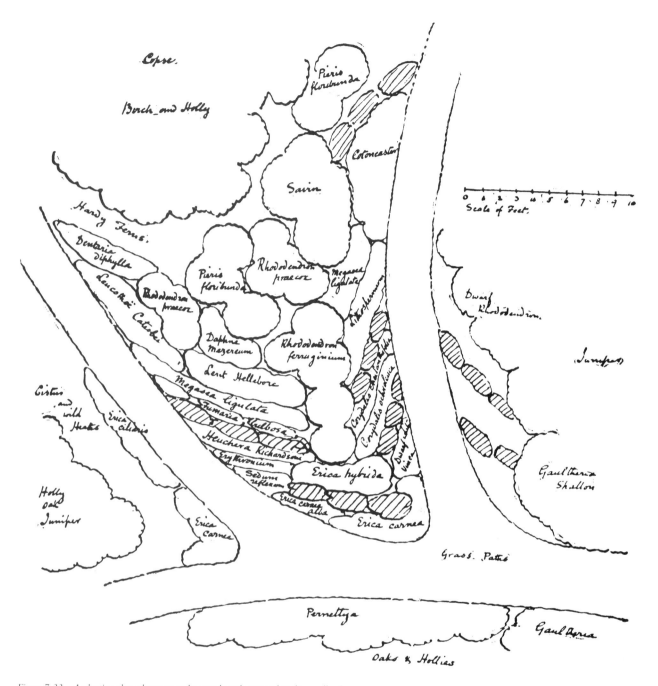

Figure 7.33   A planting plan where two paths ascend south-eastward to the woodland.

The Main Wood Walk (25 on Figure 7.1)

Opposite the garden door, across the South Terrace and lawn, a broad Walk led some four hundred feet into the wood to be terminated by a "fine old Scotch Fir" *(Pinus sylvestris)*. This pine and one other were all that remained of the old plantation and had originally been spared the axe on account of their deformity which made them worthless for timber, and later were kept for their pictorial effect. From here the house was framed by birch and rhododendrons flanking the Walk (Figure 7.34),

which had been laid out some years before the house was built. At the northern end, towards the house grew a number of silver birch and some fine hollies. The beautiful association of the birch and the dark green of the holly was enough to prompt a decision to plant groups of rhododendrons (Figure 7.35); mostly the pink 'Bianchi,'[54] the salmon 'Mrs R S Holford' and the whites 'Album Elegans' and 'Album Grandiflorum'. These plantings, ten feet apart (Miss Jekyll was later to regret that they had not been fifteen feet[55]), did not

Figure 7.34   Munstead Wood from the Main Woodland Walk.

extend along the whole length of the ride but faded out into more natural plantings. In spring beneath the sweet chestnuts at the southern end the ground was carpeted with 'poets narcissus' *(Narcissus poeticus)* followed by lily of the valley with clouds of amelanchier flowers above. Later, as the season progressed, the natural growth of bracken filled the space between broad patches of ornamental brambles, *Rubus nutkanus* and *Rubus odoratus.*[56]

Figure 7.35   Rhododendrons in the Main Woodland Walk.

More Rhododendrons

Miss Jekyll loved rhododendrons. After her death, Sir Edwin Lutyens wrote of their first meeting at Littleworth Cross, "the silver kettle and conversation reflecting rhododendrons."[57] With her fine sense of colour she could not abide the indiscriminate way in which they were so often grouped. Distrusting catalogue descriptions she visited all the best nurseries, in those days found close at hand in Bagshot, and walked the nursery fields. From observations made there she was able to divide up the colours into groups, and planted only crimsons with some claret and true pink, scarlet rose with salmon, and clear purple grouped with lilac whites.

A second, smaller, path ran south-west from the Main Wood Walk and it was here she planted the crimson, claret and pure pink rhododendrons. She chose hybrids such as 'John Waterer', a fine red still grown today, 'Alarm', a good crimson with a white throat, a variety called 'Nigrescens', a dark claret colour, and a fine pure pink, 'Bianchi' which in her day was never very popular and is sadly no longer available. She also planted the fine hybrid 'Lady

Figure 7.36 Near the Fern and Lily Walks to Munstead Wood.

Eleanor Cathcart', the flower of which so resembles a pelargonium. Still further to the west under the deeper shade of the sweet chestnuts she planted groups of purple and lilac white rhododendrons. The deep shade she felt, would make the purples seem richer and to dispel any feeling of gloom she added large amounts of white which the impressionists regarded as the colour of light itself. The purples were mostly *Rhododendron ponticum* seedlings selected in the nursery to which she added some plants of the double flowered *R.fastuosum* 'Florepleno' and the hybrid 'Everestianum'. In all about forty bushes were planted and by the end of her life they had filled out to make quite large plantations.

A River of Daffodils (26 on Figure 7.1)

Miss Jekyll wrote that long before the land came into her possession it had once been rough moorland. In the eighteenth century smuggling was rife along the Sussex coast and the heath, being a convenient distance from Guildford and no doubt the prying eyes of the Excise, was a useful place to hide a haul brought from Shoreham over the Downs. The ground to this day shows the remnants of many packhorse and cart tracks, although some of these ruts and depressions could have been made when the pine wood was felled and the timber dragged to waggons which probably stood in Heath Lane.[58]

Some of these depressions were visible from the house a little to the east of the Main Wood Walk and it occurred to Miss Jekyll that they could be quite effectively utilized if planted with daffodils. So, in the early years of the century, she put in a few hundred bulbs of *Narcissus horsfieldii* (a form of *Narcissus bicolor*). Her plan succeeded for as she later wrote the effect was that of a little river of daffodils flowing out of the wood.

The Fern and Lily Walks
(27 on Figure 7.1)

To the east of the place where the "River of Daffodils" flowed onto the South Lawn began one of the woodland paths, known as the Fern Walk. It lay roughly opposite the porch which projected from the house across the eastern end of the Terrace. Here the lawn had given way to a swathe of planting round the porch which included some silver birch, but was mostly oaks, hollies, and some cistus, with an undergrowth of gaultheria and andromeda to the right. Another path left the bottom of the Fern Walk, mounted two rough stone steps and skirted the shrubs, doubling back northwards to join the entrance path by way of a

few more steps. Off this path two further paths led back towards the woodland on the right, and at their fork an April Garden was skilfully created by using large stones, placed with great care to suggest a natural outcrop of rock (Figure 7.36). The result was so successful that this convenient accident of nature prompted many envious remarks from visitors.[59]

On the Fern Walk the ground was slightly higher to the right hand side and to turn this to advantage hollow bays a few yards across were scooped out, cutting back the natural growth of whortleberry but leaving some as promontories between the plantings of ferns. The large amount of sand excavated was used to cover paths and was replaced by even larger quantities of leaf mould, although the bays were left slightly lower than the path in the hope that this would allow the surface water to drain into them.[60] There grew ferns of every conceivable type, with large quantities of hartstongue, polypody and hard fern. Miss Jekyll grouped clumps of trillium, the gift of an American friend (possibly Mrs. Francis King), with drifts of *Smilacina bilfolia* and Solomon's Seal beyond. At the back grew the natural covering of bracken with here and there stately spires of white foxgloves, and beyond large hollies which looked splendid with the silver birch.

Further on one of the broad woodland walks known as the Lily Walk, which ran north-east south-west, joined the Fern Walk and ran towards the second large Scots pine used as a focus for three paths. The Lily Walk probably derived its name from plantings of the giant lily (*Cardiocrinum giganteum*). They were placed in large straggling groups and some considerable effort was needed to grow them with any degree of success on Munstead's very light sandy soil. Pits were dug twelve feet across and three feet deep and were filled with all manner of garden rubbish to within a foot of the top, the remainder being filled with good garden compost into which the young bulbs were planted.[61]

Such descriptions cannot possibly convey the thought and trouble that went into creating all the woodland paths. Each had a carefully worked out character distinct from all the others, and each was used to display a different range of plants. Many people think that woodland gardening requires very little skill and is easy to master. It is in fact the hardest form of gardening to do well since its success lies in appearing as though it were not gardened at all. In such art Gertrude Jekyll with her fine taste was a pioneer.

An Azalea Clearing (28 on Figure 7.1)

Miss Jekyll's azalea plantings were nearly all Ghent hybrids, with some *Azalea occidentalis,* and large amounts of the common yellow azalea, *Azalea pontica* (now *Rhododendron luteum*). The original plantings were made in the late 1890s but a further bed beneath the shade of a large beech was added in the mid 1920s.[62]

The colours began with a patch of the white 'Daviesii' planted in the fork of the path. The right hand path led into pinks and reds, while the other to the left and east led into the yellows. The yellows were composed of a large number of *A. pontica* to which were added the hybrids 'Narcissifolia', with its long trumpet flower, 'Nancy Waterer', a fine rich yellow and the deeper 'Ellen Cuthbert'. These led on to 'Princeps', a deep yellow with a red throat and to the bright orange 'Gloria Mundi'.

The other path began with a pale pink called 'Incana', followed by 'Bijou de Gendbrugge', the slightly deeper pink 'Marie Ardente' and the rosy pink 'Fama', which is always covered in flower. After a short gap the reds came into view and here such hybrids as 'Grandeur Triomphant', a strong red with bronze tinted foliage, 'Antoinette' and the magnificent later flowering 'Sang de Gendbrugge' were all liberally used. Amongst all the azaleas, groups of *Cistus laurifolius, C. cyprius* and *C. formosus* were added for further interest later in the year.[63]

The Heath Garden (29 on Figure 7.1)

The paths in the Azalea Clearing came together and emerged at the Heath Garden which Miss Jekyll created in 1913 just before the outbreak of the Great War. Quite a large space measuring about three hundred by two hundred feet was cleared of trees and the natural growth of heath, bracken and whortleberry was cleared in some areas but retained in others to form "tongues" around which the planting was carried out (Figure 7.37).

For winter colour *Erica carnea* and hybrids were

Figure 7.37   The Heath Garden.

used together with some tall *Erica lusitancia* and the taller *Erica stricta*. *Erica carnea* was planted to form a continuous mass with each group thinning into the next. Near the path were extensive plantings of a white variety of Irish heath and some pains were taken to make it resemble a moorland track by adding patches of varieties of *Erica cinerea* in pale pink and white leading to patches of *Erica tetralix* backed by drifts of Cornish heather (*Erica vagans*). When the nursery plants had been laid out they didn't fill the ground so a friendly Lord of the Manor allowed her to collect some young plants of the wild heaths, *Erica cinerea*, *Erica tetralix* and *Calluna vulgaris,* which all grew locally and to increase the natural look she added wood sage (*Teucrium scorodonium*), harebells and the blue sheep's-bit scabious (*Jasione montana*).[64]

Miss Jekyll's Staff

Although Munstead Wood extended to over fifteen acres it was worked with a small staff. Over the years it has been stated that Miss Jekyll employed a huge staff, which is quite untrue. The origins of the confusion lie in an exaggerated remark made by Sir Edwin Lutyens to his wife, Lady Emily. After staying at Munstead in 1933 he wrote that it was sad to see the state of the garden but this could not be avoided as there was "no Bumps and no longer the 11 Essential gardeners."[65]

When Miss Jekyll died in 1932 the garden was run by her Head Gardener and was worked by just two men, Arthur Berry and Frank Young, while the kitchen gardens were worked by William Berry (Arthur Berry's son) and an old man from Busbridge called Bailey. When Frank Young, whom I knew quite well through the kindness of some good friends, first went to work for Miss Jekyll in 1926 the kitchen gardens were worked by Fred Boxal and William Hawkes who both died before Miss Jekyll. Miss Jekyll also kept a pony, not only as a means of transport but also to pull the lawnmower, and so a groom, Jarot, was employed. The house staff consisted of a cook, Mary Irons who had been with her for many years, as had the lady's maid Florence Hayter, but the housemaid, Mary Platt, was a more recent recruit. A daily help, whose identity is unfortunately not known, was also employed.[66]

The former Head Gardener Albert Zumbach was Swiss. He came to work for Miss Jekyll in November 1893 and only retired in 1927. Zumbach had been a retainer of Jacques and Leonie Blumenthal who maintained a summer home at Les Avants above Lake Geneva which was known to all their many guests as the 'Châlet'.

Perhaps his contribution to the efficient running of Munstead Wood is summed up best by Francis Jekyll who wrote that "he maintained unbroken the harmony of her garden staff, and succeeded in giving her, for over thirty years, what she appreciated as the rarest of all services – intelligent obedience untainted by ideas at variance with her own."[67]

Each morning at ten o'clock the Head Gardener went up to the workshop for his orders. These were not day-to-day instructions; as most of the gardeners had been with her for so long that they didn't need to be told what jobs to do, but were of a more specific nature. Perhaps Miss Jekyll intended to work in the garden after lunch and would require some assistance or maybe she had decided to move or modify some planting and wished to make arrangements for this work to be carried out. She also drew up planting plans for the borders which would be given to the Head Gardener for him to take the appropriate action. These were drawn on cartridge paper and marked off every 10 feet. It is interesting to note that only Frank Young and the Head Gardener could read or write.[68]

Miss Jekyll did not as a rule, except when planting out was being done, work in the garden herself in the morning but spent the time working on her correspondence, in itself a considerable undertaking. At noon each day Frank Young collected the post from the workshop door and would take it to the Bramley Cross Road box to catch the lunch time collection.

After the Great War Miss Jekyll continued to design gardens completing more than 120 garden commissions and wrote over 550 articles.

In the spring of 1932 she was in poor health and confined to bed but the gardeners carried her downstairs on one bright day so that she could admire the Primrose Garden from a wheelchair, a gift from Sir Edwin. Her health rapidly declined after the death of her younger brother Sir Herbert, in September 1932, and on the eighth of December sometime in the evening she died, peacefully, in the arms of her maid Florence Hayter. The gardeners raked the lawns for moss with which to line the grave and the following Monday they performed their last service by acting as pall bearers and laid their mistress to rest.[69]

Perhaps Sir Edwin Lutyens best summed up Miss Jekyll's long and eventful life when, writing after her death, he said she possessed "a clear logical brain, without favour or fear, save of God, for whose knowledge she for ever searched and which she now for ever shares".[70]

8

The Plant Nursery at Munstead Wood

Michael Tooley

Introduction

In 1897 Theresa Earle wrote:

"....Miss Jekyll of Munstead Wood.... now sells her surplus plants, all more or less suited to light soils, to the management of which she has for many years past given special attention."[1]

This informs us of several little known facts about Miss Jekyll. Firstly, she had been cultivating plants for many years and horticulture was not a pursuit superseding painting, embroidery and interior decoration. Secondly, the plants she cultivated were particularly well suited to the light sandy soils that were characteristic of Munstead Heath and elsewhere in the Weald of Sussex and Kent. Thirdly, she was selling plants and this meant that she was no longer an amateur and could not exhibit plants at the Royal Horticultural Society's or other societies' shows as an amateur. It is noticeable that the first book of hers to be published in 1899, *Wood and Garden,* about a third of which had appeared as notes in *The Guardian Newspaper* in 1896 and 1897, carried the subtitle "notes and thoughts, practical and critical, of a working amateur." In her second book, *Home and Garden,* published in 1900, she omitted the word amateur from the subtitle.

In 1885 the editor of *The Gardeners' Chronicle* had put the question "what is an amateur?" and derived an answer from the regulations for exhibitions put forward by the National Auricula and Carnation and Picotee Society that, "no person shall be allowed to compete as an amateur who publishes a list of plants for sale, or who advertises them in any form whatever, with the exception of seedlings of his own raising."[2] Miss Jekyll not only sold plants from 1897 but also published a list of plants for sale from her nursery at Munstead Wood.

The fourth fact arising from the quotation from Mrs. Earle's book is that Miss Jekyll at the age of 54 had begun a new professional career by selling plants from her nursery. She ran the nursery for 35 years from 1897 until 1932, and after her death it was run for a further 9 years by her nephew, Francis Jekyll.[3] The plant nursery operated for at least 45 years, shorter than many contemporary nurseries such as Barr's, Jackman's or Paul's, but longer than others such as Col. Grey's Hocker Edge Nursery at Cranbrook.[4] The success of the nursery side of Miss Jekyll's business required a knowledge of plants and particularly their cultural needs and a ready outlet for the plants.

Miss Jekyll and horticulture

Miss Jekyll's knowledge of garden plants arose from her accumulated knowledge of wild plants that she identified by matching a specimen with the drawings of plants in the Rev. C. A. Johns' *Flowers of the Field,*[5] just as we might match specimens today with drawings by Stella Ross Craig or by the Rev. Keble Martin. She informs us that she had three copies of *Flowers of the Field,* one copy of which she wore out by constant use. By close observation, collection, identification and drawing, she became conversant not only with the British flora but also the floras of Europe and North Africa. In her library at Munstead Wood were county floras of Devon, Dorset, Hampshire, Somerset, Westmorland and Wiltshire, Fiori's *Flora Italiana Illustrata* and *Flora Analitica d'Italia* and Hegi's *Illustrierte Flora von Mittel Europa.*[6]

The collection of wild plants and their use in gardens had begun to alarm botanists and horticulturists to the extent that editorials in *The*

Left: Carpenteria californica at Munstead, June 27, 1886.

Gardeners' Chronicle and *The Times* in 1885 were critical of this destructive activity both in Britain and in Switzerland. The Council of the Midland Union of Natural History Societies, based at Mason College (now Birmingham University) gave examples of the ravages of professional plant hunters, who offered for sale species of orchids and saxifrages from 2s (10p) to 5s (25p) per 100, and invited tenders for daffodils and primroses per 100,000.[7] In Switzerland Sir Alfred Wills noted that increasing numbers of professional plant hunters were penetrating remote alpine regions to collect plants to sell to tourists and were destroying many plants at the stations where they were recorded to enhance the rarity and value of the plants collected.[8] In Switzerland a solution was proposed by Miss Jekyll's friend M. Henri Correvon who founded *L'Association pour la Protection des Plantes*, which used part of his garden, *Jardin Alpin d'Acclimatation* in Geneva, to germinate the seed of rare alpines and pot them up for sale at low prices. Miss Jekyll must have been aware of these concerns and the solutions proposed in England and Switzerland but in the years up to 1885 both she and William Robinson were collecting plants from the wild in large numbers and assessing their value as garden plants.

In 1881 Miss Jekyll sent to the offices of *The Garden* several plants for identification. They included 4 species of orchid amongst which was a specimen of the rare Early Spider Orchid. From plants collected in Switzerland she sent *Primula villosa* and from the Pyrenees *Fritillaria pyrenaica*.[9] Her use of rare native plants was approved by the reviewer of William Robinson's recently published book on *The English Flower Garden* in 1884: he noted that Robinson, "strongly urges planting in groups, especially dwarf and choice plants to produce an effect, rather than dotting about.... Those who have seen.... the colony of Pyrola rotundifolia at Munstead.... well know the value of this advice."[10] Only two years earlier, Miss Jekyll had sent specimens of the larger wintergreen to the offices of *The Garden* for identification. An idea of the scale of the transfer of this plant from the wild to garden cultivation can be gained from extracts from letters that Miss Jekyll was writing to William Robinson in the 1880s:

> Nov. 1 – "I have been planting some three hundred little Pyrolas. They make a carpet among the biggest stones and heaths in the Alpine Garden, and are put in in the most approved fashion in a hard slit in the ground, plant put in rather deep and very firmly trodden up, indeed I doubt if anything was ever planted *so firmly*."

> Nov. 6 – "It will be interesting to test the two Pyrolas – I was working in the old rockery today and have prepared a place next to the old clump, sinking a stone on end as a wall between the two that their roots may not run together."[11]

She was also intent on collecting *Convolvulus (Calystegia) soldanella*, the Sea Bindweed, and *Scilla autumnalis*, the Autumnal Squill, and responded exultantly to William Robinson's letter:

> "What a good find! I wish I had been there. I should have yelled with delight and made a war dance – Why do they flower so late? Send any number of thousands to go into nursery for your future use, but do get some sort of digger and let the poor things have roots."[12]

It was not only from the British Isles that she was collecting native plants but also from Switzerland, North Africa and the Eastern Mediterranean, as well as from islands in the Mediterranean – Rhodes, Malta, Sardinia and Capri. It was from

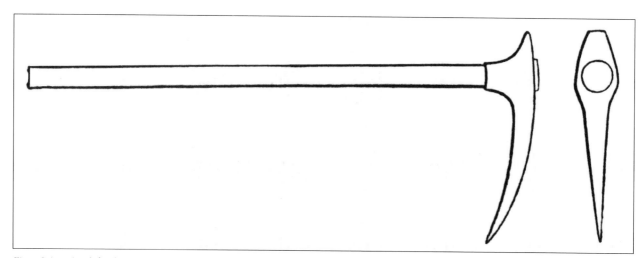

Figure 8.1   A pick for plant collecting designed by Gertrude Jekyll.

Figure 8.2   Caricatures of Gertrude Jekyll by Lionel Benson.

Capri that she wrote William Robinson in December 1883 extolling the virtues of the flora and describing the methods by which she collected plants from awkward and inaccessible places:

> "As for the plants, it is a kind of intoxication to get into a wilderness of olive and myrtle, orange and prickly pear, and the rough ground clothed with Smilax, Cyclamens and Rosemary, and the many aromatic plants that grow in Mediterranean islands, only one has to go carefully for one comes suddenly to *nasty places* when one looks over and sees the sea a thousand feet below! I hope to bring home some useful plants; my little tool has covered itself in glory, you should have seen it today picking and chipping out of the crevices of a cliff of white marble some sturdy plants of *Campanula fragilis* – it abounds near the sea."[12]

She recommended for plant collecting a pick that she had designed and had made by James Jackson of Bramley (Figure 8.1). The iron head was 8 inches long and the haft 22 inches long. She described the pick as working "more quickly and powerfully than anything of the trowel family. A Crocus Imperati or a Cyclamen neapolitanum comes up with a single, light, one-handed stroke, and a whole day's work does not stain or blister a woman's hand. The handle is of just such a length that it can be used with both hands or one only, and it is a great advantage, when climbing about nasty places, where one must hold on with one hand to rock or bush, to be able to get at some

desirable plant in a rockery fissure 1½ feet beyond handreach. The tool is also a great help in climbing upwards; the point digs firmly, with an anchor-like grip into earth or rock, and as the head cannot possibly pull off, the whole weight of the body may be safely trusted to it."[13]

Armed with this tool and a truck many plants were recovered from "nasty places" in the Swiss Alps, Southern Italy and Capri, packed and sent back to Munstead (Figure 8.2). But once back at Munstead the plants had to be properly cultivated and Miss Jekyll's knowledge of their cultural requirements was second to none. The landscape gardener and author William Goldring noted that, "Miss Jekyll is an advocate for good cultivation, and likes to see plants individually attain full growth."[14] In the hardy plant border at Munstead (See Figures 2.9, 2.10), which was 270 feet long and 14 feet wide, she grew several species of Red Hot Poker (*Kniphofia*) in deep, light soil. *K. uvaria* was planted in bold masses measuring some 9 feet by 5 feet, and in a dry season produced 100 flower spikes 5 feet high. *K. uvaria* 'Nobilis' had flower spikes a foot long.[15] In the same border *Lobelia splendens* was grown in a drift covering three square yards, the ox-eye daisy *Chrysanthemum (Leucanthemum) maximum* grew over four feet high and Tiger lilies had stems 8 feet high.[15] The cultivation and propagation of the giant Himalayan lily, *Lilium (Cardiocrinum) giganteum* in light woodland required special attention at Munstead (Figure 8.3). It was introduced from Nepal in 1852 as a tender cool greenhouse plant but was grown out of doors not only in the south of England by Charles Noble at Bagshot[16] but also at Gordon Castle in Banff[17] in the late 1870s. Miss Jekyll began growing it in the 1880s and in the sandy soil of Munstead Heath pits 12 feet across and 3 feet deep were excavated and filled in the late autumn with dahlia tops and half hardy annuals cut up and trampled. The upper foot was filled with compost and the shallowly-planted bulbs covered with leaves.[18] After flowering the bulb collapses and the plant has to be lifted and the offsets recovered and replanted (Figure 8.4). Miss Jekyll described how she sawed off one of the 9 feet high stems, with a basal diameter of 2½ inches, and recovered from the hollow stem "a pint of water, smelling sweet like cider, tasting vinous but with a bitter after taste."[19]

Another two plants, introduced from California and of doubtful hardiness, that were well-cultivated, observed, described, drawn and photographed at Munstead, were *Romneya coulteri* (Figure 8.5) introduced in 1875 and *Carpenteria*

Figure 8.4 *Root of Giant Lily showing offsets.*

Figure 8.3 *The Giant Lily at Munstead Wood with Miss Jekyll's gardener, Peter Brown, in monk's habit.*

californica (Figure 8.6) in 1880. The Rev. C. Wolley Dod noted in 1885 of the former that "this beautiful Californian poppy is without doubt a difficult plant for cold soils and cloudy climates, but it ought not to be despaired of without a trial, and it is worth the trouble it gives."[20] He saw it flowering at Munstead where it was growing in warm sandy soil and was drawn in 1884.[21] Two years later Miss Jekyll extolled its merits as a cut flower with a delicate perfume, as well as an outdoor plant of "supreme and stately beauty."[22]

Seedlings of *Carpenteria* were obtained from Mrs. Davidson of Salisbury in 1883; two plants survived out of doors and a third had flowered in a cool greenhouse by 1885.[23] Miss Jekyll was probably the first to flower the plant out of doors in 1886 and she was described as "the most successful cultivator" of it.[24] Again it was the dry, warm, sandy soil at Munstead that benefitted the plant. In 1888 she exhibited the plant in flower at a meeting of the Floral Committee of the Royal Horticultural Society in the Drill Hall, Westminster, and was awarded a First Class Certificate.[25]

Throughout the 1880s she was selecting and cultivating a range of hardy plants that formed the core of the plant nursery at Munstead and subsequently at Munstead Wood.

Miss Jekyll's plant nursery

It is clear that the reserve garden at Munstead

Figure 8.5   Romneya coulteri at Munstead, 20 July 1884.

[House], described with a plan by William Goldring in 1882, and the description and plan employed by William Robinson in 1883 in *The English Flower Garden* ,[26] was Miss Jekyll's first plant nursery: "Such a garden as this is of the greatest importance, for it is not only a never-failing source of cut flowers, but also of great value as a nursery where plants can be reared or divided for stocking the other parts of the garden." William Robinson used this reserve garden for his collection of plants until he bought Gravetye Manor in 1885. Miss Jekyll received plants for Robinson from Woolson's nursery in Passaic, New Jersey, in 1883 and remarked how well they had travelled packed in moist *Sphagnum*.[27] An illustration in one of the letters to William Robinson shows bags of daffodils "ready at any time for planting," boxes of trillium and bloodroot in the cellar and a marginal gloss, "when you are straight would like to be attended to" and sacks of grape hyacinth, fritillarias, white anemone 'Bride', white gladiolus 'Bride' and pink wood hyacinth awaiting his collection (Figure 8.6). Whilst the garden and nursery at Munstead [House] were being maintained Miss Jekyll had bought fifteen acres of ground at O.S. – the Other Side of the road – and to be called Munstead Wood. Here the ground was laid out before the house was built and it is significant that the first buildings on the site were the tool shed, workshop, potting and packing sheds and stable, in addition to the small house known as the 'Hut'.

At Munstead Wood the reserve garden was adjacent to the September borders that ran from the Iris and Lupin borders towards the orchard. But in one of the notebooks in Godalming Museum[28] she refers to a "Top Nursery" and a "Lower Nursery" and elsewhere areas were set aside for nursery stock and individual plants were noted for sale. Examples from this notebook, kept in the 1920s, indicate that the whole of the Munstead Wood ground was not only a series of gardens but also the nursery: hence, "irises in cage", "irises in Spring Garden", "irises in quantity in End Road border", "asters by faggot

stack", "daffodils in long bed by Asparagus 1928", "in lower end Road Border Tradescantia light blue opposite last Phormium". The stock list for beeches shows that they were self sown seedlings earmarked by Miss Jekyll for sale: "1 by Dovecote, 1 small by periwinkle, 1 up same path, 2 in Nar poeticus, 1 by little Daffs, 1 just behind, 2 middle trees, 2 beyond Old Scotch, 4 by Foxglove hollow, 2 right and left going down path towards entrance, 1 back of yews by entrance." This made a stock of 18 available but she concluded her notes, "probably others higher in ground". The stock lists for hollyhocks from 1922 to 1927 (Table 8.1) show the scale of propagation of only one group of plants in the nursery although the range of plants offered was surprisingly limited.

Only one copy of the plant catalogue is known to exist.[29] It is a slight pamphlet entitled "Some of the Best Hardy Plants for Border, Shrubbery and Rock Garden grown by Miss Jekyll, Munstead Wood, Godalming". It comprises 15 pages measuring 14 x 21.6cm and includes sections on border and shrubbery plants (10 pages, 234 genera, species and varieties listed), some sweet herbs and old plants of English gardens (1 page, 20), alpine and other small plants suited to the rock garden (4 pages, 70). In addition the Munstead flower basket and Munstead Wood potpourri were offered for sale. The 324 plants listed were those that were available in "large or fair quantity." Additional plants were available but nonetheless the list of plants offered was small. The reason for this may be that these plants were the ones used most often by Miss Jekyll in planting plans and she knew that if she supplied both plan and plants the effect desired would be realised. A gardener or another plant nursery would substitute another variety if the one specified was not available and the overall effect would be diluted or lost. To encourage her clients to purchase plants from her nursery she offered them more cheaply than her competitors. Her first letter to Mrs. Barnes-Brand of Woodhouse Copse, Holmbury St Mary in 1926 sought a fee of 5 guineas for a plan of the double borders and, in addition, the

Table 8.1 Munstead Wood. Stock lists of Hollyhocks 1922-1927

	1922	1923	1924	1925		1926	1927	
				Spring	Autumn		Spring	Autumn
'Pink Beauty'	250	110	128	18	50	198	24	–
Dark	80	18	100	0	5	–	–	60
Red	140	160	60	0	12	18	–	24
White	110	70	12	4	8	30	12	100
Yellow	25	6	50	2	7	30	–	40
Rose	–	–	30	6	–	–	–	–
Crimson	–	–	–	–	–	40	6	–

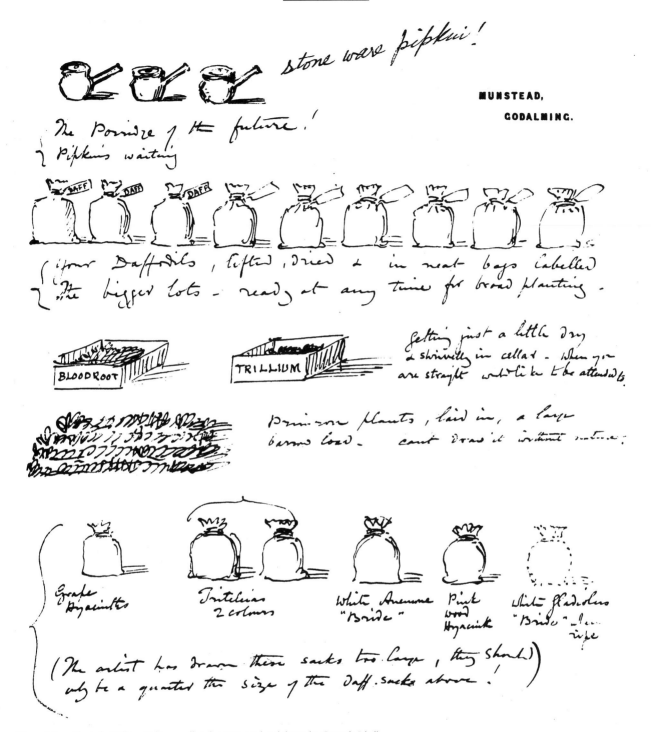

Figure 8.6   Plants for William Robinson collected at Munstead and drawn by Gertrude Jekyll.

following offer of plants: "If you have no reserve of plants and would like me to supply them or partly, I can do it a good deal to your advantage as to price and strength compared with the usual nurseries".[30] As late as March 1932 Miss Jekyll wrote Mrs. Barnes-Brand: "I have a splendid list of good hardy plants, and bigger plants and at lower prices than the nurseries."[30]

The scale and mode of operations of the plant nursery is provided by the account books at Godalming Museum[31] and these, together with the lists of commissions,[32] show that she designed and provided plants for 398 projects, of which 166 were in Surrey (see Gertrude Jekyll's Garden Plans and Surrey Gardens, p.125 and Garden Plans p.200).

There are 37 account books covering the period from 1903 until 1929. Each account book contains details of several commissions. Each commission is identified by the name of the property followed by the client's and gardener's name and address. The name of the nearest railway station is given. For large commissions such as King Edward VII Sanatorium the names and addresses of the architect, contractor, clerk of works and engineer are also listed.

All the borders on the plans were numbered or lettered and listed under these numbers or letters were the plants required. Miss Jekyll used a standard notation throughout the account books, employing coloured ink or crayon lines to indicate plant availability or status of the account. For Highmount, Guildford,[33] the notation was explicit:

> "A single ink line round names of plants are those wanted to be ordered from Jackmans. A single green line – small shrubs that went all together from here. A double ink line Lilies that I obtained from Wallace and elsewhere. A red chalk line all round. Plants owing that will be sent in Spring. Diagonal Blue crayon line – to book. Diagonal red crayon line – paid."

About 5 miles south of Munstead Wood, at Chiddingfold, were the extensive Japanese Nurseries of V.N. Gauntlett and Co. A comparison of the prices they were charging for plants in 1910 with the prices charged by Miss Jekyll for the same species or variety of plant confirms the offer of cheaper plant prices that she made to her clients.[34] The following examples show the extent to which Miss Jekyll was undercutting the commercial nurseries.

The range of prices quoted and charged by Miss Jekyll in the Account Books shows that she was discriminating between clients. Mr. Edward Hudson, owner of *Country Life,* for whom she designed four gardens and who published nine of her books, was charged significantly less than Mr. Roger Fry for the garden at Durbins or Lord Rendel at Hatchlands.[35] Some of the commissions for the early years of the nursery and especially for 1910 and 1911 are described here, and these give an indication of the scale of operations at the plant nursery.

Commissions

Just over a third of Miss Jekyll's commissions were in Surrey and the majority was in the home counties. However there are gardens designed by Miss Jekyll in most counties in the British Isles, and she received commissions from clients in France, Germany, Yugoslavia and the United States of America. The garden of the Viceroy's House in New Delhi may also owe something to Miss Jekyll, for not only were Lutyens' plans amongst the drawings at Berkeley[36] but also in Francis Jekyll's memoir there is a reference to Miss Jekyll making some "small trees for the Delhi model."[37]

By 1905 the Munstead Wood plant nursery had been in operation for eight years and fifty-four design commissions had been completed, several in association with distinguished architects such as Edwin Lutyens, Robert Lorimer, Walter Brierley and Ernest George. All but one were for private clients, but in April 1905 Miss Jekyll began work on her first public commission – the King Edward VII Sanatorium for patients suffering from pulmonary tuberculosis. The hospital and layout of the grounds and beds were designed by H. Percy Adams, of the architectural practice Adams, Holden and Pearson, and Miss Jekyll was responsible for the plantings and supplying the plants. The sanatorium

Table 8.2 Comparative prices for plants in 1910

	Gauntlett	Jekyll
Armeria	8d each	0.5d each
Centranthus	1s 0d	4d
Cerastium tomentosum	8d	1d
Digitalis	6d	2d
Eryngium oliverianum	9d	1d to 9d
Gypsophila	9d	3d
Iberis	8d	3d to 6d
Lupinus arboreus	1s	6d
L. polyphyllus	9d	6d
Meconopsis cambrica	1s 6d	1d
Nepeta mussinii	8d	2d, 4d and 5d
Olearia Hastii	1s 6d	6d
Peony	1s 6d	1s 6d
Sedum spurium	8d	1d, 2d

(1 shilling = 5 pence: 6d = 2.5 pence)

was opened by the King on 14 June 1906 and Miss Jekyll was there.[38] The months leading up to the opening ceremony were times of phrenetic activity on Miss Jekyll's part. The sanatorium was on a south-facing slope that lent itself to terracing. There were seven gardens, each with a distinctive character, and no less than 49 beds. In addition there were over 1200 feet of stone walls to plant up and the piers on the building itself were wired up for planting. In 1905 Miss Jekyll met the Advisory Committee on site on three occasions and the gardener, Mr. E.R. Squelch, visited her at Munstead Wood. She charged £26.5.0 (£26.25) for the designs and working plans, £78.4.1 (£78.20) for the plants for the walls and borders above them and £74.15.5 (£74.77) for shrubs and plants for the beds elsewhere in the garden.[39]

The majority of the plants came from Miss Jekyll's nursery but the rhododendrons came from Jackman's and other plants from Waterer's. The tools came from Messrs. Gill and Carling and all were paid as subcontractors by Miss Jekyll.[39] In the first four months of 1906 instructions and plants were sent every few days to the Clerk of Works, Mr. Atkinson, and the letters often included a note to the gardener – "Kindly hand the note enclosed to Squelch." On 8 January 1906 she wrote "I have today put on rail the rest of the plants for Rhododendron bank," and later in the same letter: "I propose to send on *Wednesday* plants for 41 West & East, 48 West & East and low wall between Bed 38 – corner & edge. Beds 44-44-46, and on *Friday* – for Bed 45 – Clumps 49A & 49B." On 14 January she wrote, "I pushed on last evening, in order to send you today, plans for 34-35, 35-36 for which I hope to send the plants early in the week . . . I also send plan for forecourt. . ." On 27 January she wrote in the evening, "I am sending tracings of Wall G & steps at end, Wall H & border above, Border 11 under Wall L, with Wall L east & border (10) below it, Garden 7 East.".... "I will also – if the weather hold open – collect on Monday, ready to send Tuesday by evening goods train, plants for Wall G & steps, Wall H, Border 11 under wall & Border 10 and Wall L east."[40]

Whilst this work was in progress Miss Jekyll was also working on the plans and sending plants to Tylney Hall in Winchfield, Hampshire and Loseley Park near Guildford in Surrey. A month before the opening of King Edward VII Sanatorium she had travelled by train north to Belford with Edwin Lutyens *en route* for Holy Island where she began to plan the planting of the walled castle garden, The Stank and Beblow Hill.[41] This work was scaled down and delayed until 1910 and 1911 when she had in hand no less than twenty-eight commissions, for twenty-two of which she sent out plants from the nursery.

In 1910 plans or plants or both went to:

Durbins, Guildford, Surrey., Mr. Roger Fry[a,b].
Shepherd's Well, Forest Row, Sussex. Mrs. Frost[a].
Great Roke, Witley, Surrey. Mrs. Dixon[b].
Corner House, Beckenham, Kent.
Mrs. Francis Hooper[b].
Old Croft, Godalming, Surrey. Rev. D. Hyland[a,b].
St. Edmund's Catholic Church, Godalming, Surrey[a].
Culmer Corner, Witley, Surrey. Mr. J.E. Eastwood. (Possibly The Nurses' House)[a,b,c].
Angerton, Morpeth, Northumberland.
Mrs. Straker[a,c].
Heywood, Abbeyleix, Ireland.
Colonel William Hutcheson Poë[a]
Lillingstone Dayrell, Buckinghamshire.
Hon. Mrs. Douglas-Pennant[a,b].
Renishaw, Derbyshire. Sir George Sitwell[a,b,c].
West Surrey Golf Club, Secretary's House, Milford, Surrey, Mr. J.H. Eastwood[a,b].
Rignalls, Great Missenden, Buckinghamshire.
Sir Felix Semon[a,b,c].
Durmast, Burley, Hampshire. Miss Baring[a,b].
Stubbings, Maidenhead, Berkshire. Mr. Eric Smith[b].
Highmount, Guildford, Surrey. Mr. Walter Neall[a,b,c].
Stilemans, Godalming, Surrey. Dr. E.P. Arnold[a,b,c].
Lindisfarne Castle, Holy Island, Northumberland.
Mr. E. Hudson[a,b,c].

In 1911 plans, plants or both went to:
Fairhill, Berkhamstead, Hertfordshire.
Mr. W.S. Cohen[a,b,c].
Amersfoort, Berkhamstead, Hertfordshire.
Mr. W.S. Cohen[a,b,c].
Struy Lodge, Beauly, Scotland.
Countess of Derby[a,b,c].
Chart Cottage, Seal, Sevenoaks, Kent.
Mr. Bernard Blunt[a,b,c].
Drumbanagher, Newry, Ireland.
Lady Muriel Close[a].
Hydon Ridge, Hambledon, Surrey.
Mr. C.E. Denny[a,b,c].
Newnham College, Cambridge. Miss Clough[a,b,c].
Lenton Hurst, Nottingham. Mrs. Player[a].
Putteridge Park, Luton, Bedfordshire.
Mr. Felix Cassel[a,b].
Vann, Hambledon, Surrey. Mr. W.D. Caroë[a,b].
Woodcote, Whitchurch, Hampshire.,
Mr. R.F. Nicholson[a,c] [42].

Some of these commissions began earlier than 1909, such as Rignalls and Highmount, but plans and plants were still being supplied in 1910. Whereas others such as Stilemans and Lindisfarne continued into the 1920s. Some of the commissions were in the form of quotations, such as Stubbings and Newnham College, Cambridge, and were not realised. Little or nothing is known of the commission for Lady Muriel Close of Drumbanagher near Newry and for Mrs. Player at Lenton Hurst, Nottingham. Of the balance, plans were sent and plants from the nursery followed. At the same time she was writing articles for *Country Life* and *The Garden* and preparing the text and illustrations with Lawrence Weaver for *Gardens for Small Country Houses*.[43]

Roger Fry, the artist and art critic, the Slade Professor of Fine Art at Cambridge University and founder of the Omega workshop, visited Miss Jekyll at Munstead Wood on six occasions between 26 May 1909 and 16 November 1911[44] to discuss the layout and planting of the garden at Durbins in Guildford, the land for which he had paid £600 in 1908.[45] The land was purchased and the house built to provide "the best chance for Helen [Fry] . . . to have a more or less country life without the excitement of London."[45] The garden was on five levels facing south to south-west, sheltered to the north and east and with excellent views. The first terrace was of gravel, the second of sand, reached by a flight of circular steps in bargate stone. Rectangular beds were planted with yuccas and grey-leaved plants such as *Santolina*. A flight of stone steps led to a pergola on a lower level and this grass terrace contained a rectangular lily pond: at the foot of the wall was a bed with soft fruit and adjacent to the axial path were beds of herbaceous perennials. A grass bank separated the fourth from the fifth terrace where there was a tennis lawn and vegetable garden.[46]

On 27 May 1911 Miss Jekyll sent some 600 plants from the Munstead Wood Nursery to Durbins. The plants included 18 *Yucca filamentosa*, 42 *Santolina* and 54 *Nepeta*. For the walls, *Corydalis, Armeria,* crimson *Sedum spurium* and *S. ewersii, campanulas, phlox* and white, pink and lemon-white snapdragon were sent. Unfortunately the order of white and pale pink snapdragons, numbering 154, was not filled and Miss Jekyll wrote to offer them in 1912 and in compensation to provide the wall plants in September 1911. Notwithstanding these problems the garden was enjoyed as it matured, by all who saw it. In the summer of 1913 Rose Sidgwick,[47] a lecturer at the University of Birmingham and friend of Roger Fry's sister, Margery, stayed at Durbins, and wrote Margery:

"what a delicious grey garden . . . The garden blazed at me down the hill with a blue positively alarming . . . anchusa Dropmore, each flower pure gem blue . . . and that grey white soil sets it off. The rest was masses of Canterbury bells, purple, white, pink; catmint in great mats; and monthly roses in full bloom, growing in a sweet and humble way like a hardy perennial among them. I spent most of the time when nothing else was happening looking down at the pretty pure sequences of colour on the grey white and the ponds."[48]

Even Roger Fry's daughter, Pamela, was moved at the age of 15 to write about the garden in 1917:

"You can't imagine anything so magnificent than the garden is here now. Everything is growing in a disorderly luxuriance. There are great hedges of monthly roses in the midst of which native irises grow. The pond is jewelled with water lilies . . ."[49]

All the plants for Durbins were supplied from the nursery ground at Munstead Wood but for other commissions Miss Jekyll recommended that a local nursery be used for plants she could not provide, or she bought in plants from nurserymen elsewhere in Surrey.

At Renishaw plantings were designed by Miss Jekyll and whilst she supplied many of the plants others, such as *Clematis Jackmanii,* were bought in and the gardener Ernest de Taeye sowed seed sent by Miss Jekyll from Munstead Wood that she had bought from Suttons. Plans were drawn up by Miss Jekyll for the Tank Garden, the Lawn Garden and The Green or Long Alley. For the Lawn Garden over 1250 plants were sent between 22 February and 15 March 1910 from her nursery. They included over 250 of her "special strain" of snapdragons such as pale pink, middle pink, rosy morn, tall white, and lemon white, and 480 *Stachys*.[50] For the Long Alley the rectangular and circular beds were planted up with marigolds, maize, cannas and dahlias.[51] The effect was startling. Osbert Sitwell wrote:

"The garden was in gala this year. Over the rounded top of an ancient holly, which grows against one of the angles of the house, where it jutted forward, the lawns lay spread in their richest, fullest beauty. The hedges had grown and were by now substantial, and the whole design, the counterpoint of bright mown grass and deep shade, of water and of trees, had settled down, and looked as if it had existed always. This year, within the mysterious fullness of their setting, this year, in the ultimate Edwardian summer, the flowers had attained a peculiar richness typical of the epoch, for Lutyens's old friend and mentor, Miss Jekyll, had been sent the plan of the garden beds by my father and had issued her decrees for them: they were to be filled only with blossoms of blue and orange and lemon yellow, in another with French eighteenth century blues and pinks."[52]

The following year, 1911, plants continued to issue from the nursery in even greater numbers. To Hydon Ridge, Hambledon, over 1130 plants were sent out in November and December 1911 and the majority went "Sat. Nov. 25 before dinner".[53] The only plants she could not supply to Mr. Denny were 27 yews, 55 hollies, 4 box and 1 laburnum and the yews and hollies were bought in from Walter Slocock at the Goldsworth Old Nurseries – from late October until early December. She was also supplying another large commission at Berkhamstead in Hertfordshire: almost 3000 plants were sent to Mr. W.S. Cohen and the only plants she could not supply here were 2 *Polygonum baldschuanicum* and 2 box.[53]   For these two commissions alone the following shrubs and herbaceous plants were sent in large numbers: 388 Iris, 278 Stachys, 214 London Pride, 176 Asarum, 144 Solomon's Seal, 72 Clematis, 69 China roses, 63 Male Fern, 62 Cistus, 61 Hollyhocks, 53 Nepeta, 51 Dicentra, 37 Viburnum, 32 Libertia, 19 Yucca, 14 Olearia, *inter alia*.

The few commissions described here for 1905, 1910 and 1911 show that not long after the plant nursery was established Miss Jekyll was supplying most of the plants required by her clients. The scale of the operations was unexpectedly large and Miss Jekyll managed them efficiently, effectively and with extraordinary industry, participating in all aspects of the activities of the nursery, whether propagation and planting out, lifting and packing plants for despatch, sending out accounts, corresponding with clients, gardeners or their agents, designing the plantings and drafting the plans herself, as well as training the clients' gardeners. It is no small wonder that there was little time to receive visitors and that she exhorted friends and visitors "to be allowed to retain a somewhat larger measure of peace and privacy."[54] Mrs. Amy Barnes-Brand was intrigued to know how Miss Jekyll managed to do so much work and, having asked her, the following exchange took place:

"By not going to Tea Parties," said Miss Jekyll.

Mrs. Barnes-Brand replied, "I don't go to tea parties," to which Miss Jekyll responded, "Ah, but you are married, and that is one person's occupation."[55]

Conclusion

Rather late in her life Miss Jekyll began the plant nursery at Munstead Wood as a commercial venture. She had been designing gardens for friends and relatives for at least twenty years before this, and had used the reserve garden at Munstead House as a plant nursery, where she propagated plants and held them for friends such as William Robinson. She had collected plants from the wild in Britain and elsewhere in Europe, and tested them as garden plants and for hardiness. She collected and improved some twenty-eight herbaceous perennials (see Chapter 9), and used many of them in the garden commissions. She observed the plants closely in their native habitats and cultivated them better than most. The rock gardens she constructed for the alpine plants collected in the Alps, Snowdonia and in the Scottish mountains were mistaken for natural outcrops, and again were based on close observation of natural situations translated into garden settings.

The occasion for the establishment of the nursery arose from the need to ensure that the right variety of plant was used, so that the effect aimed for in the plans was realised. It was also commercially astute to supply both plan and plants, and Miss Jekyll added an irresistible offer that the plants she could supply were stronger and cheaper than the nurseries with whom she was competing, but whom she employed as sub-contractors if she could not supply the plants required.

The number of plants that went out from the Munstead Wood nursery was remarkable: many thousands were despatched each planting season. This implies that additional gardening staff would have to be taken on to enlarge the establishment. Nevertheless Miss Jekyll had no foreman and was engaged not only in the nursery itself, but also in the packing shed. She made up the bills, kept the account books and visited many of the sites where the gardens she had designed were being laid out: on occasions, as at the King Edward VII Sanatorium, Lindisfarne Castle and Hydon Heath (1915), she helped with the planting.

The plant nursery at Munstead Wood, like everything that Miss Jekyll assayed and pursued was, in George Leslie's words, "carried on with perfect method and completeness."[56]

Gertrude Jekyll's Surrey Gardens

This list of 166 commissions on gardens is based on several sources but it cannot be regarded as definitive. Miss Jekyll's nursery account books at Godalming Museum cover the period from about 1893 until 1929 and in some cases only a client's name or a house name is given, for example Miss C. D. Richards 1914, T. P. Whateley Esq., Mrs. Waterlow, Mrs. Schluter. In the case of Mr. Whateley, Mrs. J. Charman was able to identify the garden at Trenance, Summerhouse Road, Godalming, but the gardens of most of these clients cannot be identified at present and some may not be in Surrey. Six commissions have no dates (n.d.) and are listed after 1932. The county boundary used is the one in existence in 1932.

Sources:

1. Jekyll, F. 1934. Garden Plans. In, Jekyll, F. 1934. Gertrude Jekyll: a memoir. London, Jonathan Cape. pp. 208-233, and Index, pp. 241-5.

2. Reef Point Gardens, Collection of Designs by Gertrude Jekyll. University of California, Berkeley, United States of America.

3. Godalming Museum, 109a High Street, Godalming, Surrey.

4. Jekyll, G. 1908. Children and Gardens. London, Country Life.

c.1854	Bramley House.[4]
1877	Munstead House, Godalming.[1]
1881	Gishurst Cottage, Weybridge.[1] Wisley.[1]
1883	Munstead Wood, Godalming.[2] Great Enton, Witley.[1]
1884	Lower Eashing, Godalming.[1]
1885	Hangerfield, Witley.[1]
1888	Knole, Cranleigh.[1]
1890	Munstead, Godalming.[1]
1891	Crooksbury House, Farnham.[1,2] The Hermitage, Effingham.[1,2]
1892	Wood End, Witley[1]
1893	Chinthurst, Wonersh.[1,2] Winkworth Farm, Hascombe.[1]
1894	Ruckmans, Oakwood Park.[1]
1895	The Vicarage, Witley.[1] Banacle Copse, Culmer, Witley.[1,2] Banacle Edge, Witley.[1] Mayhurst, Maybury Hill.[1] The Lodge, Thames Ditton.[1] Lascombe, Puttenham.[1] Munstead Corner, Godalming.[1]
1896	Charterhouse, Godalming.[1,2] Milford House, Milford.[1] Thorncombe Park, Bramley.[1,2,3]
1897	Hillside, Godalming.[1] Burrows Cross, Shere.[1] Fulbrook House, Elstead.[1] Whinfold, Hascombe.[1,2]

1898	Charterhouse, Godalming.[1,2] Westaway, Godalming.[1] Normanswood, Farnham.[1]
1899	Munstead Rough, Godalming.[1,2] Little Tangley, Guildford.[1,2,3] Orchards, Godalming.[1] Tigbourne Court, Witley.[1] Goddards, Abinger Common.[1]
1900	Hatchlands, Guildford.[1,2]
1901	High Barn, Hascombe.[1,2] Fisher's Hill, Woking.[1,2] Prior's Wood, Godalming.[1,2] Camilla Lacey, Dorking.[1,2] Enton Lodge, Witley.[1,2]
1902	Hale House, Ockley.[1,2] New Place, Haslemere.[1,2] Friar's Hill, Elstead.[1,2] Leybourne, Witley.[1,2] Sutton Place, Guildford.[1,2] Munstead Grange, Godalming.[1,2,3]
1903	Hall Place, Shackleford, Godalming.[1,2] Hughes Memorial Wesleyan Church, Godalming.[1,2] Warren Lodge, Witley.[1,2] Westbrook, Godalming.[1,3]
1904	Osbrooks, Capel.[1,2] Field Place, Dunsfold.[1,2] Busbridge Park, Godalming.[1,2,3] Millmead, Bramley.[1,2,3]
1905	Bramley House.[1,2] The Grange, Hindhead, Haslemere.[1,2] Church Road, Purley.[1,2] Loseley Park, Guildford.[1,2] Tarn Moor, Witley.[1]
1906	Busbridge Rectory.[1,2,3] Ceasar's Camp, Wimbledon Common.[1,2] The Moorings, Hindhead, Haslemere.[1,2]
1907	Firgrove, Godalming.[1,2,3] Copyhold Cottage, Haslemere.[3] Uplands, Brook, Witley.[1,2,3] Braboeuf Estate, Guildown, Guildford.[1,2]
1908	South Corner, Wimbledon.[3] Whiteways, Brockham Green.[3] Duffell, Brockham Green.[3] Peperharow Park, Godalming.[1,2] King's Sanatorium, Milford.[3]
1909	Frensham Place, Frensham.[1,2] Heatherside House, Camberley.[1,2,3] Highmount, Fort Road, Guildford.[1,2,3] Stilemans, Godalming.[1,2,3] Woodruffe, Worplesdon Hill, Brookwood.[1,2]
1910	Durbins, Guildford.[1,3] Great Roke, Witley.[1,3] St. Edmund's Catholic Church, Godalming.[1,3] Old Croft, Godalming.[1,3] Culmer Corner, Culmer, Witley.[1,2] West Surrey Golf Club, Milford.[3]
1911	Hydon Ridge, Hambledon.[1,2,3] Vann, Hambledon.[1,3]
1912	Munstead Grange, Godalming.[1,2,3] The Grange, Hindhead.[1,3] Monkswood, Godalming.[1,2,3] Merrow Croft, Guildford.[1,2,3] Phillips Memorial, Godalming.[1,2,3]
1913	Munstead Oaks.[1,2,3] Kilnfield, Puttenham.[3] Warren Hurst, Ashtead.[1,2,3] Hascombe Grange, Godalming.[1,2] The Copse, Brook, Godalming.[1,2] Heath Cottage, Puttenham, Guildford.[1,2] Nurse's House, Culmer, Witley.[1,2,3] Merton Park, Mostyn Road.[1,3]
1914	Bowerbank, Wimbledon.[1,2,3] Gorse Bank,

Enton Green, Witley.[1] Lukyns, Eshurst.[1,2] Godalming Police Station.[1] Trenance, Busbridge.[3] Busbridge Rectory, Godalming.[12]

1915 Hydon Heath, Hambledon.[1] Kings Arms Hotel, Godalming.[1] Highlands, Haslemere.[1,2] Garden Court, Guildford.[1,2] Munstead Grange.[3] Lower House, Bowlhead Green, Witley.[1,2]

1916 New Chapel House, Lingfield.[1,2,3] Lower House, Witley.[1,2,3]

1918 Kilmeena, West Byfleet.[1,2,3] Burgate, Dunsfold.[1,2]

1919 Normanswood, Farnham.[1] Puttenham Priory.[1,2]

1920 Heath House, Headley, Epsom.[1,2,3] Old Broom Hall & Broomhall: Club Grounds, Teddington.[3] Walsham House, Elstead.[1,2] Kingswood, Shere.[1,2] Kingswood, Gomshall.[3] Broad Oak, Seale, Farnham.[1] Grayswood Hill, Haslemere.[1,2,3] Foyle Riding Farm, Oxted.[1] Compton, War Memorial.[1] Golands House, New Chapel, Lingfield.[1,2,3] Kew, 61 The Avenue.[1]

1921 Bradstone Brook, Guildford.[1,2,3] Hill Top, Fort Road, Guildford.[1,2,3] Little Tangley.[3] Tangley Way, Blackheath, Guildford.[1,2] Upper Ifold

House, Dunsfold.[1,2,3] Quedley, Haslemere.[3]

1922 Busbridge War Memorial.[1] Enton Hall, Witley.[1,2,3] Hascombe Court.[1,2,3] Burningfold Farm, Dunsfold.[1,2,3] Great House, Hambledon.[1,2,3]

1923 Fox Hill, Elstead.[1,2] Southernway, St. Martha's, Guildford.[1,2,3] Great Meadow, Hambledon.[3] Holmwood, Hambledon.[1,2,3]

1924 North Munstead, Godalming.[1,2,3] Sullingstead, Hascombe.[1] Hall's Cottage, Frensham.[1]

1925 Widford, Wydown Road, Haslemere.[1,2,3]

1926 Three Fords, Send.[1,2] Woodhouse Copse, Holmbury St. Mary.[1,2,3] Roysted, Highdown Heath, Godalming.[1,2,3]

1928 Cottage Wood, Walton-on-Thames.[3] Valewood Farm, Haslemere.[1] Bridge Farm, Byfleet.[3]

1929 Reflections, Echo Pit Road, Guildford.[1] Marylands, Hurtwood.[1,2]

1931 Little Wisset, Hook Heath Road, Woking.[1,2] Springwood, Godalming.[1]

1932 Cottage Wood, Walton-on-Thames.[1,2n.d] The Dormy House, Walton Heath.[n.d.] Wood Lea, Virginia Water.[2,3n.d.] Pasture Wood, Holmbury St. Mary.[2n.d.] Richmond.[2 n.d.] Crossways Cottage.[2n.d.] Chisbury.[2]

Hascombe Court, near Godalming, Surrey, designed by Sir Edwin Lutyens' pupil John Duke Coleridge for Sir John Jarvis. Clare Nauheim (Lady Railing) drew the garden plans and Gertrude Jekyll, the planting plans in 1922. Drawn by Rosanna Tooley August 1985.

9

Plants selected and bred by Miss Jekyll

Michael Tooley

Introduction

Showy, flowering plants are a joy in the wild. They have been collected for hundreds of years and have been cultivated in gardens. Both in the wild and in gardens, increasing numbers have become rare and then extinct. It is extraordinary that the total number of species of flowering plants on the earth is not known, but estimates of about a quarter of a million are common, and it has been estimated that by the middle of the next century 10% may be extinct.[1] In western medicine, we use chemicals from 700 plants and, for example, an alkaloid, Vinchristine, from the Madagascan periwinkle, *Catharanthus roseus,* has been used successfully to treat children suffering from a form of leukaemia.[2]

Plants from the temperate world have been selected not only for their curative properties but also for their beauty of form, leaf and flower to enrich the pleasure gardens and landscapes of Britain, and in many cases , such as the Horse Chestnut and the Cedar of Lebanon, have been saved from near extinction in their home areas by introductions to western Europe, and are now found throughout the temperate world.

For many years, gardeners, including Miss Jekyll, have introduced plants from the wild to gardens and varieties and cultivars have appeared in large numbers in nursery catalogues, especially in the nineteenth and early twentieth centuries. But the numbers and varieties of garden plants are also subject to extinction as the result of changes of fashion, genetic instability, disease and economics.[3]

Concern about the considerable loss of garden plants available to the gardener and horticulturalist led to the establishment in 1978 of the National Council for the Conservation of Plants and Gardens (NCCPG), and Christopher Brickell and Fay Sharman have drawn attention to the scale of the problem and the need to conserve garden plants.[4]

Miss Jekyll would have been sympathetic towards the aims and objectives of the NCCPG, for not only had she rescued plants from cottage gardens, but also had selected and bred plants, and introduced them to gardeners and horticulturalists through her plant nursery at Munstead Wood (see Chapter 8). She wrote in 1929: "there is now such a wealth of flowering plants available for our gardens that it becomes almost a difficulty to make a choice without leaving out a number of good things that may be considered essential. Seventy years ago it was quite another matter, and yet it seems strange that there are a certain number of highly desirable plants that were then in favour, and that we should still consider to be among the best, which have passed out of cultivation or can only rarely be heard of."[5]

Having collected plants from the wild in Britain, Italy, Algeria and elsewhere, selected them for their hardiness and improved them, she tried to ensure that they were conserved by sending specimens to Kew.[6] She had discovered a prostrate form of rosemary and *Lithospermum rosmarinifolium* on a coastal cliff in Capri in 1883 and sent plants to William Robinson and to the Royal Botanic Gardens, Kew.[7] In addition plants she had selected and bred, such as the Munstead Poppies and the bellflower *Campanula persicifolia*, were sent to Kew in 1883 and *Lupinus polyphyllus* Munstead variety in 1917.[8] However none of these has survived

Left: Figure 9.1 Campanula alpina by Gertrude Jekyll.

there, and are lost to gardens everywhere in the temperate world.

Miss Jekyll selected the best forms of garden plants by close observation over a long period of time, and described the process of selection in *Wood and Garden* and *Home and Garden*:

"By this time [c.1873] I was steadily collecting hardy garden plants wherever I could find them, mostly from cottage gardens. Many of them were still unknown to me by name, but as the collection increased I began to compare and discriminate, and of various kinds of one plant to throw out the worse and retain the better and to train myself to see what made a good garden plant . . ."[9]

". . . the stores of the rubbish heap were much enriched by the many plants that seemed unworthy, or of which better garden kinds could be had, so all my older clumps of Michaelmas Daisies found their way there . . . and a whole set of the oldest of the garden forms of the albiflora Peonies as well as many other unworthy individuals."[10]

It is a curious fact that little is known about the plants she bred and introduced to the trade, except for the cultivars that are still available. Even these are not listed in F.A. Stafleu and R.S. Cowan's book on *Taxonomic Literature*[11], published in 1979, and the entry under herbarium and types is given as "unknown".

The objective of this contribution is to provide details of the 'unknown' types of plants selected and bred by Miss Jekyll, and of plants named after her, to give the first date of introduction or description and to indicate the awards received.

The starting point for the list, as with most things appertaining to the life and work of Miss Jekyll, is the biography by her nephew:

Table 9.1 Plants selected and bred by or named after Gertrude Jekyll

Antirrhinum 'Pale Pink'	1911
Aquilegia vulgaris 'Munstead White'	1884
Aster 'Munstead Purple'	1911
Aster 'Peperharow'	1882
Campanula persicifolia 'Chauderon'	1883
C. latifolia macrantha alba	1933
Cardamine pratensis fl. pl. 'Miss Jekyll' A.M. 1896	1896
Cheiranthus mutabilis 'Munstead'	1916
Chrysanthemum maximum 'Munstead'	1898
Digitalis 'Munstead White'	1887
Helianthus 'Munstead Primrose'	1898
Helleborus orientalis 'Gertrude Jekyll'	1884
Lavandula spica 'Munstead' A.M. 1916 and 1963, H. C. 1961	1916
Lunaria annua 'Munstead Purple'	1908
Lupinus polyphyllus 'Munstead Beauty', 'Munstead Blue' A.M. 1931	1924
Lupinus polyphyllus 'Munstead White'	1924
Narcissus 'Gertrude Jekyll'	1882
Nigella damascena 'Miss Jekyll, Blue', 'Miss Jekyll, Dark Blue' and 'Miss Jekyll, White'	1900
Paeonia decora 'Gertrude Jekyll'	1898
Papaver nudicaule Munstead poppies & 'Munstead White'	1883
Papaver somniferum 'Munstead Cream Pink'	1917
Primula cortusoides Jekyllae	1885
Primula 'Munstead Bunch' Bronze Banksian Medal 1900	1886
Primula 'Munstead Early White'	1890
Primula 'Sultan'	1901
Pulmonaria angustifolia azurea 'Munstead Blue'	1919
Rose 'Gertrude Jekyll'	1986
Sedum telephium 'Munstead Red'	1916
Vinca minor 'Gertrude Jekyll' A.G.M. 1962	1885
Viola 'Jackanapes' A.M. 1899, 1931. H.C. 1898, 1922	1888

Royal Horticultural Society Awards: A.M. Award of Merit; H.C. Highly Commended; A.G.M. Award of Garden Merit.

"To these years [1902-1906] also belong her intensive labours in the cultivation and improvement of particular species, such as the Polyanthus Primulas, since known as 'Munstead Primroses' throughout the gardening world. . . . Many other garden favourites such as Lent Hellebores, Nigellas, Aquilegias, double pink Poppies and white Foxgloves, owe their present state of perfection to the selective breeding carried on at Munstead under her supervision."[12]

However, this list is incomplete and the dates are too late. The second source was The Royal Horticultural Society's consolidated *List of Awards* that covered the period during which Miss Jekyll was selecting and improving garden cultivars.[13] The third source was the gardening journals, especially *The Garden* and *The Gardeners' Chronicle*. The fourth source was the nursery catalogues of Barr and Son and Carters and the fifth source was the Munstead Wood plant catalogue.[14]

The list of plants (Table 9.1) is based on these five sources, but it is not claimed to be definitive. Miss Jekyll did not herself promote or greatly publicise the plants she had improved and it was left to friends, such as George Paul, or the plant nurseries to submit them for consideration for an award by The Royal Horticultural Society.

Description of plants selected and bred by Miss Jekyll or named after her

Antirrhinum 'Pale Pink' and "my special strain"[15]

Miss Jekyll wrote Sir George Sitwell's gardener, Mr. Ernest de Taeye, in March 1911, "the snapdragons (my special strain) for the altered planting and also for the original planting I would send at planting time – viz. end of May or early June". They included pale pink, middle pink, rosy morn, tall white and lemon white, and, altogether over 250 plants were sent from the Munstead Wood nursery (see Chapter 10).

By 1911 Miss Jekyll had perfected the strain, and used snapdragons in many situations at Munstead Wood and in her garden commissions. In the main flower border at Munstead Wood tall yellow and white snapdragons were used and in August these "spire up four feet high." The following month "tall white snapdragons, five feet high, show finely among the gracefully curved leaves of the blue Lyme-grass." As with other plants, Miss Jekyll pulled down the tall snapdragons to cover the adjacent bare ground with flowering shoots.

Snapdragons were also grown in dry stone walls at Munstead Wood: "Snapdragons are grand wall-plants, both in sun and shade. I think the tender colourings, white, yellow, and pinkish are the most suitable for the cool exposure, and the fine dark crimson reds and mixed colourings for the warm one."

The white snapdragon grown by Miss Jekyll may have been a form named by J. T. Bennett-Poë 'The Swan.'

Miss Jekyll not only supplied many snapdragon plants to her clients, but also recommended seed from Suttons, whose nursery she visited on 9 August 1902, and described the antirrhinums she saw there, including 'Rosy Morn' – "a flower of refined beauty ... white flushed with tender pink, with a yellow lip."

Aquilegia vulgaris 'Munstead White'[16]

The first unnamed reference but apparently to this form of *Aquilegia* is in *The Garden* for 1881. Miss Jekyll had sent a collection of sweet peas, columbines, briar roses, and dog lilies to the editor, William Robinson, who described them in the editorial:

". . .a stately bunch of white single garden Columbine, so large and free that it reminded one of the white Rocky Mountain Columbine, but this common single Columbine is so easily grown that it has the advantage over the rarer kind."

It was described again, but not named, in 1884:

"A white Columbine has been sent to us by Miss Jekyll from Munstead, who considers it a very beautiful variety. The flowers are the counterpart of those of *A. coerulea,* but they are pure white save the faintest suggestion of mauve on the outer sepals. From the tip of the spurs to the anthers the flowers measure $3\frac{1}{4}$ inches, and the habit of the plant is dwarf and graceful. It has been raised from seed and is surely one that should be perpetuated and grown largely, as it is far more beautiful than any white form of the common Columbine (A. vulgaris)."

It was first named as *Aquilegia* 'Munstead White' in 1887 and again in 1890 in *The Garden*. In 1891, a reference was made to a Munstead Giant-type of *Aquilegia*.

Seed was offered for sale by Barrs in 1898 when it was described as a fine white single. Barr's submitted seed for the *Aquilegia* trial at The Royal Horticultural Society's garden at Wisley in 1913 and 'Munstead White' received a commendation. Unlike most Aquilegias, 'Munstead White' showed little variation and was true. Barrs submitted seed again at the *Aquilegia* trials at Wisley in 1927 and 'Munstead White' was listed in the short-spurred varieties' category. The flower size was given as 1⅞ inch and the spur ½ inch long. The flower was creamy white. In the monograph on *Aquilegia* in 1901, Irving includes *Aquilegia* 'Munstead White' as one of the better known forms and equates it with *A. vulgaris grandiflora alba* – "a very fine pure white form."

It was described by H. Avray Tipping in 1933: "A good selection of single ones is again in favour and especially a white variety long ago selected by Gertrude Jekyll and called Munstead White. The pendant petals open wide and rise up to short spurs ending in an inward curve, which makes the entire form one of finished and graceful reticence..."

It was available in 1992 from 13 nurseries as *A. vulgaris* 'Nivea' ('Munstead White').

Aster 'Munstead Purple' and Aster 'Peperharow'[17]

Miss Jekyll devoted two double borders at Munstead Wood to Michaelmas Daisies: one was between the house and the pergola, parallel to the nut-walk, whereas the other divided the plant-nursery or kitchen garden between the orchard and the iris and lupin borders. Plans of the Michaelmas Daisy borders were described and published, and one of the cultivars developed by Miss Jekyll was used in planting commissions and was available commercially from another nursery. Curiously, only the dwarf *Aster alpinus* was offered for sale in the Munstead Wood plant catalogue.

Aster 'Munstead Purple' was used by Miss Jekyll in one of the Michaelmas Daisy borders at Amersfort, Berkhamsted in 1911, and in Barr's *Hardy Perennials*

Catalogue for 1916 it was offered for sale at 9d each and described as "rich purple, dark stems. Sept. 4ft."

There is only a single reference to Aster 'Peperharow' and this is in an article by the Rev. C. Wolley Dod in *The Gardeners' Chronicle* in 1882:

"I have three Asters which nearly resemble it [A. Archer Hind], both in colour and habit, one was sent me by Miss Jekyll, who calls it Peperharow, from a village of that name in Surrey, in a cottage garden of which she found it."

Campanula persicifolia 'Chauderon'[18]

Miss Jekyll used Campanulas extensively in woodland plantings, in shady borders and in open, sunny situations in rockeries. She photographed them and made a collection of drawings which are botanically accurate. From a sketchbook of drawings in the Lindley Library, *Campanula alpina* and *C. allionii* (syn. *C. alpestris*) are reproduced here (Figures 9.1 & 9.2)

The peach-leaved bell flower (*C. persicifloia*) was collected by Miss Jekyll from the Gorge du Chaudron between Glion and Sonzier at the north-east end of Lake Geneva. It was probably collected during one of her visits to Jacques and Leonie Blumenthal's Châlet near Sonzier in 1873, 1876, or 1879,[18] and may have been a garden escape.

It was described in the Munstead Wood catalogue as "a fine variety, originally collected by Miss Jekyll in the Alps, and improved by garden culture. The stalk is slender and graceful, and the flowers larger than in the usual garden kinds." There is no reference to this cultivar in her friend Henri Correvon's description of the genus *Campanula* published in 1901, when it was already in the plant nursery at Munstead.

Figure 9.2   Campanula allionii by Gertrude Jekyll.

Portion of flower-stem of a fine variety of Campanu'a persicifolia (colour bright blue-purple).

Figure 9.3   Campanula persicifolia 'Chauderon.'

The only description was published in *The Garden*, with an illustration, in 1883, probably shortly after she had collected it (Figure 9.3). A scholarly description is given by Miss Jekyll:

"A fine variety of Campanula persicifolia, 4 feet high, blooming long and late, still in flower (September 7) and likely to bloom for another fortnight, but coming into flower when the ordinary garden kinds are going out of bloom. There is a large variety of persicifolia figured in Curtis's *Botanical Magazine* Vol. xii, p.397, and C. persicifolia maxima nearly agreeing with my flower in general dimensions, but different in form, being of a broad cup or bowl shape with the edges of the segments very slightly turned outwards; whereas this flower has a true bell shape, with the segments of the corollas from the point of junction prolonged outwards and then recurved, this outer part projecting five-eights of an inch beyond the rim of the bell, and giving the flower its handsome, wide-spreading character."

Seed of a pure white form of another species of *Campanula, C. latifolia macrantha*, selected by Miss Jekyll was offered for sale by Carters in 1933.

Cardamine pratensis flore-pleno 'Miss Jekyll'[19]

The double form of Lady's Smock or Cuckoo flower was first described by the Rev. C. Wolley Dod in 1881 as "an interesting plant both for its peculiar power of producing young plants on the edges of the leaves when detached...., and from the frequency with which it bears double flowers in the wild state .... about four miles from Malpas there is a warm wet meadow sheltered by woods where it grows in great abundance, and nearly all the flowers are double. In this form it makes a fine garden plant for a moist retentive soil.... the tendency to double.... is confined to the light-coloured variety, the darker flowers being single." Miss Jekyll recounted in *Home and Garden* how a friend bought a double variety and introduced it to a meadow with the single wild form, where it spread. Miss Jekyll visited this meadow every spring and noted to her delight "one plant of a much deeper colour, quite a pretty and desirable variety from the type, that has proved a good garden plant." This must have been in 1894 or 1895, because in 1896, her friend, Mr. George Paul of Messrs. Paul and Son of The Old Nurseries, Cheshunt, exhibited a pale lilac doubled flowered variety at the Royal Horticultural Society's Floral Committee meeting in the Drill Hall, Westminster, under the name *Cardamine pratensis* fl. pl. Miss Jekyll and received an Award of Merit.

It was described by Miss Jekyll in *Wall and Water Gardens* in 1901 and in articles in *Country Life* in 1911 and 1923 and there is a photograph in *Home and Garden*. Curiously, the photograph in volume 3 of the photograph albums at the University of California, Berkeley, is missing. Plants of *C. pratensis flore-pleno* are still available from many nurseries, but Miss Jekyll's cultivar is lost.

Cheiranthus mutabilis 'Munstead'[20]

Miss Jekyll devoted a chapter in *Home and Garden* to a garden of wall flowers and described the great variations in habit and flower colour that arose from self sown seedlings on the dry, sandy soil of Munstead Wood. One seedling she described with a flower that was a "full clear orange colour, more deeply tinged to the outer margins of the petals with faint thin lines of rich mahogany, that increase in width of line and depth of colour as they reach the petal's outer edge, till, joining together, the whole edge is of this strong rich colour." Drifts of pale lemon, yellow, brown and purple wall flowers were planted in the spring garden of Munstead Wood, in associations such as spring bitter vetch, purple wall flower and honesty, or brown wall

Figure 9.4   *'White foxgloves at the edge of the fir wood.'*

flowers with red tulips and bright, mahogany coloured crown imperials. A favourite perennial double wall flower was described by Miss Jekyll in 1928 as a "bushy, half-woody plant that goes on for years; just a little tender, and likes to have its back against a warm wall." But the 'Munstead' cultivar was described in Barr's catalogue in 1916 as a "rich purple, shot with bronze" flowering from May until August and growing to about 1 foot in height. This form is smaller than the species *C. semperflorens*. She opined in 1922 that a good purple wallflower was wanted: "a purple inclining towards blue rather than towards red," and that such a purple would be bred.

Chrysanthemum maximum 'Munstead'[21]

In the great new borders, known as 'The Yew Hedges', at Blagdon, Northumberland, designed by Miss Jekyll in 1929 and running from near the house west to the walled garden, some plantings of *Chrysanthemum maximum* were proposed. They were backed by *Aconitum napellus* and Aster Rycroft. Lady Ridley wrote that "the borders.... will be *quite* lovely and are exactly what I wanted", but she questioned the use of *C. maximum*: "The

only thing I am not quite happy about is, is the Chrysanthemum maximus. The one we have now in the garden is a large, and (I think) rather ugly big white daisy – & it grows about 6 foot high – this would completely hide anything behind it – (such as the asters & aconites in B. I.) but perhaps there are more than one variety of Chrys. max. and you are thinking of a different one". Miss Jekyll replied six days later: "The Chrysanthemum maximum that you have is evidently one of the coarse growing kinds that I much dislike. The one I have is the best I have ever seen, is about 2ft. to 2ft. 6" high with no look of coarseness. In fact it is known in the trade as the Munstead variety."

It is not listed in Miss Jekyll's catalogue but she described it in *The Garden* in 1920. It was offered for sale by Barrs in 1898 and 1899 but with no description.

Digitalis 'Munstead White'[22]

White foxgloves were valuable for Miss Jekyll not only in woodland but also in the June garden of the Hut. In the woodland of Munstead Wood she described the Fern Walk and "to right and left, white Foxgloves spire up among the Bracken". A photograph in *Wood and Garden* shows the effectiveness of this composition (Figure 9.4). Propagation was effected by sowing seed where tree stumps had been grubbed up: "....one forgets all about them, till two years afterwards there are the stately Foxgloves. It is good to see their strong spikes of solid bloom standing six to seven feet high...." Quite a different association was created in the June garden, where to the west of the Hut it was grown with irises, *Anchusa azurea* 'Dropmore' and *Aruncus sylvester*. To the north, against a hedge of *Mahonia*, giant hogweeds and white foxgloves were grown.

Miss Jekyll first described the white foxgloves in *The Garden* in 1887: "Our strain – pure white colour with dark leaves.... and making a quantity of good, free-flowering side growth after the main flowering stem has been cut away.... bush foxgloves, though not so graceful as foxgloves in single spires in June, are not plants to be despised in August." She wrote about the Munstead strain of foxgloves in journal articles in 1918, 1919, 1920, 1927 and the year of her death in 1932, in addition to numerous references in *Wood and Garden, Home and Garden* and *Colour Schemes for the Flower Garden*. Seed of 'Munstead White' was offered for sale by Carters in 1933, with the following description: "for wild gardens or woodland walks, selected by Miss Gertrude Jekyll at Munstead Wood."

Helianthus 'Munstead Primrose'[23]

Miss Jekyll's use of the perennial sunflowers was inventive and clever. She described using *H. orgyalis* to fill the space left by *Achillea* and *Eryngium* by pulling it down over these moribund perennials to form a sheet of bloom in September. H. 'Munstead Primrose' however is an annual sunflower, referred to only once by Miss Jekyll, and grown in association with *Artemisia lactiflora*. It was described in Barr's Seed Guide in 1898 as a novelty and in 1899 as "a very effective plant with flowers seven inches across, of a beautiful soft primrose, with handsome dark centre, 4ft."

Helleborus orientalis 'Gertrude Jekyll'[24]

Miss Jekyll grew Lent Hellebores in the borders of the nut walk at Munstead Wood and her stock came from Mr. Archer-Hind's garden in Devon, via her friend Mr. Peter Barr. She also grew them in the spring garden. The cultivar was offered for sale by Barr's and was described first in 1884 as "flowers large, pure white, the finest of all the white varieties (new)". A single plant cost 10s 6d in 1884, and 7s 6d in 1888: by 1895 it was being offered at 2s 6d. and by 1916 it was offered at 9d.

Lavandula spica 'Munstead', Large-flowered 'Munstead Dwarf'[25]

Lavender and Rosemary were two shrubs from the Mediterranean region that Miss Jekyll planted around her house and used in commissions wherever appropriate. Together "they agree in their homely beauty and their beneficence of enduring fragrance," she wrote in 1900. At Munstead Wood, she used lavender in two ways : the first was as hedges from which the flowers were cut and these were found in a garden adjacent to the potting shed, the second was in association with other plants in the grey garden. She described the dwarf lavender in 1914: "Much use is made of a dwarf kind of Lavender that is also among the best of the July flowers. The whole size of the plant is about one-third that of the ordinary kind; the flowers are darker in colour and the time of blooming a good month earlier. It has a different use in gardening, as the flowers, being more crowded and of a deeper tint, make a distinct colour effect. Besides its border use, it is a plant for dry banks, tops of rock work and dry walling." It was offered for sale in the Munstead Wood plant nursery at 9d. and 1/- each and was described as "Lavender, Munstead Large-Flowered Early Dwarf; large sweet-scented flowers in abundance, quite a month earlier than the common lavender, height not exceeding 1ft; valuable for massing in small beds, fronts of borders, rock gardens, etc."

It received an Award of Merit from the Floral Committee of the Royal Horticultural Society in 1916, and the recommendation read: To Lavender 'Barrs Large-flowered Munstead Dwarf' (votes 13 for, 4 against), from Messrs. Barr, Taplow. A very free-flowering variety of dwarf bushy habit. The flowers are of large size, very sweetly scented; and are borne on stems about 8 inches long." It was sold in the section under "new and rare hardy plants for 1916." In 1933 it was offered for sale by Carters and was described as "a dwarf of exceptional merit, making large compact plants about 15 in. high which look well at all seasons. The flowers are a very deep blue and make a splendid edging for borders." The 'Munstead' variety was submitted by George Jackman and Son of Woking for the Wisley Trials of 1961, when it was Highly Commended, and in 1963 it received an Award of Merit for the second time. This cultivar is still widely available.

Lunaria annua 'Munstead Purple'[26]

In 1933 Carters of Raynes Park, London, published the third edition of *The Blue Book of Gardening* and offered a form of Honesty called "Munstead

Figure 9.5   Narcissus 'Gertrude Jekyll.'

It was exhibited by Miss Jekyll at the Royal Horticultural Society on 11 May 1915. Seed of "Munstead Purple" was available from Unwins and from Thompson and Morgan until the 1980s, but it is now no longer available.

Lupinus polyphyllus 'Munstead Blue',
'Munstead White' and 'Munstead Beauty'[27]

The year before she died, Miss Jekyll would have been pleased to learn that the perennial lupin she had selected and refined at Munstead had received an Award of Merit from Floral Committee A of the Royal Horticultural Society on 16 June 1931. It had been raised by her friend Miss Willmott and submitted by Messrs. W. H. Simpson & Sons of Birmingham. In 1930 it had received a commendation, and Simpson & Sons had offered it for sale as 'Munstead Blue' – china blue, with a lighter standard, and in 1938 as 'Munstead', and described the colour as "lavender". It was described in the Munstead Wood catalogue as 'Munstead Beauty' – the finest light purple Lupin,' and sold at 1/- each. It was displayed in the Iris and Lupin borders at Munstead Wood and an autochrome was published as the frontispiece and on the dust jacket of *Gardens for Small Country Houses* in 1912 and another view as the frontispiece in *The Hardy Flower Book* in 1913 (See Figure 7.17 & 7.18).

In 1924 Miss Jekyll had designed a garden for Hall's Cottage, Frensham, at the request of the architect Mr. Harold Falkner. He was a regular visitor to Munstead Wood from 1900 onwards and has given a description of the lupin borders. "Lupins have been since developed by Mr. George Russell, and have achieved some notoriety and brilliance, but I do not think they were ever better grown than in this border, particularly Munstead blue which was probably a species, with very large fat flowers of forget-me-not blue and medium spikes, and Munstead white which was really a cream with white-wings and thick petalled bells." This is the only reference to a white form of the Munstead lupins.

Narcissus 'Gertrude Jekyll'[28]

This daffodil was raised by the Rev. J. G. Nelson of Aldborough, Norfolk, and the flower illustrated in *The Garden* in 1883 (Figure 9.5). Dr. F. W. Burbidge of Trinity College, Dublin reproduced a letter from the Rev. Nelson who described how it acquired its name. "Mr. Peter Barr calls it Gertrude Jekyll, he, good man, having got into a mess by naming one Narcissus after two ladies. I got him out of his

Purple". It was described as a "giant form... raised by Miss Jekyll, V. M. H., in her delightful garden at Munstead Wood; the large bright rosy well-formed flowers are of great substance and quite distinct. Grand for semi-wild gardens and spring bedding."

Miss Jekyll extolled the virtues of Honesty in the spring garden: "biennials are usually associated with annuals, and one may mention the usefulness of the Purple Rocket and the darker kind of purple Honesty (*Lunaria*). The two plants are much alike, both in colour and habit, and are of great use in the back regions of any garden scheme of which the time is the month of May."

In *Children and Gardens*, when it was first described by her, it was the seed pods that attracted her attention: "I must say I do like the silvery Honesty." She kept the middle papery partition, having discarded the seeds : "it is of a delicate texture, half transparent, and has the silvery-satin lustre that makes it such a pretty thing set up in a room in some handsome blue-and-white Chinese jar or Japanese bronze."

trouble by giving him leave to name mine after one of them". Dr. Burbidge described it as "amongst the boldest and most beautiful of the Aldborough Daffodils, this is one of the best, and I think the best of all those which I have actually seen". He went on, "it is so beautiful in form and its colour so delicately soft and pure that one cannot but regret that it is so far unobtainable 'either for love or money". The gracefully nodding flower was described as "soft maize-coloured". The perianth segments cluster around the corona in a cup-like manner, which is long and cylindrical with a most elegantly fringed mouth. Dr Burbidge gave a fuller description in 1882: "a fine, bold and distinct flower of a clear sulphur-yellow, stained or suffused with gamboge-yellow. The trunk or corona is 2 inches in length, also clear sulphur, with a deeper coloured rim. It has a beeswax-like odour, which suggests its

being related to N. moschatus, but the perianth and trunk are of a firmer texture. Indeed in form and size the flower is that of N. bicolor Horsfieldii, but, as we have already shown, the colour is very different. It is named Gertrude Jekyll, in compliment to a lover of hardy flowers."

It was listed in T. Moore & P. Barr's *Nomenclature of Narcissus* in 1884 as Narcissus Pseudo-Narcissus Major Gertrude Jekyll, and in P. Barr's booklet on the Narcissus where it was described as one of the major varieties of the Ajax or Trumpet division, "perianth and trumpet almost uniform sulphur, very distinct." Other major varieties listed by Barr included Little Princess, which resembled Gertrude Jekyll, Shirley Hibberd, Mrs. Shirley Hibberd, Joseph Chamberlain and John Nelson. Narcissus Gertrude Jekyll appears never to have been offered

Figure 9.6   Love-in-a-Mist and Devil-in-a-Bush.

for sale by Barr's, and has vanished from cultivation.

Nigella damescena 'Miss Jekyll Blue', 'Miss Jekyll, Dark Blue', 'Miss Jekyll, White'[29]

Love-in-a-Mist and the dwarf Munstead lavender are the two plants still available that are associated with Miss Jekyll. She described the discovery of Love-in-a-Mist in a small garden and deemed it to be "of a type that I thought extremely desirable, with a double flower of just the right degree, and of an unusually fine colour. I was fortunate enough to get some seed, and have never grown any other, nor have I ever seen elsewhere any that I think can compare with it." It was described in the *Gardeners' Chronicle* in 1884, where it had been discovered in an "old fashioned Kentish garden." The vernacular names are Love-in-a-Mist and Devil-in-a-Bush, the latter of which was regarded as a misnomer. However Miss Jekyll thinks the first name belongs to the flower, and the second to the seed pod, and in *Children and Gardens* photographs by Miss Jekyll are reproduced to show the appropriateness of the names (Figure 9.6).

At the trials of Annuals at Wisley in 1909, both Barr's and Dobbie's submitted seed and the plant was described as "1½ foot, erect, branched; flowers blue, freely produced." The following year, at the trials of Miscellaneous Annuals, Barr's submitted *Nigella* "Miss Jekyll Improved" which had large cornflower blue flowers borne on long stems. It was offered for sale by Barr's in 1916 and described as "specially selected," with "long stems bearing large semi-double flowers of a lovely tender blue, nestling in a fine feathery foliage." She recommended the use of Love-in-a-Mist and other half-hardy annuals to fill the spaces in the hardy flower border for two or three years before the perennials became established.

Two forms of *Nigella* were noted by H. Avray Tipping in 1933: "A taller blue is Love-in-the-Mist. The type... produces mere grey-blue flowers. But by careful selection Gertrude Jekyll fixed a real sky blue variety and from that a deep blue has been obtained. Thus both 'Miss Jekyll Blue' and 'Miss Jekyll, Dark Blue' are now found under Nigella in the seedlists." In Carters' seed list of that year not only are these two described, but also a white form.

Paeonia decora 'Gertrude Jekyll'[30]

At the end of the nineteenth century Miss Jekyll devoted a garden to peonies. It was immediately north of the wall that backed the long flower borders and west of the spring garden. It was a triangular plot of ground, bounded by walls of different heights, but affording protection to the three classes of peonies that were grown there: tree peonies, Chinese peonies and old garden peonies. They were grown with Lent Hellebores and, as she explained, "they are agreed in their liking for deeply-worked ground with an admixture of loam and lime, for shelter and for rich feeding; and the Paeony clumps, set, as it were in picture frames of the lower-growing Hellebores, are seen to all the more advantage."

Miss Jekyll's collection of Paeony species came from Mr. Barr. "I wished to have them, not for the sake of making a collection, but in order to see which were the ones I should like best to grow as garden flowers." However many were discarded "because of the raw magenta colour of the bloom, one or two only that had this defect being reprieved on account of their handsome foliage and habit. Prominent among these was *P. decora*, with bluish foliage handsomely displayed, the whole plant looking strong and neat and well-dressed." So *P. decora*, described by Stern as "a great red-flowered paeony" was grown by Miss Jekyll

Papaver nudicaule.

Figure 9.7   Papaver nudicaule.

only for its foliage, like many other plants she used such as *Heuchera* and *Stachys*. However the cultivar 'Gertrude Jekyll' was sold by Barr's in 1898 and in 1899 as "rich crimson, single flowers, habit very graceful."

Papaver nudicaule 'Munstead Poppies' and 'Munstead White'[31]

Of the genus Papaver Miss Jekyll wrote: "poppies provide our gardens with beautiful and brilliant flowers in a great variety of form and colour, both among the kinds that are of annual lifetime only and those that are perennial." In the hardy flower border at Munstead Wood Miss Jekyll planted Oriental Poppies with Red Hot Pokers, the foliage of which covered the space left by the poppies. Elsewhere she grew drifts of Oriental Poppies, and beside them *Gypsophila paniculata* to occupy the space left by the moribund poppies, into which she led nasturtiums to cover the brown-coloured seed heads.

Another perennial poppy was *P. nudicaule* (Figure 9.7). Miss Jekyll was regarded as the best exponent of culture and display of this poppy. "By far the best results as regards growing the Iceland Poppy that we have seen are in the garden at Munstead, near Godalming, where Miss Jekyll pays special attention to this plant. Her plan is to save seeds from the white and vermilion varieties, but she always has amongst the resulting seedlings a proportion of the typical yellow kind. On the light warm soil at Munstead this poppy is thoroughly at home, and during several months from late in the spring till late in summer, it forms one of the chief features of the garden. Miss Jekyll does not confine herself to a few plants here and there, but makes large beds, consisting of the different colours mixed, the result being a most beautiful display." These are the 'Munstead Poppies' first described in 1884 (Figure 9.8). "The orange-red shades are extremely brilliant, and a number of flowering plants together light up the whole surroundings. There is also a pure white, but Miss Jekyll is inclined to regard this as being different from the yellow and orange-red forms. It is certainly less robust, but very chaste and lovely. These 'Munstead Poppies' are remarkable for their large size, being fully twice the ordinary size, a circumstance doubtless due to liberal cultivation..... A bed of Iceland Poppies seen on a sunny morning in June, with their cup-like flowers glistening like satin in the sun is one of the most charming sights a garden can afford."

Miss Jekyll grew a white form of *P. alpinum* at Munstead, which she thought was botanically

Figure 9.8   The Iceland Poppy (Papaver nudicaule) at Munstead.

inseparable from *P. nudicaule*. A white form of the Iceland Poppy, known as 'Munstead White' was grown by Miss Jekyll and was first described by William Robinson in 1883 and by W. Baylor Hartland in 1887 from his nursery at Temple Hill in Cork, Ireland. In 1883, Robinson wrote "the white (album) variety of P. nudicaule is comparatively rare, but Miss Jekyll has grown it this season at Munstead.... This is a delicately beautiful variety, the satiny white flowers of which are as plentifully produced as in the other forms of P. nudicaule." A large form of the white Iceland Poppy was obtained by Miss Jekyll from Mrs. Davidson and known at Munstead by her name. The 'Munstead Poppies' were offered for sale by Barr and Son first in 1884 and later in 1898 and 1899. In 1884 the colours were described as "various shades from pale lemon to orange scarlet, in 1899 "various shades from white to pale lemon, orange and orange-red." The description continues, "it is impossible to overestimate the value and beauty of this Poppy, which produces its graceful flowers in great abundance from May to September. For cutting no poppies are more prized." Miss Jekyll had demonstrated in the early 1880s that, contrary to expectation, these poppies could be picked and displayed: she wrote, "if the flowers are cut early every morning soon after expansion, they endure fresh and fair several days in vases indoors."

Papaver somniferum 'Munstead Cream Pink'[32]

Miss Jekyll argued that improvement of annual poppies, amongst others, could be achieved by rigid selection. She was particularly fond of the annual cornfield poppy, *Papaver rhoeas*, that had been improved by the Rev. W. Wilks, and was known after the village where he had been a priest. The Shirley Poppies superseded the French Poppies that Miss Jekyll had used in the flower border at Munstead in 1883. An insight into the procedures involved in "rigid selection" in the last quarter of the nineteenth century are given by the Rev. Wilks and no doubt Miss Jekyll practised them also:

> "In the summer of (I think) 1879 or 1880 I noticed in a wilderness corner of my garden, among a patch of field Poppies, one bloom with a narrow white edge. I marked it with a bit of wool, and saved the seed-capsule. The seed was sown the next year, and I obtained varieties with deeper white edges and some of a paler scarlet colour. Of these I marked and kept the best. The next year the flowers got still paler colours and wider white edges. In 1883, I began to see that the presence of black, either at the base of the petals or in the stamens, was a great disfigurement; I therefore pulled up and destroyed every plant having black in it, and in order to get the black out of the strain I used to get up a few minutes before the bees were about (4 a.m.); and have continued this work of selecting the most beautiful flowers for seed, and have ruthlessly destroyed all plants which showed even a symptom of black however lovely they might otherwise be."

In 1917, at the trials of annual poppies at Wisley, Messrs. Carters submitted seed of a double "flesh pink" opium poppy called 'Munstead Cream Pink'. It was described as a paeony-flowered poppy growing to 3 feet with a pink and flesh pink double flower 4½ to 5 inches. Messrs. Carters submitted it again at the trails in 1927, but on neither occasion was an award made. Miss Jekyll described the poppy in 1924 and again in 1932 shortly before she died. "Among the finest" of the Opium Poppies "is one with wide guard petals, but is otherwise fully double, but not overcrowded. The colour is a full

pink of a soft creamy quality". Seed was offered for sale by Carters in 1933 for 1/- (5p) a packet, and described as "a lovely double, selected by Miss Jekyll, and so requires no further recommendation."

Primula cortusoides Jekyllae[33]

Miss Jekyll would have obtained a description of *P. cortusoides* from *The Gardeners' Chronicle* in 1881 and from George Nicholson's *Dictionary of Gardening* of 1888, where it was described as having bright rose-coloured flowers on scapes 6" long, flowering in early summer, and with leaves on stalks. It was introduced from Siberia in 1794. However only two references have been found of this variety of *P. cortusoides*, both of them by Mr. Daniel Dewar of the Royal Botanic Gardens, Kew. During a visit to Munstead in 1885 Mr. Dewar identified and named this variety. Subsequently he described it:

> "Its origin appears to be lost in obscurity, and the name rotundifolia was, however, suggested, but as it clearly belongs to the Chinese and not to the Indian primroses, the name suggested would hardly be consistent seeing that a Primula already bears that name. Primula cortusoides var. Jekyllae seems the best name for this new Primrose, as it has affinity with P. cortusoides, though distinct both in the leaves, flowers and time of flowering. It is in full flower now (12 September 1885), and has been for the last month. It is a great acquisition to the Primulas, as the flowering time of the majority of them, and cortusoides in particular, was over a month ago. The new Jekyllae grows from 6 inches to 9 inches in height, with an upright flower scape, with from four to a dozen flowers, the petals deeper cut than the ordinary cortusoides and of a pretty rosy pink colour, not unlike P. sibirica var cashmeriana of the *Botanical Magazine*. The calyx is narrower and longer and the leaves shorter and rounder, sharply and irregularly serrated and undulated, and of a light yellowish green. The older leaves are now brown round the margins and almost orbicular".

Three sources of *Primula cortusoides* are commercially available in the U.K., but *P. cortusoides Jekyllae* has vanished.

Primula 'Munstead Bunch', 'Munstead White' and 'Bunch Primrose Sultan'[34]

Of all the flowers grown by Miss Jekyll, the primrose stayed with her longest and touched her spirit. "It must have been at about seven years of age that I first learnt to know and to love a Primrose copse. Since then more than half a century has passed, and yet each spring, ...I wander into the Primrose wood, and see the pale yellow blooms, and smell their sweetest of sweet scents, and feel the warm spring air throbbing with the quickening pulse of new life, and hear the glad notes of the birds and the burden of the bees...."

One of the first references to Miss Jekyll in *The Garden* in 1881 is in association with primroses : "Ever since the dawn of spring, when Miss Jekyll sent early little tufts of primroses from a Surrey hillside, the primrose and its varieties have been a source of pleasure." By this time she had begun to select and improve the primroses and polyanthus that by the end of the century were to bear the name "Munstead". But even before this Miss Jekyll used primroses in displays at the Royal Horticultural Society halls. In 1885 Miss Jekyll included Primulas in a display at the Royal Horticultural Society for which she received a Bronze Medal. The Chairman of the Floral Committee on this occasion was Mr Shirley Hibberd. The report in *The Gardeners' Chronicle* was, on balance, favourable: "The plan was that of an undulating bank of moss, highest at one end, backed up by drooping sprays of Solomon's Seal, and of Alexandrian Laurel (Ruscus). In the moss were studded at intervals, groups of Daffodils of various kinds, of Primula rosea, P. denticulata, Heuchera, Iris stylosa, Oxlips &c. the whole group furnished a valuable lesson to flower show exhibitors, for it was evident that such an arrangement as this might frequently be adopted with great advantage, even when, as in the Rose Shows, it is desirable to have the competing kinds side by side for comparison. So far as beauty and general interest is concerned, the advantages of this plan are beyond question, though, of course, it is not always practicable. A Bronze Medal was awarded for this group – none too high a commendation." By 1886 she had already been recognised as an expert on Primulas and was invited to join the Committee organising the Primula Conference on 20-21 April. Miss Jekyll contributed an exhibition which could be seen alongside collections from Kew, Edinburgh and Glasnevin Botanic Gardens and from nurseries such as Backhouse of York, Paul of Cheshunt and Ware of Tottenham. Individual exhibitors included Mr. Loder of Floore, Mr. Llewelyn of Penllergare, Mr. G. F. Wilson of Wisley, Miss Owen of Gorey, Mr. Poë of Riverston, Nenagh and Professor Foster of Shelford, Cambridge. In the review in *The Garden* a special extended reference was made to Miss Jekyll's collection:

"Quite distinct from the rest was a charming arrangement of yellow and white Primroses and Polyanthuses on a bank of Moss. This was done by Miss Jekyll, who displayed the same exquisite taste in grouping the tints as she did in the case of her Daffodil group. Such an arrangement showed the high value of a robust strain of border Primroses for decorative effect, and what such a superb race of Primroses must look like at home in their own cosy nooks and corners at Munstead one can imagine. Would that we could see more of these beautiful informally arranged groups at flower shows than we now do."

Thus, by 1886, Miss Jekyll had perfected "a robust strain" of primroses and polyanthus both as garden plants and for cutting. The origin of this strain is given as a cross between "a named kind, called Golden Plover, and a white one, without a name, that I found in a cottage garden." Miss Jekyll and Mr. Anthony Waterer were, apparently, working along similar lines, but Miss Jekyll owned that she preferred the strain she had developed, and "Mr. Waterer, seeing them soon after, approved of them so much that he took some to work with his own."

The primroses or polyanthus produced white and yellow flowers, and Miss Jekyll noted great variation in form, colour, habit, size of eye and shape of edge. An attempt to classify them led to sixty classes, and still the variation continued, as well as the selection: "Among the seedlings (of the big yellow and white bunch Primroses) there are always a certain number that are worthless. These are pounced upon as soon as they show their bloom, and cut up for greenery to go with the cut flowers." Three distinctive forms have been described: the 'Munstead Bunch' Primroses, 'Munstead White' and 'Bunch Primrose 'Sultan'.

In 1900 Miss Jekyll was awarded the Bronze Banksian Medal for the "most glorious group of white and yellow Polyanthus Primroses (Munstead Strain)" that she exhibited at the Royal Horticultural Society. Fifteen years earlier Plate 513 in *The Garden* displayed a painting of a bunch of Miss Jekyll's yellow primroses (Figure 9.9). In 1901 Miss Jekyll submitted to the Floral Committee of the Royal Horticultural Society a form of Bunch Primrose that she called 'Sultan'. It was described as "a remarkable plant. The rich almost intense orange gold of a single flower is very fine, while the noble truss standing on stout stems of 9 inches high or more render it at once bold and telling. It is a great

Figure 9.9   Primula 'Munstead Bunch.'

step forward in this section of early spring plants." For 'Sultan' Miss Jekyll received an Award of Merit.

In 1890 Miss Jekyll described a "useful white primrose" and offered, free of charge, plants of this primrose to the first 30 applicants. One of the first recipients of this gift was Mr. S. Arnott of Carsethorn, Dumfries, who wrote in 1891: "I can speak very favourably of the variety on account of its earliness, compact habit of growth and purity of colour... If Munstead Early White should come into the market, lovers of the 'fragrant Primrose' should secure it." In 1899 he wrote that he had "lost it a year or two ago through neglect caused by illness" but it was replaced by further stock from Miss Jekyll.

'Munstead Early White' was exhibited at the Royal Horticultural Society in 1891 and at the National Auricula and Primrose Society's meeting in the Drill Hall, James Street, London on 21 April 1891.

In 1933 Carters offered seed of the 'Munstead Strain' and wrote "we have been honoured with the distribution of Miss Jekyll's famous re-selected MUNSTEAD STRAIN, which contains every possible shade of white, cream, yellow and orange. It is splendid for bedding or for growing in woodland walks and other shady positions."

The Bunch Primroses are no longer commercially available, but until 1985 Barnhaven at Brigsteer near Kendal was selling seed of 'Harvest Yellows' that were described as "direct, unadulterated descendents of Miss Jekyll's strain" and 'Winter White', "perpetuated with the yellows from the Munsteads". There was a third, 'Chartreuse', also attributed to Miss Jekyll and described as "cream, iced with pale green or white, shading to a green centre".

Pulmonaria angustifilia azurea 'Munstead Blue'[35]

This was first described by Miss Jekyll in 1919, and was offered for sale from Munstead Wood nursery as: "the rare and true kind, pure blue flowers in spring". 'Mawson's variety' was described in 1935 as, "a very free and dwarf form, also with unspotted leaves and flowers of a beautiful full-toned blue" by Michael Vaughan, who continued his description of the pulmonarias: "better even than this is another with the same plain leaves but bigger and even bluer flowers. It is, I believe, one of the many good plants which will long keep Miss Jekyll's name in grateful memory." In 1966, Thomas concluded that "'Mawson's Variety' and 'Munstead Blue' are so near as to be practically indistinguishable." However, Chittenden (1936) had distinguished between them on the grounds that the style

protruded from the mouth of the corolla in the case of Miss Jekyll's variety. *Pulmonaria angustifolia azurea* 'Munstead Blue' was available from many plant nurseries in the early 1990s, and received the Award of Merit in 1926.

Rose 'Gertrude Jekyll'[36]

This rose was bred by David Austin Roses of Albrighton, Wolverhampton and introduced in 1986. It has been described as "a rich deep warm-pink colour, sometimes almost red in cool weather, with pretty buds not unlike those of the charming Alba 'Celestial'. The fragrance is particularly powerful – the true Damask fragrance of its Portland Rose parent."

Sedum telephium 'Munstead Red'[37]

Miss Jekyll had a place for a cultivar of the native Orpine in the garden of summer flowers at Munstead Wood. She planted drifts between Penstemon, and between Geraniums and Dahlias, where it was planted for a purpose: "in several places among the reds comes a drift of a fine garden form of the native *Sedum Telephium*. The quiet grey-green of the plant turns to a subdued chocolate-red, as the large, flat flower-head is developed. The introduction of this undergrowth of quieter related colouring greatly enhanced the quality of the livelier reds and helps to put the whole thing together." For Lindisfarne she sent 24 *Sedum telephium* to fill the central island bed in 1910 and through this "undergrowth" gladioli grew in clumps.

S. telephium 'Munstead Red' was offered for sale in the Munstead Wood catalogue and by Barr's in 1916, where it is described as "rich chocolate coloured flowers, forms a good groundwork for late summer flowers of red colouring such as Cannas, Gladioli, etc., also good for rough rocky places and wild gardening at edge of woodlands. Unlike most sedums, it does well in half shade." In Barr's 1921 catalogue a sentence has been added: "a fine variety raised by Miss Jekyll, who writes: The plant has a green foliage and rich chocolate flowers and makes a good groundwork."

It is curious that there is no reference to this cultivar in Praeger's account of the *Genus Sedum* published in 1921, but in the Royal Horticultural Society's *Dictionary of Gardening* in 1951 a "good form" of *S. telephium* is given as 'Munstead Dark Red'. It is still available from plant nurseries.

Vinca minor 'Gertrude Jekyll'[38]

This periwinkle is still widely available and received an Award of Garden Merit in 1962. It was

Figure 9.10 Viola 'Jackanapes' and 'Quaker Maid' by Gertrude Jekyll.

described on only a few occasions by Miss Jekyll, and it is probably the small white periwinkle that she collected in Italy to which the name is given. She described it as having "an abundance of small flowers and a close tufty habit of growth that give it a distinct appearance and make it a very desirable garden plant." However she grew another white periwinkle in the gardens at Munstead House: "the prettiest form of the small white Vinca we have is from a friend's garden in the south of Ireland: the shape of the flower is rather rounder and richer than in the wild kinds, as it has six petals, but sometimes more and rarely five." The friend was probably Miss C. M. Owen of Gorey, Wexford, who had visited Miss Jekyll at Munstead in 1885.

Viola x williamsii 'Jackanapes'[39]

There is no description by Miss Jekyll of the bedding pansy 'Jackanapes', but at some time before 1888 she had painted it together with a white pansy called 'Quaker Maid' (Figure 9.10). The painting by Miss Jekyll had been lost but was found at Gravetye Manor. Her sister-in-law, Dame Agnes Jekyll, gave it to Mr. E. V. Lucas after Miss Jekyll died. The origin of the name is attributed by Brickell and Sharman to Miss Jekyll's "pet monkey". Miss Jekyll's menagerie of animals comprised cats, doves, owls and a donkey called Jack. It is more likely that the pansy was named after Jack who had disgraced himself by browsing one side of a rose outside the studio door of The Hut whilst logs were being unloaded. But there was another donkey called Jack at Bramley House, and it was Jack and the pony Toby who broke loose and ran amock up the High Street in Guildford, and it was perhaps Jack's naughtiness that resulted in Georgina Duff-Gordon's fall from his back that resulted in the appellant 'Jackanapes' applied not to a monkey but to the donkey Jack, at about the time that Miss Jekyll had perfected this viola.

By the end of the nineteenth century Viola 'Jackanapes' was commercially available and at the Viola Trials at Chiswick in 1898, where plants had been submitted by Mr. Forbes, it was highly commended. It was described as having a bushy habit, was very free flowering and the flowers were small, golden yellow with dark rays, the upper petals brownish crimson edged with yellow and a continuous bloomer. The following year on 11 July it received an Award of Merit from the Floral Committee of the Royal Horticultural Society. It was also submitted at the Viola Trials at Wisley in 1913, when it was noted that it was not a strong grower, and at the Trials in 1922 when it was highly commended once again. In 1931 a form of 'Jackanapes' was sent for trials by Gayborder Nurseries and received an Award of Merit. In 1992 it was available from twenty-three nurseries in the United Kingdom.

Thirty-four plants were improved by or named after Miss Jekyll or her garden at Munstead. Of these there were two annuals, Nigella 'Miss Jekyll',

Helianthus 'Munstead Primrose', one biennial, Lunaria annua 'Munstead Purple' and two shrubs, Lavandula spica 'Munstead' and Rose 'Gertrude Jekyll', of which the latter, produced 50 years after she died, should be discounted. The balance were herbaceous perennials, of which three genera contained several cultivars; Lupinus, Papaver and Primula. Only seven of these cultivars are at present (1995) commercially available; Aquilegia, Lavandula, Nigella, Pulmonaria, Sedum, Vinca and Viola. A double flowered Lady's Smock and a white Foxglove are also available, but these are probably not the cultivars selected and fixed by Miss Jekyll. The Munstead Bunch Primroses were available until recently, and were sold as 'Harvest Yellows': plants from this stock continue to be grown in the U.K., France and the U.S.A.

Miss Jekyll was conscious that a combination of fashion and economics affected the availability of garden plants with desirable qualities from cottage gardens and by giving her cultivars to botanic gardens and to friends she tried to guard against loss. However, the loss of most of her cultivars reinforces the conclusions in C. Brickell and F. Sharman's book on The Vanishing Garden: a conservation guide to garden plants[4] and in G. T. Prance[1] that the rates of extinction of both garden plants and the wild flora of the earth are increasing. The work of the NCCPG, and particularly the committed individuals amongst whom, no doubt, Miss Jekyll would be numbered, is an essential cornerstone to sustain the diversity of garden plants. Without it our gardens will become impoverished and it will be impossible to achieve the task of the restoration of gardens of historic interest.

In addition to the work of the National Council for the Conservation of Plants and Gardens in encouraging institutions and individuals to assemble and maintain collections of plants, it would be worthwhile to make collections of plants bred and improved by individuals. A garden containing the surviving plants bred by Miss Jekyll would be unique and a welcome addition to the list of gardens of special effect: drifts of white-flowered Aquilegia within parterres formed of Lavender 'Munstead'. Beds edged with Stachys and a filling of Orpine with chocolate coloured flowers are reminiscent of the planting of the Central bed at Lindisfarne. Blue-flowered lungworts and white-flowered periwinkles could be planted together in light shade. A search could then be made for the recently-lost Honesty, and some of the other lost Jekyll plants.[40]

10

Gertrude Jekyll: a gardener ahead of her time

Richard Bisgrove

All day for two days I sit on a low stool dividing the plants. A boy feeds me with armfuls of newly dug-up plants, two men are digging-in the cooling cow-dung at the farther end, and another carries away the divided plants tray-by-tray and carefully replants them.[1]

Edwin Lutyens' biographer, Christopher Hussey, considered him to be the last architect of his era, "his romantic spirit and classical ideals unable to function in a bureaucratic democracy."[2]

In the light of the opening quotation from Gertrude Jekyll's *Wood and Garden* and many more similar descriptions and her other books and articles it is easy to think of Miss Jekyll in a similar way: old fashioned even in her own lifetime, an outstanding but outdated figure of historical significance only. Why, then, has her popularity increased so spectacularly in recent years, with exhibitions, symposia and books raising her almost to the status of a cult figure?

The simple commercial answer, that copyright of her books expired in 1982,[3] is inadequate: the publishers of new editions of her works have benefitted from, not created, the growing tide of popularity evident in the hitherto unsatisfied demand for her books. Undoubtedly, the 50th anniversary of her death provided the stimulus for bringing together the many reminders of her achievements into a single year but the steady increase of interest in her work – and especially in her gardening – up to and beyond the 150th anniversary of her birth (1993) indicates more than a fleeting fashion.

A more convincing explanation for this interest is revealed by considering her work – and particularly her writing – on four levels: plantsmanship, artistry, literary ability and philosophy.

Plantsmanship

Miss Jekyll's knowledge of plants is well known and well documented.[4] As a child she learned to match the flowers she had collected with the illustrations in Johns' *Flowers of the Field*, wearing out one copy of the book and nearly exhausting two more.[5] In 1863 she went to Greece with Charles and Mary Newton, in 1868 to Italy and in 1873 to Algeria. Her accounts of each show a keen interest in the flora, and several plants in her garden clearly served to remind her of early travels. In describing the roses in her garden at Munstead she wrote "two wild roses have for me a special interest as I collected them from their rocky home in the Island of Capri"[6]; of *Iris unguicularis*: "what a delight it was to see it in its home in the hilly wastes a mile or two inland from the town of Algiers: what a paradise it was for flower rambles."[7] Nearer home, she noted that the wall pennywort growing in her stone walls was not to be found growing within Surrey but was brought back from Cornwall.[8]

As her interest in plants grew she visited shows and nurseries to study and select. She gathered paeonies, roses, narcissi, rhododendrons. She discovered particularly good forms of *Nigella damascena*[9] (Figure 9.6) and bunch-flowered primrose (*Polyanthus*. Figure 9.9)[10], and selected her own strain of delphiniums to protect herself from the vagaries of catalogue descriptions.[11] The energetic gathering of new plants was not, however, mere botanical hoarding but an attempt to know plants as thoroughly as possible in order to be able to identify the best. Most of the new plants sent or brought to Munstead Wood served ultimately to enlarge the impressive compost heaps.[12]

Left: Figure 10.1 The Virginia Cowslip at Munstead, May 1885.

In her collecting and cultivating of plants, Miss Jekyll was extraordinary only in the time and energy which she expended. Her long experience, though, with a small team of gardeners to undertake most of the physical effort, enabled her to gather an enormous fund of information on the characteristics of plants, the type of information which most of us would now glean vicariously from the steady stream of gardening literature. *Iris stylosa* thrives in poor soil and in competition, and "the more the Alströmeria grew into it on one side and *Plumbago Larpentæ* on the other the more the brave little Iris flowered."[13] After flowering from November to April "then is the time to take up old tufts and part them, and plant afresh; the old roots will have dried into brown wires, and the new will be pushing". Other plants behave differently: "The spring Bittervetch (*Orobus vernus*) … is one of the toughest plants to divide: the mass of black root is like so much wire". A sharp cold-chisel is recommended.[14] *Primula rosea* "comes up with thick clumps of matted root that is now useless. I cut off the whole mass of old root about an inch below the crown when it can easily be divided into nice little bits for replanting."[15] "Tritomas want dividing with care; it always looks as if one could pull every crown apart, but there is a tender point at the 'collar', where they easily break off short; with these it is best to chop from below."[16] "When one is digging up plants with running roots … it never does … to give a steady haul; this is sure to end in breakage, whereas a root comes up willingly and unharmed in loosened ground to a succession of firm but gentle tugs, and one soon learns to suit the weight of the pulls to the strength of the plant, and to learn its breaking strain."[17] Although beyond the scope of the present essay, such passages also serve to illustrate the complete unity of Miss Jekyll's ideas in gardening with the other arts and crafts which she practised. A cold chisel for the bitter vetch would be ready to hand in her workshop.

For handling cut flowers too, there was a storehouse of techniques: slitting hellebore stems, sealing the sappy stems of poppies, immersing artichoke leaves and crushing woody stems to prolong vase life.[18] "I grew [*Eulalia zebrina*. syn. *Miscanthus* 'Zebrinus'] for many years before finding out that the closed and rather draggled-looking heads would open perfectly in a warm room" if the uppermost leaves were taken off.[19]

The cultivation of all these plants on poor Surrey sand required much skill and effort. For the giant lily *Cardiocrinum giganteum*, "their beds are deeply excavated, and filled to within a foot of the top with any of the vegetable rubbish of which only too much accumulates in the late autumn. Holes twelve feet across and three feet deep are convenient graves for frozen Dahlia-tops and half-hardy Annuals; a quantity of such material chopped up and trampled down close forms a good subsoil that will comfort the Lily bulbs for many a year. The upper foot of soil is of good compost and, when the young bulbs are planted, the whole is covered with some inches of dead leaves that join in with the natural woodland carpet."[20]

Her whole attitude to life was expressed in the belief that things worth doing are worth doing well[21] and when, in the case of hybrid perpetual roses, she finally admitted defeat,[22] one suspects it was due at least as much to admiration of the robust older and easier roses as to the difficulties of cultivating the new.

One of the most important Things Worth Doing was looking. "Throughout my life I have found that one of the things most worth doing was to cultivate the habit of close observation…. And I know from my own case that the will and the power to observe does not depend on the possession of keen sight. For I have sight that is both painful and inadequate; short sight of the severest kind and always progressive (my natural focus is two inches) but the little I have I try to make the most of and often find that I have observed things that have escaped strong and long-sighted people."[23] Training the eye to see colour "enables one to see pictures for oneself… and the pictures so siezed by the eye and brain are the best pictures of all for they are those of the great Artist, revealed by Him direct to the seeing eye and the receiving heart."[24]

Sometimes the benefits of this training were obvious and practical: "One can hardly go into the smallest cottage garden without learning or observing something new. It may be some two plants growing beautifully together by some happy chance, or a pretty mixed tangle of creepers, or something that one always thought must have a south wall doing better on an east one."[25] More often they served to enhance the pleasure of the observer and the admiration of the Maker. In the middle of a sombre spruce wood, for example, "I see some patches and even sheets of a vivid green."

"It is the Wood-Sorrel, tenderest and loveliest of wood plants. The white flower in the mass has a slight lilac tinge; when I look close I see that this comes from the fine veining of reddish-purple colour on the white ground… the white is not very white, but about as white as the lightest part of a pearl. The downy stalk is flesh-coloured and half-transparent, and the delicately formed calyx is painted with faint tints of dull green edged with transparent greenish buff, and is based and tipped with a reddish-purple that recalls the veining of the petals. Each of these has a touch of clear yellow on its inner base that sets off the bunch of tiny white stamens."

"The brilliant yellow-green leaf is a trefoil of three broad little hearts, each joined at its point to the upright stalk by a tiny stalklet just long enough to keep the leaf-divisions well apart. In the young foliage the leaflets are pressed down to the stalk and folded together. The mature ones also fold and sleep at night. Each little heart does not fold upon itself, but each half is closely pressed against the half of its neighbour, so that the whole looks like a blunt three-winged arrow-head or bolt-head."[26]

The Virginian cowslip (Figure 10.1) receives similarly close scrutiny of its poise and delicately changing colouring[27] and *Berberis* [*Mahonia*] *aquifolium* merits two pages[28]: "every leaf is a marvel of beautiful drawing and construction" and its flowers are "fuller of bee music than any other plant then in flower". The juniper, one of her favourite plants, is extolled for six pages.[29] Always these descriptions show a keen perception of colour, texture, form and usually a relationship to the practical crafts with which Miss Jekyll was occupied. In the juniper description cited above, "each tiny, blade-like leaf has a band of dead, palest bluish-green colour on the upper surface, edged with a narrow line of dark green slightly polished; the back of the leaf is of the same full, rather dark green, with a slight polish; it looks as if the green back had been brought up over the edge of the leaf to make the dark edging on the upper surface". In describing the birch stem: "For about two feet upward from the ground... the bark is dark in colour, and lies in thick and extremely rugged upright ridges, contrasting strongly with the smooth white skin above. Where the two join, the smooth bark is parted in upright slashes through which the dark rough bark seems to swell up reminding one forcibly of the old fifteenth century German costumes where a dark velvet is arranged to rise in crumpled folds through slashings in white satin."[30] "How endlessly beautiful is the woodland in winter! Today there is a thin mist; just enough to make a background of tender blue mystery three hundred yards away, and to show any defect in the grouping of near trees. No day could be better for deciding which trees are to come down; there is not too much at a time within sight; just one good picture full and no more."[31]

This, then, is one obvious reason for Miss Jekyll's continued popularity. Her knowledge of plants was profound. She wrote gardening books which gave the sort of information missing from the normal gardening book. All gardeners have shared something of her experience. Shared experiences encourage one to read on and the education begins. It is at this point that the long essays on juniper, or mahonia or the tiny oxalis flower - remarkably potent word-pictures – have opened the eyes of many a gardener with ostensibly superior vision.

Artistry

Miss Jekyll's knowledge of plants, their characteristics and their requirements was impressive but much more important was her skill in composition or association of plants. As with her plant knowledge this was not a skill with which she considered she had been naturally endowed. It took much patient effort before, "little by little comes the power of intelligent combination, the nearest thing we can know to the mighty force of creation."[32]

Her books, her articles and her hundreds of garden plans[33] overflow with intellegent combinations. In her own woodland at Munstead, for example, winter merged into spring with "a straggling group of *Daphne Mezereum*, with some clumps of red Lent Hellebores, and, to the front, some half-connected patches of the common Dogtooth Violet;"[34] on the edge of the wood, "St Bruno's Lily and London Pride, both at their best about the second week in June ... delicate clouds of faint pink bloom ... to set off the quite different way of growth of the Anthericum;"[35] in her scheme for gardens of special colouring, "the Grey garden is seen at its best by reaching it through the orange borders . . . making the eye eagerly desirous for the complementary colour, so that . . . suddenly turning to look into the Grey garden – the effect is surprisingly – quite astonishingly – luminous and refreshing."[36]

Other combinations were devised to provide a succession of colour in the flower border: red wallflowers planted among the emerging shoots of paeonies;[37] scarlet dahlias planted over oriental poppies;[38] poppies smothered by the later growth of gypsophila which in turn acted as a support for annual nasturtiums;[39] delphiniums covered successively by everlasting pea, *Clematis jackmanii* and *C. flammula*.[40] "It must not be supposed that they are just lumped over one another so that the under ones have their leafy growth smothered. They are always being watched and, bit by bit, the earlier growths are removed as soon as their respective plants are better without them."[41] The embroidery of the border required, and received, the same dexterity as the making of a quilt.

Whether Miss Jekyll's ability was, in fact, a natural gift or merely the result of diligent practice, it was undoubtedly greatly enhanced by her years as an art student in South Kensington. Here she was exposed to the lastest ideas on colour and colour perception, and to Ruskin's writings and lectures on art in general and on William Turner in particular. Gertrude Jekyll had a special interest in Turner and spent many hours in the National Gallery studying and copying his paintings. There are obvious parallels between Turner's use of colour to create atmosphere, a sense of place and drama and Miss Jekyll's colour planning, not least in the comparison between the distribution of colour in Turner's 'Burning of the Houses of Lords and Commons'[42] and the colour scheme of the main hardy flower border at Munstead Wood, building from cool blues and greys at either end to a "gorgeous" climax of crimson, scarlet and orange in the centre. The "astonishingly luminous and refreshing effect" of moving from the orange garden to the blue garden referred to above can also be judged by viewing Turner's glowing sunsets with his ethereal dawns.

Not all effects were planned but Miss Jekyll's trained eye seized upon and stored any chance incident: "where garden melts into copse ... is a happy intergrowth of the wild Guelder-Rose, still bearing its brilliant clusters, a strong-growing and far-clambering garden form of *Rosa arvensis*, full of red hips, Sweetbriar, and Holly – a happy tangle of red-fruited bushes, all looking as if they were trying to prove, in happy emulation, which can make the bravest show of red-berried wild-flung wreath, or bending spray, or stately spire; while at their foot the bright colour is repeated by the bending, berried heads of the wild Iris, opening like fantastic dragons' mouths, and pouring out the red bead-like seeds upon the ground."[43]

This passage, like many quoted earlier, illustrates not only her appreciation of plants and plant combinations but her very considerable ability to describe them in words.

Literary Ability

Only a privileged few were able to visit Munstead Wood or to met its creator. For most, the acquaintance with Miss Jekyll was through her dozen or so books and the more than 2000 articles which she continued to produce from soon after her first meeting with William Robinson in 1875 to her death in 1932. It was her ability as a writer, even more than her skill as a gardener, which has resulted in her lasting popularity. At first casual reading her books may appear as overstuffed with words as were the Victorian drawing-rooms she disliked with ornaments. It is very clear, however, – especially to anyone seeking to extract a brief quote from her writing – that she was as painstaking with her association of words as with her grouping of plants. It is difficult to leave out a word or to extract a sentence from its paragraph without leaving a painfully ragged tear. The "fantastic dragons' mouths" of *Iris foetidissima* exactly describes the hard, sinuously edged capsules lurching on bowed stems.

Elsewhere she wrote of adonis flowers "*comfortably seated* in dense fennel-like masses of foliage,"[44] of

Figure 10.2 'Bumps' and 'Lut-Lut.'

gypsophila "like clouds of flowery mist settled down upon the flower borders. Shooting up behind and among it is a tall salmon-coloured Gladiolus."[45] (Figure 10.2). Despising exhibition dahlias with heads too heavy for their thin stalks, she considered that, "The dahlia's first duty in life is to flaunt and swagger."[46]

Careful study of her books reveals a picture strikingly similar to her gardens: carefully planned, strictly disciplined but overflowing with incident. Even the details bear striking resemblance. Compare, for example, the soft cloudlike mist of gypsophila and the "telling contrast" of shooting gladiolus with her description of work in the primrose garden which follows on immediately from the opening quotation of this essay:

> "The still air, with only the very gentlest south-westerly breath in it, brings up the mighty boom of the great ship guns from the old seaport, thirty miles away, and the pheasants answer to the sound as they do to thunder. The early summer air is of a perfect temperature, the soft coo of the wood-dove comes down from the near wood, the nightingale sings almost overhead, but – either human happiness may never be quite complete, or else one is not philosophic enough to contemn life's lesser evils, for – oh, the midges!"[47]

The balance of harmonious background and dramatic focal point – of gypsophila and gladiolus, London Pride and anthericum, cooing doves and biting midges – is central to her designs so it is amusing, and I think not too flippant, to reflect on the nature of the partnership with Lutyens which provided the stimulus for much of her later work (Figure 10.2).

Significantly, the second paragraph of *Wood and Garden* begins "I lay no claim either to literary ability or to botanical knowledge." This is not false modesty but a genuine appreciation of the hard work required in either to achieve success. She was not, perhaps, especially gifted but long, patient effort certainly imbued her with considerable skill in both and she undoubtedly knew the value of language. After a heated argument with Edwin Lutyens over a detail of his design for Munstead Wood, she wrote, "I learnt from the architect's crushed and somewhat frightened demeanour that long words certainly have their uses, if only as engines of warfare of the nature of the battering ram."[48]

Her descriptions of the sounds of building operations at Munstead Wood,[49] of the effect of a great snowstorm on a juniper colony,[50] of a small valley near her home,[51] of a workman splitting a log,[52] are word pictures of tremendous clarity and atmosphere. Atmosphere is, in fact, a very significant word as many of her descriptions and comments show a great sensitivity to the "spirit of the place": she had a deep reverence for nature and a contemplative mind and it is for this that she will eventually be recognised as being of far greater importance than a mere arranger of plants.

Philosophy

Some aspects of Miss Jekyll's outlook on life have already been touched on. She was deeply imbued with the idea that work is good for the soul: if something is worth doing, it is worth doing well. She was convinced, like other disciples of Ruskin, of the unity of art and craft. "The size of a garden has very little to do with its merit.... It is the size of [the owner's] heart and brain and goodwill that will make his garden either delightful or dull."[53] "It is not the paint that makes the picture but the brain and heart and hand of the man that uses it."[54]

The physical world was the gift of a generous Creator and, as such, was to be revered in its every detail. Sometimes her appreciation was almost mystical: "when in our hills a moss-grown thorn or juniper dies of old age the woodbine will give it a glorious burial covering the hoary branches with a freshness of young life and a generous and gladly-given wreath of sweetest bloom."[55]

Given such an attitude of life and acute awareness, each small action takes on a significance beyond common comprehension.

"What scent is so delicate as woodruff leaves? They are almost sweeter when dried, each little whorl by itself with the stalk cut away closely above and below. It is a pleasant surprise to come upon these fragrant little stars between the leaves of a book, reviving memories of rambles in Bavarian Woodlands."[56]

"Further up the Fern walk ... growing close to the ground in a tuft of dark-green moss, is an interesting plant – *Goodyera repens,* a terrestrial Orchid. One might easily pass it by, for its curiously white-veined leaves are half hidden in the moss, and its spike of pale greenish-white flower is not conspicuous; but, knowing it is there, I never pass without kneeling down, both to admire its beauty and also to ensure its well-being by a careful removal of a little of the deep moss here and there where it threatens too close an invasion:"[57] observation, admiration and cultivation in a single sentence.

Pages 98-9 of *Wood and Garden* describe the making of fern pegs from bracken, for layering carnations. After selecting, cutting and stacking the fronds in neat ridges: "Four cuts with a knife make a peg, and each frond makes three pegs in about fifteen seconds. With the fronds laid straight and handy it goes almost rhythmically, then each group of three pegs is thrown into the basket, where they clash on to the others with a hard ringing sound."

Clearly Miss Jekyll appreciated her garden and her surroundings in an extraordinarily perceptive way, and there is much pleasure to be had by borrowing from her experience when reading her books. To appreciate the full significance of her writing and the philosophy expressed therein, though, it is necessary to consider another source of inspiration, one expressed most compactly in the Epilogue of J. J. O. Simonds' *Landscape Architecture*[58] from which the following paragraph is condensed:

> "Looking back I feel extraordinarily lucky to have been in the Harvard School of Design during 1936-9 in the tumultuous years of the rebellion [in the battle of Bauhaus versus Beaux Arts]. A fervor almost religious in quality seemed to sweep the school. We determined we must seek a new philosophy. I set out once again with a fellow student to wander in search of fundamentals through Japan, Korea, China, Burma, Bali, India and up into Tibet. In the contemplative attitude of Buddhist monks we would sit for hours absorbed in the qualities of a simple courtyard space. We noted with fascination the relationship of sensitive landscape planning to the arc of the sun, the direction and force of the wind and topographical forms. Years later [while lying quietly in an American forest] I recalled the same sensation as when I had moved along the wooden-slatted promenade above the courtyard garden of the Ryoan-ji, with its beautifully spaced stone composition in an abstract panel of raked sand simulating the sea. All at once it came to me: what must count is not primarily the planned approach, the designed shapes, spaces and forms. What counts is the experience. The older, wiser cultures of the Orient have shown us that, because of the dynamic nature of their philosophies, the Taoist and Zen conceptions of perfection lay more stress upon the process through which perfection is sought than upon perfection itself."

This oriental example of carefully simplified, symbolic landscapes and the Bauhaus cry for simpler forms in building form the twin bases of modern architecture and landscape architecture. Particularly in California, where both the climate and the influence of a large Japanese population were powerful factors, a new style of house and garden emerged: simple in content, irregularly geometrical in form, "organically" growing from the site and often borrowing heavily from the Japanese vocabulary of gravel, stone, sculpture and very restrained "sculpturesque" planting. The "modern movement" or "international style" has spread in the half-century since its inception to all industrialised countries and, although in Europe the severe geometry of the Bauhaus has been more in evidence than the freer forms inspired by Japanese example, it has been interesting to watch the steady encroachment of the orient even into the hallowed grounds of the Chelsea Flower Show: bonsai in 1963, synthetic stone lanterns in 1981 and a fully fledged miniaturised rock-garden, complete with viewing pavilion, in 1983. Of course the influence is not confined to gardens: every successful "pop-star" seems to find it necessary to flee to the East, most conveniently to India, to seek a guru, while two major English houses (Mentmore Towers and Croome Court) now serve as meditative centres for those who cannot afford to travel so far and William Mason's contemplative flower garden at Nuneham is now part of the Global Retreat Centre of Brahma Kumaris University.

In England, gardens of the international style exist but the modern wave might be said to have broken its back on our shores. The pure geometry evident in John Brookes' *Room Outside* (Thames & Hudson, 1969) has been tempered by more substantial and more varied planting in his *Improve Your Lot* (Heinemann, 1977) and the effect of many borders illustrated in the latter is remarkably similar to that found in the pages of Jekyll and Weaver's *Gardens for Small Country Houses* (Country Life, 1912). Why should this be?

To anyone aware of the characteristics of the oriental garden, the close analogy between the philosophy expressed in them and in Gertrude Jekyll's writing is very evident. The quotations in this essay have been chosen to highlight the similarity but they are by no means atypical. It is interesting, therefore, to consider her own views on oriental art:

> "The elaborate system of flower arrangement practised by the Japanese shows firstly, and throughout, a recognition of beauty of line as the supreme law.... It has become a fashion to attempt to imitate this system; and among some successes at the hands of those who cannot be content with anything short of "good drawing" there are many absurd failures of those to whom it is nothing but sticking flowers and branches upright in shallow vessels.... I cannot think it will ever supersede, or even seriously compete

with, the loose and free ways of using our familiar garden flowers... in our case one whole group of motives that is absorbingly present to the mind of the Japanese decorator is absent, namely, those that have to do with traditional law and symbolism. For, happily, we can pick a bunch of Primroses in the wood and put it in water without having to consider whether we have done it in such a way as to suggest a ship coming home or a matrimonial engagement in contemplation. I do not say this in any spirit of derision, for I gladly acknowledge how much we may learn from the Japanese in the way they insist on beauty of line; but, at the same time, I cannot but rejoice that we are not hampered by other considerations than those that lead us to combine and place our flowers so as to be beautiful in themselves and fitting for our rooms."[59]

This was written in 1901, twenty-two years before Gropius' Bauhaus in Dessau and thirty-five years before Simonds arrived at Harvard. Clearly, Miss Jekyll was aware of the importance of Japanese art, and of the traditions on which it was founded, long before Simonds was born. Equally clearly, she was aware of the folly of borrowing too slavishly from other cultures.

The bowing down to a tiny terrestrial orchid, her awareness of the sound of bracken-pegs thrown in a basket, her recognition of the renewal of life as a honeysuckle wreathed a dead juniper have all the solemnity and symbolism of a tea ceremony, the raking of sand in Ryoan-ji or the contemplation of the full moon shining on almond blossom. Her acute perception of nature, the poetry with which she described what she saw and her feeling for the inseparability of art, life and religion are exactly comparable with the oriental poet/philosopher/gardener. Indeed there was even a Thunder House built into the garden wall at Munstead Wood so Miss Jekyll could watch the storms playing over the Surrey Hills (Figure 10.3).

But there were no pagodas or lanterns at Munstead, no rice-paper shoji or stepping stones arranged to represent a flight of doves. The Thunder House was built of good Surrey sandstone and in the architectural tradition of the district.

Miss Jekyll was, of course, not alone in her day in experiencing and expressing reverence for the natural world. She was one of many sensitive artist-craftsmen who collectively formed the Arts and Crafts movement. Because she worked in the garden, however, her example has a more immediate appeal than that of her contemporaries working in paints or stained glass or words alone. More than anyone else she has shown that the Arts and Crafts ideals were not merely harking backward to a golden mediaeval age: they are equally appropriate in a post-industrial society wearied by tumultuous progress and worried by the thought of man as a redundant species. Few of us can aspire to the fifteen acres and seven gardeners which Miss Jekyll found insufficient but the point is made that striving towards perfection is more important and more satisfying than achieving it, that being part of the miracle of creation is sufficient reason for being alive. Whether our estate

Figure 10.3   The Thunder House, Munstead Wood.

is a window box[60] or a few stone steps[61] there is reason to be grateful.

Miss Jekyll is already renowned for her profound knowledge of plants, for her skill in grouping them and for her ability to describe the results in words but her most durable contribution will surely be in showing that it is possible to learn from four thousand years of oriental "living-within-nature" in a completely English way. Her writing encapsulates a philosophy of life even more relevant now than when it was written eighty years ago.

Clearly, she was a gardener ahead of her time.

11

Gertrude Jekyll: a versatile photographer

Heather Angel

The reason that Gertrude Jekyll was such a multi-talented woman must, in no small way, be attributable to her ability to observe details which many others might otherwise have passed over. Her perceptive eye, enhanced by a training as an artist, is obvious from her description of how the interplay of light and shadow on tree trunks affected their colour during a ramble through a wood one April:[1]

"Where the sun catches the .... trunks it lights them in a sharp line, leaving the rest warmly dark; .... where the trees stand in shade the trunks are of a cool grey that is almost blue ..... The trunks seen .... against the sunlight look a pale greenish-brown, lighter than the shadow they cast .... the varying colourings of the trees .... offer such valuable lessons in training the eye to see the colour of objects as it appears to be; .... any one who has never gone through this kind of training could scarcely believe the difference it makes in the degree of enjoyment of .... our beautiful world. .... it enables one .... to see pictures for oneself, not merely to see objects.

It is not .... that people are unobservant, but .... (lacking) the necessary training they cannot see .... what is seen by the artist, ... only pictures .... (with) positive colour, such as a brilliant sunset, ... or a field of poppies .... To these untrained eyes .... Nature's pictorial moods .... can only be enjoyed or understood .... in the form of a painted picture by the artist who understands Nature's speech and can act as her interpreter."

This passage gives us a clear insight to the person who had the ability to select memorable images from the plethora of visual stimuli which surround us. Indeed, Gertrude Jekyll's ability to perceive at close range was fundamental to the multifarious disciplines which she pursued and perfected.

"Throughout my life I have found that one of the things most worth doing was to cultivate the habit of close observation .... the more it is exercised the easier it becomes, till it is so much part of oneself that one may observe almost critically and hardly be aware of it .... I know from my own case that the will and the power to observe does not depend on the possession of keen sight. For I have sight that is both painful and inadequate; short sight of the severest kind and always progressive (my natural focus is two inches); but the little I have I try to make the most of and often find that I have observed things that have escaped strong and long-sighted people."[2]

What is most remarkable is that she retained this observant eye throughout her life, even though she suffered from acute myopia. Maybe the reason lay in her "clear, logical brain"[3] coupled with an inquisitive mind. For example, the account of her discovery of the sensitive stamens in common barberry (*Berberis*) flowers, which she detested because of their smell:- "if ... touched ... – the slightest tickle with the end of a blade of grass is enough – they fly together to the *pistil*. It is amusing to see a flower make some quick movement."[4]

At the age of forty-one, when her eyesight was failing and she no longer painted landscapes to the extent she had done, Gertrude Jekyll took up photography. Once she had mastered the art, she was able to use her photographs as a visual notebook, for illustrating her books and articles on garden design topics as well as for communicating with her clients. Unlike the three-dimensional landscape, a two-dimensional print could be minutely studied at leisure using, if necessary, a magnifying glass.

Her skills as an artist, embroiderer, gardener, garden designer and author have been well documented, and even though a collection of copy photographs selected from six of her photo-albums now held in the College of Environmental Design Documents Collection, University of California, Berkeley, has been published,[5] they relate to her role as a designer rather than to her standing as a photographer. The albums alone contain 2151 images, some of which were published in her books and others were engraved and published in *The Garden* and several editions of *The English Flower Garden* by William Robinson. In addition there are three privately owned scrapbooks containing photographs, prints and articles on Munstead Wood. The latter "include paste-ups of articles written for *Gardening Illustrated* and *Country Life* ....."[6] with photos. However, an inscription notes the photographs which appear in these magazines were taken by the editor, Herbert Cowley. The earliest date which appears in the Berkeley albums is 25th March 1885 and the last recorded date is 19th August 1914.[7] If the ratio of pictures in these albums are indicative of her output generally, she was much more productive in the early years: almost 900 photographs were taken during the period 1885-8; whereas about 1200 pictures were amassed during the much longer period 1888-1914.[8] In the oldest albums, Gertrude Jekyll sometimes overlaid repeat prints of the same subject on top of one another. Maybe she did this to serve as a reminder of a progressive sequence as she advanced her camera technique.

Unfortunately, we glean virtually nothing about Gertrude Jekyll's photography or the equipment she used in any of her own books; however, her nephew Francis Jekyll refers briefly to her photography at Munstead House in the biography he wrote about Gertrude Jekyll.[9] "The year 1885 saw her introduction to the art of photography, then in its infancy. This soon became an absorbing interest, and, as usual, the entire process was mastered from start to finish; sinks and dark-rooms were fitted up at home, and the long series of tree and flower studies, farm buildings, and old Surrey characters which were to figure in her books began to issue from the 'shop'. Some of her earliest efforts may be seen in the illustrations to Mr Robinson's books and papers, including the *English Flower Garden*, already a classic, which reappeared every few years in a new and enlarged edition. An entry for July, 'Phot. at 4am', shows the spirit of the true enthusiast."

Photography was not, in fact, such a novel art as Francis Jekyll would lead us to believe since many years before Gertrude Jekyll took up photography, two ladies had produced memorable photographic images, one by using conventional cameras and the other without any camera at all. Julia Margaret Cameron (1815-1879),[10] like Gertrude Jekyll, turned to photography in middle age when she produced striking (some deliberately soft focus) portraits, which have been much published since her death. Until quite recently[11], Anna Atkins' (1799-1871) exquisite cyanotype (blueprint) studies (using a non-silver photographic printing process invented by Sir John Herschel in 1842) of botanical specimens (notably seaweeds) were virtually unknown and unappreciated. Yet, "she produced, with her own hands, the first published book printed and illustrated by photography"[12] in 1843, a year before the first part of Fox Talbot's classic book *The Pencil of Nature*[13] appeared. The botanical specimens were pressed and laid on the specially chemically-coated paper, exposed to the light and washed to reveal the striking white negative images against a stunning blue background.

Gertrude's younger brother Herbert Jekyll (1846-1932) was an amateur photographer, and he may well have showed her the basic rudiments of developing and printing but, no doubt Gertrude learnt much by her own trial and error. She certainly had helpful criticism from the person – possibly Herbert – who scribbled the comments "Keep the Camera level. Use rising front. Expose less. More Pyro. More bromide."[14] on the reverse of a print in her photo-albums held by the University of California.

In any event, she must have quickly mastered the chemical processes (not always grasped by people with an artistic flair) because in the very same year as she embarked on her photography, Gertrude Jekyll had a picture taken in June published the following month in William Robinson's journal *The Garden*[15] and she was one of four joint winners in a competition run by this journal[16] with the result published in October 1885. Her prize-winning pictures showed cedar-planted lawns at Peper Harow near Godalming.

Unlike Julia Margaret Cameron and Anna Atkins, who concentrated on a single photographic genre, Gertrude Jekyll was more versatile in the subjects she chose to record. They ranged from local landscapes, tree roots, county cameos, cottage ornaments, tools and old furniture to portraits, garden designs, plants, children and her beloved cats.

Figure 11.1 'Tabby and the Photograph basket.'

Her friend and collaborator, Sir Edwin Lutyens, refers to "many a voyage of discovery throughout Surrey and Sussex" with Miss Jekyll in her pony-cart[17], which she must have loaded up with camera and tripod as we would a car today. A photograph in her book *Children and Gardens* 'Tabby and the Photograph basket'[18] (Figure 11.1) is the only clue we have that she used a basket as her gadget bag because, although she repeatedly used shallow baskets as props for photographing her cats, this one is far too deep for this purpose.

Whether she used from the outset the camera left at Munstead Wood in 1932 when she died, we can only surmise. This was a Collins with a Dallmeyer lens. Charles G. Collins made six sizes of cameras from 1858 to 1909[19] and Miss Jekyll probably used a whole (dry) plate ($6^1/_2$" x $8^1/_2$") model as the largest dimensions of her original prints measure 6" x 8" (now held by the Surrey Local Studies Library in Guildford), used for publication in her book *Old West Surrey* suggest that she made same size prints, slightly cropped from the whole plate negatives. The camera conveniently came complete with a base into which the tripod legs were fitted.

The camera was used by focusing the image on a ground glass screen. It is interesting to ponder how Gertrude Jekyll managed to focus the camera; no doubt she used a magnifier to check the image on the screen, and it is possible that her camera may have been fitted with focusing stops as some were at that time.

From the time her first photograph was published as an engraving in 1885, many more appeared as engravings and later as photographic plates in both gardening journals and books. But it was not until 1899 that her first book, *Wood and Garden*, was published entirely illustrated with her own photographs. "The greater part of the photographs from which the illustrations have been prepared were done on my own ground – a space of some fifteen acres."[20] Even though she had by this time been photographing for fourteen years she was, none the less, quite modest about her photographic capabilities: "Some of them, owing to my want of technical ability as a photographer, were very weak, and have only been rendered available by the skill of the reproducer...."[21]

Figure 11.3   'Tabby takes possession.'

It is tragic we have so little factual information about Gertrude Jekyll's equipment and techniques, but even so, much can be gleaned by studying her published photographs. For the purpose of this essay, reference has been made, wherever possible, to original editions of her books since much has been lost in the more recent reproductions in fascimile editions.

Analysis of the 71 photographs which appear in *Wood and Garden* reveals the majority (68%) are of flowering plants in her own garden at Munstead Wood. In addition, there are ten plates of plants in the landscape, four of cut flowers against a uni-toned background and ten miscellaneous subjects, including people and garden buildings.

One photograph in this collection stands out above all others; this is 'Scotch firs thrown on to Frozen Water by Snowstorm.'[22] In this vertical composition, a beautiful ethereal quality of successive fainter tones receding behind an upright pine (not, in fact, a fir, *Abies*, but Scotch Pine, *Pinus sylvestris*) to the left of the frame has been captured (Figure 11.2).

Initially, it comes as something of a surprise to find no less than six photographs of wild juniper — some looking decidedly tatty after a severe snowstorm in late December 1886 — in the same book. However, when the text is read adjacent to the pictures of the damaged junipers, it is obvious that Gertrude Jekyll was quite devastated: "The great wild Junipers were the pride of our stretch of heathy waste just beyond the garden and the scene of desolation was truly piteous....."[23] This is interesting since, quoting from Elwes and Henry[3] an observation made in the early part of this century cited by Salmon in his *Flora of Surrey*[24] states: "In .... Juniper Valley 3 m E. of Godalming the Juniper attains a greater size than I have seen anywhere else in a state of nature in Great Britain. The trees .... attain 15 to 30 ft. in height". There is no trace whatsoever of a single juniper nowadays as the greensand area around Juniper Valley has been cleared of scrub and replanted with conifers. Thus, although Miss Jekyll's juniper pictures are not only striking photographs, they are of great historic interest as part of the demise of Surrey's native flora.

While many of Gertrude Jekyll's garden plant studies in *Wood and Garden* are straight forward portraits, her artistic eye framed two gems of flower studies in a woodland setting in which the flowers occupy a very small area of each picture. A horizontal study 'Daffodils in the Copse'[25] depicts the bulbs planted in hollows where one track passes beside another among birch trees, while a vertical study 'Trillium in the Wild Garden'[26] shows clumps of these woodland flowers in the lower third of the picture with birches behind.

It is surprising that the same eyes which saw and took these studies and the sensitive firs (pines) in snow should have been content to have a creased cloth as a backdrop to 'Late single tulips, breeders and Bybloemen:'[27] but maybe this was not detected as a result of her myopia?

She invariably used props when photographing children and cats; often baskets and occasionally a barrow. Two pictures of her cat, Tabby, suggest a progression in her approach to 'cats in baskets' photography. One is no more than a record of a cat asleep in a Munstead basket (designed by Gertrude Jekyll for gathering cut flowers, made locally and advertised for sale in *The Garden* magazine in 1901. A picture of an empty basket appears in one of the Berkeley photo-albums[28]) taken probably as first seen ('Tabby in the basket'[29]); while the other ('Tabby takes possession'[30]) may have been posed as the cat's head is now erect. The latter (Figure 11.3) is a charming composition of a cat also lying in a Munstead basket with hydrangea blooms at one end spilling onto the lawn in front of a wall festooned with fig leaves, which would be rated highly as photographic art today.

There are other delightful studies of children in the garden. Dorothea Strachey, aged six, appears in 'Gathering fir cones'[31] sitting on the ground to one side of a pine tree with a basket partially filled with cones. 'Rose leaves for pot pourri' shows Miss Jekyll's two nieces, Barbara and Pamela Jekyll, sitting on a terrace besides blooming lilies, with their skirts full of rose petals ready to add to the pile for drying. In both these photos considerable care and thought has been taken in framing the subjects and their situations, thereby producing unforgettable pictures.

But the most memorable of all her child studies is a picture of a child and a kitten entitled 'Dorothea and Dinah'[32] (Figure 11.4). This shows Dorothea Strachey in the Dutch Garden at Orchards, a Lutyens/Jekyll collaboration "a short mile away" from Munstead Wood, sitting on a semi-circular step with a floral garland over her shoulder and a

Figure 11.4 'Dorothea and Dinah.'

black kitten nearby. The curvaceous lines of the steps with their shallow risers are repeated with the fall of the floral garland and the curving pose of the girl's body, framed on either side by roses (a breeze has caused a slight blurring of the taller stems), creating a charming study in a summer garden, capturing a moment when neither the child nor the kitten were moving.

Many of Miss Jekyll's earlier portraits of people appear rather stiff, but it must be remembered that when she began her photography in 1885, the slow speed of the photosensitive plates then available would have necessitated an exposure of around 1 second in sunlight; whereas by the turn of the century increased speed of the film plates would have allowed an exposure of 1/100 second in sunlight.[33]

The ability to freeze motion was clearly a problem when Gertrude Jekyll encountered moving subjects. For example the picture of a man 'Cutting heath turf' on page 203 of *Old West Surrey* shows his head as blurred. She writes about the actions of her cat, Blackie, whenever he encountered catmint: "He seems to go quite crazy with delight, jumps straight up in the air and comes down flop in the middle, dances in it and twists about. ...... I wish I could have photographed him but my camera is not quick enough."[34] Beside this text is a plate of a sharp but static 'Tabby in the catmint'. However, a picture of Tabby in catmint with a blurred head survives in her photo-albums and was reproduced many years after she died[35] – although she herself clearly felt it was not worthy of publication.

Miss Jekyll's reservation about the quality of her photographs written in the preface of *Wood and Garden* is particularly illuminating when the complete set of original prints (over 300) which appeared in her book *Old West Surrey*[36] are examined. Each one is mounted on card with a printed acquisition label stating it was taken prior to 1904 (the year the book was published) and donated (to Croydon Local Studies Library) by Miss G. Jekyll in April 1908. These pictures became incorporated into the Photographic Survey and Record of Surrey, and were transferred to the Surrey Local Studies Library in Guildford in 1989.

Many of the prints have been retouched – some quite extensively – and when these are compared side by side with the plates in the first edition there is no question these were the actual prints used for this publication.

For example, 'An Old Cottage at Elstead' on page 6 has the sky painted over in white and the background to the right side of the white pinafore, worn by the person standing in the doorway,

Figure 11.5 'A Cottager's border of China Asters.'

darkened. Patches of paper have been stuck onto the lower corners of the print but this part of the picture has been cropped for reproduction in the book.

More extensive retouching has been done to 'A Cottager's border of China asters' which appears on page 275 and is reproduced here (Figure 11.5). Dark lines radiating out from the centre of the pale flower heads on the right and the rear of the patch can be detected, even in the fascimile edition, by using a magnifying glass. Conversely, all the roses around the window in 'Banksian rose around a cottage window' (Figure 11.6) seen as the lower plate on page 273, have been lightened to make them stand out more clearly from the foliage. The plant in the windows has been made more conspicuous by darkening the background around it.

Interestingly enough, the plant is identical to the one captioned 'The Window Plant' (Figure 11.7) on page 271. The lady, Mrs. Joy, tying up the plant has had her lips darkened in addition to every one of the many spots on her dress. How much simpler it would have been to ask the sitter to change her dress!

The pair of 'Eighteenth Century Stoneware Mugs' (Figure 11.8) printed above on page 143, looks as though they have been photographed against a white backcloth. In fact, they were taken against a dark brick wall and after the print was made, the edge of the mugs was outlined in white, so they could be reproduced as cut-outs in the plate. A similar treatment could have eliminated the creased cloth behind the tulips which appeared five years previously in *Wood and Garden*, but maybe Gertrude Jekyll had not considered retouching at this time?

Chains on the posts on either side of the stile in 'The Five-Barred Gate' have been obliterated for publication on page 28 of *Old West Surrey*. However, this same composition appears elsewhere[37] entitled 'Stile & Gate Hascombe Road' with the chains! This proves at least two prints were made of this subject and it is likely that the untouched one contained in Miss Jekyll's photo-album was not intended for publication.

These examples – plus many more – confirm Gertrude Jekyll's own reservations about the quality of many prints (as they emerged from the darkroom) for reproduction purposes. In many cases the retouching is quite crude, although it has been done by someone with an eye for effectively enhancing the contrast between similar toned subjects or, in some cases, reducing the contrast of light-toned background structures. While it is obvious that the retouching was not done by a professional in this field, we can only surmise whether some of this work was carried out by Miss Jekyll herself. Her artist's eye would have detected any deficiencies in contrast and her myopia may explain the unrefined retouching.

It is doubtful whether anyone else would have bothered with a trivial detail such as darkening the band on the hat as appears in 'The White Frock' on page 299. The plate entitled 'The King's Arms' on page 288 has been made from a horizontal print with the sky whitened out to about three-quarters of the way across the print. The remainder which

Figure 11.6 'Banksian Rose around a cottage window.'

Figure 11.7 *'The Window Plant.'*

has been left grey has been cropped out of the plate in the book. So, whoever did the retouching either knew the complete print was not going to be reproduced or else the blockmaker had no option but to crop the composition because the retouching was incomplete.

It is interesting that the retouching was done on the prints and not on the negative plates when it would have been possible to make repeat identical prints.

Apparently the appearance of the prints in Gertrude Jekyll's photo notebooks improved around 1901[38] when she had her first book published by *County Life* which suggests the publisher had the prints professionally made from her own negatives. Now this date is three years prior to the publication of *Old West Surrey* – by her original publisher Longmans Green & Co., who were presumably content for Miss Jekyll to do her own printing.

Not withstanding their technical quality, Gertrude Jekyll appreciated only too well the educational value of photographs. "..'I like a book with pictures' is not only an idle speech of those who open a book in order to enjoy the trivial intellectual tickling of the thing actually represented; but the illustrations ..... present aspects of things beautiful, or of matters desirable for practice, much more vividly than can be done by the unpictured text."[39]

Photographs are an invaluable tool in garden design.[40] Not only can they be used to aid the identification of plants, but also as an *aide memoire* to associated planting and as a means of making observations about the modification of existing planting schemes to clients. For gardens she was unable to visit, Gertrude Jekyll often relied on photographs to make critical observations about aspects of garden design.[41] "I venture to feel sure (the owners) will perceive my intention ..... as the suggestion of alternatives of treatment .... as might ..... be desirable in places presenting analogous conditions."[42]

Four years after Ursula, the second daughter of Edwin Lutyens, married Lord Ridley in 1924 she asked Gertrude Jekyll to design two gardens at Blagdon in Northumberland. Preliminary plans for one of these, the Quarry, were exchanged between Lady Ridley and Miss Jekyll.[43] Later Lady Ridley took photographs of this garden specifically to send to Gertrude Jekyll with her own thoughts on planting ideas. Gertrude Jekyll replied by adding her comments to the back of each print and although her sight was fading fast she was still able to interpret photographs. It makes for some interesting reading.[44] On the back of *Photograph 11* Lady Ridley (**LR**) writes: "Just showing steps up & out of quarry. Suitable bank on left for primroses or any low growing plant." **GJ**: "There are plants that would be better here than primroses – drifts of fritillary Fritillaria meleagris for spring & Colchicum autumnale for autumn."

Photograph 8 (of the quarry wall) **LR**: "Showing face of wall very suitable for any small rock plants. Would you let the ivy grow again on the bank on the top of the wall – where the earth is now rather bare?" **GJ**: "Certainly a place for some rock plants. Pile up the natural stones into a sort of small moraine – a ground work of the natural soil and grit; the stones half buried but all pointing one way as if they had slithered down. Don't abolish the ivy altogether but let it grow moderately; partly veiling the top edge of the cliff."

Photograph 9 **LR**: "Bits of this cliff are very damp – one might plant dwarf irises in the shelves & crevices." **GJ**: "Hardly the place for dwarf irises. Better for some of the good saxifrages, S. umbrosum (London Pride) perhaps best of all, or some of the white plumed kinds such as S. pyrimidalis, S. longifolia, S. cotyledon, ... There is also a beautiful short growing kind with white flowers S. Wallacia.

This would also bear a little moraine in that middle cavity.

The ivy is very good here – just right. Also at the foot of the scarp some of the mossy saxifrages would do well – S. Decopius with red flowers and S. Muscoides with white flowers." Despite her poor vision Miss Jekyll was even able to correct the identification of some of the trees in the Quarry garden using the photographs she received from Lady Ridley.[45]

Fortunately, an early colour photographic process became available in the early part of this century, so we can appreciate Gertrude Jekyll's own garden in its heyday – in colour. The autochrome plate was invented by the Lumière brothers (Auguste and Louis) in 1903 and marketed in 1907. Each plate was covered with minute grains of starch that had been dyed orange, green, and violet, in equal proportions and mixed so that the colours were evenly distributed before the plate was infilled with powdered carbon coated with emulsion. The pictures were taken using a special yellow filter. After the negative had been developed, it was reversed into a positive transparency to reveal the original colours. The autochromes with their fine grain emulsions were popular with amateur photographers, but their main disadvantage was the very slow speed. This meant that even on a sunny day, a view required an exposure of 1-2 seconds at f8 and so could only be contemplated on bright, windless days.

The autochromes (See p.6 and p.83, and Figures 7.7, 7.8, 7.9, 7.10, 7.18, 7.19 & 7.23) taken in Gertrude Jekyll's garden at Munstead Wood have been credited to her,[46] but if that is correct it is strange that she failed to make any mention about the obvious benefit of referring to reproductions of her colour schemes *in colour*. We know the last entry in the Berkeley photo-albums for her monochrome prints was made in August 1914 when she was 70 and in all probability this marked the end of her photographic period.

How then can we rate Gertrude Jekyll as a photographer? That she was accomplished, there can be no doubt, but we must remember that she was very preoccupied with her garden designs and her writing. While these activities no doubt fuelled her with ideas for photography, she could indulge only a small part of her time with a camera or working in the darkroom. She saw and used her pictures very much as a tool to illustrate her books and articles, and as a visual notebook, not as photographic art which would appeal in isolation. Having said that, there are some images which would stand up to being marketed today as photographic prints, notably: 'Scotch firs thrown on to Frozen Water by Snowstorm'[47] and 'Dorothea and Dinah.'[48]

Historically, her photographs of local scenes and traditions are a valuable record of life in rural Surrey around the turn of the century. In addition, the copious photographic record of her garden at Munstead Wood – throughout all the seasons and through the years – greatly embellishes her written descriptions of this celebrated garden.

In conclusion, our appreciation of Gertrude Jekyll's vision of late Victorian and Edwardian England is greatly enhanced when seen through her photographs, which in turn provide another facet for us to gain a better insight to the mind of this amazingly gifted and productive woman. It is worth pondering whether we would have enjoyed this legacy of her time if she had been blessed with better sight and not been forced to abandon her paintbrush for the camera? Nevertheless, as we have seen, Miss Jekyll was acutely aware that photographs greatly enhanced the appeal of her books and so she no doubt would have taken up photography for this purpose, sooner or later.

Figure 11.8 'Eighteenth Century Stoneware Mugs.'

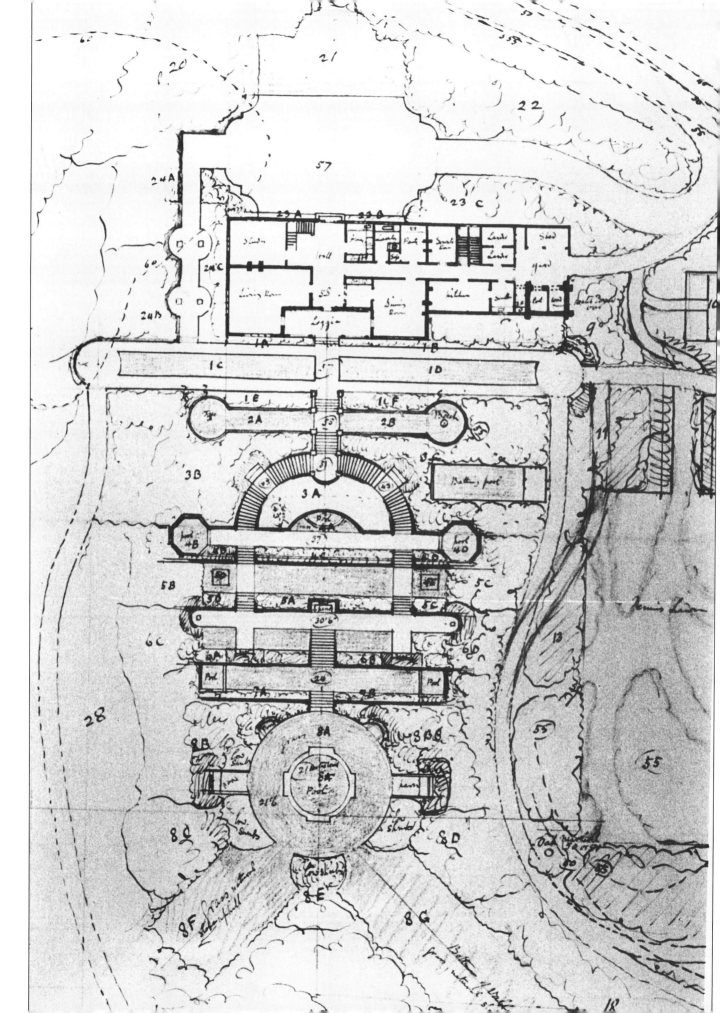

12

Gertrude Jekyll's American gardens

Susan E. Schnare and Rudy J. Favretti

Early in the twentieth century, Gertrude Jekyll's books became popular in North America;[1] and her ideas were widely accepted, especially those relating to colour, texture, massing and wild gardens and rock gardens. Several American authors, for example Mrs. Francis King, Helena Rutherford Ely and Louise Beebe Wilder, applied her ideas to North American climates, and wrote popular books about their own gardens.[1] It was never forgotten, though, that Miss Jekyll was the source of their inspiration. As Mrs. Francis King, who referred to Gertrude Jekyll as "my own adored preceptress,"[2] said, "If we take up such a book as Miss Jekyll's *Garden Ornament* and turn to the marvelous illustrations under the heading 'Steps and Balustrades' we need not make any serious mistakes."[3]

Americans chose Miss Jekyll as their gardening idol and plagued her with their pilgrimages to Munstead Wood and requests to meet her. As she wrote in a letter to a friend:

> "if I only knew who were the genuine applicants, I would still make exceptions. You can have no idea what I have suffered from Americans, Germans and journalists."[4]

Francis Jekyll concluded the biography of his aunt with a list of gardens that she had designed.[5] Amongst these are three that were designed for clients in the United States:

1914 ELMHURST, Ohio. Mr. Glendinning B. Groesbeck

1925 COTSWOLD COTTAGE, Greenwich, Conn. Mr. Stanley Resor

1926 OLD GLEBE HOUSE, Woodbury, Conn. Miss. A. B. Jennings

Each of the three gardens was of a completely different type. The garden for the Groesbecks was to be an architectural garden spanning several acres of steep slope with terraces, steps, pools, and many carefully planned herbaceous perennial borders. Along the margins of the formal garden would be planted wild gardens which would merge into the Ohio countryside.

The Resors' place was almost entirely a wild garden. Near the house there were a few perennial borders, shrubs, and fruit trees espaliered against the house, but Gertrude Jekyll concentrated on the outer part of the grounds which she planted with spring blooming shrubs and groundcover plants.

The Glebe House garden was much smaller than the other two gardens, but it may have given Gertrude Jekyll even more pleasure. She was not unaware of gardening styles in America[6] and had wondered about the cottage gardens around the old houses and why she had seen no pictures of them. The garden that she designed for the Glebe House was a cottage garden type and reflected Gertrude Jekyll's concern with fitting the style of the garden to the house.

Although Gertrude Jekyll travelled abroad frequently during her youth, with the decline of her eyesight and the building of Munstead Wood, her travelling days were curtailed. After 1904, it was a rare occasion for her to leave home at all. Still, most of her gardens were yet to be designed. These she planned through the mail without ever visiting the site. 'Toward the end of her life the owners of various gardens tried to persuade her to visit them by holding out promises of 'getting her home before sunset' etc. but none of these were to any avail.'[7] Miss Jekyll developed a routine by which she

Left: Figure 12.2 Gertrude Jekyll's first plan of Groesbeck Place, 1914.

acquired the information she needed to create gardens from a distance.

The procedure she used when designing gardens in places she never visited was *always* to ask for a surveyor's plan. She mentioned that this was not causing the owner extra expense because nobody could work without it. She also asked the owner various questions, amongst which were two outstanding: had they any specially favourite flowers which they wanted to include in their garden, and were there any opportunities for making a vista?[8]

With the surveyor's plans, photographs, and descriptions she received from her clients, Gertrude Jekyll was able to continue designing gardens until the end of her life without leaving Munstead Wood. This was also the method she used to design gardens in the United States, a country with a climate unfamiliar to her where many of the plants she used as stand-bys would not live.[9] Often the choice of plants was left in the hands of a local nurseryman and mail had to cross the ocean twice before she could get an answer to a question, but Gertrude Jekyll undertook the making of her American gardens with the same courteous deliberation with which she approached her English gardens.

Her American clients were of a type that was probably familiar to her. They were well-travelled people of wealth, taste and intelligence, who had been exposed to the lush grace of the English flower garden and recognized the genius of Gertrude Jekyll, one of its authors. They were women. Although the husband's name appeared as the owner of the garden (and he was occasionally consulted) the letters and business matters were always between his wife and Miss Jekyll. It is probable that all of her American clients had met Miss Jekyll and had tea and toured the garden at Munstead Wood. We know that two did. Two of the three received local recognition in their own right for their gardens.

Tea with Gertrude Jekyll was an impressive experience fondly remembered by her guests:

"Miss Jekyll was either in the garden or her workroom. If in her work-room she would quietly appear through the doorway on the staircase which led straight down into the sitting room...

At once you would be plunged into the business of the day ... usually some gardening topic, possibly adjoined from the last meeting, and then tea.

At tea there would often be something rather unusual, crab apple or quince jelly, or some other rare conserve (and always finger bowls for sticky fingers) and sometimes even greater oddities, such as radishes grown in leaf mould. All this was in consideration of the visitor, for Gertrude Jekyll was always on saccharined tea and one biscuit."[10]

Both Helen Resor and Annie Burr Jennings expressed their appreciation of meeting Gertrude Jekyll and having tea with her in their letters asking her to design their gardens. Although there is no such letter in existence from Grace Groesbeck, it is likely she also met Miss Jekyll and enjoyed her tea and company. Grace Groesbeck's admiration for Gertrude Jekyll is obvious in the one letter in the Groesbeck garden file, and in her house (Figure 12.1) which strongly resembles Munstead Wood.

If Grace Groesbeck visited Gertrude Jekyll it would have been before 1914, when the First World War began. That was also the year Gertrude Jekyll began drawing plans for the Groesbecks' gardens. Grace, perhaps accompanied by her husband, Glendinning, would have met a woman who was still quite strong and energetic. As part of her war effort in 1915, Gertrude Jekyll worked with a group of boy scouts "to clear away undergrowth and arrange a neat system of paths" to serve as look-out stations in the Surrey countryside.[11] Stanley and Helen Resor and Miss Annie Burr Jennings, with their visits in 1925 and 1926 respectively, would have found a person in her eighties, whose day was scheduled and visitors carefully screened to protect her from over-exertion and to allow her to work during her most productive hours. She would have been much like the person Russell Page met the year before she died:

"A dumpy figure in a heavy gardener's apron, her vitality shining from a face half concealed behind two pairs of spectacles and a battered and yellowed straw hat."[12]

Through the material in the Groesbeck, Resor and Glebe House files in the Documents Collection of the College of Environmental Design at the University of California, Berkeley, and copies of the rough drafts of plans (the final draft would have been sent to the client), and through visits to the sites of the gardens and information supplied by local sources, it has been possible to recreate the following portraits of the three American gardens, designed by Gertrude Jekyll, and their owners.

The Groesbeck Place

In October of 1914 plans for the gardens of Mr. and Mrs. Glendinning B. Groesbeck's Perintown,

Figure 12.1   Groesbeck Place, Perintown, Clermont, Ohio.

Ohio estate were underway. It was Gertrude Jekyll's first American garden and preceded her popularity and the popularity of the herbaceous, perennial border in America. While America was still in the grips of the Victorian style of gardening, Grace Groesbeck had become a model of what countless other women would become in the 1920s, a devotee of Gertrude Jekyll, dwelling on every word in her books and believing in her own capability to wield a trowel. A letter from Grace Groesbeck to Gertrude Jekyll, which discusses the proposed sites for the house and other buildings, demonstrates the absolute faith which the Groesbecks had in Gertrude Jekyll and her work:

"My dear Miss Jekyll

"Your letter of Oct. 31st received, Mr. Groesbeck and I have come to the conclusion that your idea of the position for the house is best and will ask you to go ahead with your original plan of placing it at the head of the main valley."

"In regard to the other buildings, we had thought of putting them in some other place with the exception of the pump house suggested in one of your previous letters. We plan to have gate posts at the foot of the hill where the road enters and had thought of having a gardener's cottage at or near the entrance but I want you to understand that we do not wish to thrust our ideas upon you but to have you feel perfectly free to work out the plan in any way you think best as of course your ideas are infinitely better and we have perfect confidence in whatever you decide is best."[13]

So Gertrude Jekyll proceeded to design twenty-four plans for terraces, borders, tanks, pools, rock gardens, paved areas, wild gardens, and woodland walks and steps. All this for a house in a unique position at the head of a valley with a moderately steep slope with a hazy vista of the Ohio countryside, which was to be viewed over terraces lined with perennial borders and at the bottom a rose garden. It was to be an architectural garden with vases, statues, walks, steps, and paving near the house, merging into the surrounding woods with the wild gardens and marginal plantings for which Gertrude Jekyll was famous. (Figures 12.2 and 12.3.)

As the contractors had not yet visited the site when Gertrude Jekyll was asked to begin planning, the Groesbecks would not have known if there was any problem with the location they had chosen. It is likely the ground would not support a building, because the house was finally built on a level site at least a hundred yards away. The sandy soil of that locality had eroded, and collapsed slopes near the proposed site suggest a problem with soil stability. As far as can be observed from the existing plans and the remaining garden walks and beds, no attempt to match the plans designed by Gertrude Jekyll to the new site was made. The house was not completed until after 1920[14] and perhaps by that time Grace Groesbeck felt challenged to design her own gardens. In any case, the gardens at the Groesbeck place were admirably designed and became famous locally for their beauty, but they were not designed by Gertrude Jekyll.

The plans designed by Gertrude Jekyll are misleadingly labelled 'Elmhurst', which was the name of the Victorian mansion built by Glendinning's grandfather, William Groesbeck in 1870. "W. S. Groesbeck was said to have been a great horticulturalist, [but] ... the heyday of 'Elmhurst' passed with the century and the deaths of its original owners."[15] The property was subdivided several times between 1904 and 1920 and then the house was torn down in 1941 and the remaining piece of land was divided into six more lots. The furnishings of the house such as the large gilt French doors and gilt mirrors, were donated to the Cincinnati Art Museum where they are on exhibit. As it was explained by a neighbour:

> "It was always our understanding that the Telford (Glen's father) Groesbecks were not well off, but lived on the inheritance from his father... I do know that when the house was torn down the furnishings inside were exactly the same as when the house was built, the rumor being that the Telford Groesbecks did not have the money to redecorate at any time."[16]

The inheritance on which the Groesbecks lived was the result of the years of hard work of William Groesbeck, an attorney. He was famous as an orator and one of his great victories was as the defence counsel at the impeachment trial of President Andrew Johnson. Late in his life he was offered the opportunity to be nominated as a candidate for the Presidency, which he declined.[17]

By the time Glendinning had grown up the family fortune was in the same state of decline as the

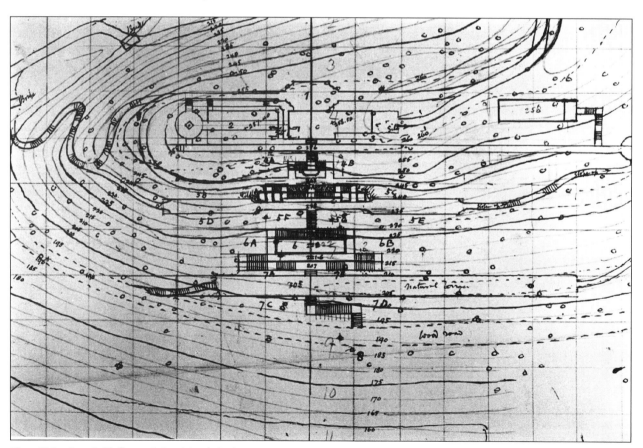

Figure 12.3   Gertrude Jekyll's second plan of Groesbeck Place, 1915.

house. After their marriage he and Grace lived in an apartment in 'Elmhurst' while they planned their own house and garden, and it was from 'Elmhurst' that Grace wrote to Gertrude Jekyll. But although the plans are labelled 'Elmhurst', they are obviously for the property in Perintown: they are of a house not yet built, are surrounded by woods and fields, and show the topography of the area where the Groesbeck house stands today.

With the Groesbeck fortune in a sorry state, Glendinning made a good choice of a wife. Grace Espy Seele was the daughter of a well-respected eye, ear, and throat doctor in Cincinnati, and her wealth, mostly in stocks and bonds, amounted to millions of dollars.[18] Although her interests were wide and varied, ranging from the Audubon Society to activities in support of many musical societies, it was for her gardening that she became reknowned. She had been a founding member of the Cincinnati Garden Club and her Perintown estate became locally renown as 'one of Clermont's [the county's] foremost gardens.'[19] Her gardening staff usually consisted of three full-time gardeners, but in the 1950s it dwindled to one man, who received occasional help from his son. Throughout the garden's prime, during the 1920s and 1930s, Grace and her gardens received many visits from members of the Cincinnati Garden Club.[20]

From the architectural features which still exist, it is clear Grace Groesbeck's gardens did deserve the recognition they were given. The plants, with the exception of some yews in front of the house, and a few others, have gone, but all the flower beds are still delineated by granite curbs. A remarkable formal rose garden, consisting of twenty-five pillars of grey limestone and red-brown slate tiles with which the house was built encircle concentric beds for roses. At one time the pillars were linked together by chains probably festooned with garlands of climbing roses or possibly wisteria in Beatrix Farrand's style. Now chainless and with empty beds, the pillars stand separately and mysteriously, with the impelling allure of a classical ruin. Paths lead out from the rose garden in four directions. One goes to the house, two lead to woodland walks, but the fourth is the beginning of what was a walk between very deep herbaceous perennial borders approximately one hundred feet long. On the West end of the house is a very lovely six-foot high stone wall which curves back and forth marking the northern edge of the West garden. Near this a small depression lined with stones with the end of a pipe visible at the bottom, thought to be a drainage hole, is more likely to

have been a small dipping pool. A drainage pipe would have been run to the other side of the wall and not have emptied into the garden. To the West of the front entrance a couple of steps lead down into a sunken garden, paved with grey granite, which is interrupted in a few sections to leave beds in which to plant.

During the thirties there was a divorce, which left Grace free to spend the rest of her life living in her beautiful country house with her servants, reading, walking in the woods, gardening, and visiting her nearest neighbours, the Krippendorfs.[21]

Mr Krippendorf, made famous by Elizabeth Lawrence's books, was also a gardener and owned all of Gertrude Jekyll's books, but his main interest was nature, especially that which surrounded his home. His land was left to become a nature centre after his death, which may have given Grace the idea to leave her estate to the Cincinnati Chapter of the Girl Scouts of America, who had no need of the property, and could not afford the expense of maintaining it. After Grace's death in 1956, the girl scouts occasionally used the estate for camping but besides removing the gold bathroom fixtures, little was done to change or maintian it. In the mid-1960s it was sold to the Presbyterian Church.

As Wildwood Christian Education Center, as it has been renamed, the estate is now used for conferences and as a summer camp for children. In the past ten years the few remaining iris and peonies have disappeared from the site of the herbaceous borders, and overgrown shrubs have been cut back or removed. The stone pillars of the formal rose garden now stand over empty beds with a camp fire pit as their central focus.

The Home of Stanley and Helen Resor

Nine years elapsed between the Groesbeck garden and Gertrude Jekyll's next American garden. In the summer of 1925, Stanley and Helen Resor, who had a special interest in gardens, toured Great Britain. It was through the good offices of one of the editors of *Homes and Gardens*, Miss Woolrich, that they met Miss Jekyll. Ellen Woolrich was a close friend, and later wife of Edward Hudson, owner and editor of *Country Life*. Edward Hudson wrote the following letter to Miss Jekyll on July 25, 1924:

> "Some American friends of Miss Woolrich, one of the editors of Homes & Gardens, Mr. and Mrs. Stanley Resor, are over in England and they want to see some gardens on not too big a scale. They are desirous of laying-out a garden in America and from what Miss Woolrich tells me

Figure 12.4 *Cotswold Cottage, Greenwich, Connecticut, 1924.*

they would like your advice from a professional point of view as to the laying out of this New York garden. Miss Woolrich says that Mr. and Mrs. Resor are quite charming people and I should be glad to hear if you would mind their coming down to see you and the Munstead Wood gardens and if they could possibly go on to Sir Herbert Jekyll's garden (Munstead House) I am sure they would much appreciate it. I am giving them an introduction to Mr. Thackery Turner and I am also sending them to see one

or two small gardens I know which are rather exceptionally good."[22]

Upon their return to New York, the Resors engaged Gertrude Jekyll to design a garden for their new 'Cotswold Cottage', in Greenwich, Connecticut(Figure 12.4). The garden was planned to put on a good show in the spring, as the Resors usually spent their summers travelling.[23] It was mainly a wild garden consisting primarily of flowering shrubs and trees, such as azaleas, rhododendrons and dogwoods (Figure 12.5). Near the house were paved areas with small flower beds and against the house were espaliered fruit trees (Figure 12.6). Where low growth was desired, vinca, cotoneaster, and trailing vines such as Virginia creeper and clematis were planted. Gertrude Jekyll specified: 'No grass'.[24]

The letters between Helen Resor and Gertrude Jekyll, written during the course of the planning of the garden, show that indeed the Resors were a charming couple and they were no less charmed by Miss Jekyll. Mrs Resor concludes her first letter:

"Mr. Resor and I consider our afternoon with you the happiest time that we experienced in the seven weeks we were abroad and we have told many people that the outstanding

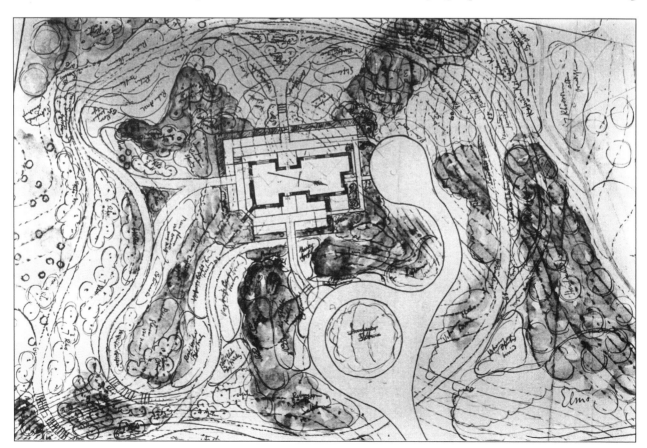

Figure 12.5 *Gertrude Jekyll's plan of the grounds of Cotswold Cottage, 1925.*

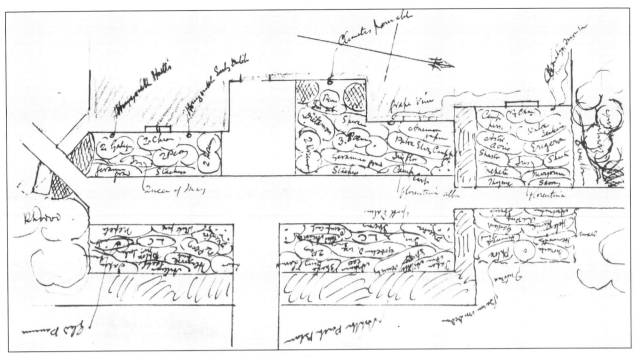

Figure 12.6   Gertrude Jekyll's plan of flower beds on the east side of Cotswold Cottage.

personality among the hundreds of people we met was Miss Gertrude Jekyll. We shall always be greatly indebted to you for the time you gave us."[25]

In response, Gertrude Jekyll wrote several letters to the Resors in which she questioned them on several points and carefully explained the reasons behind the plans she had made for their garden:

"I have put China roses (the Common Pink or Monthly Rose) in front of windows. It is delightful to see these pretty things in one's foreground when looking out."[26]

"The planting I have shown for the outer grounds you must please take as a general suggestion only but at any rate it is so arranged that it leaves the directions of the good views unblocked. It is always best to plant good groups of one thing at a time."

"The outer paths should have no formal edging; in fact it would be best if the path was merely cleaned so that one can see where it is intended to be with any low plants coming to the edge, but nothing hard or clearly defined. It is so much the character of a wild garden that it should look like informal tracks or ways in wild ground."

"Where steps are marked I may not have shown just the number required, but it is always pleasant where the gradients allow to have the treads (wide) and the risers low – so that one can almost run up and down."[27]

Several times Gertrude Jekyll suggested an American nurseryman be consulted in the choice of plants, particularly evergreens, as she was not sure what would survive American winters.

"But so many of the useful evergreens, Box, Holly, (Lime) trees, Bay and various Laurels do not seem to be available to you and I must leave the decision to local knowledge."[28]

In response to an inquiry about her charges, Gertrude Jekyll replied: "I can't give a definite answer about terms as I don't know how much work would be involved but I may say my fee will be anything from 20 to 30 guineas."[29] In the 1920s with a pound equal to $4.87, and a guinea no longer minted but used as a unit of account worth 21s. (£1.1s.0d.), very roughly 20 to 30 guineas would have been worth $100 to $150. Considering the transplanting of a large elm to the north side of the house was costing Mr. Resor $10,000,[30] this was a very reasonable rate.

In 1931 Mrs. Resor's sister and her husband, Mrs. and Mr. Duble, moved into the gardener's cottage which was attached to the garage and remodelled the whole place to match the main house. The landscaping around the cottage was done by Miss Isabella Pendleton, who often talked of her admiration of Gertrude Jekyll's work.[31] Miss Pendleton, a 1917 graduate of Lowthorpe School,[32] became a member of the American Society of Landscape Architects in 1933.[33] Throughout the 1930s she worked frequently for the Resors and the Dubles, mostly it seems adjusting the landscape to alterations and additions to the buildings. The changes she made to the landscape, such as espaliered apples and pears against a new potting shed,[34] appear to have been in sympathy with the plan designed by Gertrude Jekyll.

When the Dubles moved out of the cottage sixteen years later, it and seven or eight acres were sold, but the main house remained in the Resor family until the 1960s when Helen and Stanley died. Since then the changes to the landscape have been drastic, mostly because of a lack of awareness of the original concept and a twentieth-century emphasis on ease of maintenance. A swimming pool was put in, but it is hidden from view from the front by the potting shed with its overgrown shrubs. Some of the paving around the house remains, but there are no flower beds. Aged rhododendrons remain between the house and the shallow brook on the east, and here and there the remains of walks may be seen, filled for the most part with brush and debris. In May 1980 three lovely dogwoods were to be seen blossoming in the midst of dense underbrush. They can be located on Gertrude Jekyll's plan, as can a cotoneaster in front of the house, a viburnum in the woods, and many other shrubs. But for the most part, the rolling acres around the house, once lush with azaleas, roses and clematis so suited to the English cottage, are nothing but mown grass. It is so commonplace and characterless, compared to the landscape which can be imagined from the plan, that one cannot help but realize how right Gertrude Jekyll was when she said, "*No grass.*"

The Old Glebe House

In 1892 three priests of the Episcopal diocese purchased the Old Glebe House in Woodbury, Connecticut as a gift for the Bishop of Connecticut. The Glebe House is a lovely old house, the earliest portions of which were built about 1690. Historically it is important to the Episcopal Church as in 1783 it was the site of the election of their first American bishop, Samuel Seabury.[35]

The fate of Glebe House was under consideration for nearly thirty years after its purchase. One proposal was to tear down the structure and place a monument on the site. Finally in 1923 a committee was formed to restore the Glebe House. By 1925 their objective had been reached, and the house was opened to the public. The Seabury Society for the Preservation of the Glebe House was then formed for the sole purpose of overseeing

the maintenance and care of the building[36] (Figure 12.7).

Miss Annie Burr Jennings was one of the founding members of The Seabury Society.[37] Neither Episcopalian nor a resident of Woodbury, she was a wealthy, public-spirited woman from Fairfield, Connecticut. Her father was Oliver Burr Jennings, who in partnership with J. D. Rockefeller, founded Standard Oil Company. Miss Jennings often used her wealth to benefit others, donating land for a public high school, beach and bird sanctuary for the citizens of Fairfield.[38] She was very much interested in education and politics, and was a member, if not an officer, of such organizations as the Daughters of the American Revolution, Fairfield Historical Society, and Fairfield Garden Club, Mt. Vernon Ladies Association, and the Garden Club of America. On her death in 1939 many churches, hospitals, educational facilities, and charitable organizations received generous amounts of money from her will.[39]

In her home town of Fairfield, Miss Jennings was best known for her garden, which she designed to surround her house, 'Sunnieholme', built in 1908. The garden, open to the public free of charge, was worthy of mention in the Massachusetts Horticultural Society's *Gardener's Travel Book* published in 1938:

"The garden of Miss Annie B. Jennings on the Old Post Road in the centre of town is open to the public at all times throughout the summer without charge. It is a large and very beautiful garden."[40]

One of Miss Jennings's greatest delights was her yearly trip abroad. In the summer of 1926, she and her brother, Walter Jennings and his wife made a trip to England. The high point of the trip for Miss Jennings was an afternoon and tea with Gertrude Jekyll at Munstead Wood. Upon her return to Fairfield Miss Jennings sent the following letter to Gertrude Jekyll on November 8, 1926:

"You remember, I hope, our visit when I, with my brother Walter Jennings and his wife, had that delightful afternoon and tea with you.

As soon as I returned I took up the matter of the Glebe House, that I told you about. We had organized a committee for the restoration of this old house and we have now, inasmuch as it has been restored, a committee for the preservation of it and it has been agreed by the committee that we should have an old fashioned garden there. I am sending you a plan of the Glebe House, and also some extracts from newspapers. These extracts give a photograph of

Figure 12.7   Members of the Seabury Society in front of the newly restored Glebe House in the early 1920s.

the house and I am sending you also measurements of the land.

You can take your time in making a plan for an old fashioned garden for this Glebe House and I have permission to go ahead with the arrangements, and I, personally, shall be responsible for the expense of these details. So kindly send me your bill when you have completed this work...

I hope that you are well and that you are going to have a very pleasant winter. With the highest regard."[41]

What Annie Burr Jennings did not mention in her letter was that the Glebe House was not without a garden. Miss Amy L. Cogswell of Norwich, Connecticut, a graduate and retired director of Lowthorpe School,[42] had been hired earlier that year to design and install a garden there. The plans were completed in September 1926 and that October the plants, which had been ordered from Bay State Nursery, arrived and were planted. The garden Amy Cogswell designed was in a small area on the south side of the house. She divided this area

into four small beds of equal size, separated by walks, edged with box, and filled with perennials. To the side of that she put in a short walk with herbaceous borders on either side.

On 12 October, between September when Amy Cogswell's plans were completed and 27 October when the plants ordered for the garden arrived, a letter from Miss Annie Burr Jennings concerning the matter of installing a garden at the Glebe House was read at a meeting of the Seabury Society. "Miss Jennings... ready to pay for the making of such a garden if the Society would undertake its maintenance. It was unanimously voted that her offer be accepted with thanks."[43]

The plans that were sent to Miss Jekyll included the portion newly designed by Amy Cogswell. In a letter written 6 December 1926, Gertrude Jekyll said of it: "the little paved garden to the South – it looks nicely done and fills that angle well – It is satisfactory as is or does it want altering or renewing?"[44] The reply came back from Miss Jennings's secretary, "Yes, this needs renewing."[45] The designing of the grounds of the Glebe House

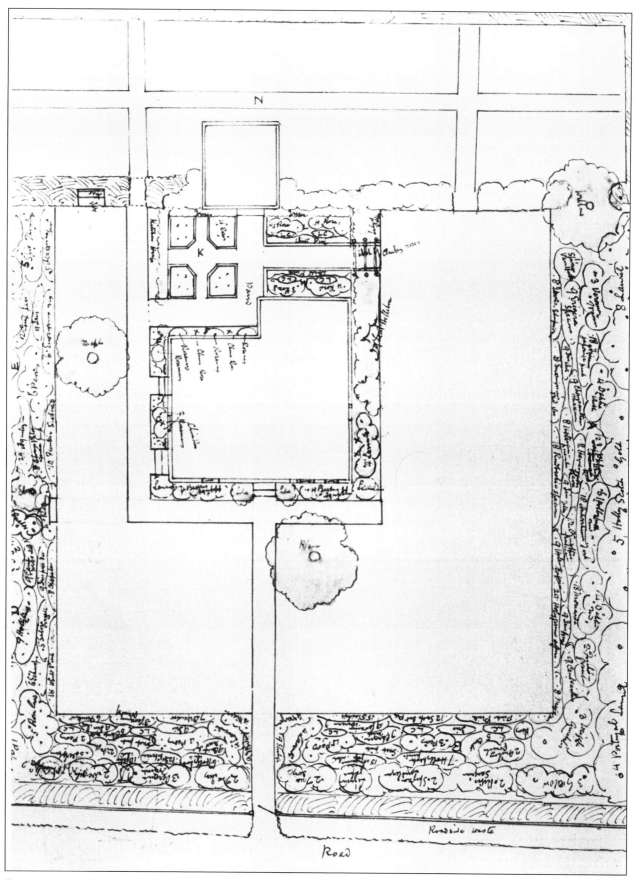

Figure 12.8   Gertrude Jekyll's plan for the Glebe House garden, 1927.

went on through the winter. In April of 1927, the plans (Figure 12.8) were received from Miss Jekyll, and Amy Cogswell was employed to install the garden. The minutes of the 28 June 1927 meeting of the Seabury Society reported: "The garden at the Glebe House has been installed by Miss Cogswell in accord with Miss Jennings's gift and is growing well."[46] The Pomperaug Valley Garden Club at that time offered to take on the responsibility for the care of the garden. "Their offer was accepted with thanks."[47]

In a letter to Mrs Francis King around 1913, Gertrude Jekyll thanked her for a book on American gardens and expressed puzzlement over the apparent dearth of cottage type gardens in the United States:

> "It is good to see how seriously good gardening is being practiced on your side and how neither pains nor cost are spared. If one may criticize, it is only that in many cases there is too much ornamental detail crowded together, so that the eye is bewildered by too many objects of interest being in sight at the same time..."

> "I was hoping to see an illustration of some reproduction of a quiet English garden such as I think must exist or have been made in connection with houses of the old Colonial type. This I think best for the northern states, for the time when these houses were built was one of singular refinement in all matters of building and decoration – there was that delightful combination of dignity, modesty and restfulness that made itself felt through everything, and this is more than ever needful in these days of painful overstrain."[48]

She may have still had this concern in mind when she began work on the garden for the Old Glebe House in Connecticut. Miss Jennings had stated that this was to be an old-fashioned garden, and Gertrude Jekyll designed a garden she considered suitable for an old country house. She began by fencing in the yard:

> "The first thing that strikes me is the need for comfortable enclosure and for this purpose some solid evergreens in the East and West and low hedges to the North and South."[49]

> "What is the usual fencing from the road – nothing shows from the illustrations. The usual thing for this class of house in England for the last 200 years is a fencing of upright slats about $2\frac{1}{2}$ inch thick pointed at the top either hardwood – oak for preference – or white painted with posts at intervals of about 9 feet with a gate of the same, and inside an evergreen

hedge – the fence set back about 3 feet from the actual road."[50]

Between the hedges and the lawn she placed deep borders filled with old-fashioned perennials: hollyhocks, delphiniums, columbine, lavender and iris, but instead of planting them in the old-fashioned haphazard manner, she arranged them carefully in accordance with her own principles of garden design. Drifts of good numbers of plants of one kind and colour are in evidence throughout the plan for the borders.

In her small beds and border-lined walk, Miss Amy L. Cogswell had crowded small groups of a wide variety of perennials, including the more recent introductions, such as the oriental poppy, which Gertrude Jekyll avoided. This area was replanted mostly to roses. The small beds were to hold four roses of the same kind.

By October 1927, the minutes of the Glebe House Committee report the Pomperaug Valley Garden Club had withdrawn its offer to care for the garden. Only one more mention of the Glebe House garden is to be found. A newspaper clipping in the Glebe House collection tells that in November of 1927 Miss Edith Beach of West Hartford was exhibiting her water-colour paintings of the Glebe House garden.

The garden was neglected from 1927 until the end of the 1950s, when Ethel Reinberg, a local woman, appointed herself its guardian. Ironically the only plans left on the premises (the plans she used to replant the garden) were those of Amy Cogswell. Any remnants of the garden donated by Annie Burr Jennings were not noticed, and Gertrude Jekyll's connection with the Glebe House was lost until 1980 when research for this study uncovered the plans and correspondence at the University of California, Berkeley. In the 1990s a group of local volunteers began to recreate the garden, and today the Glebe House is surrounded by walks, lawns, and perennial borders much like those Miss Jekyll envisioned.

Gertrude Jekyll served as an important role model for the many amateur and professional women landscape designers who created beautiful gardens throughout the country early in the twentieth century. In what was perhaps the richest period of gardening in the United States, excellent design blended with exquisite plantsmanship. For the most part extensive perennial gardens have disappeared, but the lasting impact of her work may still be seen in the garden design of today and in the perennials used, as well as in the resurgence of interest in her books and ideas.

13

A pair of gardening boots worn by Gertrude Jekyll

June Swann

No carpenter likes a new plane; no house painter likes a new brush. It is the same with tools as with clothes; the familiar ease can only come of use and better acquaintance. I suppose no horse likes a new collar; I am quite sure I do not like new boots! Gertrude Jekyll, 1900.[1]

In the first place the technical details, which are essential to understanding the boots, are given:-

Guildford Museum LG 1417/1 & 2 (1 = left) ?pre 1885 - 1932.

These are a pair of *Men's* Balmoral boots (Figure 13.1).

Colour: Now black, but possibly originally brown, because stitched with red thread, but see black tongue. Dark brown facing extension-repair

Material: Leather, grain out.

Toe: Shallow square, rounded corners. Steel toe plate attached on sole with 5 nails. Left boot has 1" toe spring, right $^3/_{16}$".

Heel: 1" stacked leather, with small pieces chipped out on the sides in wear: mainly on the inside of the left boot, outside of the right. No wheeling visible due to the amount of dubbin/polish.

Top piece: leather, probably repaired. Steel "horseshoe" attached with 5 nails.

Sole: shaped right/left. $^1/_2$ – sole repairs, nailed at waist; right boot also has a $^1/_8$" screw and larger $^3/_{16}$" screw at the inside corner, obviously amateur work. Rather clumsy toe bit repair under plate on left boot which distorts the boot, making the sole project obliquely $^5/_8$"

beyond the upper at the toe and also making it appear larger than the right. Right boot has a row of hobnails round edge and three rows up the centre, one of which is overlapped by the toe plate which must therefore be a later addition. The hobs are very worn and additional hobs, less worn, have been nailed between the rows.

The left sole has much more irregular hobnailing (Figure 13.2), with some of the original rows worn down to pinheads, with the outer row less worn. There are at least three lots of studding done at different dates.

Slightly domed waist, with knife cuts visible, marking the position of each heel, which probably indicate that the boots have had through-sole repairs. Worn outdoors, with some mud[2] adhering between the hobs and on the top piece of golosh.

Construction: welted, stitched in channel, @ about 7 to 1" on the left, though the right may have only 5. The welt is broken on the left boot at the outside joint, and restitched @ 8 to 1".

Upper: Ankle high. Front lace over unlined tongue of black grain leather; this colour is unlikely to have been used on a brown boot. The original lace holes are covered with two pieces of brown leather, $1^3/_8$" wide, rather coarsely stitched on, which extend each side of the original leg by $^1/_2$". This may have been done because of excessive wear, though it is unlikely the leg would have been extended a full inch if extra size were not also required. There are 8 pairs of eyelets in the extensions, the middle two on the inside of the left boot

Left: *Figure 13.1 Gertrude Jekyll's Balmoral boots, photographed at St. Aidan's College, Durham during the 50th Anniversary Exhibition, 1982.*

176

Figure 13.2   The sole of the left boot.

being larger than the rest, presumably a replacement. The laces are of flat leather, $\frac{1}{8}$" wide, each end with a $\frac{1}{2}$" spiral wire tag. A short end of the lace leads from the bottom pair of eyelets straight to the top, while the long end was threaded ladder-pattern through the next three lower pairs of eyelets, presumably as when last removed, and similar to the Nicholson painting. Full golosh, with the only seams, oblique, in the centre of each side. The leg is finely stitched in red thread, @ 16 to 1". This represents fine closing work. The left boot has a repair patch $1\frac{1}{4}$" x 1" let into the top of the golosh over the back strap, stitched @ about 10 to 1".

Lining: Fawn strong twill cloth remains over the back strap, top and part of the sides, the rest having been worn away. There is no sign of a loop to pull on, nor of maker's label or other markings; i.e. the boots were probably bespoke. Leather $\frac{1}{2}$-sock over the insole, and evidence for wet and dirt, giving the impression that the insides were no longer comfortable. The lace was probably not long enough to fasten to the top with a loop round the ankle, though there is a faint impression that this method had been used with an earlier, longer lace.

Decoration: Upper stitched with red thread, which is unusual at this date.

Size: Left: sole 11" (about $10\frac{1}{2}$" insole); 4" wide at tread (upper about $3\frac{5}{8}$"). Right: sole $10\frac{9}{16}$" (about $10\frac{1}{4}$" insole); width as for left. The left now looks bigger, but before repairs, they were probably a matched pair. The length is sufficient for a small-footed man, or a healthy length for a woman, but there is evidence at the left heel and right toe that they were slightly short for her. They are very wide for even a late-Victorian woman.

Comment

The most obvious impression is of a shabby, well worn pair of masculine boots with multiple repairs. First as to their shabbiness this is probably the result of regular dubbinings[3] to keep the leather waterproof and supple: dubbin does not take a polish. However little attempt was made to ensure that all mud was removed before treatment and certainly some dirt has gathered on the greasy surface. So the boots were kept serviceable, without undue care as to appearance.

This is borne out too by the apparent difference between right and left, due to differential repairs. But they do suggest either a woman who insisted on having the cobbler do the minimum, or a rather

Figure 13.3   Gertrude Jekyll at Higham Bury, Pulloxhill, Bedfordshire.

slovenly cobbler, or indeed possibly an amateur repairer. It is unlikely that the screws would have been inserted by even the poorest grade of cobbler and a handyman or carpenter is more likely.

They have certainly too seen many years of wear. The initial date of making is not easy to ascertain. Although the name Balmoral was first associated with boots in 1851 the style of front lace boot with a golosh (as now recognised by this term) may have first appeared in the late 1820s, and J. Sparkes Hall certainly exhibited an elastic side boot with golosh in the Balmoral style at the Great Exhibition of 1851. After Queen Victoria bought the Balmoral estate in 1852 there are many more uses of the term, though not all Balmoral boots listed in catalogues then had the golosh. The style made an elegant boot, snugly fitting round the top of the golosh, which also gave it extra strength and resistance to water penetration. It was most fashionable at the end of the nineteenth century and especially during the years up to the First World War, the formal colour being black, with brown for sporting and more casual wear. The feature of the rounded, square toe and the hint of brown suggests a date of *c.* 1885 (Figure 13.3) when the toe shape was narrowing to a blunter point and brown was just starting to become fashionable.

They continued in use and had degenerated to gardening boots some time before October 1920 when William Nicholson began to paint them (Figure 13.4): they are already then shown with a gaping hole at the toe of the left boot (it may only be the toe plate unattached), and indeed looking quite derelict or, one might say, full of character. The offending toe plate was replaced after 1920, rather clumsily, or it may well have been that the plate had damaged the sole beneath it so much that it needed piercing to make it strong enough to re-attach the plate.

The amount of repairs will surprise modern readers. The eyelet extensions suggest room for extra socks to protect against the worn lining, or perhaps swollen ankles? But the boots during their lifetime saw the demise of the handsewn shoemaker, as mechanisation and large-scale factory production squeezed him out of the trade. Those that survived turned more and more to repairing, and for many years, virtually until the end of Miss Jekyll's life, there would have been handsewing men capable of doing the highly skilled repairs to keep these boots wearable for so many years. Unfortunately the skills were dying by the time of the Second World War, after which attitudes changed and interminable repairs were no

longer either possible or acceptable.

Unfortunately too, it appears from the quality of the work that Miss Jekyll did not continue to have close access to a skilled man. From other surviving footwear worn by the gentry and aristocracy, some of which are repaired almost as much, it is obvious there was no stigma in repairs. In fact it was considered wasteful to discard footwear until it could be repaired no more, though much-repaired footwear was usually handed down the social scale before it reached the state of these boots. It was normal until the 1960s to expect a good pair of men's boots to last at least twenty years, and the record for continuous, though part-time wear, must be the Victorian slippers in Northampton Museum worn by father and son for 62 years.

The problem of the boots' possible masculine origin is not easily solved. Marguerite Steen in *William Nicholson* describes them as, "The old pair of army boots, in which she trudged about her gardens, are invested with so much of her own character, that they seem to have a life of their own."[4]

The catalogue[5] of the Tate Gallery, which houses the Nicholson painting, which he entitled "Miss Jekyll's Gardening Boots" (Figure 13.4), also calls them an "old pair of army boots", presumably on the evidence of a letter from him: "I didn't entirely waste the daylight, as I painted her Army boots and gave the result to N. Ned (Sir Edwin Lutyens) presented the portrait to the Tate."[6] Nicholson had been commissioned by Lutyens to paint Miss Jekyll but she had refused to waste the brief hours of daylight in October-November of 1920 in sitting to him. He obviously turned those hours to good account. Mary Lutyens, writing about her father in 1980, says:

"Nicholson also painted at the same time a portrait of her gardening boots which he gave to my father; they seemed an integral part of her. My mother gave the picture of the boots to the Tate after my father's death (1944) . . . It should really be hung in the National Portrait Gallery as a predella to the portrait."[7]

She also commented:

"I wish the picture had never been given away." (The portrait, given by Lutyens to the Tate in 1922, was transferred to the National Portrait Gallery in 1947).

The boots were offered to the Tate and the National Portrait Gallery, but correspondence makes it clear that no art gallery would consider having the real boots in proximity to the work of art. This has been to the advantage of Guildford Museum, where they are proudly displayed with other Jekyll memorabilia. For at the wearer's death in 1932, her gardening boots and tools were still by the back door. Her nephew sent them to the garden designer Mrs Nellie B. Allen in New York, "because I consider you, among all American visitors, loved her most." Mrs. Allen finally sent them to Guildford in 1956.[8]

This was not the first footwear to be painted by Nicholson. In 1918 he had painted 'Dancing Pumps', now in the Courtauld Gallery, and 'Miss Simpson's Boots' in 1919. He may have been influenced by earlier precedents, for Miss Jekyll's have a certain affinity with Van Gogh's memorable paintings of his and his brother's boots in the 1880s.

I can find no records of Balmoral boots being used as army boots though the hobnailing, toe and heel plates obviously suggest military influence: they might very well have been added at the time of the Boer or First World War. Although Miss Jekyll's father never saw active service one of her brothers,

Edward, was a captain in the Guards, retiring about 1889 and another, Herbert, was a colonel in the Royal Engineers, retiring to Godalming about 1895. It would be interesting to ascertain the size of his foot to see if they could possibly have been made for him: he may have kept them for unofficial wear. The military influence would have been strong and she may just have decided to have a similar pair of practical boots made.[9] They bear no resemblance to even the most practical Balmoral boots made for women in the late nineteenth century, which is of some significance in the years leading to the Suffragette movement. It needed a woman of Miss Jekyll's strength to flaunt convention then.

Miss Jekyll had commented: "I suppose no horse likes a new collar; I am quite sure I do not like new boots!"[1] – which we might all have guessed from this splendid pair, which as Nicholson saw, tells us so much more about this incredible woman than her rather frosty portrait: almost as much as the gardens themselves.

Figure 13.4   Gertrude Jekyll's boots by William Nicholson.

Figure 14.1 *Golden Wedding anniversary group at Munstead House, taken in early January 1932.*

1 David McKenna 2 Reginald McKenna 3 Lord Monteagle (Tom Spring-Rice) 4 Pamela McKenna 5 Francis Jekyll 6 Agnes Jekyll 7 Richard Howes (butler)
8 Herbert Jekyll 9 Guy McLaren 10 Barbara Freyberg 11 Paul Freyberg 12 Bernard Freyberg 13 Martin McLaren 14 Frank Mathews (chauffeur) 15 (maid)
16 Nanny Brown 17 Mrs Symons (cook) 18 Ernest Sherlock (gardener) 19 Miss Murray (Agnes's maid) 20 (maid) 21 (footman) 22 Muriel Tolly (Barbara's maid).

14

Postscript: A personal recollection by

David McKenna

Figure 14.2 David and Michael McKenna by the Tank at Munstead Wood.

It was about 1916 that my brother and I, two small boys aged 6 and 5, first became conscious of Aunt Gertrude, as she was invariably and respectfully know to us. She was in fact our great-aunt; and in those war years it had become the habit for us to spend much of each summer at Munstead House, the home of our grandparents Herbert and Agnes Jekyll, Gertrude's brother and sister-in-law.

Munstead House and Munstead Wood, where Gertrude lived, were adjoining properties separated only by a minor un-tarred road which led eventually to Guildford, the route 'by the lanes' as it was called to distinguish it from the main tarred road to Godalming. Together the two properties formed an unspoilt Jekyll enclave, and although there were other neighbours, they did not impinge unduly upon the close family circle.

I cannot recollect any first encounters with Aunt Gertrude, when we might have been formally introduced. Rather, we had just slipped imperceptibly into the general Munstead scene. We had, however, been well briefed by our grandmother. Aunt Gertrude was very fond of cats of which she had many, but like our grandfather disliked noise. It was a case of 'little boys were to be seen and not heard.' Our main function in that scene was to act as errand boys, for there was a fairly constant exchange of minor items between Munstead House and Munstead Wood; a pot of homemade jam one way, and a plant the other; and there were always notes, as the telephone did not loom large, if indeed it loomed at all, as a means of communication. For us, an errand to Munstead Wood was a little adventure (Figure 14.2).

First, there was, just over the road, the locked door in the close-boarded fence which surrounded

Munstead Wood. This meant climbing up the bank on which the fence stood, and reaching over the fence to find the key on the nails behind the door post. Entry having been effected, the door having been locked again and the key put back, then came the short trek through the woods to the garden. As likely as not, Aunt Gertrude would be found at work in the garden, a wide-brimmed hat on her head, and draped with her gardener's apron, with its large pouch containing all the worker's necessities. We would present our basket. If there was a note, she would open it and say if there was to be an answer. If not, she would say, "Run along now and take the pot of jam to Florrie". If there was anything to go back, she would say "I will be with you in a few minutes in the house to give you something to take back to your granny." Occasionally she might pause for a little instruction; for little boys, besides being seen, could be instructed. She would tell us what she was doing and why; she would introduce us to the trug basket, explaining its particular shape, and the different tools with their use. It was all very businesslike. To us she appeared austere but kindly, with a nice twinkle in her eye. Time, however, was not to be frittered away in needless pleasantries.

After the war, our visits to Munstead, although frequent, were much less prolonged. No more were we parked out with the grandparents for months at a time. We ceased to be an integral part of the daily Munstead scene, and became instead weekend visitors, along with our parents, during school holidays. We slipped into a new routine which was centred, as far as Aunt Gertrude was concerned, upon Sundays. By then, Aunt Gertrude was not herself a churchgoer, but there was always a Munstead House church party for 11 am Matins at Busbridge Church, consisting at least of Granny and Grandpapa, any grandsons, and those of the grown-up weekenders who felt inclined to go, if only to support Grandpapa who read the lessons.

After church, the party would saunter back to Munstead House through Aunt Gertrude's garden, entering it at the bottom end, near her Thunder-house on the wall, and pay a call upon the great lady. The grown-ups would cluster round her at one end of her sitting-room; but before settling down to the week's gossip, Aunt Gertrude would move to a side-table and pour into a tumbler for each of us some of her home-made raspberry vinegar, topped up with water. It was delicious. And that was our cue to keep ourselves to ourselves, whispering perhaps together, in the far corner of the room, while the grown-ups sat themselves down with Aunt Gertrude at the opposite end. Very occasionally, during this phase, if the church party was down to the minimum, we might be summoned, after we had had our raspberry vinegar, and given a little instruction, say, in undoing and doing up parcels. "Do not cut string if you can help it; untie it, and wind it up round your fingers into neat little bundles for subsequent use." Her demonstration of doing up parcels – no sellotape in those days – was a lesson never to be forgotten.

The Sunday call would last about half an hour, after which the church party would continue their saunter through the woods back to Munstead House for a sybaritic luncheon, always on Sundays at a quarter to two.

A few years later, as we entered our 'teens, the pattern of our lives changed again, and although there continued to be regular visits to Munstead, they took place much less frequently. By then, Aunt Gertrude was entering her eighties, and was becoming more and more a recluse. She did not join the Golden Anniversary Group at Munstead House (Figure 14.1). Half a century earlier Gertrude's mother, Julia Jekyll, had written to her son Herbert, Gertrude's favourite brother, who was a Sapper Officer, then serving in the Gold Coast:

> "As I sit at breakfast in the entrance room I look south and picture to myself what you and Gertrude [who was then in Algeria] may be about – she enjoying herself to the top of her being, you, by this time hard at work, for I fancy you must have landed yesterday or the day before. She is still studying harmony with Mr. Blumenthal, and says she is quite bewildered with all she wants to do, and see. Between the attractions of music, metal work and nature, I am afraid she won't give as much time to painting as one could wish, but she must follow her own inclinations..."

Gertrude had done just that. But now there seemed no longer much taste for new experience. In her last decade, it is sad, though perhaps understandable, that we, moving rapidly through the school to the University stage, never seemed able to build up a new and exciting relationship with such a remarkable person. She remained as ever the kindly, much revered but formidable great-aunt; while in her presence we remained children, to be seen and not heard, and occasionally to be instructed.

Bibliography

Margaret Hastings and Michael Tooley

Books

† Published posthumously

1883 Colour in the Flower Garden. In W. Robinson. 1883. *The English Flower Garden.* London, John Murray. pp. cx-cxii.

1899 *Wood & Garden: notes & thoughts - practical & critical of a working amateur.* Incorporating articles printed in *The Guardian Newspaper* as "Notes from Garden & Woodland", 1896-1897. London, Longmans, Green & Co. xvi + 286.

1900 *Home & Garden: notes and thoughts - practical and critical of a worker in both.* London, Longmans, Green & Co. xv + 301.

1901 *Lilies for English Gardens: A guide for amateurs.* Compiled from information previously published in *The Garden* with the addition of some original chapters. London, Country Life, and George Newnes xii + 72.

1901 *Wall and Water Gardens.* London, Country Life Ltd. and George Newnes Ltd. xiv + 177.

1901 Preface in E.T. Cook. 1901. *Gardening for Beginners: A Handbook to the garden.* London, Country Life and George Newnes v-vi.

1902 *Roses for English Gardens* (with Edward Mawley). London, Country Life and George Newnes xvi + 166.

1904 *Old West Surrey: Some Notes and Memories.* London, Longmans, Green & Co. xx + 320.

1904 *Some English Gardens.* After drawings by George S. Elgood, R.I., with Notes by Gertrude Jekyll. London, Longmans, Green & Co. xii + 131.

1907 *Flower Decoration in the House.* London, Country Life and George Newnes xi + 98.

1908 *Colour in the Flower Garden.* London, Country Life and George Newnes xiv + 148.

1908 *Children and Gardens.* London, Country Life and George Newnes xx + 110.

1911 Preface in W. Miller. 1911. *The Charm of English Gardens.* London, Hodder & Stoughton vii-x.

1912 *Gardens for Small Country Houses* (with Sir Lawrence Weaver). London, Country Life and George Newnes xvi + 260.

1913 *Wall and Water Gardens: With Chapters on the Rock-Garden and the Heath-Garden.* 5th ed., revised. London, Country Life xvi + 214.

1914 *Colour Schemes for the Flower Garden* (originally published (1908) as *Colour in the Flower Garden*). London, Country Life xvi + 159.

1915 Preface in Mrs Francis King. 1915. *The Well Considered Garden.* New York, Charles Scribner's Sons. x.

1916 *Annuals and Biennials: The Best Annual and Biennial Plants and their Uses in the garden.* With cultural notes by E. H. Jenkins. London, Country Life and George Newnes xiv + 174.

1918 *Garden Ornament.* London, Country Life and George Newnes xii + 460.

1918 *Public Parks and Gardens.* Burnley, The Civic Arts Association. 12 pp.

1921 Garden Design on Old-Fashioned Lines. In E.T. Ellis (ed.) *Black's Gardening Dictionary.* London, A. C. Black pp. 383-384.

1921 Garden Planning. In E.T. Ellis (ed.) *Black's Gardening Dictionary.* London, A.C. Black pp. 408-409.

1921 The Garden Summerhouse. In E.T. Ellis (ed.) *Black's Gardening Dictionary.* London, A.C. Black pp. 416-7.

1921 Old-Fashioned Flowers. In E.T. Ellis (ed.) *Black's Gardening Dictionary.* London, A.C. Black pp. 692-6.

1921 Potpourri. In E.T. Ellis (ed.) *Black's Gardening Dictionary.* London, A.C. Black p. 815.

1921 The Water Garden. In E.T. Ellis (ed.) *Black's Gardening Dictionary.* London, A.C. Black pp. 1149-51.

1924 Introduction. In G. F. Tinley, T. Humphreys and W. Irving. 1924. *Colour Planning of the Garden.* London, T. C. & E. C. Jack ix-xvii.

1924 The Garden. In A.C. Benson and Lawrence Weaver. 1924. *The Book of the Queen's Dolls' House.* London, Methuen and Co. p. 151.

1925 *Old English Household Life: Some account of Cottage objects and Country folk.* Incorporating material from "Old West Surrey". London, B.T. Batsford ix + 222.

1927 Preface in Mrs. Francis King. *The Flower Garden Day by Day.* New York, Frederic A. Stokes Co.

1927 *Garden Ornament* (with Christopher Hussey). 2nd ed., revised. London, Country Life x + 438.

1928 *The Old Garden Roses. In The Gardener's Year Book 1928.* London, Phillip Allen & Co. pp. 223-5.

1928 Garden Design on Old-Fashioned Lines. In, E. T. Ellis (ed.) *Black's Gardening Dictionary* Second edition. London, A.C. Black pp. 383-4.

1928 The Garden Planning: aims to be kept in view. In, E. T. Ellis (ed.). *Black's Gardening Dictionary.* Second edition. London. A.C. Black pp. 408-9.

1928 The Garden Summerhouse. In, E. T. Ellis (eds.). *Black's Gardening Dictionary.* Second edition. London, A.C. Black pp. 416-7.

1928 Old-Fashioned Flowers. In, E. T. Ellis (ed) *Black's Gardening Dictionary.* Second edition. London, A.C. Black pp. 692-6.

1928 Potpourri. In, E. T. Ellis (ed.) *Black's Gardening Dictionary.* Second edition. London, A. C. Black Ltd. p. 815.

1928 The Water Garden. In, E. T. Ellis (ed.). *Black's Gardening Dictionary.* Second edition. London, A.C. Black pp. 1149-51.

1931 Gertrude Jekyll (1843-). In Ernest Nelmes and William Cuthbertson (compilers). 1931. *Curtis's Botanical Magazine Dedications, 1827-1927.* London, Bernard Quaritch pp. 392-4.

†1933 *Wall, Water and Woodland Gardens: Including the Rock-Garden & the Heath-Garden.* 8th ed., revised of "Wall & Water Garden" with a chapter on the Asiatic Primulas by G.C. Taylor. London, Country Life xvi + 246.

†1936 Planting a Garden. In, *The Gardener's Companion* (reprinted from *Home and Garden*, 1900). London, J. M. Dent & Co. pp. 270-2.

†1936   The Common Speedwell. In, *The Gardener's Companion* (reprinted from *Home and Garden*, 1900). London, J. M. Dent & Co. p. 367.

†1937   *A Gardener's Testament. A selection of Articles and Notes.* Edited by Francis Jekyll and G. C. Taylor. London, Country Life xiv + 258.

†1939   *Old English Household Life* (with Sydney Robert Jones). London, B. T. Batsford viii + 120.

†1947   A fox hunt at Munstead Wood. 1925. In H. M. Larner 1947. *Busbridge, Godalming, Surrey. A history, ancient and modern.* Cambridge, St Tibbs Press (Cambridge Chronicle Ltd.). pp. 58-9.

†1947   Some Trees of our neighbourhood. 1923. In, H. M. Larner (ed.) 1947. *Busbridge, Godalming, Surrey. A history, ancient and modern.* Cambridge, St Tibbs Press (Cambridge Chronicle Ltd.). pp. 68-73.

†1966   *On Gardening.* London, Studio Vista. 283 pp. Introduction by Elizabeth Lawrence.

†1983   *Gertrude Jekyll on Gardening.* Edited with a Commentary by Penelope Hobhouse. London, National Trust and William Collins. 336 pp.

†1984   *The making of a garden.* An anthology of her writings, illustrated with her own photographs and drawings, and watercolours by contemporary artists, compiled by Cherry Lewis. Woodbridge, Antique Collectors' Club. 169 pp.

Articles

†Published posthumously

A, Article; N, Note; C, Correspondence

1881   Some plants from Algeria. *The Garden* **19** (483), 202 A.
1881   Spring flowers and the frost. *The Garden* **19** (484), 233 A.
1881   Brown Cos Lettuce. *The Garden* **19** (487), 312 N.
1881   Culture of Clematises. *Gardening Illustrated* **3** (114), 126 A.
1881   Sweet Peas. *The Garden* **19** (499), 589 N.
1881   Show Roses. *The Garden* **20** (502), 7 A.
1881   Carnations in Italy. *The Garden* **20** (507), 137 N.
1881   An October nosegay. *The Garden* **20** (517), 408 N.
1881   Flowers and plants in the house. *The Garden* **20** (519), 449 A.
1881   Flowers and plants in the house. *The Garden* **20** (520), 471 A.
1881   Flowers and plants in the house. *The Garden* **20** (521), 489 A.
1881   Flowers and plants in the house. *The Garden* **20** (522), 510 A.
1881   Flowers and plants in the house. *The Garden* **20** (523), 532-3 A.
1881   Flowers and plants in the house. *The Garden* **20** (524), 554 A.
1881   Flowers and plants in the house. *The Garden* **20** (525), 573 A.
1881   Flowers and plants in the house. *The Garden* **20** (526), 574 A.
1881   Red Spider on Violets. *The Garden* **20** (527), 601-2 A.
1881   Flowers and plants in the house. *The Garden* **20** (527), 617 A.
1881   Flowers and plants in the house. *The Garden* **20** (528), 637 A.
1882   Flowers and plants in the house. *The Garden* **21** (529), 7 A.
1882   Brown Cos Lettuce. *Gardening Illustrated* **3** (149), 553 N.
1882   Flowers and plants in the house. *The Garden* **21** (530), 29 A.
1882   Flowers and plants in the house. *The Garden* **21** (531), 47 A.
1882   Flowers and plants in the house. *The Garden* **21** (532), 65 A.
1882   Winter - Scented plants. *The Garden* **21** (533), 71 A.
1882   Flowers and plants in the house. *The Garden* **21** (533), 85 A.
1882   Flowers and plants in the house. *The Garden* **21** (534), 102-3 A.
1882   Flowers and plants in the house. *The Garden* **21** (535), 119 A.
1882   Flowers and plants in the house. *The Garden* **21** (536), 135 A.
1882   Flowers and plants in the house. *The Garden* **21** (537), 151 A.
1882   Flowers and plants in the house. *The Garden* **21** (538), 167 A.

1882   Wild Flowers in the House. *Gardening Illustrated* **4** (158), 25 A.
1882   Flowers and plants in the house. *The Garden* **21** (539), 185 A.
1882   Flowers and plants in the house. *The Garden* **21** (540), 205 A.
1882   Flowers and plants in the house. *The Garden* **21** (541), 221 A.
1882   Wild Flowers in the House. *Gardening Illustrated* **4** (161), 61 A.
1882   Flowers and plants in the house. *The Garden* **21** (542), 241 A.
1882   Flowers and plants in the house. *The Garden* **21** (543), 261 A.
1882   Wild Flowers in the House. *Gardening Illustrated* **4** (163), 85 A.
1882   Flowers and plants in the house. *The Garden* **21** (544), 281 A.
1882   Flowers and plants in the house. *The Garden* **21** (545), 297 A.
1882   Flowers and plants in the house. *The Garden* **21** (546), 317 A.
1882   Flowers and plants in the house. *The Garden* **21** (547), 333 A.
1882   Wild Flowers in the House. *Gardening Illustrated* **4** (167), 133 A.
1882   Flowers and plants in the house. *The Garden* **21** (548), 353 A.
1882   Enjoyable Winter Gardens (Conservatories). *The Garden* **21** (549), 357 A.
1882   Flowers and plants in the house. *The Garden* **21** (549), 373 A.
1882   Flowers and plants in the house. *The Garden* **21** (550), 391 A.
1882   Flowers and plants in the house. *The Garden* **21** (551), 411 A.
1882   Wild Flowers in the House. *Gardening Illustrated* **4** (171), 182 A.
1882   Flowers and plants in the house. *The Garden* **21** (552), 429 A.
1882   Wild Flowers in the House. *Gardening Illustrated* **4** (172), 194 A.
1882   Flowers and plants in the house. *The Garden* **21** (553), 449 A.
1882   Wild Flowers in the House. *Gardening Illustrated* **4** (174), A.
1882   Flowers and plants in the house. *The Garden* **21** (556), 53 A.
1882   Wild Flowers in the House. *Gardening Illustrated* **4** (176), 241 A.
1882   Flowers and plants in the house. *The Garden* **22** (557), 75 A.
1882   Wild Flowers in the House. *Gardening Illustrated* **4** (177), 253 A.
1882   Flowers and plants in the house. *The Garden* **22** (558), 102 A.
1882   Flowers and plants in the house. *The Garden* **22** (560), 150 A.
1882   Flowers and plants in the house. *The Garden* **22** (561), 172 A.
1882   Colour in the Flower Garden. *The Garden* **22** (562), 177 A.
1882   Flowers and plants in the house. *The Garden* **22** (562), 193 A.
1882   Wild Flowers in the House. *Gardening Illustrated* **4** (182), 313 A.
1882   Flowers and plants in the house. *The Garden* **22** (563), 214 A.
1882   Flowers and plants in the house. *The Garden* **22** (564), 236 A.
1882   Flowers and plants in the house. *The Garden* **22** (565), 246 A.
1882   Flowers and plants in the house. *The Garden* **22** (566), 279 A.
1882   Flowers and plants in the house. *The Garden* **22** (567), 289 A.
1882   Flowers and plants in the house. *The Garden* **22** (568), 319 A.
1882   Flowers and plants in the house. *The Garden* **22** (569), 330 A.
1882   Flowers and plants in the house. *The Garden* **22** (570), 363 A.
1882   Wild Flowers in the House. *Gardening Illustrated* **4** (190), 409 A.
1882   Colour in the Flower Garden. *The Garden* **22** (575), 470-1 A.
1882   Daphne indica planted out. *The Garden* **22** (576), 477 N.
1882   Tall Border Plants. *The Garden* **22** (576), 490 A.
1882   Hardy flowers in Winter. *The Garden* **22** (576), 491 N.
1883   Narcissus monophyllus. *The Garden* **22** (585), 115 N.
1883   Anemone fulgens. *The Garden* **23** (591), 245 A.
1883   Ornithogalum nutans. *The Garden* **23** (596), 362-3 N.
1883   Lotier cultive. *Gardening Illustrated* **5** (216), 93 N.
1883   Anemone apennina. *The Garden* **23** (597), 379 N.
1883   Androsace carnea. *The Garden* **23** (598), 400 N.
1883   Flowers and plants in rooms. *Gardening Illustrated* **5** (218), 121 A.
1883   Diseased vines. *The Garden* **23** (605), 575 N.
1883   Some July Flowers. *The Garden* **24** (609), 50 A.

1883	Peach-leaved bellflower. *The Garden* **24** (611), 84 N.
1883	Large white alpine poppy. *The Garden* **24** (611), 84 N.
1883	Varieties of the white Lily. *The Garden* **24** (611), 84 N.
1883	Alstroemerias. *The Garden* **24** (611), 86 N.
1883	Carnation Lady Agnes. *The Garden* **24** (614), 157 N.
1883	Carnation Grenadin. *The Garden* **24** (616), 196 N.
1883	Campanula persicifolia. *The Garden* **24** (617), 219 A.
1883	Flowers and plants in rooms. *Gardening Illustrated* **5** (237), 326 N.
1883	Gentiana Andrewsi. *The Garden* **24** (623), 357 N.
1883	Sedum Sieboldi. *The Garden* **24** (623), 357 N.
1883	October in the alpine garden. *The Garden* **24** (624), 379 A.
1883	Iris stylosa. *The Garden* **24** (626), 432 N.
1883	The Oriental poppies. *The Garden* **24** (627), 459 A.
1883	Cotoneasters. *Gardening Illustrated* **5** (246), 433 N.
1883	Tall Border Plants. *Gardening Illustrated* **5** (247), 444-5 A.
1884	An English Garden two centuries ago. *Pall Mall Gazette* September or October.
1884	Notes from Capri. *The Garden* **25** (635), 33 A.
1884	A Pretty Violet. *The Garden* **25** (638), 96 N.
1884	A Handy Tool for Plant Collecting. *The Garden* **25** (641), 174 A.
1884	Iris stylosa. *The Garden* **25** (643), 220 N.
1884	Climbers on Trees. *The Garden* **25** (653), 425 A.
1884	Schizanthus Grahami. *The Garden* **25** (655), 466 N.
1884	Three Important Annuals. *The Garden* **25** (655), 470 A.
1884	Orobus canescens. *The Garden* **25** (656), 486 N.
1884	Senecio abrotanifolius. *The Garden* **25** (656), 486 N.
1884	Ixia crateroides. *The Garden* **25** (656), 486 N.
1884	Erigeron aurantiacus. *The Garden* **25** (656), 486 N.
1884	Rosa Brunoniana. *The Garden* **25** (657), 506 N.
1884	Small white Carnation Pink. *The Garden* **25** (657), 510 N.
1884	Border Pink Lady Fitzhardinge. *The Garden* **26** (659), 2 N.
1884	Some July Flowers. *Gardening Illustrated* **6** (280), 217-8 A.
1884	White Carnation Pink. *The Garden* **26** (662), 67 A.
1884	Rosa Brunoniana. *The Garden* **26** (663), 87 A.
1884	Autumn Sown Annuals. *The Garden* **26** (665), 125 A.
1884	The Oriental Poppies. *Gardening Illustrated* **6** (290), 349 A.
1884	An English garden two centuries ago. *The Garden* **26** (670), 243-244 A.
1884	A neglected native shrub (Viburnum opulus). *The Garden* **26** (671), 267 N.
1884	Some Fair Autumn Flowers. *The Garden* **26** (672), 290 N.
1884	A garden picture. *The Garden* **26** (673), 313 N.
1884	Tea Roses in Cottage Gardens. *The Garden* **26** (676), 377 N.
1884	Notes from Munstead. *The Garden* **26** (677), 392 N.
1884	The Shamrock Pea (Parochetus) in autumn. *The Garden* **26** (677), 396 N.
1884	Exeter Apple Fair. *The Garden* **26** (677), 399-400 A.
1884	Aubretia olympica. *The Garden* **26** (679), 432 N.
1884	Linaria anticaria. *The Garden* **26** (679), 436 N.
1884	Polygonum vaccinifolium. *The Garden* **26** (679), 436 N.
1884	Autumn Flowers. *The Garden* **26** (680), 452 N.
1884	Some Winter Roses. *The Garden* **26** (683), 530 N.
1884	Rosa Brunoniana. *Gardening Illustrated* **6** (303), 529 N.
1884	Garden and Landscape in Winter. *The Garden* **26** (684), 531 A.
1885	Polygala Chamaebuxus. *The Garden* **27** (686), 31-2 N.
1885	Alexandrian Laurel (Ruscus Racemosus). *The Garden* **27** (687), 43 A.
1885	Plants now in flower in open air. *The Garden* **27** (690), 100 N.
1885	Spring in Winter. *The Garden* **27** (692), 141 A.
1885	Iris tuberosa. *The Garden* **27** (695), 208 N.
1885	Chinodoxa sardensis. *The Garden* **27** (695), 208 N.
1885	Iris reticulata. *The Garden* **27** (695), 208 N.
1885	Winter Pansies. *The Garden* **27** (697), 262 N.
1885	Colour in Flowers. *The Garden* **27** (698), 277-8 A.
1885	Easter Notes. *The Garden* **27** (699), 303 A.
1885	The Lesser Periwinkles. *The Garden* **27** (701), 359 A.
1885	Iris tuberosa. *The Garden* **27** (701), 378 N.
1885	Erythronium grandiflorum. *The Garden* **27** (702), 392 N.
1885	American Asarums. *The Garden* **27** (702), 392 N.
1885	The Virginian Cowslip (Mertensia (Pulmonaria) Virginica). *The Garden* **27** (702), 393 N.
1885	Iris stylosa. *The Garden* **27** (703), 412 N.
1885	Railway Gardening. *The Garden* **27** (704), 435-6 A.
1885	The Double White Pinks. *Gardening Illustrated* **7** (330), 222 N.
1885	The great Mulleins. *The Garden* **28** (712), 40 N.
1885	Opium Poppies. *The Garden* **28** (713), 57 A.
1885	Carpenteria Californica. *The Garden* **28** (713), 64 N.
1885	Oenothera Lamarckiana for house decoration. *Gardening Illustrated* **7** (333), 293 N.
1885	Large root growths on bulbs. *The Garden* **28** (714), 82 N.
1885	Cistuses. *The Garden* **28** (714), 92 N.
1885	Autumn Sown Annuals. *Gardening Illustrated* **7** (336), 330 N.
1885	Tinted Carrot Leaves. *The Garden* **28** (719), 231 N.
1885	Dinner Table Decoration. *The Garden* **28** (720), 252 A.
1885	Herbertia Pulchella. *The Garden* **28** (721), 269 A.
1885	Colchicums and Tunica saxifraga. *The Garden* **28** (723), 308 N.
1885	Bedding or not Bedding. *The Garden* **28** (727), 428 N.
1885	Carpeting Bulb Beds. *The Garden* **28** (733), 577 A.
1886	Corbularia monophylla. *The Garden* **29** (743), 140 N.
1886	Romneya Coulteri. *The Garden* **29** (746), 207 N.
1886	A beautiful Tulip (Tulipa Schrenki). *The Garden* **29** (752), 342 N.
1886	Neopolitan Violets. *The Garden* **29** (752), 348 A.
1886	Centaurea montana. *The Garden* **29** (759), 528 N.
1886	Romneya Coulteri. *The Garden* **30** (764), 26 N.
1886	Cistuses. *Gardening Illustrated* **8** (383), 236 N.
1887	Carpenteria Californica. *The Garden* **31** (794), 130 N.
1887	Scotch Briars. *The Garden* **31** (814), 572 N.
1887	The Sun and the Poppies. *The Garden* **31** (814), 581 N.
1887	White foxgloves. *The Garden* **32** (820), 103 N.
1887	How to keep up a supply of Cut Flowers. *Gardening Illustrated* **9** (433), 214 A.
1887	Shrubs for window boxes. *Gardening Illustrated* **9** (450), 455 A.
1887	Clove carnation – Paul Engleheart. *The Gardeners' Chronicle* **2**, 409.
1888	A large Scilla bifolia. *The Garden* **33** (856), 335 N.
1888	Carpenteria californica. *The Garden* **34** (871), 75 N.
1888	Cistus algarvensis. *The Garden* **34** (874), 165 N.
1888	Clove carnation – Paul Engleheart. *The Garden* **34** (874), 165 N.
1888	Lilium giganteum. *The Garden* **34** (879), 269 N.
1888	A fine white snapdragon. *The Garden* **34** (880), 293 A.
1888	Lilium giganteum. *The Garden* **34** (884), 395-6 N.
1888	Chrysanthemum Cottage Pink. *The Garden* **34** (887), 456 N.
1889	Chrysanthemum Cottage Pink. *The Garden* **35** (897), 69 A.
1889	Lilium giganteum. *The Garden* **35** (901), 165 A.

1889 A place where 'nothing would grow'. *The Garden* **35** (908), 331 A.

1889 Berkeley Castle, Gloucester. *The Garden* **35** (916), 525 A.

1889 Some June Flowers in Surrey. *The Garden* **35** (917), 565 N.

1889 Wallflowers on dry soils. *The Garden* **36** (929), 226 N.

1890 Sweet-scented shrubbery beds. *The Garden* **37** (953), 169 A.

1890 Rhododendrons grouped for colour. *The Garden* **37** ((960), 335-6 A.

1890 A useful white primrose. *The Garden* **37** ((964), 448 A.

1890 Plants for a grave. *The Garden* **37** ((968), 532 N.

1891 The picturesque use of hardy summer perennial plants. *Journal of the Royal Horticultural Society* **13** (3), 324-8 A.

1891 Protection of tender shrubs on walls. *The Garden* **39** (1015), 410 A.

1891 Gardens of one flower. *The Garden* **40** (1026), 64 N.

1891 A good Rock Garden (Miss Ewart's, Coneyhurst, Surrey). *The Garden* **40** (1044), 473 N.

1891 Garland Rose. *The Garden* **40** (1045), 482, 489 N.

1891 Verbascum phlomoides. *The Garden* **40** (1048), 561 N.

1892 Lilium giganteum. *The Garden* **41** (1053), 88 N.

1892 Cottage Roses. *The Garden* **42** (1078), 43 N.

1892 A plea for a good Pink. *The Garden* **42** (1079), 69-70 N.

1892 The Black and White Pink and other flowers. *The Garden* **42** (1082), 131 A.

1893 Yucca pendula. *The Garden* **43** (1124), 455 N.

1893 Review of "Further recollections of a happy life" by Miss Marianne North. Macmillan and Co., London. *The Garden* **44** (1131), 88.

1894 House Decoration. *National Review* **24**, 519-529 A.

1895 Registering frost. *The Garden* **47** (1209), 52 N.

1895 Wood sorrel. *The Garden* **47** (1214), 129 N.

1895 Spring bitter vetch. *The Garden* **47** (1217), 186 N.

1896 White french willow. *The Garden* **50** (1309), 504 N.

1896 Notes from Garden and Woodland I. *The Guardian Newspaper* **51** (1) (2626), 499450 A.

1896 Notes from Garden and Woodland II. *The Guardian Newspaper* **51** (1) (2629), 610-611 A.

1896 Notes from Garden and Woodland III. *The Guardian Newspaper* **51** (1) (2633), 792 A.

1896 Notes from Garden and Woodland IV. *The Guardian Newspaper* **51** (1) (2637), 951 A.

1896 Gardens & Garden Craft. *The Edinburgh Review or Critical Journal* **184** (377), 161-184 A.

1896 Notes from Garden and Woodland V. *The Guardian Newspaper* **51** (2) (2641), 1106 A.

1896 Notes from Garden and Woodland VI. *The Guardian Newspaper* **51** (2) (2644) 1221 A.

1896 Notes from Garden and Woodland VII. *The Guardian Newspaper* **51** (2) (2647), 1317-8 A.

1896 Notes from Garden and Woodland VIII. *The Guardian Newspaper* **51** (2) (2652), 1483 A.

1896 Notes from Garden and Woodland IX. *The Guardian Newspaper* **51** (2) (2657), 1755-6 A.

1896 Notes from Garden and Woodland X. *The Guardian Newspaper* **51** (2) (2663), 2028 A.

1897 Notes from Garden and Woodland XI. *The Guardian Newspaper* **51** (1) (2668), 99 A.

1897 Notes from Garden and Woodland XII. *The Guardian Newspaper* **51** (1) (2672), 268 A.

1897 Notes from Garden and Woodland XIII. *The Guardian Newspaper* **52** (1) (2674), 355 A.

1897 Notes from Garden and Woodland XIV. *The Guardian Newspaper* **52** (1) (2683), 691 A.

1897 Notes from Garden and Woodland XV. *The Guardian Newspaper* **52** (1) (2688), 919 A.

1897 Notes from Garden and Woodland XVI. *The Guardian Newspaper* **52** (2) (2694), 1145-6 A.

1897 A neglected native evergreen. *The Garden* **51** (1321), 183 A.

1897 Good climbing roses. *The Garden* **51** (1333), 414-5.

1898 Hardy-plant borders (with H. Selfe-Leonard). *Journal of the Royal Horticultural Society* **21** (3), 433441 A.

1899 Snapdragons. *English Life March*.000.

1900 Althaea ficifolia. *The Garden* **57** (1468), 3 N.

1900 Narcissus pallidus praecox. *The Garden* **57** (1475), 148 N.

1900 Hardy vines for the South of England. *The Garden* **57** (1479), 225 N.

1900 Narcissus pallidus praecox. *The Garden* **57** (1480), 246 N.

1900 Field flowers in the house. *Ladies Field* **10** (118), 13 A.

1900 Cosmos bipinnatus. *The Garden* **57** (1492), 462 N.

1900 Formal gardening merging into free. *The Garden* **58** (1504), 197-8 A.

1900 Formal gardening merging into free. *The Garden* **58** (1505), 223-4 A.

1900 Cut flowers in the house. *Ladies Field* **11** (131), 68 A.

1900 Wild flowers in the house. *Ladies Field* **11** (140), 400 A.

1900 Wild flowers in the house. *Ladies Field* **11** (143), 546 A.

1900 Winter window-boxes in London. *Ladies Field* **11** (144), 36 A.

1901 Winter bouquet. *Ladies Field* **12** (150), 279 A.

1901 Orchards Surrey. The Residence of Mr. William Chance. *Country Life* **10** (243), 272-9 A.

1901 Two grand Autumn flowers. *Ladies Field* **15** (187), 181 A.

1902 The pergola in English gardens - its making and planting. *Journal of the Royal Horticultural Society* **27** (1), 93-97 A.

1902 The Primrose Garden. *Country Life* **11** (276), 491-2 A.

1902 Roses for Decoration. *The Garden* **62** (1598), 13 A.

1902 From the Mountains I. *The Garden* **62** (1599), 32 A.

1902 Mountain Flowers II. *The Garden* **62** (1603), 97-8 A.

1902 Mountain Flowers III. *The Garden* **62** (1606), 152 A.

1902 Mountain Flowers IV. *The Garden* **62** (1607), 160 A.

1902 Nursery Gardens: China Asters & Antirrhinums. *The Garden* **62** (1610), 218-9 A.

1902 Dahlias & hardy plants – Visits to Nurseries. *The Garden* **62** (1612), 252 A.

1902 The Pergola in English gardens. *The Garden* **62** (1616), 326-7 A.

1902 The Pergola in English gardens. *The Garden* **62** (1617), 343-4 A.

1902-3 The Garden Roses. *Journal of the Royal Horticultural Society* **27** (2/3), 503 4 A.

1903 The reafforestation of Hainault Forest. *Country Life* **13** (314), 634 C.

1903 Greenhouse Flags. *The Garden* **63** (1629), 85-6 N.

1903 Horticultural Club. *The Garden* **63** (1629), 85-6 N.

1903 Penzance Briars on Manetti stock. *The Garden* **63** (1629), 85-6 N.

1903 Yuccas in the rockery. *The Garden* **63** (1629), 85-6 N.

1903 The Bunch Primroses. *Country Life* **13** (330), 574 A.

1903 The Best Sweet Peas. *The Garden* **63** (1642), 308 N.

1903 The beauties of Rose foliage. *The Garden* **63** (1642), 308 N.

1903 Large-leaved Saxifrages. *The Garden* **63** (1642), 308 N.

1903 Horse chestnuts layering themselves. *The Garden* **63** (1642), 308 N.

1903 Colour in the Spring Garden. *The Garden* **63** (1645), 363 A.

1903 Phlox Avalanche. *The Garden* **63** (1647), 405 N.

1903 Rose Pompon de Bourgoyne. *The Garden* **63** (1648), 421 N.

1903 The Garland Rose. *The Garden* **64** (1650), 11 N.

1903 A well coloured flower border. *The Garden* **64** (1673), 405 A.

1904 Technical education – vegetable culture. Details of a course of 6 lectures on "Vegetables and their culture" by A. Dean, F.R.H.S. in the Parish Room, Busbridge. *Busbridge Parish Magazine* **6** (1), n.p. A.

1904 Studies of Flowers and Fruit. *Country Life* **15** (388), 833-5 A.

1904 The Late Dean of Rochester. *Country Life* **16** (400), 359 A.

1905 Wall Gardening – Snapdragons (Antirrhinums). *The Garden* **67** (1729), 7 N.

1905 Arranging Fruit and Flowers. *The Garden* **67** (1729), 9 A.

1905 A Colour Scheme. *The Garden* **67** (1729), 10 N.

1905 Arranging Fruit & Flowers. *The Garden* **67** (1730), 20-1 A.

1905 Bee balm & Bees. *The Garden* **67** (1739), 157 N.

1905 Anemone Hepatica. *The Garden* **67** (1740), 179 A.

1905 Ivy & its many ways. *Country Life* **17** (440), 833-4 A.

1905 A Definite Purpose in Gardening I. *The World* (1624), 287 A.

1905 A Definite Purpose in Gardening II. *The World* (1625), 323 A.

1905 A Definite Purpose in Gardening III. *The World* (1626), 359 A.

1905 The Bulbous Plants of Spring and Early Summer. *The World* (1630), 504 A.

1905 The Bulbous Plants of Summer & Autumn. *The World* (1631), 548 A.

1905 Borders of Spring and Early Summer. *The Garden* **68** (1770), 257 A.

1905 Awards in the Flower Border Competition. *The Garden* **68** (1776), 346 A.

1906 St. Catherine's Court - I. Somersetshire. The Seat of the Hon. Mrs. Paley. *Country Life* **20** (516), 738-746.

1907 How to make a Commonplace Garden a Paradise. *Daily Mail* (3440), 11 A.

1908 Roses in Wild Woodland. *The National Rose Society Rose Annual* **84-5** A.

1909 The streamside Garden. *Country Life* **25** (632), 245-6 A.

1909 Colour Nomenclature. *The Garden* **73** (1978), 501 A.

1910 Shrubs with scented leaves. *Country Life* **27** (696), 678 A.

1910 Heath Path. *Country Life* **27** (700), 820 A.

1910 Weeping roses. *Country Life* **27** (702), 920 A.

1910 Rock wall Edgings. *Country Life* **28** (704), 29-30 A.

1910 Michaelmas Daisies. *Country Life* **28** (722), 659-60 A.

1910 Warley Gardens in Spring and Summer. *Country Life* **28** (723), 689-91 A.

1910 Rose Garden at St. Fagan's Castle. *Country Life* **28** (724), 713-4.

1911 A garden of sweet scents. *Country Life* **29** (731), 8-9.

1911 Some winter effects of flower & shrub. *Country Life* **29** (733), 104-5 A.

1911 Hollyhocks. *Country Life* **29** (738), 284-5 A.

1911 Borders of Annuals. *Country Life* **29** (740), 340-1 A.

1911 Gardening on corrugated iron. *Country Life* **29** (743), 466 A.

1911 Edging to Roses. *The Garden* **75** (2055), 162 C.

1911 Winter effects at Belton, Lincolnshire. *Country Life* **29** (744), 483-4 A.

1911 Bog Gardens. *Country Life* **29** (749), 670-1 A.

1911 A wild fern garden. *Country Life* **29** (751), 740-1 A.

1911 Colour groupings of some May Tulips. *The Garden* **75** (2064), 273 A.

1911 The making of pot-pourri. *Country Life* **30** (759), 150-1 A.

1911 The Pictorial use of Bedding Plants. *Country Life* **30** (765), 350-1 A.

1911 Historical Notes on Garden Ornament. *Country Life* **30** (774), 662-4 A.

1911 Historical Notes on Garden Ornament. *Country Life* **30** (775), 701-2 A.

1912 The Garland Rose. *The Garden* **76** (2099), 75 N.

1912 Plants for a Blue Garden. *The Garden* **76** (2099), 75 N.

1912 Bed of Tuberous Begonias. *The Garden* **76** (2099), 75 N.

1912 Clematis Flammula. *The Garden* **76** (2099), 75 N.

1912 Romneya Coulteri. *The Garden* **76** (2099), 75 N.

1912 Winter Jasmine. *The Garden* **76** (2100), 87 N.

1912 Shrubs under Deodar. *The Garden* **76** (2100), 87 N.

1912 White Rose for London. *The Garden* **76** (2100), 87 N.

1912 Fuchsias. *The Garden* **76** (2100), 87 N.

1912 Snow and Seeds. *The Garden* **76** (2100), 87 N.

1912 Roses and Clematis on fence. *The Garden* **76** (2100), 87 N.

1912 Weeping Standard Roses. *Country Life* **31** (790), 288-9.

1912 The hardy flower border. *Country Life* **31** (796), 514-5.

1912 An April Garden. *Country Life* **31** (799), 611-12.

1912 A Self-Sown Wood. *Country Life* **31** (802), 735-6.

1912 Garden Roses. *Country Life* **31** (809), 5-7.

1912 Gardens for Small Country Houses. Millmead Bramley, Surrey. *Country Life* **32** (825), 7★-11★ A.

1912 A June border of Irises & Lupines. *The Garden* **76** (2144), 639 A.

1913 Primulas from a garden point of view. *Journal of the Royal Horticultural Society* **39** (1), 1914 A.

1913 How to make & plant a streamside Garden. *The Garden* **77** (2147), 20-1 A.

1913 How to grow Holly-hocks. *The Garden* **77** (2153), 99 A.

1913 Primroses and Polyanthuses. *The Garden* **77** (2161), 194-5 A.

1913 Two good April plants. (Erythronium giganteum and Corydalis cheilanthifolia). *Country Life* **33** (850), 576 A.

1913 Grouping Flowers for Colour. *The Garden* **77** (2167), 276 A.

1913 Grouping for Colour. *The Garden* **77** (2169), 298 C.

1913 Notes from Wisley – Primula japonica. *The Garden* **77** (2169), 302 N.

1913 Notes from Wisley – Rambler Roses. *The Garden* **77** (2169), 302 N.

1913 Notes from Wisley – Tree Lupines. *The Garden* **77** (2169), 302 N.

1913 Eremuri in the Wild Garden. *The Garden* **77** (2170), 315 A.

1913 Some good Summer Flowers. *The Garden* **77** (2173), 349 A.

1913 A natural colour study. *Country Life* **34** (863), 87 N.

1913 Planting in dry walls. *Country Life* **34** (866), 189-90 A.

1913 Scentless Musk. *The Garden* **77** (2178), 406 N.

1913 Convolvulus Heavenly Blue. *The Garden* **77** (2179), 419 N.

1913 Annuals for filling flower-borders. *The Garden* **77** (2185), 495 A.

1913 Designing a Rose Garden. *The Garden* **77** (2186), 508 A.

1913 Funkia grandiflora. *Gardening Illustrated* **35** (1809), 719 N.

1914 A Cottage Home in Somerset. *The Garden* **78** (2198), 8 N.

1914 November Hardy Chrysanthemums. *The Garden* **78** (2199), 18 C.

1914 Two Excellent Kales. *The Garden* **78** (2200), 30 N.

1914 Sparassis crispa. *Country Life* **35** (891), 160-1 A.

1914 Wild Gardening in Rocky Sites. *Gardening Illustrated* **36** (1821), 71 A.

1914 Planting a carriage drive. *Country Life* **35** (892), 190.

1914 The National Trust & Hydon Heath. *Country Life* **35** (893), 228-9.

1914 British Flowering Plants (Review). *Country Life* **35** (901), 521.

1914 Corydalis cheilanthifolia. *The Garden* **78** (2213), 191 C.

1914 Salvia farinacea. *The Garden* **78** (2216), 226 C.

1914 Planting for Autumn effect. *Country Life* **35** (905), 664.

1914 A newly made garden at Sandbourne, Worcestershire. *Country Life* **36** (921), 290-2 A.

1914 Wild and Garden Roses (review of 'The Genus Rosa' by Ellen Willmott F.L.S., London, Murray 1910-14). *The Quarterly Review* **221** (441), 363-375 A.

1914 Planting in dry walls. *The Garden* **78** (2237), 485 A.

1914 Bulbous plants in grass and woodland. *Country Life* **36** (926), 465 A.

1914 Moss on Tennis Court. *The Garden* **78** (2242), 540 C.

1914 British Flowering Plants (Review). *Country Life* **36** (931), 622-3.

1914 Aubrietias in the Spring Garden. *The Garden* **78** (2247), 598 A.

1915 A self-sown Wood. *The Garden* **79** (2252), 34 A.

1915 The Five-Barred Gate. *Country Life* **37** (943), 151-2 A.

1915 Evergreens on walls in winter. *Country Life* **37** (945), 202 A.

1915 The Double Chamomile. *The Garden* **79** (2259), 110 C.

1915 Evergreens on walls in Winter. *The Garden* **79** (2259), 114-5 A.

1915 Planted banks as hedges. *Country Life* **37** (949), 3334.

1915 Careers for Women – Landscape Gardening. *Ladies Field* **69** (895), 534-5 A.

1915 A newly made garden at Sandbourne, Worcestershire. *The Garden* **79** (2270), 244-5 A.

1915 Sun Roses. *The Garden* **79** (2273), 288 C.

1915 Simply planted pergolas. *Country Life* **37** (962), 808 A.

1915 Undesirable Plants. *The Garden* **79** (2274), 300-1 C.

1915 Mr. Thackeray Turner's Garden at Westbrook, Surrey. *Country Life* **38** (968), 119-121.

1915 An interesting Surrey garden. *The Garden* **79** (2283), 411-2 A.

1915 Michaelmas Daisies. *The Garden* **79** (2287), 460-1 A.

1915 The Water Elder. *The Garden* **79** (2288), 469 N.

1915 A Young Heath Garden. *Country Life* **38** (978), 464.

1915 The Willow Gentian (Gentiana asclepiadea). *The Garden* **79** (2290), 492 A.

1915 Clematis Flammula in the flower border. *The Garden* **79** (2290), 498 N.

1915 Planting a Carriage Drive. *The Garden* **79** (2291), 508 A.

1915 Borders of Michaelmas Daisies. *Gardening Illustrated* **37** (1911), 640 A.

1915 A pretty Combination. *The Garden* **79** (2301), 622 C.

1916 The green things of the Winter garden. *Country Life* **39** (995), 151 A.

1916 Snowdrops. *Country Life* **39** (998), 237-8 A.

1916 Spring Crocuses. *Country Life* **39** (999), 264-6 A.

1916 Some Sheltering devices. *The Garden* **80** (2311), 117 A.

1916 A Nut Walk. *The Garden* **80** (2312), 128 A.

1916 Early Irises. *Country Life* **39** (1001), 336-7 A.

1916 The early Anemones. *Country Life* **39** (1002), 363-4.

1916 The North border. *The Garden* **80** (2315), 155 A.

1916 Spring cyclamens and grape hyacinths. *Country Life* **39** (1005), 444-5 A.

1916 Planting for Autumn effect. *The Garden* **80** (2317), 183 A.

1916 Pulmonaria angustifolia. *The Garden* **80** (2318), 190 C.

1916 Women as gardeners. *Country Life* **39** (1008), 541-2 A.

1916 China Roses. *The Garden* **80** (2323), 253 N.

1916 Spring flowers in a Surrey garden. *Country Life* **39** (1013), 706-8 A.

1916 Nandina domestica. *The Garden* **80** (2325), 284 N.

1916 A Young Heath Garden. *The Garden* **80** (2326), 296 A.

1916 The Guelder Rose. *Country Life* **40** (1018), 38 A.

1916 An early Summer border. *Country Life* **40** (1018), 38 A.

1916 The "Petits Soins" of a garden. *The Garden* **80** (2330), 347-8 A.

1916 Shrubbery edges. *Country Life* **40** (1020), 105 A.

1916 Clary (Salvia Sclarea). *The Garden* **80** (2333), 381 A.

1916 Genista virgata. *The Garden* **80** (2333), 384 N.

1916 A July flower border *Country Life* **40** (1022), 161-2 A.

1916 Some flowering shrubs of late July. *The Garden* **80** (2335), 405 A.

1916 Summer flowers carefully arranged. *Country Life* **40** (1027), 303-4 A.

1916 The garden at Frant Court Sussex. *The Garden* **80** (2341), 476 A.

1916 The use of grey foliage with border plants. *Country Life* **40** (1031), 401-2 A.

1916 A border of Lupine & Iris. *The Garden* **80** (2343), 503 A.

1916 Fuchsia gracilis. *The Garden* **80** (2345), 522 C.

1916 Sparassis crispa. *The Garden* **80** (2345), 528 A.

1916 Guelder Rose in Autumn. *The Garden* **80** (2347), 544 C.

1916 A July Flower Border. *The Garden* **80** (2347), 548 A.

1916 September flowers. *Country Life* **40** (1036), 580-1 A.

1916 Clematis Vitalba in seed. *The Garden* **80** (2349), 568 C.

1917 The fate of the south border. *The Garden* **81** (2357), 20 C.

1917 An Ever-Blooming Geum. *The Garden* **81** (2362), 64 C.

1917 Gladioli. *Country Life* **41** (1051), 178-9 A.

1917 The fate of the South border. *Country Life* **41** (1051), 179 A.

1917 Mache. *The Garden* **81** (2363), 73 C.

1917 The paint-pot in the garden. *Country Life* **41** (1052), 209-210.

1917 To save potatoes. *Country Life* **41** (1054), 258 A.

1917 To save potatoes. *The Garden* **81** (2367), 106 A.

1917 Swedes Cabbages and Turnip. *The Garden* **81** (2369), 121 C.

1917 The promise of fruit. *Country Life* **41** (1064), 526 A.

1917 Cutting back Hardy Plants. *The Garden* **81** (2376), 196 C.

1917 Rhubarb Leaves. *The Garden* **81** (2376), 197 A.

1917 Plants in steps and pavements. *Country Life* **41** (1065), 553-4 A.

1917 The earliest Roses. *The Garden* **81** (2377), 208 C.

1917 Spring flowers. *Country Life* **41** (1066), 577 A.

1917 Long stemmed Roses for cutting. *The Garden* **81** (2378), 220 C.

1917 Scilla italica alba. *The Garden* **81** (2380), 245 C.

1917 Kitchen Garden Notes. *The Garden* **81** (2381), 260 A.

1917 A well shaped garden trowel. *The Garden* **81** (2382), 273 N.

1917 Garden Labels. *The Garden* **81** (2382), 273 N.

1917 A graceful American Bramble. *The Garden* **81** (2383), 280 C.

1917 A red Arum. *The Garden* **81** (2383), 280 C.

1917 The South border for utility. *The Garden* **81** (2385), 304 C.

1917 A Handsome Striped Grass. *The Garden* **81** (2385), 311 N.

1917 The making of pot-pourri. *Country Life* **42** (1074), 115-6.

1917 Some good Gooseberries. *The Garden* **81** (2386), 321 N.

1917 The making of pot-pourri. *The Garden* **81** (2386), 324-5 A.

1917 Some American peat shrubs. *Country Life* **42** (1075), 139-140 A.

1917 The Effect of Heavy Rain. *The Garden* **81** (2387), 334 A.

1917 The Yellow Austrian Briar (Rosa foetida = Rosa lutea). *The Garden* **81** (2388), 348 N.

1917 Chantarelle (Cantharellus cibarius). *The Garden* **81** (2390), 371 N.

1917 Veronica Traversii. *The Garden* **81** (2391), 383 C.

1917 Heracleum mantegazzianum. *The Garden* **81** (2391), 387 N.

1917 Plants in steps & pavements. *The Garden* **81** (2393), 407-8 A.

1917 Two good Sea Hollies. *The Garden* **81** (2393), 411-2 A.

1917 Plants for shrubbery edges. *Country Life* **42** (1084), 356 A.

1917 Gentiana asclepiadea (The Willow Gentian). *The Garden* **81** (2396), 441 N.

1917 Some Garden Roses. *The Garden* **81** (2398), 468-9 A.

1917 The Survivors. *The Garden* **81** (2398), 472 N.

1917 Sweet Corn. *The Garden* **81** (2402), 523 N.

1917 Hardy Azaleas. *Country Life* **42** (1092), 78★, A.

1917 Hardy Azaleas. *Gardening Illustrated* **39** (2025), 693 A.

1918 An instructive failure with dried plums. *The Garden* **82** (2408), 17 N.

1918 Impatiens Roylei. *The Garden* **82** (2411), 59 N.

1918 Clematis montana and its many uses. *Country Life* **43** (1100), 114-5 A.

1918 Pink Snapdragons. *The Garden* **82** (2412), 70 N.

1918 Some Hardy Annuals. *The Garden* **82** (2412), 71 A.

1918 The making of Pot-pourri. *The National Rose Society Rose Annual* **46** (2363), 95-8 A.

1918 Trientalis. *The Garden* **82** (2416), 119 N.

1918 Daphne pontica. *The Garden* **82** (2416), 119 N.

1918 Helxine Soleirolii. *The Garden* **82** (2416), 119 N.

1918 Early flowering Cosmos. *The Garden* **82** (2416), 119 N.

1918 Christmas Roses. *The Garden* **82** (2416), 119 N.

1918 Pimpernel (Salad Burnet). *The Garden* **82** (2416), 119 N.

1918 Spring Crocuses. *The Garden* **82** (2417), 125 A.

1918 The early Anemones. *The Garden* **82** (2417), 125-6 A.

1918 Viburnum opulus. *The Garden* **82** (2418), 130 C.

1918 Iris stylosa. *The Garden* **82** (2420), 148 N.

1918 Plant names. *The Garden* **82** (2420), 148 N.

1918 Omphalodes verna. *The Garden* **82** (2427), 209 N.

1918 Corydalis ochroleuca. *The Garden* **82** (2428), 217 C.

1918 Sorrel milk soup. *The Garden* **82** (2428), 217 C.

1918 Akebia quinata. *The Garden* **82** (2428), 218 N.

1918 Trillium grandiflorum. *Country Life* **43** (1118), 537 A.

1918 A handsome fern. *The Garden* **82** (2429), 224 C.

1918 Saxifraga cymbalaria. *The Garden* **82** (2430), 233 C.

1918 Exochorda grandiflora. *The Garden* **82** (2431), 240 C.

1918 Munstead Bunch Primroses. *The Garden* **82** (2431), 242 A.

1918 Phlox stellaria. *The Garden* **82** (2432), 249 C

1918 Some of the new Bearded Irises. *The Garden* **82** (2432), 251 A.

1918 Paeonia officinalis. *The Garden* **82** (2433), 257 C.

1918 Trientalis europaea. *The Garden* **82** (2434), 266 C.

1918 Cornus canadensis. *The Garden* **82** (2434), 266 C.

1918 Some Old Garden Roses. *The Garden* **82** (2434), 270 A.

1918 Seseli gummiferum. *The Garden* **82** (2435), 279 N.

1918 Pot Pourri. *Ladies Field* **82** (1062), 167 A.

1918 Some of the Hardy Sages. *The Garden* **82** (2436), 289- 290 A.

1918 Rose Aglaia. *The Garden* **82** (2437), 296 N.

1918 A useful maincrop pea. *The Garden* **82** (2438), 302 C.

1918 Onions for seed. *The Garden* **82** (2439), 311 C.

1918 Sparaxis pulcherrima. *The Garden* **82** (2440), 325 N.

1918 A White Cottage Balsam. *Gardening Illustrated* **40** (233), 420 C.

1918 Camouflage. *The Garden* **82** (2441), 332 A.

1918 Calycanthus occidentalis. *The Garden* **82** (2442), 337 C.

1918 Lettuce Stalks as Ginger. *The Garden* **82** (2442), 337 C.

1918 White Foxglove. *The Garden* **82** (2443), 346-7 A.

1918 Hydrangea Hortensia. *The Garden* **82** 2444), 353 C.

1918 Gladioli. *The Garden* **82** (2444), 355 A.

1918 Roadside and hedgerow timber. *Country Life* **44** (1134), 266-7 A.

1918 The Judas Tree in fruit. *The Garden* **82** (2446), 376 N.

1918 A heath garden in West Surrey. *Country Life* **44** (1135), 281 A.

1918 Rambling rose Lady Godiva. *The Garden* **82** (2447), 386-7 C.

1918 Ways of using green tomatoes. *The Garden* **82** (2448), 398 A.

1918 Aster corymbosus. *The Garden* **82** (2449), 403 C.

1918 Welwitschia mirabilis. *The Garden* **82** (2451), 418 C.

1918 The wooden rake. *The Garden* **82** (2452), 427 C.

1918 A hybrid clematis. *The Garden* **82** (2455), 455 N.

1918 The Re-creation of Gardens. *Country Life* **44** (1144), 512-4 A.

1918 Some evergreens for poor soils. *The Garden* **82** (2456), 461 A.

1918 Bambusa Metake. *The Garden* **82** 2457), 467 C.

1918 Hardy ferns in Winter. *Country Life* **44** (1146), 586 A.

1918 Hardy Azaleas. *The Garden* **82** (2458), 478 A.

1919 Stobaea purpurea. *The Garden* **83** (2459), 4 C.

1919 Sparassis crispa. *Country Life* **45** (1148), 26 A.

1919 Clubbing in Honesty. *The Garden* **83** (2460), 10 C.

1919 Digging fork converted to Drag. *The Garden* **83** (2461), 19C.

1919 A June flower border. *The Garden* **83** (2464), 51 N.

1919 The Nut Walk. *The Garden* **83** (2464), 52 A.

1919 Useful plums. *The Garden* **83** (2465), 67 C.

1919 Thalictrum aquilegifolium purpureum. Country Life 45 (1154), 184 A.

1919 Clematis Montana & its many uses. *The Garden* **83** (2466), 80 A.

1919 White Weigela. Country Life 45 (1155), 203 A.

1919 White Foxgloves. *The Garden* **83** (2467), 92 N.

1919 Green wood on the fire. *The Garden* **83** (2468), 102 C.

1919 Flowers from seed for the coming Summer. *Country Life* **45** (1157), 262-3 A.

1919 The Rot pit. *The Garden* **83** (2469), 123. N.

1919 Millmead, Bramley Surrey. *The Garden* **83** (2470), 130-1 A.

1919 Colour in the Flower Garden I. *Country Life* **45** (1159), 308-9 A.

1919 Colour in the Flower Garden II. *Country Life* **45** (1160), 348-9 A.

1919 Some interesting Annuals. *The Garden* **83** (2475), 191 N.

1919 Spring Flowers in a Surrey Garden. *The Garden* **83** (2476), 204-5 A.

1919 Plants for edgings. *The Garden* **83** (2477), 216 A.

1919 Platycodon mariesii. *The Garden* **83** (2478), 226 N.

1919 Olearia stellulata. *The Garden* **83** (2480), 251 C.

1919 Colour in the small garden. *Our Homes & Gardens* **1** (1), 20-1 A.

1919 Pulmonaria azurea. *The Garden* **83** (2482), 274 C.

1919 White Weigela. *The Garden* **83** (2482), 280 N.

1919 A garden of Summer Flowers. *Ladies Field* **86** (1109), 18 A.

1919 To follow Oriental Poppies. *The Garden* **83** (2483), 288 C.

1919 Crowning the Colours. *The Garden* **83** (2485), 312 C.

1919 Cistus Florentinus. *The Garden* **83** (2486), 325 C.

1919 Pyrus Maulei. *The Garden* **83** (2487), 337 C.

1919 A bedding Pelargonium newly planted. *The Garden* **83** (2487), 343 N.

1919 Carpeting plants for Rosebeds. *The Garden* **83** (2490), 372 C.

1919 Rosa gallica. *Country Life* **46** (1181), 249.

1919 Solanum jasminoides. *The Garden* **83** (2493), 410 N.

1919 Cistus Cyprius. *The Garden* **83** (2494), 421 N.

1919 Wood Sage. *The Garden* **83** (2494), 426 N.

1919 Wasp Stings. *The Garden* **83** (2495), 434 C.

1919 September Flowers. *The Garden* **83** (2495), 438 A.

1919 Colour in the flower border. *The Garden* **83** (2496), 450 A.

1919 Some Tea Roses. *The Garden* **83** (2498), 470-1 A.

1919 A pretty Fuchsia. *The Garden* **83** (2499), 484-5 N.

1919 September Flowers. *The Garden* **83** (2499), 485 A.

1919 Nandina domestica. *The Garden* **83** (2500), 492 C.

1919 Clerodendron foetidum. *The Garden* **83** (2501), 506 N.

1919 Helianthus rigidus. *The Garden* **83** (2501), 507 N.

1919 Rosa microphylla. *The Garden* **83** (2501), 510 N.

1919 Lilium superbum. *The Garden* **83** (2502), 519 N.

1919 Rosa Evangeline. *The Garden* **83** (2502), 521 N.

1919 Some Aims in Gardening. *Bulletin of the Garden Club of America.* **Nov.** (1), 7-10 A.

1919 Clematis flammula. *The Garden* **83** (2503), 530 N.

1919 Crocus speciosus & sweet alyssum. *The Garden* **83** (2504), 541 C.

1919 October flowers. *The Garden* **83** (2505), 554 N.

1919 Vine Chasselas Gros Coulard. *The Garden* **83** (2505), 559 N.

1919 Hydrangea Hortensia. *Country Life* **46** (1196), 790 A.

1919 Rosa gallica. *The Garden* **83** (2508), 592 N.

1919 Macartney rose. *The Garden* **83** (2509), 606 N.

1919 Hydrangea & Ivy Geranium. *The Garden* **83** (2510), 613 C.

1919 Mistletoe (Viscum album). *The Garden* **83** (2510), 614 N.

1920 A garden of Spring Flowers. *Bulletin of the Garden Club of America* **Jan** (2), 3-7 A.

1920 Hydrangea Hortensia. *The Garden* **84** (2511), 2 C.

1920 A colour border for August. *The Garden* **84** (2511), 5-6 A.

1920 Some False Ideals. *The Garden* **84** (2515), 56 A.

1920 Scotch Briars. *The Garden* **84** (2515), 57 N.

1920 Some uses of grey plants. *Country Life* **47** (1206), 196 A.

1920 Megasea cordifolia major. *The Garden* **84** (2519), 106 N.

1920 The flower border. *Bulletin of the Garden Club of America* Mar (2) New Series, 5-8 A.

1920 Woodland Roses. *The National Rose Society Rose Annual*, pp. 29-30 A.

1920 Sweet Bay. *The Garden* **84** (2521), 129 N.

1920 St. Helena Violet. *The Garden* **84** (2522), 140 C.

1920 Myrtus ugni. *The Garden* **84** (2523), 153 C.

1920 Stephandra flexuosa. *Country Life* **47** (1212), 403 A.

1920 Iris stylosa. *The Garden* **84** (2524), 164 C.

1920 A bird scare. *The Garden* **84** (2524), 165 C.

1920 A good Megasea. *The Garden* **84** (2525), 177 C.

1920 Lent Hellebores. *Country Life* **47** (1214), 473 A.

1920 Lent Hellebores. *The Garden* **84** (2526), 195 A.

1920 The Chopping Bench. *The Garden* **84** (2528), 217 A.

1920 Wild Gardening. *Bulletin of the Garden Club of America* May (4) New Series, 5-9 A.

1920 Corydalis cheilanthifolia. *The Garden* **84** (2529), 234 N.

1920 Narcissus Johnstoni. *The Garden* **84** (2530), 255 N.

1920 Erythronium giganteum. *The Garden* **84** (2531), 272 N.

1920 Oriental Poppy Perry's White. *The Garden* **84** (2535), 313 N.

1920 Rolling steps. *The Garden* **84** (2535), 315 N.

1920 The Primrose Garden. *The Garden* **84** (2536), 328 N.

1920 Scilla italica alba. *The Garden* **84** (2537), 333 N.

1920 London Pride. *The Garden* **84** (2537), 334 N.

1920 Two roses of Northern Asia (Rosa hugonis & Rosa altaica). *Country Life* **48** (1226), 32 A.

1920 Andromeda (Pieris) Floribunda. *The Garden* **84** (2539), 359 N.

1920 White Foxgloves. *The Garden* **84** (2539), 361 N.

1920 The Willow Gentian (Gentiana asclepiadea). *The Garden* **84** (2544), 417 N.

1920 Two Eyening Primroses. *The Garden* **84** (2545), 429 N.

1920 Ways & Means in the Garden. *Bulletin of the Garden Club of America.* Sep (6), 4-5 A.

1920 Two roses of northern Asia. *The Garden* **84** (2546), 441 N.

1920 Anemone sylvestris. *The Garden* **84** (2548), 465 N.

1920 Chrysanthemum maximum. *The Garden* **84** (2548), 467 N.

1920 Yew Hedge. *The Garden* **84** , 493 A.

1920 Michaelmas Daisies. *Country Life* **48** (1237), 370 A.

1920 Sweet Alyssum & Catmint. *The Garden* **84** (2559), 597 N.

1920 Star Dahlias. *The Garden* **84** (2561), 601 N.

1920 Poterium obtusum. *The Garden* **84** (2561), 619 N.

1920 A simple slug trap. *The Garden* **84** (2562), 630 N.

1921 The Conservatory or Winter Garden. *Bulletin of the Garden Club of America* Jan (8), 2-6 A.

1921 Borders of Annuals. *The Garden* **85** (2565), 30 A.

1921 Annuals to sow in heat. *The Garden* **85** (2565), 32 A.

1921 Annuals for Sunny & Shady Places. *The Garden* **85** (2566), 54 A.

1921 A plea for the Laurel. *The Garden* **85** (2567), 68 A.

1921 Border Plants that succeed best. *The Garden* **85** (2573), 126 A.

1921 How a little August garden was made effective with Pink and Purple flowers. *The Garden* **85** (2574), 148-149 A.

1921 Mulleins pulled down. *The Garden* **85** (2587), 306 A.

1921 The use of grey foliage. *Country Life* **49**, 1vi A.

1921 Small London Gardens. *Country Life* **50** (1292), 458-9 A.

1922 The taller Campanulas. *The Garden* **86** (2633), 210 A.

1922 Some of the lesser Campanulas. *The Garden* **86** (2634), 227 A.

1922 Wallflowers in the Spring garden. *The Garden* **86** (2636), 246 A.

1922 Primroses. *The Garden* **86** (2636), 245 N.

1922 Colour effects in the flower garden. *The Garden* **86** (2638), 277 A.

1922 Bedding out. *The Garden* **86** (2640), 305-6 A.

1922 Colour effects in the flower garden. *The Garden* **86** (2640), 307 C.

1922 The Iris garden. *Country Life* **51** (1329), 850-2 A.

1922 A beautiful cherry. *The Garden* **86** (2641), 317 A.

1922 A suggestion for garden plots. *Country Life* **52** (1331), 29 A.

1922 Flowers in the rain. *The Garden* **86** (2646), 387 A.

1922 Regulating the flower border. *The Garden* **86** (2647), 397-8 A.

1922 Colour effects in the flower garden. *The Garden* **86** (2647), 398 N.

1922 The joys of observation. *Country Life* **52** (1336), 177 A.

1922 Why "Amethystine"? *The Garden* **86** (2648), 418 C.

1922 A blue border. *Country Life* **52** (1337), 218-9 A.

1922 Why "Amethystine"? *Country Life* **52** (1337), 223 A.

1922 Colour effects in the late Summer Border. *The Garden* **86** (2651), 452 A.

1922 Sweet Peas. *The Garden* **86** (2651), 455 C.

1922 Hardy Crinums. *The Garden* **86** (2653), 482 C.

1922 The reconstruction of a Nottinghamshire garden. Bulcote Manor. *Country Life* **52** (1342), 385 A.

1922 Some colour effects in the flower garden. *The Garden* **86** (2653), 495 A.

1922 Alliums in the flower garden. *The Garden* **86** (2657), 531 A.

1922 Iberis sempervirens and others. *Country Life* **52** (1347), 554-5 A.

1922 The grey border for late Summer. *Country Life* **52** (1353), 776-7 A.

1923 Some trees of our neighbourhood. *Busbridge Parish Magazine* **25** (10), n.p. A.

1923 Garden notes. *Country Life* **51** (1360), 113.

1923 Grouping of hardy bulbs. Country Life 53 (1361), 156-7 A.

1923 Garden notes. *Country Life* **53** (1362), 182-7 A.

1923 Garden notes. *Country Life* **53** (1364), 239-40 A.

1923 Garden notes. *Country Life* **53** (1366), 326 A.

1923 Mistletoe as a spring plant and other notes. *Country Life* **53** (1368), 396 A.

1923 Garden notes. *Country Life* **53** (1372), 543 A.

1923 A Primrose Garden. *Country Life* **53** (1373), 568-9 A.

1923 Heaths and aubrietas. *Country Life* **53** (1373), 569 A.

1923 How to use Spring flowers. *Country Life* **53** (1375), 643 A.

1923 Munstead Bunch Primroses. *The Garden* **87** (2688), 256-7 A.

1923 Waterside planting. *Country Life* **53** (1377), 713 A.

1923 Erinus alpinus. *The Garden* **87** (2689), 279 C.

1923 Clematis Flammula. *The Garden* **87** (2690), 297 C.

1923 Whitebeam (Pyrus Aria). *The Garden* **87** (2691), 310 C.

1923 Garden notes. *Country Life* **53** (1382), 931-2 A.

1923 The old roses. *Country Life* **54** (1385), 91-2 A.

1923 The Azalea garden. *Country Life* **54** (1390), 258-9 A.

1923 Gardening Among Stones. *Homes & Gardens* **5** Sept 120-1 A.

1923 Fruit on the dinner table. *Country Life* **54** (1392), 322 A.

1923 Bunch primroses. *Country Life* **54** (1395), 418-9 A.

1923 A flower border for the whole Summer. *Gardening Illustrated* **45** (2332), 717 A.

1923 Old-fashioned Roses. *The Garden* **87** (2713), 587-8 A.

1923 Some Horticultural Indiscretions. *The Garden* **87** (2714), 607-8 A.

1923 Calluna Vulgaris. *Gardening Illustrated* **45** (2334), 754 N.

1923 Yuccas in the flower border. *Gardening Illustrated* **45** (2337), 801 A.

1923 Grey foliage in the flower border. *Gardening Illustrated* **45** (2338), 820 N.

1924 Mothering Sunday. *Busbridge Parish Magazine* **26** (3), n.p. A.

1924 Trachymene caerulea. *Gardening Illustrated* **46** (2339), 3 C.

1924 Crinum Powelli. *Gardening Illustrated* **46** (2341), 37 N.

1924 White beam. *Gardening Illustrated* **46** (2342), 50 N.

1924 Some Annuals for cutting. *Country Life* **55** (1412), 142 A.

1924 Garden Borders. *Homes & Gardens* **5** Feb, 285-7 A.

1924 Borders round a house. *Gardening Illustrated* **46** (2343), 68 A.

1924 Some desirable Annuals. *The Garden* **88** (2724), 58-9 A.

1924 Borders of late Summer Flowers. *Gardening Illustrated* **46** (2347), 128 N.

1924 Some Desirable Annuals & Biennials. *English Life* **2** (4), 210-1 A.

1924 Forsythia Suspensa. *Gardening Illustrated* **46** (2351), 183 N.

1924 Doronicum Caucasicum as cut flowers. *Gardening Illustrated* **46** (2351), 183 N.

1924 Rabbit-proof plants. *The Garden* **88** (2732), 213 C.

1924 How to Run a Garden party. *Gardening Illustrated* **46** (2353), 216 A.

1924 An outdoor sitting-place. *Country Life* **55** (1423), 581 A.

1924 Some garden ornaments & accessories. *The Garden* **88** (2736), 282-3 A.

1924 Some decorative Aspects of Gardening. *The Empire Review* **39** (280), 532-9 A.

1924 Magnolia conspicua. *Gardening Illustrated* **46** (2358), 293 N.

1924 Magnolia stellata. *Gardening Illustrated* **46** (2359), 310 N.

1924 The Phillips Memorial at Godalming. *Gardening Illustrated* **46** (2362), 351 A.

1924 New Zealand flax *Gardening Illustrated* **46** , 353.

1924 A River of Daffodils. *Gardening Illustrated* **46** (2362), 363 N.

1924 Euphorbia Wulfenii. *Gardening Illustrated* **46** (2363), 368 C.

1924 A Cypress Hedge. *Gardening Illustrated* **46** (2363), 375 A.

1924 Ghent Azaleas. *Gardening Illustrated* **46** (2364), 389 N.

1924 Iris Alcazar. *Gardening Illustrated* **46** (2364), 389 N.

1924 Midsummer in the Garden. *Country Life* **55** (1434), 1055-6.

1924 Rhododendrons. *Gardening Illustrated* **46** (2365), 400 C.

1924 Steps to a Seed Room. *Gardening Illustrated* **46** (2367), 442 N.

1924 Summer Borders. *The Garden* **88** (2748), 495-6 A.

1924 Iris Pallida Dalmatica. *Gardening Illustrated* **46** (2368), 452 N.

1924 Flower Jars at a War Memorial. *Gardening Illustrated* **46** (2368), 453 C.

1924 Viburnum Plicatum. *Gardening Illustrated* **46** (2368), 455 N.

1924 Border Campanulas. *The Garden* **88** (2749), 515-6 A.

1924 Children & Gardens. *Homes & Gardens* **6 Aug,** 109-110 A.

1924 Poppies. *Country Life* **56** (1439), 174-5 A.

1924 Iris Sibirica. *Gardening Illustrated* **46** (2370), 487 A.

1924 Potpourri. *Gardening Illustrated* **46** (2371), 498 N.

1924 Spiraea Van Houttei. *Gardening Illustrated* **46** (2371), 499 N.

1924 Some hints for the flower border. *Gardening Illustrated* **46** (2371), 499 A.

1924 Borders of June Flowers. *Gardening Illustrated* **46** (2372), 517 N.

1924 The Austrian Briar. *Gardening Illustrated* **46** (2373), 524 N.

1924 Megasea Cordifolia M. Purpurea. *Gardening Illustrated* **46** (2373), 530 N.

1924 Rosa sinica Anemone. *Gardening Illustrated* **46** (2374), 544 N.

1924 Romneya Coulteri. *Gardening Illustrated* **46** (2376), 573 N.

1924 A Garden Gateway. *Gardening Illustrated* **46** (2376), 577 N.

1924 Crinum Powelli. *Gardening Illustrated* **46** (2377), 588 N.

1924 The August border. *Gardening Illustrated* **46** (2378), 605 N.

1924 Eryngium and White Pea. *Gardening Illustrated* **46** (2378), 605 N.

1924 Aretotis and Gazania. *Gardening Illustrated* **46** (2379), 619 N.

1924 A Double Border of late Summer Flowers. *Gardening Illustrated* **46** (2379), 622 N.

1924 Yuccas. *Gardening Illustrated* **46** (2380), 633 N.

1924 Blues and mauves in the garden. *Country Life* **56** (1450), 602.

1924 Sorb Apple. *Gardening Illustrated* **46** (2382), 666 C.

1924 Some problems of the flower border. *Gardening Illustrated* **16 August**.000.

1924 Snap Dragons in a dry wall. *Gardening Illustrated* **46** (2382), 667 N.

1924 Tritomas in the flower border. *Gardening Illustrated* **46** (2382), 668 N.

1924 Glyceria aquatica fol. var. *Gardening Illustrated* **46** (2383), 683 C.

1924 Olearia Haasti. *Gardening Illustrated* **46** (2383), 689 N.

1924 Yucca filamentosa. *Gardening Illustrated* **46** (2384), 699 C.

1924 Wall plants for an eastern exposure. *Gardening Illustrated* **46** (2385), 723 N.

1924 The Azalea Garden. *Gardening Illustrated* **46** (2386), 737 N.

1924 Polygonum campanulatum. *Gardening Illustrated* **46** (2387), 755 N.

1924 Rhododendron Mrs. R. H. Holford. *Gardening Illustrated* **46** (2388), 767 C.

1924 Old Apple trees. *Gardening Illustrated* **46** (2389), 780 N.

1924 Jelly from Mountain Ash berries. *Gardening Illustrated* **46** (2389), 780 N.

1924 The Flower Garden – a Quiet Entrance. *Gardening Illustrated* **46** (2389), 782 N.

1925 A fox hunt at Munstead Wood. *Busbridge Parish Magazine* **27** (3), n.p. A.

1925 The August Borders. *Gardening Illustrated* **47** (2392), 25 A.

1925 Waterers Laburnum. *Gardening Illustrated* **47** (2395), 65 N.

1925 The Herbaceous border. *The Field* **145** (3763), 3 (suppl.) A.

1925 Salvia Sclarea in the Flower Border. *Gardening Illustrated* **47** (2397), 97 N.

1925 A Garden in the making. *Gardening Illustrated* **47** (2397), 101 A.

1925 Spring planting of Summer Flower Borders. *Gardening Illustrated* **47** (2401), 166 A.

1925 A weed as Salad. *Gardening Illustrated* **47** (2401), 174 C.

1925 The ordinary garden. *Homes & Gardens* **6 April**, 395-8 A.

1925 Corydalis cheilanthifolia. *Gardening Illustrated* **47** (2411), 321 N.

1925 The between plants. *Gardening Illustrated* **47** (2414), 376 N.

1925 Olearia Gunniana. *Gardening Illustrated* **47** (2415), 401 N.

1925 Iris Alcazar. *Gardening Illustrated* **47** (2416), 417 N.

1925 Scots pine on a chimney. *The Garden* **89** (2798), 381 C.

1925 Iron Garden Gates. *The Garden* **89** (2799), 390-1 A.

1925 A well set up exhibit. *The Garden* **89** (2799), 398 C.

1925 Azalea Occidentalis. *Gardening Illustrated* **47** (2418), 444 N.

1925 Salvia Sclarea. *Gardening Illustrated* **47** (2419), 465 N.

1925 Senecia Greyi. *Gardening Illustrated* **47** (2420), 483 N.

1925 Rose Mme. Plantier. *Gardening Illustrated* **47** (2421), 491 C.

1925 White flowers in the woodland. *The Garden* **89** (2803), 441 A.

1925 Planting against a house. *Gardening Illustrated* **47** (2423), 519 N.

1925 Campanula lactiflora syn. celtidifolia. *Gardening Illustrated* **47** (2424), 527 C.

1925 Rose Lady Curzon. *Gardening Illustrated* **47** (2424), 532 N.

1925 Crinum Powelli. *Gardening Illustrated* **47** (2427), 555 C.

1925 Ivy Geranium Mme. Crousse. *Gardening Illustrated* **47** (2427), 561 N.

1925 Yucca Filamentosa. *Gardening Illustrated* **47** (2429), 587 N.

1925 Scabiosa graminifolia. *Gardening Illustrated* **47** (2430), 599 N.

1925 Cistus cyprius. *Gardening Illustrated* **47** , 601.

1925 Truth in Advertising. *Gardening Illustrated* **47** (2431), 615 C.

1925 Rosa Alba and its varieties. *Gardening Illustrated* **47** (2432), 634 N.

1925 Rose species by the sea. *Gardening Illustrated* **47** (2434), 660 C.

1925 Garden Craftsmanship in Yew & Box. *English Life* **5** (6), 436-9 A.

1925 September in the flower border. *Gardening Illustrated* **47** (2435), 680 N.

1925 The best Eryngiums. *Gardening Illustrated* **47** (2437), 709 N.

1925 Godetia Double Rose. *Gardening Illustrated* **47** (2438), 725 C.

1925 Solanum jasminoides. *Gardening Illustrated* **47** (2439), 741 N.

1925 Tritomas in the flower border. *Gardening Illustrated* **47** (2439), 742 N.

1925 Othonnopsis cheirifolia. *Gardening Illustrated* **47** (2440), 757 N.

1925 Flowering Shrubs in the Flower Border. *Gardening Illustrated* **47** (2441), 776 N.

1925 Nemophila insignis. *Gardening Illustrated* **47** (2442), 785 N.

1925 Oenothera Lamarckiana. *Gardening Illustrated* **47** (2442), 787 N.

1926 The church and churchyard. *Busbridge Parish Magazine* **27** (3), n.p. A.

1926 An old book of flower pictures. *Country Life* **59** (1516), 121-2.

1926 Clematis Jouiniana. *Gardening Illustrated* **48** (2449), 98 N.

1926 In a West Surrey garden. *Gardening Illustrated* **48** (2450), 116 N.

1926 In a West Surrey garden. *Gardening Illustrated* **48** (2452), 149 N.

1926 Lent Hellebores as cut flowers. *Gardening Illustrated* **48** (2453), 162 A.

1926 Pieris japonica. *Gardening Illustrated* **48** (2454), 179 N.

1926 Narcissus pallidus praecox. *Gardening Illustrated* **48** (2455), 194 N.

1926 Lawn and Woodland. *Gardening Illustrated* **48** (2455), 196 A.

1926 Doronicum Caucasicum. *Gardening Illustrated* **48** (2455), 206 N.

1926 Annuals as cut flowers. *English Life* **6** (5), 323-5 A.

1926 Rhododendron praecox. *Gardening Illustrated* **48** (2456), 209 N.

1926 The Lesser Trumpet Daffodils. *Gardening Illustrated* **48** (2457), 223 A.

1926 Helenium pumilum & its companions. *Gardening Illustrated* **48** (2457), 231 A.

1926 Mistaken spelling in plant names. *Gardening Illustrated* **48** (2464), 305 N.

1926 Obituary: John T Bennett-Poe. *Gardening Illustrated* **48** (2464), 312 A.

1926 Tulip Mrs Hoog. *Gardening Illustrated* **48** (2465), 373 N.

1926 The Framed Picture. *Gardening Illustrated* **48** , 391.

1926 Hardy plants with handsome foliage. *Gardening Illustrated* **48** (2474), 467 A.

1926 Verbascum olympicum. *Gardening Illustrated* **48** (2474), 467 N.

1926 Asphodelus ramosus. *Gardening Illustrated* **48** (2474), 469 N.

1926 In the Spring Garden. *Gardening Illustrated* **48** (2477), 517 A.

1926 To Redeem Unsightliness. *English Life* **7** (4), 300 A.

1926 A scarlet border. *Gardening Illustrated* **48** (2478), 543 N.

1926 Penstemons. *Gardening Illustrated* **48** (2478), 532 N.

1926 Alstroemeria chilensis. *Gardening Illustrated* **48** (2480), 563 N.

1926 The Primrose Garden. *Gardening Illustrated* **48** , 565.

1926 Dwarf lavender. *Gardening Illustrated* **48** (2480), 569 N.

1926 Hydrangea aborescens grandiflora. *Gardening Illustrated* **48** (2481), 579 N.

1926 The Joy of making a New Garden. *The Garden* **90** (2860), 535-6 A.

1926 In the Heath Garden. *Gardening Illustrated* **48** (2482), 597 N.

1926 Natural planting. *Gardening Illustrated* **48** (2482), 601 N.

1926 The Joy of making a New Garden. *The Garden* **90** (2861), 551-2 A.

1926 Campanula lactiflora. *Gardening Illustrated* **48** (2483), 609N.

1926 The joy of making a New Garden. *The Garden* **90** (2862), 569 A.

1926 A Design for a Small Garden. *The Garden* **90** (2863), 581 A.

1926 The Joy of making a New Garden. *The Garden* **90** (2864), 599 A.

1926 The rolling steps. *Gardening Illustrated* **48** (2486), 651 N.

1926 Grey foliage in the flower garden. *Bulletin of the Garden Club of America* Nov. (12) 3rd Series, 9-10 A.

1926 Pyrethrum uliginosum with Michaelmas Daisies. *Gardening Illustrated* **48** (2487), 671 A.

1926 The Joy of making a New Garden. *The Garden* **90** (2866), 630 A.

1926 Heracleum mantegazzianum. *Gardening Illustrated* **48** (2488), 683 N.

1926 The Joy of making a New Garden. *The Garden* **90** (2868), 661 A.

1926 Cedronella Triphylla. *Gardening Illustrated* **48** (2491), 725 N.

1926 The late Michaelmas Daisies. *Gardening Illustrated* **48** (2491), 729 N.

1926 The Joy of making a New Garden. *The Garden* **90** (2870), 692 A.

1926 Clematis Flammula. *Gardening Illustrated* **48** (2492), 744 N.

1926 My Christmas Garden. *Daily Express* (8317), 8 A.

1927 Plants in pots. *Gardening Illustrated* **49** (2495), 3 N.

1927 Grey Foliage in the flower border. *Gardening Illustrated* **49** (2495), 7 N.

1927 The Joy of making a New Garden. *The Garden* **90** (2874), 2 A.

1927 Polygonum molle. *Gardening Illustrated* **49** (2496), 21 N.

1927 Spiders and Pernettya. *Gardening Illustrated* **49** (2497), 36 N.

1927 The Joy of making a New Garden. *The Garden* **91** (2876), 35 A.

1927 Foliage plants for shrub edges. *Gardening Illustrated* **49** (2499), 68 A.

1927 Pyrethrum uliginosum with Michaelmas Daisies. *Gardening Illustrated* **49** (2501), 93 N.

1927 The Joy of making a New Garden. *The Garden* **91** (2880), 99 A.

1927 Grey foliage on a low wall. *Gardening Illustrated* **49** (2502), 113 N.

1927 Scabiosa Columbaria. *Gardening Illustrated* **49** (2505), 156 N.

1927 Clematis paniculata. *Gardening Illustrated* **49** (2506), 167 N.

1927 The Joy of making a New Garden. *The Garden* **91** (2885), 189 A.

1927 Salvia Sclarea. *Gardening Illustrated* **49** (2509), 217 N.

1927 Gladioli in the Summer Garden. *Gardening Illustrated* **49** (2509), 221 N.

1927 My Easter Garden. *Daily Express* (8412), 8 A.

1927 Polygonum campanulatum. Gardening Illustrated 49 (2511), 249 N.

1927 A Decorative Annual for edging. *The Garden* **91** (2892), 297 N.

1927 A Decorative shrub – Clethra Alnifolia. *The Garden* **91** (2893), 313 N.

1927 An admirable rockery plant (Arenaria montana). *The Garden* **91** (2893), 313 N.

1927 A Quick growing Clematis – Clematis vitalba. *The Garden* **91** (2894), 328 N.

1927 The care of the flower border. *The Garden* **91** (2895), 341 A.

1927 Ivy Geranium Mme. Crousse. *The Garden* **91** (2895), 343 N.

1927 Campanula pyramidalis. *The Garden* **91** (2895), 344 N.

1927 Early Michaelmas Daisies. *Gardening Illustrated* **49** (2519), 371 A.

1927 Iris Alcazar. *Gardening Illustrated* **49** (2519), 372 C.

1927 Ornithogalum nutans. *Gardening Illustrated* **49** (2519), 377 N.

1927 Crocus speciosus & Koniga maritima. *Gardening Illustrated* **49** (2519), 381 N.

1927 Nemophila insignis. *Gardening Illustrated* **49** (2521), 406 N.

1927 The June Borders. *Gardening Illustrated* **49** 2521), 407 A.

1927 Inchmury – a fine Garden Pink. *Gardening Illustrated* **49** (2522), 421 N.

1927 Some of the Sweetest Roses. *Gardening Illustrated* **49** (2522), 424 A.

1927 Viburnum plicatum. *Gardening Illustrated* **49** (2523), 441 N.

1927 Grey Foliage in Garden Effects. *The Garden* **91** (2902), 467 N.

1927 Gallon Rhododendron ferrugineum. *Gardening Illustrated* **49** (2524), 448 C.

1927 Kalmia latifolia. *Gardening Illustrated* **49** (2524), 450 A.

1927 Allium nigrum var. album. *Gardening Illustrated* **49** (2524), 451 N.

1927 Rose Parfum de l'Haye. *Gardening Illustrated* **49** (2525), 464 C.

1927 A neglected Rhododendron. *Gardening Illustrated* **49** (2525), 468 N.

1927 Foxglove Munstead white. *Gardening Illustrated* **49** (2525), 469 N.

1927 Rosa polyantha fi. pl. *Gardening Illustrated* **49** (2526), 485 N.

1927 Azaleas in woodland. *Gardening Illustrated* **49** (2526), 487 N.

1927 Libertia formosa. *Gardening Illustrated* **49** (2528), 515 N.

1927 Geranium ibericum platyphyllum. *Gardening Illustrated* **49** (2528), 516 N.

1927 Omphalodes linifolia (Venus Navelwort). *Gardening Illustrated* **49** (2528), 519 N.

1927 Miss Jekyll & her Flower Garden (foreword by Miss Willmott). Paper read at a meeting of The Garden Club. *Gardening Illustrated* **49** (2529), 531-4.

1927 Rose Euphrosyne. *Gardening Illustrated* **49** (2530), 550 N.

1927 A plant worth reviving – Salvia Sclarea. *The Garden* **91** (2911), 609N.

1927 Monk's Rhubarb. *Gardening Illustrated* **49** (2535), 623 C.

1927 The Heath Garden. *Gardening Illustrated* **49** (2535), 629 N.

1927 The Yew Cat. *Gardening Illustrated* **49** (2536), 641 N.

1927 White Crinum Powelli. *Gardening Illustrated* **49** (2436), 642 N.

1927 Rose Fimbriata. *Gardening Illustrated* **49** (2537), 657 N.

1927 Rosa Flora. *Gardening Illustrated* **49** (2537), 657 N.

1927 High Mount, Guildford I. *Gardening Illustrated* **49** (2537), 660-1 A.

1927 High Mount, Guildford II. *Gardening Illustrated* **49** (2538), 674-5 A.

1927 Spiraea Aruncus. *Gardening Illustrated* **49** (2541), 725 N.

1927 The Grey Garden. *Gardening Illustrated* **49** (2542), 738-9 A.

1927 Hardiness of Gazania. *Gardening Illustrated* **49** (2542), 741 N.

1927 Ophiopogon Jaburan. *Gardening Illustrated* **49** (2542), 741 N.

1927 From Indoors – Looking Out. *Gardening Illustrated* **49** (2543), 751 N.

1927 A freak Helenium. *Gardening Illustrated* **49** (2544), 764 C.

1927 A well placed fig. *Gardening Illustrated* **49** (2544), 767 N.

1927 Rosemary growing in masonry. *Gardening Illustrated* **49** (2545), 783 N.

1927 Ligustrum Japonicum. *Gardening Illustrated* **49** (2546), 796 N.

1927 Corydalis ochroleuca. *Gardening Illustrated* **49** (2546), 805 N.

1927 Apple wood. *Gardening Illustrated* **49** (2547), 810 C.

1928 Climbing plants for cottage gardens. *Busbridge Parish Magazine* **30** (6), n.p. A.

1928 Climbing plants for cottage gardens. *Busbridge Parish Magazine* **30** (7), n.p. A.

1928 The changes of fashion in gardening. The Nineteenth Century and After 104 (618), 195-9 A.

1928 A grouping of Dahlias. *Gardening Illustrated* **50** (2549), 19 N.

1928 Spiraea Aruncus. *Gardening Illustrated* **50** (2549), 20 N.

1928 Tree Ivy. *Gardening Illustrated* **50** (2549), 21 N.

1928 A hybrid Musk Rose. *Gardening Illustrated* **50** (2549), 29 N.

1928 Aesculus parviflora. *Gardening Illustrated* **50** (2553), 78 N.

1928 Hollyhock Pink Beauty. *Gardening Illustrated* **50** (2553), 80 N.

1928 The earliest flowers for cutting. *Gardening Illustrated* **50** (2557), 141 A.

1928 Narcissus pallidus praecox. *Gardening Illustrated* **50** , 240.

1928 Alexandrian Laurel. *Gardening Illustrated* **50** (2565), 271 N.

1928 Leucotfloe Axillaris. *Gardening Illustrated* **50** (2567), 309~N.

1928 The Nutwalk in Spring. *Gardening Illustrated* **50** (2568), 324 N.

1928 The way in. *Gardening Illustrated* **50** (2569), 347 N.

1928 Arum Italicum. *Gardening Illustrated* **50** (2569), 347 N.

1928 Tulips in the Spring Garden. *Gardening Illustrated* **50** (2570), 363 A.

1928 Foamflower (Tiarella cordifolia) *Gardening Illustrated* **50** , 369.

1928 A June Garden. *Country Life* **63** (1639), lvi (suppl.).

1928 Corydalis Solida. *Gardening Illustrated* **50** (2572), 392 N.

1928 The Primrose Garden. *Gardening Illustrated* **50** (2572), 397 N.

1928 Pyrus Malus Floribunda. *Gardening Illustrated* **50** (2572), 398 N.

1928 Choisya Ternata. *Gardening Illustrated* **50** (2572), 399 N.

1928 Double Cuckoo Flower (Cardamine pratense fl. pl.). *Gardening Illustrated* **50** (2573), 408 N.

1928 Plants on steps. *Gardening Illustrated* **50** (2573), 410 N.

1928 Trillium grandiflorum. *Gardening Illustrated* **50** (2573), 411 N.

1928 The steps to the loft. *Gardening Illustrated* **50** , 425.

1928 Pieris floribunda. *Gardening Illustrated* **50** , 427.

1928 Salvia sclarea. *Gardening Illustrated* **50** , 506.

1928 Spiraea discolor. *Gardening Illustrated* **50** (2579), 513 N.

1928 Romneya Coulteri. *Gardening Illustrated* **50** (2580), 525 N.

1928 Alstroemeria chilensis. *Gardening Illustrated* **50** (2580), 529 N.

1928 Verbascum Chaixi. *Gardening Illustrated* **50** (2582), 558 N.

1928 Campanula lactiflora. *Gardening Illustrated* **50** (2583), 571 N.

1928 Penstemon Heterophyllus. *Gardening Illustrated* **50** (2583), 573 N.

1928 Ivy Geranium Mme Crousse. *Gardening Illustrated* **50** (2585), 609 N.

1928 A July flower border. *Gardening Illustrated* **50** , 641.

1928 Heracleum mantegazzianum. *Gardening Illustrated* **50** (2591), 657 N.

1928 Garden Plants of Seventy Years ago. The New Flora and Silva 1 (1), 4-8 A.

1928 Peroffskya atriplicifolia. *Gardening Illustrated* **50** (2591), 703 N.

1928 Acanthus Spinosus. *Gardening Illustrated* **50** (2593), 732 N.

1928 Clematis Flammula. *Gardening Illustrated* **50** (2594), 748 N.

1928 Double Tropaeolum. *Gardening Illustrated* **50** (2594), 754 N.

1928 Campanula Isophylla alba. *Gardening Illustrated* **50** (2595), 762 C.

1928 Gaultheria Shallon. *Gardening Illustrated* **50** (2596), 779 N.

1928 Musk mallow. *Gardening Illustrated* **50** (2597), 800 N.

1928 Hydrangea arborescens grandiflora. *Gardening Illustrated* **50** (2598), 813 N.

1928 Barberry jelly. *Gardening Illustrated* **50** (2599), 825 C.

1928 Gentiana asclepiadea. *Gardening Illustrated* **50** (2599), 835 N.

1929 Colour in garden planning. *Journal of the Royal Horticultural Society* **54** (2), 282-3 A.

1929 Aster Corymbosus. *Gardening Illustrated* **51** (2600), 8 N.

1929 The Mulberry & the Flower Border. *Gardening Illustrated* **51** (2602), 35 N.

1929 Laurus nobilis. *Gardening Illustrated* **51** (2610), 177 N.

1929 Colour in the flower border. *Gardening Illustrated* **51** (2611), 204A.

1929 Star Dahlia. *Gardening Illustrated* **51** (2612), 213 N.

1929 Dahlias grouped for colour. *Gardening Illustrated* **51** (2614), 248 N.

1929 Dahlias in the Flower Border. *Gardening Illustrated* **51** (2620), 372 N.

1929 Guelder Rose: a snow storm in June. *Gardening Illustrated* **51** (2625), 449 N.

1929 Sea Kale. *Gardening Illustrated* **51** (2626), 461 N.

1929 Lupin Munstead Strain. *Gardening Illustrated* **51** (2627), 477 N.

1929 Iris Quaker Lady. *Gardening Illustrated* **51** (2627), 479 N.

1929 Rheum Undulatum. *Gardening Illustrated* **51** (2628), 497 N.

1929 Kalmia latifolia. *Gardening Illustrated* **51** (2629), 513 N.

1929 Colour names & descriptions. *Gardening Illustrated* **51** (2630), 525-6 A.

1929 Oriental Poppies in the flower border. *Gardening Illustrated* **51** (2630), 527 C.

1929 Garden Weeds. *Gardening Illustrated* **51** (2631), 543 C.

1929 Thalictrum aquilegifolium puepureum. *Gardening Illustrated* **51** (2631), 547 N.

1929 Asarum europaeum. *Gardening Illustrated* **51** , 564.

1929 Fuchsias as potting plants. *Gardening Illustrated* **51** (2632), 565 N.

1929 Viburnum plicatum. *Gardening Illustrated* **51** (2633), 578 N.

1929 Othonnopsis cheirifolia. *Gardening Illustrated* **51** (2634), 594 N.

1929 Azaleas. *Gardening Illustrated* **51** (2635), 615 N.

1929 Iris Pallida Dalmatica. *Gardening Illustrated* **51** (2636), 627 N.

1929 Hop (Humulus lupulus). *Gardening Illustrated* **51** (2637), 641 N.

1929 Flavour in Gooseberries. *Gardening Illustrated* **51** (2638), 656 C.

1929 Ceanothus Gloire de Versailles. *Gardening Illustrated* **51** (2638), 665 N.

1929 The Garden Cottage. *Gardening Illustrated* **51** (2639), 675 N.

1929 Gladiolus as a cut flower. *Gardening Illustrated* **51** (2640), 699 N.

1929 Rhododendrons. *Gardening Illustrated* **51** (2641), 712 N.

1929 Clematis Davidiana. *Gardening Illustrated* **51** (2642), 724 N.

1929 Double Tropaeolum. *Gardening Illustrated* **51** (2643), 737 C.

1929 Gloxinias. *Gardening Illustrated* **51** , 739 N.

1929 The August Borders. *Gardening Illustrated* **51** (2646), 788 N.

1929 Morning Glory. *Gardening Illustrated* **51** (2647), 806 N.

1929 The end of the South border. *Gardening Illustrated* **51** (2648), 823 N.

1929 Border phloxes. *Gardening Illustrated* **51** (2648), 825 N.

1929 A flood incident. *Gardening Illustrated* **51** (2649), 832 C.

1929 Peltaria alliacea. *Gardening Illustrated* **51** (2649), 835 N.

1929 Rock Roses. *Daily Express* (9243), 13 A.

1929 Olearia Haastii. *Gardening Illustrated* **51** (2651), 864 N.

1930 Aster Corymbosus. *Gardening Illustrated* **52** (2653), 20 N.

1930 Green oranges. *Gardening Illustrated* **52** (2668), 267 C.

1930 The Primrose Garden. *Gardening Illustrated* **52** (2671), 312 N.

1930 The Nut Walk. *Gardening Illustrated* **52** (2672), 349 N.

1930 The Broadleaved Saxifrages. *Gardening Illustrated* **52** (2673), 361 N.

1930 Narcissus Johnstoni. *Gardening Illustrated* **52** (2674), 374 C.

1930 Magnolias stellata & conspicua. *Gardening Illustrated* **52** (2674), 381 N.

1930 Viburnum Carlesii. *Gardening Illustrated* **52** (2676), 407 N.

1930 The Spring garden. *Gardening Illustrated* **52** (2677), 418 C.

1930 Aubrietias in the rockwall. *Gardening Illustrated* **52** (2672), 434 C.

1930 Erythronium giganteum. *Gardening Illustrated* **52** (2673), 455 N.

1930 Campanula lactiflora syn. celtidifolia. *Gardening Illustrated* **52** (2683) 517 N.

1930 Rose Blush Rambler. *Gardening Illustrated* **52** (2683), 525 N.

1930 Rose Zephyrine Drouhin. *Gardening Illustrated* **52** (2684), 541 N.

1930 Alstroemeria pelegrina alba. *Gardening Illustrated* **52** (2685), 545 N.

1930 Bedding plants. *Gardening Illustrated* **52** (2685), 548 A.

1930 Ceanothus Gloire de Versailles. *Gardening Illustrated* **52** (2686), 569 N.

1930 Chrysanthemum maximum. *Gardening Illustrated* **52** (2687), 589 N.

1930 That Blue Pea. *Gardening Illustrated* **52** (2688), 595 C.

1930 Hydrangea aborescens var. grandiflora. *Gardening Illustrated* **52** (2688), 597 N.

1930 How good to eat Gooseberries. *Gardening Illustrated* **52** (2688), 606 N.

1930 Galega officinalis. *Gardening Illustrated* **52** (2689), 612 N.

1930 Nordmannia cordifolia syn. Borago orientale. *Gardening Illustrated* **52** (2689), 616 N.

1930 Some good Yuccas. *Gardening Illustrated* **52** (2690), 627 N.

1930 Romneya Coulteri. *Gardening Illustrated* **52** (2690), 629 N.

1930 Hydrangea Hortensia. *Gardening Illustrated* **52** (2691), 640 C.

1930 Erigeron speciosus. *Gardening Illustrated* **52** (2691), 642 N.

1930 Helenium pumilum. *Gardening Illustrated* **52** (2692), 657 N.

1930 Some old garden Roses. *Gardening Illustrated* **52** (2692), 659 N.

1930 Eryngium oliverianum. *Gardening Illustrated* **52** (2693), 675 N.

1930 Flowers in the garden landscape. *Gardening Illustrated* **52** (2693), 683 N.

1930 Eupatorium purpureum. *Gardening Illustrated* **52** (2693), 683 N.

1930 Pachysandra terminalis. *Gardening Illustrated* **52** (2694), 692 C.

1930 Nicotiana affinis. *Gardening Illustrated* **52** (2695), 709 N.

1930 Annual Chrysanthemums & Nigella. *Gardening Illustrated* **52** (2695), 714 N.

1930 Flower borders in September. *Gardening Illustrated* **52** (2696), 729 N.

1930 Ipomoea rubro-caerulea. *Gardening Illustrated* **52** (2697), 740 C.

1930 The Grey Garden. *Gardening Illustrated* **52** (2698), 759 N.

1930 Michaelmas Daisies. *Gardening Illustrated* **52** (2699), 775 N.

1930 Sedum Sieboldi. *Gardening Illustrated* **52** (2700), 790 N.

1930 Dearth of Mushrooms. *Gardening Illustrated* **52** (2701), 806 C.

1930 Evergreens for decoration. *Gardening Illustrated* **52** (2702), 827 A.

1930 The Grey Garden from above. *Gardening Illustrated* **52** (2703), 843 N.

1931 The Yule Log. *Gardening Illustrated* **52** (2704), 5 A.

1931 Native Ferns in the Garden I. *Gardening Illustrated* **53** (2704), 11 A.

1931 Native Ferns in the Garden II. *Gardening Illustrated* **53** (2705), 25 A.

1931 Native Ferns in the Garden III. *Gardening Illustrated* **53** (2706), 37 A.

1931 Native Ferns in the Garden IV. *Gardening Illustrated* **53** (2707), 61 A.

1931 Fungi and Trees. *Gardening Illustrated* **53** (2716), 195 N.

1931 Ornithogalum nutans & some Megaseas. *Gardening Illustrated* **53** (2721), 272 A.

1931 Vinca Minor. *Gardening Illustrated* **53** (2722), 289 C.

1931 Sowing Anemone seeds. *Gardening Illustrated* **53** (2723), 317 N.

1931 Vinca Minor. *Gardening Illustrated* **53** (2727), 371 C.

1931 Dentaria diphylla. *Gardening Illustrated* **53** (2730), 412 C.

1931 Asarum europaeum. *Gardening Illustrated* **53** (2731), 436 N.

1931 Potpourri. *Gardening Illustrated* **53** (2733), 460 N.

1931 A garden landscape. *Gardening Illustrated* **53** 594.

1931 Vaccinium Corymbosum *Gardening Illustrated* **53** (2743), 607 N.

1931 Primula Florindae. *Gardening Illustrated* **53** (2745), 637 N.

1931 Guelder-rose on wall. *Gardening Illustrated* **53** (2748), 683 N.

1931 Planting against a house. *Gardening Illustrated* **53** (2748), 683 N.

1931 Struthiopteris germanica (Shuttlecock Fern). *Gardening Illustrated* **53** 693.

1931 Lilies in woodland edges. *Gardening Illustrated* **53** (2750), 715 N.

1932 White Foxgloves in woodland. *Gardening Illustrated* **54** (2757), 20 N.

1932 Between shrubs and lawn. *Gardening Illustrated* **54** (2761), 81 N.

1932 Chimonanthus fragrans. *Gardening Illustrated* **54** (2762), 90N.

1932 Iris stylosa in Algiers. *Gardening Illustrated* **54** (2765), 165 A.

1932 Hollyhock Pink Beauty. *Gardening Illustrated* **54** (2768), 181 N.

1932 The care of Nuts. *Gardening Illustrated* **54** (2769), 199 N.

1932 Male Fern and Campanula. *Gardening Illustrated* **54** (2774), 277 N.

1932 Heracleum mantegazzianum. *Gardening Illustrated* **54** (2775), 295 N.

1932 Plants for steep river bank. *Gardening Illustrated* **54** (2781), 382 C.

1932 Rosa microphylla. *Gardening Illustrated* **54** (2782), 394 N.

1932 Rose arches. *Gardening Illustrated* **54** (2789), 511 N.

1932 Bee and Wasp stings. *Gardening Illustrated* **54** (2790), 518 C.

1932 A neglected Strawberry. *Gardening Illustrated* **54** (2790), 518 C.

1932 Campanula lactiflora. *Gardening Illustrated* **54** (2790), 518 C.

1932 Spiraea Filipendula fl. pl. *Gardening Illustrated* **54** (2790), 527 N.

1932 Cream Pink Poppy. *Gardening Illustrated* **54** (2791), 537 N.

1932 Senecio Greyi. *Gardening Illustrated* **54** (2792), 549 N.

1932 Rose Lady Curzon. *Gardening Illustrated* **54** (2793), 561 N.

1932 White Foxgloves. *Gardening Illustrated* **54** (2794), 582 N.

1932 Flowering shrubs in the flower border. *Gardening Illustrated* **54** (2795), 596 A.

1932 The Grey garden. *Gardening Illustrated* **54** (2797), 623 N.

1932 Wild Thyme on the steps. *Gardening Illustrated* **54** (2798), 637 N.

1932 The Court and its planting. *Gardening Illustrated* **54** (2799), 655 A.

1932 Various corners in the garden. *Gardening Illustrated* **54** (2800), 665 N.

1932 Clematis Jouiniana. *Gardening Illustrated* **54** (2800), 669 N.

1932 Lonicera tragophylla. *Gardening Illustrated* **54** (2802), 678 C.

1932 A bed of Pinks. *Gardening Illustrated* **54** (2802), 687 N.

1932 The South border door. *Gardening Illustrated* **54** (2803), 711 A.

1932 Some recollections of Bramley in my young days. *Bramley Parish Magazine.* September 1p.

1932 Recollections of old Bramley. *Bramley Parish Magazine.* October 1p.

†1932 Recollections of old Bramley. *Bramley Parish Magazine.* December 1p.

†1933 Old Bramley. *Bramley Parish Magazine.* February 1p.

†1933 Old Bramley. *Bramley Parish Magazine.* March 1p.

†1933 Old Bramley. *Bramley Parish Magazine.* April 1p.

†1937 Formal Gardens. In, Jekyll, F. and Taylor, G. C. (eds.) *A Gardener's Testament.* London, Country Life. pp. 73-82.

†1937 Terraced gardens. In, Jekyll, F. and Taylor, G. C. (eds.) *A Gardener's Testament.* London, Country Life. p. 82-86.

†1937 June and July borders. In, Jekyll, F. and Taylor, G. C. (eds.) *A Gardener's Testament.* London, Country Life. p 121.

†1937 The grey garden. In, Jekyll, F. and Taylor, G. C. (eds.) *A Gardener's Testament.* London, Country Life. pp. 178-180.

†1937 Suggestions for the decorative use of some garden roses. In, Jekyll, F. and Taylor, G. C. (eds.). *A Gardener's Testament.* London, Country Life. pp. 204-7.

†1937 In a primrose wood. In, Jekyll, F. and Taylor, G. C. (eds.) *A Gardener's Testament.* London, Country Life. pp. 321-2.

Gertrude Jekyll's Garden Plans

Michael Tooley

There has been much debate and discussion about the number of Miss Jekyll's garden commissions. It is unlikely that this debate will be concluded, but as new information emerges more and more commissions have been added to Francis Jekyll's list of 1934, even though the aim of his list was "the inclusion of every locality for which evidence can be traced of Gertrude Jekyll's consultation either from diaries and personal sources or from the plans themselves preserved at Munstead."[1]

Francis Jekyll's list is the starting point, but with additions from the Munstead Wood account books at Godalming Museum[3] and the Documents Collection, College of Environmental Design, University of California, Berkeley, U.S.A.[2] Francis Jekyll listed 340 commissions, and with the additions listed here the number stands at 398.

The format of this revised list is the same as the one given by Francis Jekyll: the year of the commission is followed by the address and the client's name. Additional dates are given after the client's name, if Miss Jekyll was consulted subsequently. For the sources, see page 125.

A. Dated Commissions

1868   WARGRAVE HILL, Wargrave, Berkshire. Capt. E. J. Jekyll.

1870   ROCHDALE, a window box.

1870   PHILLIMORE'S SPRING, Crazies Hill, Berkshire.

1877   MUNSTEAD HOUSE, Godalming, Surrey. Mrs. J. Jekyll.

1877   SCALANDS, Robertsbridge, Sussex. Mme. Bodichon.

1880   LE CHALET, Sonzier, Les Avants, Switzerland. M. Jacques Blumenthal.

1881   GISHURST COTTAGE, The Heath, Weybridge, Surrey. Mr. G. F. Wilson.

1881   WISLEY, Surrey. Mr. G. F. Wilson.

1882   LONGWOOD PARK, Winchester, Hampshire. Countess of Northesk.

1882   OAKLANDS, Cranleigh, Surrey. Mrs. Thompson Hankey.

1883   GREAT ENTON, Witley, Surrey. Mr. J. H. Eastwood.

1884   LOWER EASHING, Godalming, Surrey. Mr. Turnbull.

1884   SUTTON, Ashley Road, Bowdon, Cheshire. Mr. R. Okell.

1884   THE NORTH CANONRY, Salisbury, Wiltshire. The Rev. Canon Swayne.

1885   HANGERFIELD, Witley, Surrey. Capt. Crawfurd.

1887   75 TILEHURST ROAD, Reading, Berkshire. Mr. A. C. Bartholomew.

1888   KNOLE, Cranleigh, Surrey. Sir George Bonham.

1890   MUNSTEAD, Godalming, Surrey. Mr. H. Shearburn.

1890   LLANFAWR, Holyhead, Anglesey, Wales. Miss Jane Adeane.

1890   GLOTTENHAM, Robertsbridge, Sussex. Mr. B. Leigh Smith.

1890   HARBLEDOWN LODGE, Canterbury, Kent. Canon Holland.

1891   CROOKSBURY HOUSE, Farnham, Surrey. Mr. A. W. Chapman.

1891   THE HERMITAGE, Effingham, Surrey. Miss Susan Muir Mackenzie.

1892   WOOD END, Witley, Surrey. Lady Stewart.

1892   ASTON ROWANT, Oxon. Sir W. Chichele-Plowden.

1892   ENBRIDGE LODGE, Kingsclere, Hampshire. Mr. Grant.

1893   CHINTHURST, Wonersh, Surrey. Miss Guthrie (1893). Hon. Mrs. Wilbraham Cooper (1903).

1893   EAST HADDON HALL, Northamptonshire. Mr. C. Guthrie.

1893   WOODSIDE, Chenies, Bucks. Adeline Duchess of Bedford.

1893   WINKWORTH FARM, Hascombe, Surrey. Mrs. Lushington.

1894   RUCKMANS, Oakwood Park, Surrey. Miss Lyell.

1895   TILECOTES, Marlow, Buckinghamshire. Mr. Graves.

1895   THE VICARAGE, Witley, Surrey. Rev. J. E. Eddis.

1895   BANACLE COPSE, Culmer, Witley, Surrey. Mrs. Sheppard.

1895   BANACLE EDGE, Witley, Surrey. Dr Theodore Williams.

1895   MAYHURST, Maybury Hill, Woking, Surrey. Miss Graham.

1895   STRATTON AUDLEY, Bicester, Oxon. Col. G. Gosling.

1895   GAZELY, Marlow, Buckinghamshire. Rev. M. Graves.

1895   SEYMOUR COURT, Marlow, Buckinghamshire. Mr. T. Wethered.

1895   STRATTON PARK, Micheldever, Hampshire. Earl of Northbrook.

1895   THE LODGE, Thames Ditton, Surrey. Sir Guy Campbell.

1895   LASCOMBE, Puttenham, Surrey. Col. Spencer.

1895   MUNSTEAD CORNER, Godalming, Surrey. Mr. C. D. Heatley.

1896   CHARTERHOUSE, Godalming, Surrey. Rev. W. H. Evans. 1898

1896   MILFORD HOUSE, Milford, Surrey. Mr. Robert Webb.

1896   THORNCOMBE PARK, Bramley, Surrey. Mr. E. R. Fisher-Rowe.

1896   BEAR PLACE, Twyford, Berkshire. Mr. Henry Nicholl.

1897   HILLSIDE, Godalming, Surrey. Mr. Gedley Robinson.

1897   BERRY DOWN, Basingstoke, Hampshire. Mr. Archibald Grove.

1897   BURROWS CROSS, Shere, Surrey. Hon. Emily Lawless.

1897   FULBROOK HOUSE, Elstead, Surrey. Mr. G. Streatfield.

1897   WHINFOLD, Hascombe, Surrey. Mr. Lionel Benson.

1898   WEST DEAN PARK, Chichester, Sussex. Mr. William James.

1898   THE HEADMASTER'S GARDEN, Charterhouse, Godalming, Surrey. Rev. Gerald Rendall.

1898   WESTAWAY, Godalming, Surrey. Mrs. Fleming.

1898   NORMANSWOOD, Farnham, Surrey. Mrs. Russell.

1898   MINNICKFOLD, Dorking, Surrey. Mrs. McLaren.

1899   MUNSTEAD ROUGH, Godalming, Surrey. Mr. W. R. Pullman.

1899   LITTLE TANGLEY, Guildford, Surrey. Mr. Cowley Lambert (1899)
Mrs. Hopper (1908)
Miss Simson (1921)

1899   ORCHARDS, Godalming, Surrey. Sir William Chance.

1899   TIGBOURNE COURT, Witley, Surrey. Mr. E. Horne.

1899 GODDARDS, Abinger Common, Surrey. Sir F. Mirrielees.

1899 THE DEANERY GARDEN, Sonning, Berkshire. Mr. E. Hudson.

1900 HATCHLANDS, Guildford, Surrey. Lord Rendel & Mr. H. Goodhart-Rendel. 1913, 1914.

1901 HIGH BARN, Hascombe, Surrey. Hon. S. Pleydell-Bouverie.

1901 FISHER'S HILL, Hook Heath, Woking, Surrey. Right Hon. Gerald Balfour.

1901 PRIOR'S WOOD, Godalming, Surrey. Mr. Leonard Huxley.

1901 CAMILLA LACEY, Dorking, Surrey. Mr. E. Leverton Harris. 1907

1901 ENTON LODGE, Witley, Surrey. Mr. J. H. Eastwood.

1901 HANLEY COURT, Bewdley, Worcestershire. Mrs. Wakeman-Newport.

1902 CHESWICK, Hedgerley Dean, Buckinghamshire. Mr. E. T. Cook.

1902 TILTING GREEN, Arundel Castle, Sussex. Duke of Norfolk.

1902 HALE HOUSE, Ockley, Surrey. Mrs. Powell.

1902 NEW PLACE, Haslemere, Surrey. Mr. A. M. S. Methuen.

1902 TRESSERVE, Aix-les-Bains, Sevoire, France. Mr. J. Bellingham.

1902 FRIAR'S HILL, Elstead, Surrey. Mrs. Davidson.

1902 GLENAPP CASTLE, Ballantrae, Ayrshire, Scotland. Mrs. Stock.

1902 LEYBOURNE, Witley, Surrey. Sir Owen Roberts.

1902 SUTTON PLACE, Guildford, Surrey. Lady Northcliffe.

1902 MUNSTEAD GRANGE, Godalming, Surrey. Mrs. E. W. Mountford (1902).
Mr. S. F. Staples (1912).

1902 COTMATON, Lindfield, Sussex. Miss Kate Leslie.

1902 MUNSTEAD GRANGE, Godalming, Surrey. Mr. S. F. Staples (1912)
Mrs. E. W. Mountford (1902)

1903 HALL PLACE, Shackleford, Godalming, Surrey. Mr. E. Horne.

1903 HUGHES MEMORIAL, Wesleyan Church, Godalming, Surrey.

1903 MONKTON, Singleton, Sussex. Mr. William James.

1903 PAPILLON HALL, Market Harborough, Leicestershire. Mr. Frank Belville.

1903 Sir Thomas Dirk Lander.

1903 WARREN LODGE, Witley, Surrey. Mr. R. Webb.

1903 Sir K. Muir Mackenzie

1903 NETTLESTONE

1903 Mrs. Balfour

1904 LE BOIS DES MOUTIERS, Varengeville, Dieppe, France. M. Guillaume Mallet.

1904 OSBROOKS, Capel, Surrey. Mrs. Schluter. 1908

1904 FIELD PLACE, Dunsfold, Surrey. Mrs. Bateson.

1904 BUSBRIDGE PARK, Godalming, Surrey. Mr. P. N. Graham.

1904 BRACKENBROUGH, Calthwaite, Cumberland. Mrs. Harris.

1904 MILLMEAD, Snowdenham Lane, Bramley, Surrey. Miss G. Jekyll. 1906, 1907

1905 BRAMLEY HOUSE, Bramley, Surrey. Col. Ricardo.

1905 MARSH COURT, Stockbridge, Hampshire. Mr. H. Johnston. 1907, 1915

1905 THE GRANGE, Hindhead, Haslemere, Surrey. Mrs. Crossley. 1912

1905 ASHBY ST. LEDGERS, Northamptonshire. Hon. Ivor Guest.

1905 CHURCH ROAD, Purley, Surrey. Mrs. Watson.

1905 LOSELEY PARK, Guildford, Surrey. Mrs. More Molyneux. (Plans made for Miss M. H. Dodge) 1906

1905 NEWLANDBURN, Mid Lothian, Scotland. Lord Ruthven.

1905 ST. GEORGE'S PLACE, York. Mr. W. H. Brierley.

1905 TARN MOOR, Witley, Surrey. Mr. Dunn.

1905 POLLARD'S PARK, Chalfont St. Giles, Buckinghamshire. Mr. A. Grove. 1906

1905 ESHOLT, Near Sheffield, Yorkshire. Mr. A. J. Hobson.

1906 TYLNEY HALL, Winchfield, Hampshire. Mrs. Lionel Philips.

1906 HIGHCROFT, Burley, Hampshire. Miss Sarrin.

1906 FOLLY FARM, Sulhampstead, Berkshire. Mr. C. C. Cochrane. 1907
Mr. Z. Merton (1916).

1906 THORPE HALL, Louth, Lincolnshire. Mrs. Brackenbury.

1906 BARTON ST. MARY, East Grinstead, Sussex. Mr. Munro Miller. 1907

1906 CEASAR'S CAMP, Wimbledon Common, Surrey. Sir George Gibb.

1906 THE MOORINGS, Hindhead, Haslemere, Surrey. Mrs. Russell.

1906 NEW PLACE, Shedfield, Hampshire.
Mrs. A. S. Franklyn.

1906 EARTHAM HOUSE, Chichester, Sussex. Sir W. Bird.

1906 BUSBRIDGE RECTORY, Godalming, Surrey. Rev. E. Larner (1914).

1906 COWORTH PARK, Sunningdale, Berkshire. Lady Alice Stanley.

1906 UPLANDS, Brook, Witley, Surrey. Mr. & Mrs. Arnold Williams. 1907

1907 LAMBAY CASTLE, Lambay Island, Ireland. Lord Revelstoke.

1907 HEATHCOTE, Ilkley, Yorkshire. Mr. Hemingway.

1907 SUNNINGDALE, Surrey. Mr. A. Spencer.

1907 FIRGROVE, Godalming, Surrey. Mr. Alfred W. Mellersh.

1907 LITTLE HAY, Burley, Ringwood, Hampshire. Lady Isobel Ryder.

1907 BISHOPTHORPE PADDOCK, York. Mr. A. T. Watson. Mr. Green.

1907 DYKE NOOK LODGE, Whalley Road, Accrington, Lancashire. Mr. H. V. Blake.

1907 LETCHWORTH GARDEN CITY, Hertfordshire. Mrs. Firth.

1907 BRABOEUF ESTATE, Guildown, Guildford, Surrey. Mrs. Bowes Watson.

1907 DURMAST, Burley, Hampshire. Miss Baring.

1907 KNEBWORTH PARK, Hertfordshire. Earl of Lytton.

1907 CLOSE WALKS, Midhurst, Sussex. Rev. F. Tatchell.

1907 LITTLECOTE, Lindfield, Sussex. Miss Kate Leslie.

1907 OAK LEE, Lindfield, Sussex. Miss Kate Leslie.

1907 MONKTON, Farleigh, Bradford on Avon, Wiltshire. Mr. L. Thornton.

1908 POLLARD'S WOOD, Fernhurst, Surrey. Mr. J. E. Forbes.

1908 HESTERCOMBE, Kingston, Somerset. Hon. E. W. B. Portman. 1904, 1907

1908 HOLLINGTON HOUSE, Newbury, Berkshire. Mr. E. Fergus Kelly. 1909

1908 PINECROFT, Graffham, Petworth, Sussex. Mrs. Powell.

1908 PEPERHAROW PARK, Godalming, Surrey. Earl of Midleton.

1908 KING EDWARD VII'S SANATORIUM, Midhurst, Sussex.

1908 UPTON GREY, The Old Manor House, Winchfield, Hampshire. Mr. Charles Holme, Mr. Best. 1909

1908	ASHWELL BURY HOUSE, Baldock, Hertfordshire. Mrs. Wolverley Fordham.
1908	RUNTON OLD HALL, Cromer, Norfolk. Mr. Bertram Hawker. 1909
1909	HENLEY PARK, Henley-on-Thames, Oxon. Mrs. Reade Revell.
1909	LEES COURT, Faversham, Kent. Mrs. Reginald Halsey.
1909	MOULSFORD MANOR, Berkshire. Mrs. Mayo Robson.
1909	PRESADDFED, Valley, Holyhead, Angelsey, Wales. Mrs. W. Fox-Pitt.
1909	RIGNALLS, Great Missenden, Buckinghamshire. Sir Felix Semon.
1909	FRENSHAM PLACE, Frensham, Surrey. Sir Arthur Pearson.
1909	HEATHERSIDE HOUSE, Camberley, Surrey. Mrs. Walter Leaf.
1909	HIGHMOUNT, Fort Road, Guildford, Surrey. Mr. Walter Neall. 1910
1909	STILEMANS, Godalming, Surrey. Dr E. P. Arnold. 1910, 1924
1909	NASHDOM, Taplow, Buckinghamshire. Princess Alexis Dolgorouki.
1909	WOODRUFFE, Worplesdon Hill, Brookwood, Surrey. Mrs. Johnstone.
1909	TEMPLE DINSLEY, Hitchin, Hertfordshire. Mr. H. G. Fenwick.
1910	DURBINS, Guildford, Surrey. Mr. Roger Fry.
1910	SHEPHERD'S WELL, Forest Row, Sussex. Mrs. Frost.
1910	GREAT ROKE, Witley, Surrey. Mrs. Dixon.
1910	CORNER HOUSE, Beckenham, Kent. Mr. Francis Hooper.
1910	ST. EDMUND'S CATHOLIC CHURCH, Godalming, Surrey.
1910	OLD CROFT, Godalming, Surrey. Rev. D. Hyland.
1910	CULMER, Witley, Surrey. Mr. J. E. Eastwood.
1910	ANGERTON, Morpeth, Northumberland. Mrs. Straker.
1910	HEYWOOD, Abbeyleix, Queen's County, Ireland. Sir E. Hutcheson Poë, Bart.
1910	LILLINGSTON DAYRELL, Buckinghamshire. Hon. Mrs. Douglas-Pennant.
1910	RENISHAW, Derbyshire. Sir G. Sitwell, Bart.
1915	RIGNALL WOOD & RIGNALL LODGE.
1910	SECRETARY'S HOUSE, West Surrey Golf Club, Milford, Surrey. Mr. J. H. Eastwood.
1910	STUBBINGS, Maidenhead, Berks. Mr. Eric Smith.
1910	LINDISFARNE CASTLE, Holy Island, Northumberland. Mr. E. Hudson. (1910) Mr. O. Falk (1923)
191	FAIRHILL, Berkhamsted, Hertfordshire. Mr. W. S. Cohen.
1911	AMERSFOORT, Berkhamsted, Hertfordshire. Mr. Walter Cohen.
1911	STRUY LODGE, Beauly, Scotland. Countess of Derby.
1911	CHART COTTAGE, Seal, Sevenoaks, Kent. Mr. Bernard Blunt.
1911	DRUMBANAGHER, Newry, Ireland. Lady Muriel Close.
1911	HYDON RIDGE, Hambledon, Surrey. Mr. C. E. Denny. 1912
1911	SIDGWICK MEMORIAL, Newnham College, Cambridge. Miss Clough.
1911	LENTON HURST, Nottingham. Mrs. Player.
1911	PUTTERIDGE PARK, Luton, Bedfordshire. Sir F. Cassel.
1911	VANN, Hambledon, Surrey. Mr. W. D. Caroë.
1911	WOODCOTE, Whitchurch, Hampshire. Mr. R. F. Nicholson.
1912	BURGH HOUSE, Well Walk, Hampstead, London N.W. Dr Williamson.
1912	SANDBOURNE, Bewdley, Worcestershire. Mrs. Louisa Wakeman-Newport.
1912	MONKSWOOD, Godalming, Surrey. Mr. J. A. Moir.
1912	TOWNHILL PARK, Bitterne, Southampton, Hampshire. Lord Swaythling.
1912	MERROW CROFT, Guildford, Surrey. Mrs. Pike Pease.
1912	PHILLIPS MEMORIAL, Godalming, Surrey. Borough of Godalming. 1914
1912	CHALFONT PARK, Gerrards Cross, Buckinghamshire. Mrs. Edgar.
1913	MUNSTEAD OAKS, Godalming, Surrey. Lady Victoria Fisher-Rowe.
1913	WARREN HURST, Ashtead, Surrey. Mrs. Henry Sams.
1913	FULMER COURT, Buckinghamshire. Mrs. Oswald Watt.
1913	HASCOMBE GRANGE, Godalming, Surrey. Mrs. Henderson.
1913	THE COPSE, Brook, Godalming, Surrey. Mr. R. W. Williamson.
1913	HEATH COTTAGE, Puttenham, Guildford, Surrey. Mr. Bruce Gosling.
1913	WATERSIDE COPSE, Liphook, Hampshire. Mr. A. H. Scott.
1913	NURSE'S HOUSE, Culmer, Witley, Surrey. Mr. J. H. Eastwood.
1913	ORCHARDS, Little Kingshill, Great Missenden, Buckinghamshire. (later BRAMLEYS) Mr. Ernest Willmott.
1913	MOSTYN ROAD, Merton Park, Surrey. Mr. G. H. Hadfield.
1913	OROSZVÁR, Móson Megye, Hungary. Princess Stephanie of Belgium & Countess de Longay.
1913	KILNFIELD, Puttenham, Surrey. Mr. G. Bruce Gosling.
1913	FRANT COURT, Tunbridge Wells, Kent. Miss Thornton. 1914
1914	BOWERBANK, Wimbledon, London S.W. Mr. Arthur Carr.
1914	GORSE BANK, Enton Green, Witley, Surrey. Mr. P. Whateley.
1914	FIELD HOUSE, Clent, Stourbridge, Worcestershire. A. Colin Kenrick.
1914	ELMHURST, Ohio, U.S.A. Mr. Glendinning B. Groesbeck.
1914	LUKYNS, Ewhurst, Surrey. Mrs. Dugald Clerk.
1914	HAWKLEY HURST, Petersfield, Hampshire. Mrs. Clive Davies.
1914	LITTLE ASTON, near Lichfield, Staffordshire. Mr. J. H. Birch.
1914	CLOGRENNAN TERRACE, Ennis Road, Limerick, Ireland. Mrs. Handyside.
1914	GODALMING POLICE STATION, Godalming, Surrey.
1914	Miss C. D. Richards
1915	HYDON HEATH, Hambledon, Surrey. National Trust.
1915	KING'S ARMS HOTEL, Godalming, Surrey. Miss Botham.
1915	HIGHLANDS, Haslemere, Surrey. Hon. Mrs. E. Gibson.
1915	CASTLE DROGO, Drewsteignton, Devon. Mr. J. C. Drewe.
1915	GARDEN COURT, Guildford, Surrey. Mr. H. G. Steele.
1915	MAUSOLEUM, Golder's Green Cemetery. Mr. R. H. Philipson.
1916	KESTON, High View Road, Sidcup, Kent. Mr. F. Eastwood.
1916	LITTLE CUMBRAE ISLAND, Bute, Scotland. Mr. Evelyn S. Parker.
1916	LOWER HOUSE, Bowlhead Green, Witley, Surrey. Lady Guillemard.
1916	KEYHAM HALL, Leicester. Mrs. Baxter.
1916	FELBRIDGE PLACE, East Grinstead, Sussex. Mr. H. Rudd.
1916	NEW CHAPEL HOUSE, Lingfield, Surrey. Mr. H. Rudd.
1916	80 CHESTERTON ROAD, Cambridge. Rev. C. M. Rice.
1916	BRIDGE FARM, Byfleet, Surrey.

1917	BARRINGTON COURT, Ilminster, Somerset. Colonel and Mrs. Lyle.
1917	23 VALE AVENUE, Chelsea, London S.W. Lady Helena Acland Hood.
1918	HOLYWELL COURT, Cliff Road, Eastbourne, Sussex. Mrs. Hornby Lewis.
1918	KILMEENA, West Byfleet, Surrey. Mr. F. Littleboy.
1918	BORLASES, Twyford, Berkshire. Mr. N. L. Davidson.
1918	LEIGH MANOR, Cuckfield, Sussex. Sir W. Chance.
1918	BURGATE, Dunsfold, Surrey. Mrs. Bateson. 1919
1918	WAR CEMETERIES. Auchonvillers, Gezaincourt, Corbie La Neuville, Hersin, Fienvillers, Trouville, Warlincourt Halte, Daours.
	War Graves Commission.
1918	ORCHARDS. Lady Elizabeth Taylor.
1919	ALMSHOUSES AND RECTORY, Basildon, Pangbourne, Berkshire. Capt. J. A. Morrison.
1919	WOOD END, Ascot, Surrey. Mr. J. B. Stevenson.
1919	WHITE HOUSE, Wrotham, Kent. Miss M. Rowe and Miss Edith Taylor. 1920
1919	FAWKEWOOD, Sevenoaks, Kent. Mrs. Best.
1919	CHESTERTON OLD HALL, Bridgnorth, Salop. Mrs. Thompson.
1919	TUNWORTH DOWN, Basingstoke, Hampshire. Mrs. Claud Chichester. 1920
1919	NORMANSWOOD, Farnham, Surrey. Miss Russell.
1919	THE OLD PARSONAGE, Gresford, Denbigh, Wales. Mr. G. C. Bushby.
1919	MARKS DANES, Bruton, Somerset. Mrs. Torrance.
1919	PUTTENHAM PRIORY, Surrey. Mr. C. F. Wood.
1919	PEDNOR HOUSE, Chesham, Buckinghamshire. Mr. H. S. Harrington.
1919	BRAMBLETYE, East Grinstead, Sussex. Mrs. Guy Nevill.
1919	CHAMBERLAYNES, Bere Regis, Near Wareham, Dorset. Mrs. J. Edmonds.
1920	HEATH HOUSE, Headley, Epsom, Surrey. Mr. E. Hudson.
1920	LEYS CASTLE, Inverness, Scotland. Mrs. Ogilvie.
1920	WALSHAM HOUSE, Elstead, Surrey. A. C. Kenrick. 1921, 1923, 1924, 1926, 1927
1920	MOUNT STEWART, Newtownards, Co. Down, Ireland. Marchioness of Londonderry.
1920	DIDSWELL PLACE, Welwyn, Hertfordshire. Mrs. Buckley.
1920	KINGSWOOD, Shere, Surrey. Mr. J. W. B. Sexton.
1920	DUNGARTH, Honley, Huddersfield, Yorkshire. Mrs. James Sykes.
1920	GIRTON COLLEGE, Cambridge. Lady Stephen.
1920	BOVERIDGE PARK, Cranborne, Dorset. Mr. C. W. Gordon.
1920	BROAD OAK, Seale, Farnham, Surrey. Lady Mayo Robson.
1920	CAEN WOOD TOWERS, Highgate, London N. Lady Waley Cohen.
1920	GRAYSWOOD HILL, Haslemere, Surrey. Mr. W. J. H. Whittall. 1923, 1925
1920	COPFORD HALL, Colchester, Essex. Mrs. Brancker.
1920	FOYLE RIDING FARM, Oxted, Surrey. Mr. A. C. Houghton.
1920	38 HAMILTON TERRACE, London N.W.8. Sir L. Weaver.
1920	PENHEALE MANOR, Egloskerry, Cornwall. Capt. N. Colville.
1920	WAR MEMORIAL, Compton, Surrey.
1920	CHOWNES MEAD, Cuckfield, Sussex. Mr. K. M. Carlisle.
1920	BUTTS GATE, Wisborough Green, Sussex. The Misses Davidson.
1920	GOLANDS HOUSE, New Chapel, Lingfield, Surrey. Mr. H. Rudd.
1920	61 THE AVENUE, Kew, Surrey. Mr. E. Jekyll.
1921	CAPTAIN BIRD'S GRAVE, Chatham Cemetery, Mainstone Road, Chatham, Kent.
1921	WILMSLOW PARK, Oaklands, Wilmslow, Cheshire. Mr. H. O. Wood.
1921	PALACE COTTAGE, Beaulieu, Hampshire. Mrs. Stuart Wortley.
1921	DRAYTON WOOD, Drayton, Norfolk. Lieut. Col. O'Meara. 1922
1921	BRADSTONE BROOK, Guildford, Surrey. Mrs. C. M. Wigan. 1922
1921	CAMLEY HOUSE, Maidenhead Thicket. Mr. Rothbart.
1921	HILL TOP, Fort Road, Guildford, Surrey. Mrs. Walter Neall. 1922
1921	IDE HILL, Sevenoaks, Kent. National Trust.
1921	TANGLEY WAY, Blackheath, Guildford, Surrey. Mr. J. W. Kennedy. 1922
1921	YEW TREE HALL, Forest Row, Sussex. Miss Rumbold.
1921	UPPER IFOLD HOUSE, Dunsfold, Sussex. Lady Cynthia Mosley. 1922
1921	28 ALBANY PARK ROAD, London. Mr. R. Antill.
1921	QUEDLEY, Shottermill, Haslemere, Surrey. Mrs. Ericsson.
1922	RIDGEWAY, Tittlerow, Maidenhead, Berkshire. Mr. L. Gilau.
1922	WAR MEMORIAL IN CHURCHYARD, Busbridge, Surrey.
1922	ENTON HALL, Witley, Surrey. Major S. Chichester.
1922	COURT LODGE, Knockholt, Kent. Mrs. Langley Smithers.
1922	HASCOMBE COURT, Godalming, Surrey. Sir John Jarvis, Bart. 1923
1922	WATLINGTON PARK, Oxon. Viscount Esher. 1923
1922	BURNINGFOLD FARM, Dunsfold. Mr. R. R. Faber. 1923
1922	FISHERS, Wisborough Green, Sussex. Capt. J. W. Greenhill, R.N.
1922	BULCOTE MANOR, Nottinghamshire. Col. B. E. Bailey.
1922	GREAT HOUSE, Hambledon, Surrey. Mrs. Readhead.
1922	THATCHED HOUSE
1923	OLD PARSONAGE, Otford, Kent. Mr. Allan Aynesworth.
1923	172 PRENTON ROAD, Birkenhead, Cheshire. Mr. N. F. Dean.
1923	FOX HILL, Elstead, Surrey. Mrs. Hamilton.
1923	STANSTEAD HOUSE, Glemsford, Suffolk. Mrs. Bird.
1923	LAINSTON HOUSE, Winchester, Hampshire. Mr. Harvey.
1923	WINCHESTER WAR MEMORIAL, Hampshire. Winchester School.
1923	AMPORT ST. MARY, Hampshire. Mrs. Whitburn.
1923	DURFORD EDGE, Petersfield, Hampshire. Mr. J. P. Gabbatt. 1924, 1926
1923	WILBRAHAM HOUSE, Wilbraham Place, Sloane Street, London S.W. Mr. Lindley Scott, M.D.
1923	35 HAMILTON TERRACE, London N.W.8. Mr. W. M. Foster.
1923	SOUTHERNWAY, St. Martha's, Guildford, Surrey. Sir John Snell.
1923	FOX STEEP, Crazies Hill, Wargrave, Berkshire. Mrs. Van den Bergh.
1923	HOLMWOOD, Hambledon, Surrey. Mrs. Wentworth Martin.
1923	17 RAUCHSTRASSE, Berlin, Germany.
1923	KEDLESTON HALL, Derbyshire. Earl Curzon.
1924	KILDONAN, Barrhill, Ayrshire, Scotland. Mrs. Euan Wallace.
1924	FISHER'S GATE, Withyham, Sussex. Countess De La Warr.

1924   HILLSIDE, Penarth, Glamorgan, Wales. Mr. J. Croisdale Kirk.

1924   NORTH MUNSTEAD, Godalming, Surrey. Capt. Sampson.

1924   PARC DES SPORTS, Versailles, France. Mr. J. H. Hyde.

1924   150 BALSHAGRAY AVENUE, Jordanhill, Glasgow, Scotland. Miss Mary Stuart.

1924   LITTLE MUNTON, Sunningdale, Berkshire. Mrs. Acland Hood.

1924   NURSERIES, Solihull, Warwickshire. Messrs. Hewitt & Co.

1924   SULLINGSTEAD, Hascombe, Surrey. Sir Charles Cook.

1924   HALL'S COTTAGE, Frensham, Surrey. Mr. H. Falkner.

1924   57, ELMSTEAD LANE, Chislehurst, Kent. Mr. E. Borthwick.

1924   THE QUEEN'S DOLLS' HOUSE. H. M. The Queen.

1924   APPLETREE FARM.

1925   GREENWICH, Conn., U.S.A. Mr. Stanley Resor.

1925   BURNT AXON, Burley, Hampshire. Col. H. B. Strang.

1925   WIDFORD, Wydown Road, Haslemere, Surrey. Mr. H. A. Barrett.

1925   WILDERNESSE, Sevenoaks, Kent. Mr. L. M. Faulkner.

1925   SOUTH AFRICAN WAR MEMORIAL, Delville Wood, France.

1925   STOWELL HALL, Templecombe, Somerset. Mrs. McCreery.

1925   COMBEND MANOR, Sapperton, Gloucestershire. Mr. Asa Lingard.

1925   HURSLEY PARK, Winchester, Hampshire. Sir George Cowper.

1925   MERDON MANOR, Hursley, Winchester, Hampshire. Capt. Cowper.

1925   LITTLE BEVERLEY, Canterbury, Kent. Miss Taylor.

1925   STONEPITTS, Seal, Sevenoaks, Kent. Lady Rhondda and Mrs. Archdale.

1925   GLEBE HOUSE, Cornwood, Devon. Mr. Allan Aynesworth.

1925   THE OLD LIGHTHOUSE, St. Margaret's at Cliffe, Kent. Sir W. Beardsell.

1925   THE COURT, St. Fagan's, Cardiff, Wales. Lady Llewellyn. 1926, 1927, 1928

1925   REDCLIFF, Whittingehame, Prestonkirk, Scotland. Mr. R. A. L. Balfour.

1925   GLEDSTONE HALL, Near Skipton, Yorkshire. Sir Amos Nelson. 1926

1926   WOODLANDS, Saltburn-by-Sea, Yorkshire. Mr. C. W. Littleboy.

1926   BESTBEECH ST. MARY, Wadhurst, Sussex. Mr. Julian Leacock. 1927, 1928

1926   THREE FORDS, Send, Surrey. Mrs. Claud Serocold.

1926   MELLS PARK, Somerset. Right Hon. Reginald McKenna.

1926   BONALY TOWER, Colinton, Scotland. Mrs. Ogilvie.

1926   WOODHOUSE COPSE, Holmbury St. Mary, Surrey. Mr. W. Barnes Brand. 1927, 1929

1926   ROYSTED, Highdown Heath, Godalming, Surrey. Mrs. Sessions and H. J. Shindler.

1926   SOUTH LUFFENHAM HALL, near Stamford, Rutland. Mrs Nugent Allfrey.

1926   ICKWELL HOUSE, Biggleswade, Bedfordshire. Col. Hayward Wells. 1928, 1931

1926   OLD GLEBE HOUSE, Woodbury, Conn., U.S.A. Miss A. B. Jennings.

1926   WEST BARSHAM, Norfolk. Mr. J. A. Keith. 1927

1926   BEACON HOUSE, Droxford, Hampshire. Mrs. Douglas Hamilton.

1927   THE MARCHES, Willowbrook, Eton, Berkshire. Mr. E. L. Vaughan.

1927   THE PRIORY, Seaview, Isle of Wight.

1927   LITTLE HALING, Denham, Buckinghamshire. Mrs. Acland Wood.

1928   THE VICARAGE, Milford-on-Sea, Hampshire.

1928   BELGRADE, Yugoslavia, Postfach 109. M.S. Ilitch.

1928   HILL HALL, Theydon Mount, Epping, Essex. Lady Hudson.

1928   LEW TRENCHARD, Lew Down, Devon. Mr. F. Baring-Gould.

1928   FASLANE, Gairloch, Helensburgh, Scotland. Mrs. Macfarlan.

1928   PONDS, Seer Green, Beaconsfield, Buckinghamshire. Mrs. James Goff.

1928   VALEWOOD FARM, Haslemere, Surrey. Mr. Oliver Hill.

1928   BLAGDON, Seaton Burn, Northumberland. Viscount Ridley. 1929

1928   5 HALL PARK AVENUE, Westcliff-on-Sea, Essex. Mr. W. Bruce Peart.

1928   PLUMPTON PLACE, Sussex. Mr. E. Hudson.

1928   THE PRIORY, Hitchin, Hertfordshire. Lady Hudson.

1928   STROOD PARK, Horsham, Sussex. Mrs. Buckley.

1928   LITTLE HOE.

1928   LITTLE HOE, Rake Hanger, Petersfield, Hampshire. Mr. Gabbatt.

1929   SHORNCLIFFE CAMP, Moore Barracks. Lieut. Col. Freyberg.

1929   REFLECTIONS, Echo Pit Road, Guildford, Surrey. Mrs. Tucker.

1929   MARYLANDS, Hurtwood, Surrey. Mr. & Mrs. Warner. 1930

1929   WANGFORD HALL, Brandon, Suffolk. Mrs. Temple Richards.

1931   LITTLE WISSET, Hook Heath Road, Woking, Surrey. Miss Bayley.

1931   SPRINGWOOD, Godalming, Surrey. Dr S. Wilkinson.

1931   LEGH MANOR. Mr. M. H. Kent.

1932   COTTAGE WOOD, Walton-on-Thames, Surrey. Mr. D. E. Round.

B. Undated Commissions

AMESBURY ABBEY. Col. Sir Edmund Antrobus.

BOSINTON HALL, Rugby, Warwickshire. Mrs. Shaw.

CHISBURY. C. D. Heatley.

COTTAGE WOOD, Walton-on-Thames. Mr. D. E. Round.

CROSSWAYS COTTAGE. Mrs. Pullman.

DUFFELL, Brockham Green, Betchworth. Mrs. Davidson

GREAT MEADOW, Hambledon, Surrey.

KING GEORGE V SANATORIUM, Milford, Surrey.

MILTON COURT

PASTURE WOOD, Surrey. Mr. R. Potter.

PLACE OF TILLIEFOURNE, Kemsay, Aberdeen, Scotland. Mrs. Smithson for Mrs. Moncrief Peterson.

RICHMOND. H. Percy Adams.

RIGNALL LODGE.

THE HOME FARM, Sandling, Hythe, Kent. Mrs. Hallam Murray.

SOUTH CORNER, Wimbledon, London SW. Lady Gibb.

TRENANCE, Summerhouse Road, Godalming, Surrey. Mr. T. P. Whately.

WESTBROOK.

WHITEWAYS, Brockham Green, Betchworth. Mrs. Williamson

WOOD LEA, Virginia Water. Mrs. Bartlett.

WRYSTONE, Manator, Devon. Mrs. Galsworthy.

Mrs. F. Lyell

Mrs. Richardson

Mrs. Waterlow

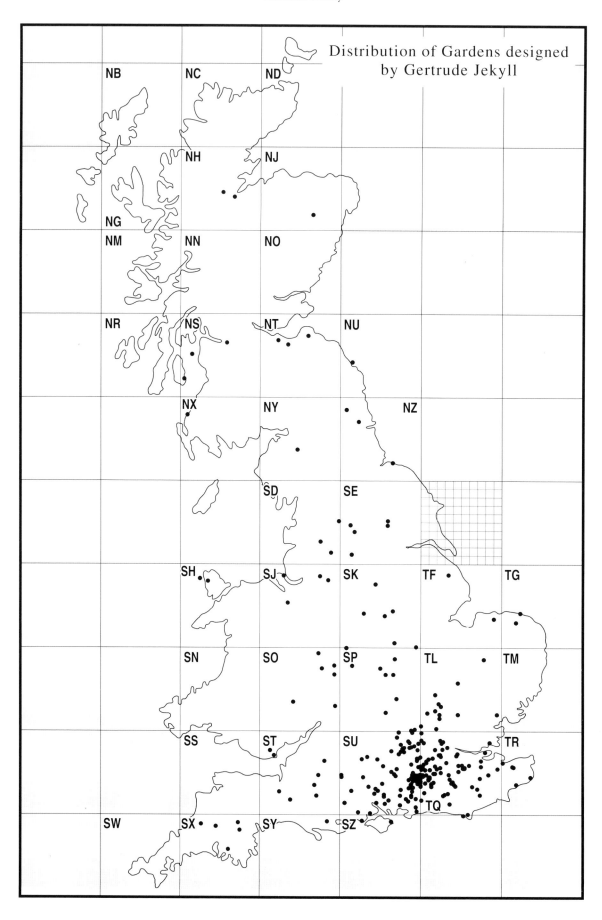

Distribution of Gardens designed by Gertrude Jekyll

Distribution of gardens designed by Gertrude Jekyll in England, Wales and Scotland.

Michael Tooley

The Map has been divided into 100 km squares identified by two letters according to the convention of the Ordnance Survey. Each 100 km square is divided into a hundred 10 km squares. A combination of letters and digits provides a grid reference for each garden within a 10 or 1 km square. A distribution map for south-east England has been published in P.F. Brandon 1979 'The diffusion of designed landscapes in south-east England. In, H.S.A. Fox and R.A. Butlin (eds.) *Change in the Countryside* London p.181.

CODE	NAME	DATE
NH 520 460	Struy Lodge	1911
NH 680 400	Leys Castle	1920
NJ 650 190	Place of Tilliefoure	undated
NS 030 210	Kildonan	1924
NS 140 510	Little Cumbrae Island	1916
NS 240 890	Faslane	1928
NS 590 650	150 Balshagray Avenue, Glasgow	1924
NT 210 690	Bonaly Tower	1926
NT 360 620	Newlandburn	1905
NT 600 730	Redcliff	1925
NU 126 434	Lindisfarne Castle	1910
NX 090 800	Glenapp Castle	1902
NY 470 380	Brackenbrough	1904
NZ 090 850	Angerton	1910
NZ 215 771	Blagdon	1928
NZ 660 210	Woodlands	1926
SD 750 280	Dyke Nook Lodge	1907
SD 890 130	Rochdale	1870
SD 990 510	Gledstone Hall	1925
SE 110 470	Heathcote	1907
SE 130 110	Dungarth	1920
SE 180 390	Esholt	1905
SE 590 470	Bishopthorpe Paddock	1907
SE 590 510	St George's Place	1905
SH 240 820	Llanfawr	1890
SH 350 800	Presaddfed	1909
SJ 300 880	172 Prenton Road, Birkenhead	1923
SJ 350 540	The Old Parsonage, Greesford	1919
SJ 750 860	Sutton	1884
SJ 850 810	Wimslow Park	1921
SK 090 000	Little Aston	1914
SK 300 410	Kedleston Hall	1923
SK 440 770	Renishaw	1910
SK 550 390	Lenton Hurst	1911
SK 650 440	Bulcote Manor	1922
SK 670 060	Keyham Hall	1916
SK 940 010	South Luffenham Hall	1926
SO 410 350	Hanley Court	1901
SO 710 930	Chesterton Old Hall	1919
SO 780 750	Sandbourne	1912
SO 920 680	Wood End	1919
SO 920 790	Field House	1914
SO 940 030	Combend Manor	1925
SP 060 140	Boveridge Park	1920
SP 150 790	Hewitt's Nurseries, Solihull	1924
SP 500 750	Bosinton Hall	undated
SP 570 680	Ashby St Ledgers	1905
SP 580 220	Stratton Audley	1895
SP 660 680	East Haddon Hall	1893
SP 680 860	Papillon Hall	1903
SP 700 390	Lillingston Dayrell	1910
SP 890 010	Rignalls Wood & Lodge	1915
SP 920 020	Pednor House	1919
ST 110 770	The Court, St Fagan's	1925
ST 180 710	Hillside	1924
ST 240 280	Hestercombe	1908
ST 680 350	Marks Danes	1919
ST 700 220	Stowell Hall	1925
ST 710 480	Mells Park	1926
ST 800 640	Monkton	1903
SU 014 469	Bradstone Brook	1921
SU 016 480	Minnickfold	1898
SU 140 290	The North Canonry	1884
SU 210 030	Durmast	1907
SU 210 030	Little Hay	1907
SU 210 030	Highcroft	1906
SU 210 030	Burnt Axon	1925
SU 270 660	Chisbury	undated
SU 290 440	Amport St Mary	1923
SU 340 690	Folly Farm	1906
SU 350 330	Marsh Court	1905
SU 380 020	Palace Cottage	1921
SU 420 250	Merdon Manor	1925
SU 423 253	Hursley Park	1925
SU 440 310	Lainston House	1923
SU 450 140	Townhill Park	1912
SU 470 670	Hollington House	1908
SU 480 290	Winchester War Memorial	1923
SU 510 380	Stratton Park	1895
SU 520 580	Enbridge Lodge	1892
SU 540 210	Woodcote	1911
SU 542 247	Longwood Park	1882
SU 560 130	New Place	1902
SU 600 180	Beacon House	1926
SU 630 510	Berry Down	1897
SU 630 760	Almshouses & Rectory	1919
SU 670 490	Tunworth Down	1919
SU 690 480	The Old Manor House, Upton Grey	1908
SU 700 550	Tylney Hall	1906
SU 700 920	Watlington Park	1922
SU 720 720	75 Tilehurst Road, Reading	1887
SU 728 990	Aston Rowant	1892
SU 740 123	Durford Edge	1923
SU 740 230	Little Hoe	1929
SU 750 300	Lukyns	1914
SU 750 750	The Deanery Garden	1899
SU 752 848	Henley Park	1909
SU 788 793	Wargrave Hill	1868
SU 790 750	Bear Place	1896
SU 790 750	Borlases	1918
SU 790 800	Phillimore's Spring	1870
SU 790 800	Fox Steep	1923
SU 810 190	Friar's Hill	1902
SU 831 174	Monkton	1903
SU 839 882	Seymour Court	1895
SU 840 310	Waterside Copse	1913
SU 840 410	Hall's Cottage	1924
SU 840 410	Frensham Place	1909
SU 850 800	Camley House	1921
SU 850 870	Tilecotes	1895
SU 850 870	Gazely	1895
SU 879 356	The Grange	1905
SU 880 210	Close Walks	1907
SU 880 360	The Moorings	1906
SU 880 600	Heatherside House	1909
SU 880 810	Stubbings	1910
SU 887 441	Normanswood	1919
SU 889 224	King Edward VII's Sanatorium	1906
SU 890 280	Pollard's Wood	1908
SU 890 320	New Place	1902
SU 890 320	Highlands	1915
SU 890 320	Grayswood Hill	1920
SU 890 470	Broad Oak	1920
SU 890 990	Orchards (later Bramleys)	1913
SU 900 320	Valewood Farm	1928
SU 900 320	Widford	1925
SU 900 400	St Edmund's Catholic Church	1910
SU 900 430	Walsham House	1920
SU 900 500	Woodruffe	1909
SU 906 445	Fulbrook House	1897
SU 910 820	Nashdom	1909
SU 919 473	Lascombe	1895
SU 930 470	Kilnfield	1913
SU 931 192	Pinecroft	1908
SU 934 479	Puttenham Priory	1919
SU 937 438	Peperharow Park	1908
SU 939 094	Eartham House	1906
SU 940 040	Great Enton	1883
SU 940 400	Lower House	1916
SU 940 400	Great Roke	1910
SU 940 400	Banacle Copse	1895
SU 940 400	The Vicarage	1895
SU 940 400	Enton Lodge	1901
SU 940 400	Culmer	1910
SU 940 400	Nurse's House	1913
SU 940 400	Leybourne	1902
SU 940 400	Tigbourne Court	1899
SU 940 400	Wood End	1892
SU 940 400	Tarn Moor	1905

CODE	NAME	DATE	CODE	NAME	DATE	CODE	NAME	DATE
SU 940 400	Uplands	1906	SU 990 850	Fulmer Court	1913	TQ 110 440	Woodhouse Copse	1926
SU 940 400	Banacle Edge	1895	SU 991 694	Wood Lea	undated	TQ 110 450	Goddards	1899
SU 940 400	Warren Lodge	1903	SU 991 958	Pollard's Park	1905	TQ 130 320	Strood Park	1928
SU 940 420	King George V Sanatorium	undated	SU 993 433	Orchards	1913	TQ 130 360	Ruckmans	1894
SU 940 420	Secretary's House	1910	SU 996 405	Winkworth Farm	1893	TQ 130 370	Hale House	1902
SU 940 420	Milford House	1896	SX 260 880	Penheale Manor	1920	TQ 150 670	The Lodge	1895
SU 944 439	Lower Eashing	1884	SX 440 860	Lew Trenchard	1928	TQ 160 380	Osbrooks	1904
SU 944 476	Heath Cottage	1913	SX 600 590	Glebe House	1925	TQ 160 490	Camilla Lacey	1901
SU 945 400	Hangerfield	1885	SX 720 900	Castle Drogo	1915	TQ 180 580	Warren Hurst	1913
SU 948 463	Prior's Wood	1901	SX 750 810	Wrystone	undated	TQ 190 490	Duffell	undated
SU 950 640	Fox Hill	1923	SY 390 180	Barrington Court	1917	TQ 190 490	Whiteways	undated
SU 950 670	Little Munton	1924	SY 830 910	Chamberlaynes	1919	TQ 190 770	61 The Avenue	1920
SU 955 472	Compton War Memorial	1920	SZ 280 920	The Vicarage	1928	TQ 200 540	Heath House	1920
SU 958 405	Gorse Bank	1914	SZ 622 911	The Priory	1927	TQ 220 710	Caesar's Camp	1906
SU 959 466	Field Place	1904	TF 330 870	Thorpe Hall	1906	TQ 240 560	Kingswood	1920
SU 960 380	Holmwood	1923	TF 900 330	West Barsham	1926	TQ 240 710	Bowerbank	1914
SU 960 380	Hydon Ridge	1911	TG 180 130	Drayton Wood	1921	TQ 240 710	South Corner	undated
SU 960 380	Great Meadow	undated	TG 210 420	Runton Old Hall	1908	TQ 240 880	Mausoleum	1915
SU 960 390	Great House	1922	TL 000 070	Fairhill	1911	TQ 250 050	Fisher's Gate	1924
SU 960 770	The Marches	1927	TL 000 070	Amersfoort	1911	TQ 250 690	Mostyn Road	1913
SU 960 910	Ponds	1928	TL 090 210	Putteridge Park	1911	TQ 260 850	Burgh House	1912
SU 963 682	Coworth Park	1906	TL 180 240	Temple Dinsley	1909	TQ 270 770	23 Vale Avenue	1917
SU 965 451	The Headmaster's Garden, Charterhouse	1898	TL 190 030	The Priory	1928	TQ 280 220	Legh Manor	1931
SU 965 451	Charterhouse	1896	TL 210 320	Letchworth Garden City	1907	TQ 280 870	Caen Wood Towers	1920
SU 970 390	Hydon Heath	1915	TL 220 160	Didswell Place	1920	TQ 280 870	38 Hamilton Terrace	1920
SU 970 420	Enton Hall	1922	TL 220 200	Knebworth Park	1907	TQ 300 240	Chownes Mead	1920
SU 970 430	Westaway	1898	TL 240 330	Ashwell Bury House	1908	TQ 300 240	Leigh Manor	1918
SU 970 430	Munstead Oaks	1913	TL 460 020	Hill Hall	1928	TQ 310 610	Church Road	1905
SU 970 430	Hascombe Grange	1913	TL 460 580	Girton College	1920	TQ 320 800	28 Albany Park Road	1921
SU 970 430	King's Arms Hotel	1915	TL 460 580	80 Chesterton Road	1916	TQ 320 800	35 Hamilton Terrace	1923
SU 970 430	Hughes Memorial	1903	TL 460 580	Sidgwick Memorial	1911	TQ 320 800	Wilbraham House	1923
SU 970 430	Hall Place	1903	TL 780 860	Wangford Hall	1929	TQ 340 250	Littlecote	1907
SU 970 430	Godalming Police Station	1914	TL 930 220	Copford Hall	1920	TQ 340 250	Munstead Grange	1902
SU 970 430	Phillips Memorial	1912	TO 018 452	Chinthurst	1893	TQ 340 250	Oak Lee	1907
SU 970 430	Munstead Corner	1895	TO 100 420	Marylands	1929	TQ 350 480	Stanstead House	1923
SU 970 430	Monkswood	1912	TO 118 532	The Hermitage	1891	TQ 360 130	Plumpton Place	1928
SU 970 430	Roysted	1926	TO 520 550	Fawkewood	1919	TQ 360 420	Golands House	1920
SU 970 430	Old Croft	1910	TO 840 470	Crooksbury House	1891	TQ 360 420	New Chapel House	1916
SU 970 430	Hillside	1897	TQ 000 330	Upper Ifold House	1921	TQ 390 380	Felbridge Place	1916
SU 970 430	Busbridge Rectory	1906	TQ 000 340	Burningfold Farm	1922	TQ 390 380	Barton St Mary	1906
SU 970 430	North Munstead	1924	TQ 000 380	High Barn	1901	TQ 400 490	Foyle Riding Farm	1920
SU 970 430	Munstead Grange	1902	TQ 000 390	Sullingstead	1924	TQ 410 360	Brambletye	1919
SU 970 430	Firgrove	1907	TQ 000 390	Whinfold	1897	TQ 420 341	Yew Tree Hall	1921
SU 970 430	Hascombe Court	1922	TQ 000 440	Millmead	1904	TQ 440 700	57 Elmstead Lane	1924
SU 970 430	Munstead Rough	1899	TQ 000 580	Mayhurst	1895	TQ 460 720	Keston	1916
SU 970 430	Springwood	1931	TQ 007 445	Bramley House	1905	TQ 480 510	Ide Hill	1921
SU 970 430	The Copse	1913	TQ 007 610	Bridge Farm	1916	TQ 480 590	Court Lodge	1922
SU 970 470	Garden Court	1915	TQ 008 430	Thorncombe Park	1896	TQ 510 590	Old Parsonage	1922
SU 970 470	Hill Top	1921	TQ 010 170	Tilting Green	1902	TQ 530 550	Wildernesse	1925
SU 970 470	Merrow Croft	1912	TQ 010 530	Sutton Place	1902	TQ 540 560	Chart Cottage	1911
SU 970 470	Trenance	undated	TQ 010 890	Chalfont Park	1912	TQ 550 560	Stonepitts	1925
SU 970 470	Reflections	1929	TQ 010 980	Woodside	1893	TQ 590 000	Holywell Court	1918
SU 970 860	Cheswick	1902	TQ 020 480	Southernway	1923	TQ 600 590	White House	1919
SU 975 421	Busbridge Park	1904	TQ 020 550	Three Fords	1926	TQ 630 320	Bestbeech St Mary	1926
SU 977 472	Loseley Park	1905	TQ 022 461	Little Tangley	1899	TQ 700 300	Quedley	1921
SU 979 429	War Memorial	1922	TQ 035 464	Tangley Way	1921	TQ 730 230	Glottenham	1890
SU 980 370	Vann	1911	TQ 040 600	Kilmeena	1918	TQ 730 430	Scalands	1877
SU 980 380	Burgate	1918	TQ 040 860	Little Haling	1927	TQ 750 580	The Home Farm	undated
SU 980 570	Fisher's Hill	1901	TQ 050 260	Fishers	1922	TQ 750 640	Captain Bird's Grave	1921
SU 980 570	Little Wisset	1931	TQ 050 260	Butts Gate	1920	TQ 800 740	Frant Court	1914
SU 984 424	Munstead	1890	TQ 060 380	Oaklands	1882	TQ 860 850	5 Hall Park Avenue	1928
SU 985 425	Munstead House	1877	TQ 060 380	Knole	1888	TQ 950 540	Corner House	1910
SU 989 421	Stilemans	1909	TQ 060 520	Hatchlands	1900	TR 010 610	Lees Court	1909
SU 989 479	Braboeuf Estate	1907	TQ 070 470	Burrows Cross	1897	TR 130 580	Harbledown Lodge	1890
SU 990 490	Durbins	1910	TQ 070 640	Gishurst Cottage	1881	TR 150 570	Little Beverley	1925
SU 990 490	Highmount	1909	TQ 100 410	Hawkley Hurst	1914	TR 190 350	Shorncliffe Camp	1929
			TQ 100 660	Cottage Wood	undated	TR 360 440	The Old Lighthouse	1925
			TQ 110 430	Pasture Wood	undated	TU 190 440	Ickwell House	1926
						TV 520 990	West Dean Park	1898

Calendar

Gertrude Jekyll and her circle

Year	Age	Life
1843		November 29, born at 2 Grafton Street, London (Parents – Edward and Julia Jekyll. Sister Caroline aged 6; brothers Edward aged 4 and Arthur aged 2).
1844		First family visit to Seaview, Isle of Wight
1846	2	Birth of Herbert Jekyll (brother).
1847	3	Foundation of Amateur Musical Society by Edward Jekyll (father) and others. Prince Albert and The Duke of Cambridge are among its members.

The Contemporary World

1843
Queen Victoria (1819-1901) on throne since 1837.

Prime Minister: Sir Robert Peel (1788-1850), Tory, since 1841 till 1846.

British imperial expansion on four continents.

'Hungry Forties'. Depression (1841-42).

Young England Coalition forms in Parliament.

Prince Albert (1819-61) President of The Royal Society of Arts.

Robert Fortune (1813-80), botanist, visits China, newly opened after Opium War of 1842, to collect plants.

John Stuart Mill (1806-73) *A System of Logic*.

John Ruskin (1819-1900) *Modern Painters*.

George Frederick Watts (1817-1904) *Caractacus*.

Birth of Henri de Vilmorin, French nurseryman and author.

Death of John Claudius Loudon (b 1783), landscape gardener and writer.

1844
Bank Charter Act gives Bank of England monopoly on issue of bank notes.

First appearance in London of Hungarian violinist, Joseph Joachim (1831-1907).

William Henry Fox Talbot (1800-77) pioneer of photography, *The Pencil of Nature*.

J.M.W. Turner (1775-1851) *Rain, Steam and Speed - the Great Western Railway*.

Robert Chambers (1802-71) *The Vestiges of the Natural History of Creation* (proposes a theory of evolution).

1845
Irish potato crop fails; famine and emigration to America.

Formation of National Association of United Trades for Protection of Labour.

Friedrich Engels (1820-95) *The Condition of the Working Class in England*.

1846
Corn Laws repealed following Irish famine. Resignation of Peel.

Prime Minister: Lord John Russell (1792-1878), Whig, till 1852.

Robert Liston (1794-1847) performs amputation on anaesthetized patient at University College, London.

Sir John Millais (1829-96) and William Holman Hunt (1827-1910) first exhibit at the Royal Academy.

Benjamin Disraeli (1804-81), MP, statesman and novelist, *Sibyl; or The Two Nations*.

Edward Lear (1812-88), artist and author, *The Book of Nonsense*.

1847
Working day in textile mill limited to ten hours for women and children.

Band of Hope (Juvenile Temperance Organisation) founded.

				Royal Opera House opens at Covent Garden, where Gaetano Donizetti's (1797-1848) *Lucrezia Borgia* is produced.
				George Boole (1815-64) *The Mathematical Analysis of Logic*.
				William Makepeace Thackeray (1811-63) *Vanity Fair* (1847-48).
				Emily Brontë (1818-48) *Wuthering Heights*.
				Charlotte Brontë (1816-55) *Jane Eyre*.
				Alfred Tennyson (1809-92) *The Princess Varney, the Vampyre*.
				Death of Felix Mendelssohn, German composer, pianist, organist and conductor in Leipzig (aged 38), having produced *Elijah* in Birmingham in the same year.
1848	4	Moves to Bramley House, south-east of Guildford, Surrey built by Lord Egremont of Petworth.	**1848**	Republic proclaimed in Venice. Revolution in Paris; Second Republic.
				Annexation of the Orange Free State.
				Second Sikh War; British capture Punjab (1849).
				Cholera epidemic in Britain (1848-49).
				Public Health Act.
				St John's House (Anglican Order) founded to train nurses.
				Queen's College opens higher education to women.
				Pre-Raphaelite Brotherhood formed by Dante Gabriel Rossetti (1828-82) and others.
				John Stuart Mill *Principles of Political Economy*.
				Thomas Babington Macaulay (1800-59) *History of England*.
				Elizabeth Gaskell (1810-85) *Mary Barton*.
				Karl Marx (1818-83) and Friedrich Engels *Communist Manifesto*.
				Concerts in England and Scotland by Frédéric Chopin (b 1810), Polish composer and pianist.
				Birth of Sir Hubert Parry (d 1918), English composer and music administrator.
1849	5	Birth of Walter Jekyll (brother).	**1849**	Venice surrenders to the Austrians.
				Kwangsi rebellion in Southern China intensifies instability and leads to foreign intervention in Chinese affairs.
				Repeal of the Navigation Acts.
				Agricultural Crisis (1849-53).
				Bedford College for Women established. Barbara Leigh-Smith (later Mme. Bodichon) (1827-91) attends.
				Prince Albert President of the Royal Commission on the Great Exhibition (1849-51).
				Charles Dickens (1812-70) *David Copperfield*.
				Death of Frédéric Chopin.
			1850	Camillo Cavour (1810-61), Italian nationalist, becomes a minister in Piedmont.
				Public Libraries Act.
				Alfred Tennyson becomes Poet Laureate.
				William Wordsworth (1770-1850) *The Prelude*.
				Elizabeth Barrett Browning (1806-61) *Sonnets from the Portuguese*.
1851	7	Visits the zoological gardens, the British Museum and the Great Exhibition in London .	**1851**	Otto von Bismarck (1815-98) asserts Prussian rights in Frankfurt.
				Gold discovered in New South Wales and Victoria, Australia.
				Opening of the Great Exhibition, at the Crystal Palace.
				Window Tax repealed.
				Michael Faraday (1791-1867) discovers electromagnetic induction.

Cambridge University adds degree examination in natural sciences.

First submarine cables from Dover to Calais.

Harriet Taylor Mill *The Enfranchisement of Women*, published in *Westminster Review*.

John Ruskin *The King of the Golden River*.

Birth of George Elgood, British artist.

1852	8	Watches funeral procession of Duke of Wellington. Attends Faraday's lectures at the Royal Institution.	**1852**	Fall of the Second Republic in France.

Prime Minister: Earl of Derby (1799-1869), Conservative, February 23 – December 17; succeded by Earl of Aberdeen (1784-1860), heading a coalition, till 1855.

New Houses of Parliament opened.

Death of Duke of Wellington (b 1769).

1853 Under the Emperor Napoleon III (1808-73), Georges Haussmann (1809-91) rebuilds Paris.

David Livingstone's (1813-73) explorations of Africa begin.

British budget promotes free trade.

Cholera epidemic in Britain (1853-54).

Smallpox vaccination becomes compulsory.

Cheltenham Ladies College established.

Charlotte Brontë *Villette*.

1854	10	Her brother, Arthur, aged 13, leaves Harrow School to join the Royal Navy. Edward Jekyll gives lectures on the Crimean War.	**1854**	Crimean War (1854-56): France and England try to curb Russian expansion.

Earl of Cardigan leads Charge of the Light Brigade at Balaclava.

Construction of London Underground begins.

Christian Socialists establish Working Men's College, London.

Charles Dickens *Hard Times*.

Caroline Harron *English Laws for Women in the Nineteenth Century*.

1855	12	Visits Brückenau, Bavaria with her mother, sister, Caroline (Carry), and cousin Sophie Weguelin.	**1855**	Fall of Sebastopol.

Prime Minister: Viscount Palmerston (1784-1865), Liberal, till 1858.

Livingstone discovers Victoria Falls.

Australian Colonies become self governing.

Barbara Bodichon forms Married Women's Property Committee.

Friendly Societies Act.

Henry Bessemer (1813-98) invents a process to convert pig iron into steel.

1856	13	Watches ships sailing into Spithead after the Crimean War.	**1856**	Treaty of Paris.

Renewal of the War with China.

New Zealand achieves responsible self-government.

William Sterndale Bennett (1816-75) becomes conductor of the Philharmonic Society and Professor of Music at Cambridge.

Owen Jones (1809-74) *The Grammar of Ornament*.

Death of Robert Schumann (b 1810).

1857 Victoria names Albert Prince Consort.

Indian Mutiny; leading to Crown assuming direct control over India (1859) from the East India Company.

Matthew Arnold (1822-88) becomes Professor of Poetry at Oxford University, till 1867.

Thomas Hughes (1822-96) *Tom Brown's Schooldays*.

Anthony Trollope (1815-82), novelist and civil servant, *Barchester Towers*.

Hallé Orchestra founded in Manchester by Sir Charles Hallé (1819-95).

				Birth of Sir Frederick William Moore, curator of Glasnevin Botanic Garden, Dublin, and author.
			1858	Prime Minister: Earl of Derby, Conservative, till 1859.
				British Columbia becomes a Crown Colony.
				Charles Darwin (1809-82) & Alfred Russel Wallace (1823-1913) read papers at Linnaean Society – propose theory of evolution.
				Medical Act sets up General Medical Council.
				First transatlantic cable.
				London Metropolitan drainage system begun.
				Birth of Ellen Ann Willmott, gardener at Warley Place, Essex and author.
				Death of Jane Wells Loudon (b 1807), horticultural writer.
			1859	France and Piedmont defeat Austria at Solferino; Henri Dunant inspired to form the Red Cross.
				Plan proposed for South African Federation.
				Prime Minister: Viscount Palmerston, Liberal, till 1865.
				Molestation of Workmen Act allows peaceful picketing.
				London Building Workers Strike (1859-60).
				Ferdinand de Lesseps (1805-94) begins Suez Canal.
				First oil well drilled in USA
				Charles Darwin *On the Origin of Species Through Natural Selection.*
				Samuel Smiles (1812-1904) *Self-Help.*
				John Stuart Mill *On Liberty.*
				Florence Nightingale (1820-1910) *Notes on Nursing.*
				Alfred Tennyson *Idylls of the King* (1869-74).
				George Eliot (1819-80) *Adam Bede.*
				Charles Gounod (1818-93), French composer, *Faust.*
				Death of Karl Baedeker (b 1801), guidebook publisher.
			1860	Victor Emanuel proclaimed King of Italy by Giuseppe Garibaldi (1807-82).
				Italian Revolution April 1860 – February 1861.
				Treaty of Peking. – Anglo-French forces expand.
				Outbreak of Maori Wars in New Zealand.
				Nightingale Training School for nurses established.
				Robert Fortune's privately funded expedition to collect plants in Japan, following 'unequal treaties' of 1858, which opened up the country.
				I.K. Brunel (1806-59) *Great Eastern,* largest ship of century.
				John Ruskin *Unto This Last.*
				George Eliot *The Mill on the Floss.*
				Wilkie Collins (1824-89) *The Woman in White.*
				Leo Tolstoy (1828-1910) *War and Peace.*
				Death of Artur Schopenhauer (b 1788).
1861	17	Student at School of Art, South Kensington.	**1861**	Death of Prince Albert from typhoid.
				Abraham Lincoln (1809-65) President of the U.S.A.
				American Civil War commences.
				Emancipation of serfs in Russia.
				First Italian parliament in Turin.
				H.M.S. Warrior, first iron-hulled warship, powered by steam and sail.
				Sir Charles Newton (1816-94) appointed Keeper of Greek and Roman antiquities at the British Museum.
				William Morris (1834-96) founds design firm Morris, Marshall, Faulkner & Co.',

Prime Minister: Earl of Derby, Conservative, till 1859.

British Columbia becomes a Crown Colony.

Charles Darwin (1809-82) & Alfred Russel Wallace (1823-1913) read papers at Linnaean Society – propose theory of evolution.

Medical Act sets up General Medical Council.

First transatlantic cable.

London Metropolitan drainage system begun.

Birth of Ellen Ann Willmott, gardener at Warley Place, Essex and author.

Death of Jane Wells Loudon (b 1807), horticultural writer.

1859

France and Piedmont defeat Austria at Solferino; Henri Dunant inspired to form the Red Cross.

Plan proposed for South African Federation.

Prime Minister: Viscount Palmerston, Liberal, till 1865.

Molestation of Workmen Act allows peaceful picketing.

London Building Workers Strike (1859-60).

Ferdinand de Lesseps (1805-94) begins Suez Canal.

First oil well drilled in USA

Charles Darwin *On the Origin of Species Through Natural Selection.*

Samuel Smiles (1812-1904) *Self-Help.*

John Stuart Mill *On Liberty.*

Florence Nightingale (1820-1910) *Notes on Nursing.*

Alfred Tennyson *Idylls of the King* (1869-74).

George Eliot (1819-80) *Adam Bede.*

Charles Gounod (1818-93), French composer, *Faust.*

Death of Karl Baedeker (b 1801), guidebook publisher.

1860

Victor Emanuel proclaimed King of Italy by Giuseppe Garibaldi (1807-82).

Italian Revolution April 1860 – February 1861.

Treaty of Peking. – Anglo-French forces expand.

Outbreak of Maori Wars in New Zealand.

Nightingale Training School for nurses established.

Robert Fortune's privately funded expedition to collect plants in Japan, following 'unequal treaties' of 1858, which opened up the country.

I.K. Brunel (1806-59) *Great Eastern,* largest ship of century.

John Ruskin *Unto This Last.*

George Eliot *The Mill on the Floss.*

Wilkie Collins (1824-89) *The Woman in White.*

Leo Tolstoy (1828-1910) *War and Peace.*

Death of Artur Schopenhauer (b 1788).

1861   17   Student at School of Art, South Kensington.

1861

Death of Prince Albert from typhoid.

Abraham Lincoln (1809-65) President of the U.S.A.

American Civil War commences.

Emancipation of serfs in Russia.

First Italian parliament in Turin.

H.M.S. Warrior, first iron-hulled warship, powered by steam and sail.

Sir Charles Newton (1816-94) appointed Keeper of Greek and Roman antiquities at the British Museum.

William Morris (1834-96) founds design firm Morris, Marshall, Faulkner & Co.', inspiration of Arts and Crafts movement. His partners included Burne-Junes, Rossetti and Philip Webb who were also directors.

Isabella Beeton *Book of Household Management.*

Charles Dickens *Great Expectations.*

Ellen Price Wood (1814-87) *East Lynne.*

Francis Palgrave (1824-97) *Golden Treasury.*

Frederic Leighton (1830-96) *Paolo and Francesca.*

Hymns Ancient and Modern.

1862 Bismarck President of Prussia, till 1890.

Cotton famine in Lancashire caused by American Civil War.

Companies Act.

Christina Rossetti (1830-94) *Goblin Market* and other poems.

Giuseppe Verdi (1813-1901), Italian composer, visits London.

1863 **19** February 7, her brother Arthur (aged 22) drowns off New Zealand in HMS Orpheus.

October 13, leaves London with Charles and Mary Newton for Turkey, Rhodes and Greece.

December 26, arrives back at Bramley.

1863 Battle of Gettysburg.

Maximilian of Austria (b 1832) made Emperor of Mexico (executed in 1867).

Polish rising against Russia.

Cooperative Wholesale Society established.

London Underground – Metropolitan Line opened.

Charles Kingsley (1819-75) *The Water Babies.*

Frederick Walker (1840-75), English painter, exhibits *The Lost Path* at the Royal Academy.

1864 **20** August 5, night croquet party at Bramley illuminated by lamps and a large transparent owl made by Gertrude Jekyll.

Walter sent to Harrow School

1864 Cession of Schleswig-Holstein to Prussia and Austria.

First Socialist International formed.

Geneva Convention originated.

Octavia Hill (1838-1912) starts model lodgings.

John Henry Newman (1801-90) *Apologia pro vita sua.*

1865 **21** February 28, Carry marries Frederick Eden at Bramley.

May 1, painting of *Cheeky* (described as a "capitally painted small pug") accepted and hung in North Room of the Royal Academy with James McNeill Whistler's *Little White Girl* and G. D. Leslie's *The Defence of Lathom House.*

June 17, to Hatchlands.

November 17, visits John Ruskin.

Death of Mrs Spencer Montague, Edward's brother's widow, results in inheritance of Wargrave Estate.

1865 General Lee surrenders to General Grant (end of American Civil War).

President Lincoln assassinated.

Slavery abolished in U.S.A.

October 18, death of Palmerston.

Prime Minister: Earl (formerly Lord John) Russell, Liberal, October 29 1865 till 1866.

Foundation of Reform League.

Joseph Lister (1827-1912) introduces antiseptic surgery.

Gregor Mendel (1822-84) experiments on heredity.

William Booth (1829-1912) founds Salvation Army.

Algernon Charles Swinburne (1837-1909) *Atalanta in Calydon.*

Lewis Carroll (1832-98) *Alice's Adventures in Wonderland.*

Birth of Jean Sibelius, Finnish composer (d 1957).

Death of John Lindley (b 1799), Professor of Botany, University College London and Secretary of the Royal Horticultural Society.

Death of Sir Joseph Paxton (b 1801), gardener at Chatsworth, MP, who designed glass hall for the 1851 Exhibition and its transfer to Sydenham as the Crystal Palace.

Death of Sir William Jackson Hooker (b 1785), Director of Kew and author.

1866 **22** April 3, to opera with Walter, *Ballo in Maschera* by Verdi.

May 28, to International Flower Show.

August 20, to Harpton Court, Sir George Cornewall Lewis, Secretary of State for War.

1866 Prussia defeats Austria at Sadowa.

Venice secured for Italy.

Prime Minister: Earl of Derby, Conservative, June 28 till 1868.

'Black Friday' Overend and Gurney crash. Bank rate at 10%.

October 22 – December 22, to Paris with Georgina Duff Gordon, staying at 1 rue Dauphiné. Copies painting by Francia in the Louvre. Sings duets with Vivarin; lessons from Galvini.

Death of Mary Newton (b 1832).

Herbert gazetted as a Lieutenant in the Royal Engineers, having passed out with the Sword of Honour at the Royal Military Academy, Woolwich.

Crown Colony government introduced for Jamaica.

John Stuart Mill presents Women's Suffrage petition to Parliament.

Emily Davies founds London School Mistresses Association.

Last major cholera epidemic.

Atlantic telegraph cable completed.

Royal Horticultural Society purchases the late Professor Lindley's Library.

Sir Edwin Landseer (1802-73) completes lions in Trafalgar Square, at the foot of the Nelson monument.

1867 23 March 1, exhibits paintings at Society of Female Artists with Mme. Bodichon (Barbara Leigh Smith).

April 21, meets George Frederic Watts, painter and sculptor, at Dorchester House.

June 13, copies paintings by Rembrandt and Velasquez at the Royal Academy.

June 14, attends Fiori's music class.

June 16, to Dorchester House.

June 20, makes copies of G. F. Watts' *Oxen*.

August 11-20, to Harpton Court.

1867 Abyssinian War (1867-68).

W.E. Gladstone (1809-98) becomes leader of Liberal Party.

Dominion of Canada established.

Russia sells Alaska to the U.S.A. for $7,200,000.

Diamonds discovered in South Africa.

Last convict ship sent to Western Australia.

Sir Henry Irving (1838-1905), actor, makes his debut.

Matthew Arnold *Dover Beach*.

1868 24 January 6, two paintings *Neptune's Horses* and *Young Donkeys* accepted for Society of Female Artists' Exhibition in London.

January 26, leaves for Paris with Susan Muir Mackenzie, en route for Cannes, Genoa and Rome (Gigi's Academy).

April 9, returns.

April 22, packing for move to Wargrave Hill begins.

April 30, to opera *The Marriage of Figaro* by Mozart, with Miss Webb and Georgina Duff Gordon.

May 1, copies pictures at the National Gallery.

June 1, to Wargrave Hill.

June 28, Carry and Frederick Eden return to England after two years abroad.

November 30, to Cambridge to visit Walter, student at Trinity College.

December 8, to Berkeley Castle with Carry and Frederick Eden.

December 29, attends Henley Ball.

1868 Prime Minister: Benjamin Disraeli, Conservative, February 27 – December 1.

Prime Minister: W.E. Gladstone, Liberal, December 3 till 1874.

Trades Union Congress established.

Meiji Restoration leads to modernisation of Japan.

Last public hanging in England.

Robert Browning (1812-89) *The Ring and the Book*.

Wilkie Collins *The Moonstone*.

Death of Giacchino Rossini (b 1792), Italian composer.

1869 25 January 30, to pantomime at Drury Lane Theatre, *Puss in Boots*.

March, to see William Morris.

April 22-May 3, to the Fitzhardinges at Berkeley Castle, where she drew furniture and interiors.

May 19-June 7, to Cambridge.

September 22-October 4, to Bute with her mother to visit Cissy Stewart (her aunt), whom later she photographed.

December 17-22, to Berkeley Castle.

Winter – embroideries for Frederic Leighton.

1869 General Ulysses Grant (1822-85) becomes President of U.S.A.

Suez Canal opened.

Single, property-owning women achieve vote in municipal elections. Emily Davies establishes Girton College, Cambridge for women with help of Barbara Bodichon.

Sea Birds Preservation Act (first legislation to protect wild life).

J.S. Mill *The Subjection of Women*.

Matthew Arnold *Culture and Anarchy*.

Nature begins publication.

1870 26 May 19-25, to Cambridge.

July 20, to opera – *Faust* by Gounod.

November 25, starts planting at Phillimore's Spring, Wargrave.

Carry and Frederick Eden settle in Venice.

Her brother Edward marries Theresa Biel in Germany.

Paintings: *Roman Cattle*
Froggy would a-wooing go.

1870 Franco-Prussian War: Paris besieged.

Papal states join Italy.

Declaration of Papal infallibility.

British Red Cross formed by Sir Robert Loyd Lindsay, VC (subsequently partner in the Grosvenor Gallery) and others.

W.E. Forster's (1818-86) Education Act, elementary education available to all children in England & Wales.

First Married Women's Property Act.

Emily Davies takes seat on London School Board.

Dr. Thomas Barnardo (1845-1905) opens first home for orphans.

Claude Monet (1840-1926), impressionist, flees to England.

Sir Lawrence Alma-Tadema (1836-1912), Dutch artist, settles in London.

William Robinson *The Wild Garden*.

| 1871 | 27 | January 13, to Frank Buckland to collect fish casts. | | 1871 |

1871   **27**

January 13, to Frank Buckland to collect fish casts.

February 15-18, to Simeon Solomon. Caricature by Gertrude Jekyll.

April 22, to opera, *The Magic Flute* by Mozart, with Georgina Duff Gordon.

May 18, to Phillimore's Spring to sow broom and furze seeds.

May 20-24, to Cambridge.

May 24, to International Exhibition.

May 31, to Agricultural Show at Guildford.

June 12, paints Wargrave flower borders.

June 20, with Herbert to High Wycombe.

Herbert involved in building telegraph systems.

1871

Proclamation of German Empire: William I of Prussia proclaimed Emperor at Versailles. Bismarck Chancellor till 1890.

Dutch cedes Gold Coast to Britain; entire Gold Coast under British rule.

Third French Republic established.

Italian unification complete.

Stanley and Livingstone meet at Lake Tanganyika.

Mont Cenis tunnel opened.

Trade Unions legalised in Britain.

Women's Education Union founded.

The Garden founded by William Robinson.

Charles Darwin *Descent of Man*.

George Eliot *Middlemarch* (1871-72).

1872   **28**

January 27-30, to 'Mr. Watts sitting for arms'.

February 29-March 5, to Westonbirt to visit R. S. Holford and to see arboretum and new house designed by Lewis Vulliamy.

March 6, to Mr. Ruskin.

June 16-17, Hercules Brabazon at Wargrave.

July 17, to Mr. Watts.

August 18, to Little Holland House with Georgina Duff Gordon to visit G. F. Watts.

September 5, to Madame Bodichon for supper.

September 26-27, to Madame Bodichon.

October 21-November 30, with Herbert to Italy – Turin, Milan, Parma, Bologna, Ravenna, Venice – drawing.

1872

Voting by secret ballot instituted.

Slade School of Art opened to women.

Thomas Cook (1808-92), tourist pioneer, offers world tour.

Samuel Butler (1835-1902) *Erewhon*.

Birth of Ralph Vaughan Williams (d 1958), English composer.

1873   **29**

January 8-10, to Madame Bodichon, London.

February 19, to Blumenthals, Hyde Park Gate, London.

February 23-28, with Mr. Percy Wyndham to Belgrave Square.

March 17, begins table cover for Frederic Leighton.

March 18-29, to London to visit Blumenthals, Wyndhams and Weguelins.

March 25, to see Mr. Leighton, Mr. Watts and Mr. Prinsep.

April 17-19, to Madame Bodichon, London.

April 28, Walter returns home after 14 months away.

May 8, to Blumenthals, London.

May 15-16 to Blumenthals, London.

June 3-7, to Duff Gordons, London. June 4, to Horticultural Garden with Georgina Duff Gordon. June 5, paints at the National Gallery. Dines at Blumenthals wearing a ismock frock surpliceî, a present from Madame Blumenthal.

June 7, singing lesson from Fiori.

June 30, Frederic Leighton's table cover finished.

July 8-19, to Madame Bodichon at Scalands, Sussex.

August 18, to Folkestone en route to Switzerland.

August 25, to Mr. G. F. Watts.

August 26, dinner with Frederic Leighton, Georgina and Alicia Duff Gordon.

September 22, to the Chalet, Sonzier, Lake Geneva, guest of Blumenthals.

1873

Ashanti War, 1873-74. Sir Garnet Wolseley mounts expedition.

Jane Hughes Senior – first woman inspector of work houses and pauper schools.

Mary Ward and others establish lectures for ladies in Oxford.

John Stuart Mill *Autobiography*.

Walter Pater (1839-94) *Studies in the History of the Renaissance*.

Birth of Sergey Rakhmaninov (d 1943), Russian composer and pianist.

November 1-28 February 1874, leaves Marseilles for Algiers arriving on November 3, guest of the Bodichons.

November 18, Herbert leaves for Plymouth en route to the Gold Coast and the Ashanti War.

1874	30	March 1, Walter ordained at Colchester. Julia and Gertrude present.	**1874**	Prime Minister: Benjamin Disraeli, Conservative, till 1880.

1874 30 March 1, Walter ordained at Colchester. Julia and Gertrude present.

March 10-14, to Blumenthals.

April 7-11, to Blumenthals.

April 30, Walter returns home from Florence.

May 2-14, to Mme Bodichon. Decorates flat in Morpeth Terrace for Herbert.

May 10, visits Poynters, Leighton, Watts.

June 22-July 8, to Blumenthals.

August 27-28, to Chester. Eaton Hall for Duke of Westminster, supervising interior decoration.

1874 Prime Minister: Benjamin Disraeli, Conservative, till 1880.

Helen Blackburn (1842-1903), President National Woman's Suffrage Society.

Emma Paterson (1848-86) founds Women's Protective and Provident League.

John Richard Green (1837-83) *A Short History of the English People.*

Birth of Gustav Holst (d 1934), English composer.

1875 31 January 16-February 1, to Blumenthals. Visits William Robinson at the office of *The Garden.*

February 22, to Blumenthals.

April 16-May 1, to Blumenthals.

April 23, Lady Duff Gordon dies.

May 21-June 5, to Blumenthals.

June 6, at Whistler private view.

June 19-26, to Blumenthals.

July 15-19, to Cambridge.

August 13-18, to Aldermaston – the Higford Burrs.

September 3-24, to Switzerland.

December 10-21, to Blumenthals.

1875 British Government purchases shares in Suez Canal.

Peaceful picketing legalised.

First women delegates to Trades Union Congress.

Universal Postal Union founded.

Alexander Graham Bell (1847-1922) invents and patents telephone.

Morris & Co founded in place of former design company (see 1861) under William Morris's sole direction.

Foundation of the Bach Choir in London.

Bedford Park 'Garden Suburb' designed by Norman Shaw (1831-1912).

Trial by Jury, the first of a series of collaborative operas by Sir William Gilbert (1836-1911) and Sir Arthur Sullivan (1842-1900).

Ellen Terry (1847-1928) as Portia in *The Merchant of Venice.*

Birth of Maurice Ravel (d 1937), French composer.

Birth of Fritz Kreisler (d 1962), Austrian violinist and composer.

1876 32 January 10-22, to Blumenthals.

January 24-29, Herbert mends telegraphs after violent snow storm in Oxford and Gloucester.

February 8-10, to Mme Bodichon.

February 12-19 to Berkeley Castle.

March 11-25, to Blumenthals.

March 26, Edward Jekyll (father) dies and is buried at Wargrave.

April 7 and 13-15, to Bramley.

April 19-21, to Berkeley Castle with Walter.

May 11, the family moves to Bramley Vicarage.

May 18-23, to Blumenthals.

May 26, to Paultons to stay with the Sloane Stanleys.

June 8, to Anthony Waterer's garden, Knap Hill.

June 10-13, to Blumenthals.

July 6-21, to Mme Bodichon, Scalands.

August 12-October 14, with her mother and Herbert to Paris, The Châlet (guests of Blumenthals) and Venice.

1876 General Custer defeated by Sioux Indians at Little Big Horn, U.S.A.

Balkan Wars July 1876 – March 1878.

Cruelty to Animals Act creates licensing procedures.

Giuseppe Verdi's opera *Aida* at Covent Garden.

Foundation of the Grosvenor Gallery by Sir Coutts Lindsay and others.

Henry Stacy Marks (1829-98) commences wall-paintings at Eaton Hall, of Canterbury pilgrims.

James McNeill Whistler (1834-1904) decorates the Peacock Room, in London.

April 26, first complete performance of *Mass in B Minor* by the Bach Choir.

1877 33 July, sketches at Slades. Commissions from Princess of Wales, Lord Carnarvon, Lord Richard Grosvenor.

September, wagon of fruit trees arrives at Munstead from Wargrave.

1877 Queen Victoria declared Empress of India.

Transvaal annexed to British Empire.

Society for the Protection of Ancient Buildings created by William Morris, Philip Webb (1831-1915), architect and designer, and others.

Library Association founded.

Johannes Brahms (1833-96), German composer, refuses Honorary Music Degree from Cambridge University, despite popularity in England.

Anna Sewell (1820-78) *Black Beauty.*

Sir Edward Burne-Jones (1833-98), James McNeill Whistler and others exhibited at the first summer exhibition of the Grosvenor Gallery; criticism by John Ruskin.

1878	34	September 26, to Munstead for good. Begins laying out and planting the garden at Munstead House. October 11, death of George John Cayley, artist; Gertrude Jekyll designs memorial. Birth of G.N. Brandt, landscape gardener, from Copenhagen, who introduced Gertrude Jekyll's ideas to Scandinavia.	**1878**	Zulu War (1878-79). 'Dual control' of Egypt by Britain and France. Under Treaty of Berlin, Bulgaria, Romania, Serbia and Montenegro recognised; British occupied Cyprus; Austria took control of Bosnia. Renewal of Afghan Wars. Edison and Swan – first successful incandescent electric light. James O'Grady *History of Ireland.* Thomas Hardy *The Return of the Native.* Georges Bizet (1838-75) *Carmen* at Covent Garden.
1879	35	September 3-October 2, to The Châlet	**1879**	Dual Alliance, Germany and Austria-Hungary. Tay Bridge destroyed. Louis Pasteur (1822-95) identifies organisms, leading to reduction in puerperal fever. *Gardening Illustrated* founded by William Robinson. Sir George Grove (b 1820), civil engineer and musicologist writes and has published first volume of *Dictionary of Music and Musicians* (4 vols 1879-1880). George Meredith (1828-1909) *The Egoist.* Birth of John Ireland (d 1962), English composer. Death of David Moore, Curator of Glasnevin Botanic Garden, Dublin, and author. Death of Julia Margaret Cameron (b 1848), pioneer of portrait photography.
1880	36	January, William Robinson and S. Reynolds Hole visit Munstead. January 31, first reference to Gertrude Jekyll in *The Garden.* *Iris* and *Periwinkle* embroidery designs published in *Handbook of Embroidery,* by Royal School of Art-Needlework.	**1880**	Prime Minister: W.E. Gladstone, Liberal, April 23 till 1885. First Boer War, 1880-1881. Elementary Education – compulsory ages seven to ten. Gaslights start to be installed in new homes. Antonin Dvorak (1841-1904) gives concert in Birmingham Sir Hubert Parry *Prometheus Unbound.* Death of Frances Jane Hope.
1881	37	February 19, first of a series of articles in *The Garden.* June, judges at Botanic Show. July, to Brittany with the Blumenthals. August, 'making a flat Alpine garden' for G. F. Wilson at Gishurst Cottage. August 20-September 29, to The Châlet; guests include Hercules Brabazon, Princess Louise and Alexander de Wolkoff, 'making rock garden in Quarry'. December 29, Herbert marries Agnes Graham, and lives mainly in London.	**1881**	Assassination of Tsar Alexander II. De Lesseps commences work on the Panama Canal Savoy Theatre opens – first to be lit by electricity. Henry James (1843-1916) *Washington Square and Portrait of a Lady.* Death of William Andrew Nesfield (b 1794), artist and garden designer.
1882	38	August 26, William Goldring writes about the garden at Munstead (House) in *The Garden.* November 20, birth of Herbert's son, Francis Jekyll (died 1965).	**1882**	Troubles in Egypt. Britain occupies Cairo. Second Married Women's Property Act. First performance of *The Ring of the Niebelung* by Richard Wagner (1813-83) in London. Robert Louis Stevenson (1850-94) *Treasure Island.* Dictionary of *National Biography* (published 1882-91), edited by Sir Leslie Stephen (1832-1904). Birth of Princess Margaret ("Daisy"), daughter of the Duke of Connaught, gardener and painter, later Crown Princess of Sweden, at Bagshot Park. Death of Rev. John Gudgeon Nelson, horticulturist and breeder of *Narcissus.*

1883	39	January 4, plants arrive from Woolson and Co., Passaic, New Jersey, for William Robinson.	**1883**

1883   39

January 4, plants arrive from Woolson and Co., Passaic, New Jersey, for William Robinson.

January 13, daffodil "Gertrude Jekyll" raised by Rev. J. G. Nelson, named by Peter Barr.

February 5, sends William Robinson a pair of French boots.

March 31, plan of garden at Munstead (House) by Gertrude Jekyll at William Robinson's behest.

Buys 15 acres of land and begins laying out and planning 'O.S.' – on the other side of the road from Munstead House.

June 12, exhibits tall hardy plants at Royal Horticultural Society (R.H.S.) in Linnaean Society, Burlington House.

October, Reverend and Mrs. C. Wolley Dod visit Munstead.

November, contributes sections and photographs for *The English Flower Garden* by William Robinson.

December, to Capri; sends plants to William Robinson and the Royal Botanic Gardens, Kew.

1883

Lord Cromer (1841-1917) Consul General in Egypt, till 1907.

First electric tram in operation.

Sir George Grove appointed first Director of the Royal College of Music.

Electricity lights the Grosvenor Gallery, which supplies neighbouring buildings.

William Robinson *The English Flower Garden*.

Death of Rev. H. Harpur Crewe (b 1830), horticulturist.

1884   40

March 29, 43 designs for Munstead Flower Glasses which are made and sold by James Green and Nephew, London.

June 7, visit to Munstead by 50 gardeners from West Surrey.

August, corresponds with John Ruskin at Brantwood.

August 7, garden plan for Robert Okell, Bowdon, Manchester.

July 3, to Llan-fawr, Angelsey, to stay with Jane Henrietta Adeane.

October, to Berkeley Castle.

1884

Wolseley leads expedition to Khartoum to rescue General Gordon, trapped by the Mahdi's forces.

Berlin Conference defines rights of European Powers in Africa.

Third Reform Bill.

Fabian Society founded.

Octavia Hill takes charge of houses for Ecclesiastical Commission.

London Society for the Prevention of Cruelty to Children formed.

Steam turbine invented.

Death of James Henry Mangles at Valewood, Haslemere, Chairman London and South-West Railway. Collector and breeder of Rhododendrons.

1885   41

Spring, takes up photography.

Awarded a Bronze Medal by the Royal Horticultural Society for her Exhibition of Primulas.

Miss C. M. Owen of Gorey visits Munstead.

July 17, William Robinson bids successfully at auction for Gravetye Manor.

1885

Prime Minister: Marquis of Salisbury (1830-1903), Conservative, June 23 till 1886.

Khartoum relieved by Sir Garnet Wolseley, but General Gordon killed.

Foundation of Indian National Congress.

Completion of Canadian Pacific Railway.

James McNeill Whistler *Ten O' Clock* lecture, a manifesto *Art for Art's Sake*.

Birth of Duncan Grant (d 1978).

Death of Daniel Higford Burr of Aldermaston Court.

1886   42

April 21, exhibits at R.H.S., Primula conference in crush room of Royal Albert Hall. Munstead Bunch primroses on display. Award of Merit for *Cardamine pratensis* fl.pl by R.H.S. Floral Committee.

June, photographs of interiors and garden of the Blumenthals' home, 48 Hyde Park Gate, London.

Herbert reports on coastal fortifications in Gibraltar.

1886

Prime Minister: W.E. Gladstone, Liberal, February 1 – July 20.

Prime Minister: Marquis of Salisbury, Conservative, July 25 till 1892.

Upper Burma annexed by Britain.

Irish Home Rule Bill defeated in House of Commons.

Riots in Trafalgar Square to protest unemployment.

Gottlieb Daimler (1834-1900) produces first internal combustion engine.

First safety bicycles manufactured in Coventry.

Robert Louis Stevenson *The Strange Case of Dr Jekyll and Mr Hyde*.

Maria Theresa Earle *Potpourri from a Surrey Garden*

Death of Franz Liszt (b 1811), pianist and composer, after visit to London.

1887   43

April 18, photographs of pollarded willows and oak at Tangley. Photographs of Gravetye.

June 14, birth of Herbert's daughter, Barbara Jekyll (died 1973).

1887

Celebration of Queen Victoria's Golden Jubilee.

Joint Anglo-French control of the New Hebrides.

November 13, 'Bloody Sunday' riots in Trafalgar Square.

August 25 – September 22, to The Châlet.

Christmas Day, four photographs of the interior of Busbridge Church, Essex.

1888 44 G. D. Leslie's personal reminiscences of Gertrude Jekyll at Wargrave published in *Our River*.

Visits from Mrs. E.V. Boyle of Huntercombe and Sir Thomas Hanbury, Victoria Fisher-Rowe, her sister Eleanor Liddell and cousin Charles Liddell.

July 10, exhibits *Carpentaria californica* at the R.H.S. First Class Certificate.

September, Lord Wolseley and his daughter Frances, visit Munstead.

1889 45 Makes a silver paten bearing a monogram and inscription: 'So man did eat angels' food, for he sent them meat enough (Psalm 78, v.26) which is and presented by the Liddells to Witley Church.

March 10, birth of Herbert's daughter, Pamela Jekyll (died 1943).

July, photographs of Cardiocrinum with her gardener, P. Brown, in a Franciscan habit.

Museum of Science and Art purchase an iron tray and a tortoiseshell casket.

Meets Edwin Lutyens (1869 – 1944), English architect, at Harry Mangles' home, Vale-Wood, Haselmere, for the first time.

December 17, sends dovecote to Lady Wolseley.

1890 46 February 11, Herbert Jekyll elected Fellow of Royal Horticultural Society.

1891 47 To Pagenstecher's Clinic, Wiesbaden, Germany. Alexander Pagenstecher (1828-1879) had pioneered cataract operations, for which he was known internationally.

April 21, Munstead Early White Primrose displayed at the National Auricular and Primrose Society's meeting.

Barbara Bodichon dies and leaves The Poor House, Zennor, Cornwall, to Gertrude Jekyll who sold it in 1895.

1892 48 October 9, first design of `The Hut' by Edwin Lutyens.

First appearance of Edwin Lutyen's name in Munstead House Visitors book.

1888 Arthur Conan Doyle (1859-1930) *A Study in Scarlet.*

William II becomes German Emperor, "The Kaiser" (1859-1941), grandson of Queen Victoria.

London County Council created.

First large electric power station built by London Electricity Corporation (Chairman Sir Coutts Lindsay; Chief Engineer S de Ferranti).

Arts and Crafts Exhibition Society formed.

Nellie Melba (1861-1931), debut Covent Garden.

Mrs Humphry Ward (1851-1920) *Robert Elsmere.*

Oscar Wilde (1854-1900) *The Happy Prince and Other Tales.*

Rudyard Kipling (1865-1930) *Plain Tales from the Hills.*

George Bernard Shaw (1856-1950) becomes music critic on *The Star.*

1889 British South Africa Company formed by Cecil Rhodes (1853-1902) to exploit mineral resources and colonize territory.

Suicide of Crown Prince Rudolf of Austria (b 1858) at Mayerling.

Gustave Eiffel (1832-1923) builds Eiffel Tower, Paris.

G.N. Brandt, Danish horticulturist, visits Baghdad.

W.B. Yeats (1865-1939) *The Wanderings of Oisin and other Poems.*

Death of M. Chevreul (b 1786), author of *The Principles of Harmony and Contrast of Colours.*

Death of Robert Marnock (b 1800), designer of parks and gardens.

1890 Cecil Rhodes Prime Minister at the Cape

Bismarck resigns March 17: "Dropping the Pilot" caricature in *Punch.*

U.S.A. becomes the world's leading industrial power.

Forth Bridge opens.

Eleanor Marx organises first English May Day celebration.

London Underground electrification begins.

First vist to London by Jan Paderewski (1860-1941), Polish pianist, composer and statesman.

William Morris *News From Nowhere.*

James Frazer (1854-1941) *The Golden Bough.*

William Booth *In Darkest England and the Way Out.*

Death of James Shirley Hibberd (b 1825).

Death of Marianne North (b 1830), artist.

1891 Anglo-Portuguese treaty signed.

Nyasaland and the territory between Zambezi and Congo Free State becomes Northern Rhodesia.

Kelmscott Press founded by William Morris.

Oscar Wilde *Picture of Dorian Gray.*

Thomas Hardy (1840-1928) *Tess of the d'Urbervilles.*

Death of John Dando Sedding (b1838); publication of *Garden-craft Old and New.*

1892 Prime Minister: W.E. Gladstone, Liberal, August 15 till 1894.

Panama Canal – financial scandals in France; de Lesseps found guilty.

Triple Alliance: Germany, Italy and Austria.

Indian Councils Act.

James Kier Hardie (1856-1915) elected to Parliament

as Independent Labour delegate.

Sidney Webb (1859-1947) and five other Fabians elected to London County Council.

George Bernard Shaw's first play *Widower's Houses* performed.

Oscar Wilde *Lady Windermere's Fan*.

Reginald Blomfield (1856-1942) and F. Inigo Thomas *The Formal Garden in England*.

Gustav Mahler (1860-1911) conducts opera season in London.

William Morris becomes Master of the Art Workers Guild.

Peter Tchaikovsky (1840-93) *Eugene Onegin* premiere in London.

1893	49	April 27, Mr. and Mrs. Watts visit Munstead. May, first designs for Munstead Wood by Edwin Lutyens. November, Albert Zumbach from The Châlet becomes head gardener at Munstead Wood.	**1893**	Irish Home Rule Bill defeated in House of Lords. Matabele War ends in conquest by British South African Company. Court martial of Alfred Dreyfus (1859-1935). Oxford University abolishes requirement that women attending lectures be chaperoned. George Elgood – Exhibition at Fine Art Society. Studio first published. Dame Ethel Smyth (1858-1944) *Mass in D major*. Antonin Dvorak *From the New World* symphony.
1894	50	'The Hut', designed by Edwin Lutyens, built in the grounds of Munstead Wood. Publication of Joseph Jekyll's letters to Lady Gertrude Sloane Stanley, edited by Algernon Bouke.	**1894**	Prime Minister: Earl of Rosebery (1847-1929), Liberal, March 5 till 1895. Japan declares War on China and acquires Formosa (Taiwan). Armenian massacres by Turks. Birth of Prince Edward, later Duke of Windsor. Manchester Ship Canal opens. Death Duties reformed by Sir William Harcourt (1827-1904). Emmeline Pankhurst (1857-1928), suffragette, is elected to Chorlton Board of Guardians. Rene Panhard (1841-1908) launches the first automobile (France). Sir Edward Poynter (1836-1919), English painter, Director of National Gallery. Sir Hubert Parry appointed Second Director of the Royal College of Music. George A. Moore (1852-1933) *Esther Waters*. Oscar Wilde *Salome*, illustrations Aubrey Beardsley (1872-98). Rudyard Kipling *Jungle Book*.
1895	51	June, Edith Wharton and Beatrix Farrand (née Jones) visit Munstead. July, Julia Jekyll (mother) dies. Herbert and Agnes Jekyll move into Munstead House. Edward (Teddy) inherits the collection of Etruscan vases. Walter moves to Jamaica permanently.	**1895**	Prime Minister: Marquis of Salisbury, Conservative, June 25 till 1902. Joseph Chamberlain (1836-1914), Colonial Secretary. Commander in Chief of British Army. Viscount Wolseley, Secretary of State for War 1895-1900. Jameson Raid in South Africa, across Transvaal border. Malay States created. Opening of Kiel Canal. Oscar Wilde sentenced to prison. National Trust founded by Octavia Hill, Sir Robert Hunter and Canon H.D. Rawnsley. Guiglielmo Marconi (1874-1937) sends message over a mile by wireless. Wilhelm Röntgen (1845-1923) discovers X-Rays. Lumière brothers invent cinematograph. Sigmund Freud (1856-1939), first work on psycho-analysis published, *Studien uber Hysterie*.

Sir Henry Wood (1869-1944) establishes the promenade concerts in London.

H G Wells (1866-1946) *The Time Machine.*

Thomas Hardy *Jude the Obscure.*

Lady Alicia Margaret Rockley (née Amherst) *History of Gardening.*

1896 52 Construction of Munstead Wood begins.

First 16 articles in *The Guardian Newspaper,* which served as the basis for her first book, *Wood and Garden.* Long anonymous article on the history of garden design for *The Edinburgh Review.*

May 5, Award of Merit to *Cardamine pratensis* fl.pl. Miss Jekyll.

September 21, Edwin Lutyens visits Munstead House.

1896 Surrender of Jameson's Force to the Boer General Cronjé at Doorncop.

Discovery of Gold on the Klondike River, N.W. Canada.

The Ashanti conquered.

Egyptian army re-trained by Sir Herbert Kitchener (1850-1916).

Cinema begins at Empire Theatre in London.

Charles Rennie Mackintosh (1868-1928) wins competition for new Glasgow School of Art building.

Sir Edward Poynter, President of the Royal Academy, till 1918.

A.E. Housman (1859-1936), scholar and poet, *A Shropshire Lad.*

Death of William Morris.

1897 53 February 11, poem written by "Oozel that is called Bumps" entitled *The Lament of the Neglected.*

April 15, Edwin Lutyens visits Munstead Wood, "took linen with Woozle".

May 27, Edwin Lutyens visits Munstead Wood.

August 7, to Warren Lodge, Thursley, taking drawing boards, paper and instruments to Edwin Lutyens.

October 26, Awarded the Victoria Medal of Honour in Horticulture by the Royal Horticultural Society. The only other lady to be honoured was Ellen Willmott. The awards were made by Sir Trevor Lawrence. Dean Reynolds Hole responded on behalf of the amateur gardeners and described Miss Willmott as the 'Queen of Hearts' and Miss Jekyll the 'Queen of Spades'.

October 27, moves into Munstead Wood; begins to sell plants.

Collaboration with Sir Robert Lorimer on Whinfold, Hascombe for Lionel Benson.

1897 Queen Victoria's Diamond Jubilee.

Period of Indian unrest begins.

National Portrait Gallery opens.

Marriage of Lady Emily Lytton to Edwin Lutyens at St. Mary's Church, Knebworth.

Giacomo Puccini (1858-1924) *La Boheme* first performed at Covent Garden.

Country Life (Illustrated) first published by Edward Hudson.

1898 54 April, agreement with Longmans to write *Wood and Garden* to be published simultaneously in London and New York.

1898 Thomas Hardy *Wessex Poems.*

Spanish-American War: Philippines surrendered for $20 million: Philippines and Puerto Rico annexed by the U.S.A.

Anglo-Egyptian condominium proclaimed over Sudan. Anglo-French confrontation at Fashoda.

The Curies discover radium.

James McNeill Whistler formed *Académie Carmen* in Paris. W. R. Sickert (1860-1942) pupil (1898-1901).

English Folk Song Society formed.

1899 55 *Wood and Garden* published. Reports to Edwin Lutyens "the best she has written about flower borders is in the chapter called 'Flower Garden and Pergola'."

Edward Hudson, owner of *Country Life (Illustrated)* and E. T. Cook, editor of John Ruskin's collected works, visit Munstead Wood. Collaboration with Edwin Lutyens on the Deanery Garden, Sonning, for Edward Hudson, on Orchards, Godalming for Sir William Chance and on Goddards, Abinger Common for Sir F. Mirrielees.

July 11, Award of Merit for Viola 'Jackanapes'.

August 6, photographs outside Munstead House of Pamela and Barbara Jekyll, Leonard Borwick, Hercules Brabazon, and Dolly Muir Mackenzie.

1899 October 10, Boer War begins (1899-1902): after three defeats in December, Britain subsequently consolidates its hold on Southern Africa.

First motor bus in service.

Claude Monet, first paintings of garden at Giverny, France.

Harold Peto (1854-1933), landscape architect, acquires Iford Manor.

Winston Churchill (1874-1965), statesman and author, *The River War.*

Sir Edward Elgar's (1857-1934) *Enigma Variations* performed.

Edith Wharton (1861-1937), American author, *The Greater Inclination.*

		September 2-16, to Thornham. The Lutyens stay in 'Plazzo' (his nickname for Munstead Wood).		
1900	56	January, co-editor with E. T. Cook of *The Garden. Home and Garden* published. May 8, Bronze Banksian Medal for group of Munstead Bunch primroses. October 3, David Fry and Son, Godalming making Cats' House. December 8, first illustrated article on Munstead Wood in *Country Life*. Herbert appointed Secretary for the Royal Commission for the Paris Exhibition and is responsible, with Edwin Lutyens, for the British Pavilion.	**1900**	Boxer Rebellion in China. Boers attack Ladysmith. Relief of Mafeking. Emmeline Pankhurst elected to Manchester School Board. Joseph Conrad (1857-1924) *Lord Jim*. Helen Allingham paints 'The South Border', and 'Michaelmas Daisies' at Munstead Wood. Paris Exhibition. Sigmund Freud *Die Traum deutung* (The Interpretation of Dreams). *Country Life* publishes article on Munstead Wood by E. Theodore Cook, photographed by Charles Latham. Anton Chekhov (1860-1904) *Uncle Vanya*. Thomas Mawson (1861-1933), garden designer, *The Art and Craft of Garden Making*.
1901	57	*Lilies for English Gardens* and *Wall and Water Gardens* published in the Country Life Library series. July 25, to Deanery Garden, Sonning with Edward Hudson and Edwin Lutyens. Award of Merit for Munstead Bunch Primrose, The Sultan. Writes articles for *Country Life* on Orchards, Surrey. Herbert becomes Assistant Secretary of the Railway Department.	**1901**	Death of Queen Victoria, succeeded by King Edward VII (m Princess Alexandra 1863). Trans-Siberian Railway opened for single-track traffic. College for Lady Gardeners, Glynde, founded by Viscountess Wolseley. Commonwealth of Australia formed. Factory Act forbids employment of children under twelve. Rudyard Kipling *Kim*. Edward Elgar *Pomp and Circumstance* marches. Beatrix Potter (1866-1943) *The Tale of Peter Rabbit*.
1902	58	To Brides-les-Bains for a "23 days-slimming cure". July 12-August 2, last visit to the Blumenthals at The Châlet, "three weeks of blessed and kindness healing for a tired stiegel". August 9, visit to Messrs Suttons and Sons to see their China Asters and Antirrhinums. Helen Allingham paints at Munstead Wood.	**1902**	Coronation of King Edward VII. Prime Minister: Arthur Balfour (1848-1930), Conservative, till 1905. Anglo-Japanese Alliance, amplified in 1905. Treaty of Vereeniging ends Boer War. Debut in London of Enrico Caruso (1873-1921). Hillaire Beloc (1870-1953) *The Path to Rome*. Claude Debussy (1862-1918) first performance of *Pelléas et Mélisande*. Death of Cecil Rhodes, establishing Rhodes Scholarships by his will. Death of Emile Zola (b 1840).
1903	59	February 29, David Fry and Son making Pigeon House. September 4-18, to Seaview, Isle of Wight. November 3, foundation stone for King Edward VII Sanatorium laid by King Edward VII. Collaboration with H. Percy Adams. Frederick Eden writes in *Country Life* about his garden in Venice.	**1903**	Assassination of the Royal family of Serbia. First controlled flight in 'heavier-than-air machine' by Orville and Wilbur Wright at Kitty Hawk U.S.A. Bertrand Russell (1872-1970) *The Principles of Mathematics*. George E. Moore (1873-1958) *Principia Ethica*. Death of James McNeill Whistler.
1904	60	Henri Correvon visits Munstead Wood. *Old West Surrey* and *Some English Gardens* published by Longmans in London and New York. Millmead, a collaborative project with Edwin Lutyens begun. Hestercombe designs begun. April, some 'adventurous' Scandinavians visited Munstead Wood. May 16, to Trebarwith, Cornwall.	**1904**	Russo-Japanese War begins. Anglo-French Entente Cordiale. Sir John Fisher (1841-1920) First Sea Lord. Treaty with Tibet signed at Lhasa. George Samuel Elgood paintings in *Some English Gardens*. Herman Muthesius (1861-1927), the German architect, writes about Munstead Wood, after a visit, in *Landhaus und Garten*. Albert Einstein (1879-1955) *Theory of Relativity*. Edith Wharton *Italian Villas and their Gardens*. G. K. Chesterton (1874-1936) publishes book on G. F. Watts.

Death of Rev. Samuel Reynolds Hole (b 1819).

Death of Rev. Charles Wolley-Dod (b 1826).

Death of George Frederick Watts (b 1817).

1905	61	April 22, photographs of site of Millmead.	1905	January 22, 'Bloody Sunday' massacre in St. Petersburg.

1905 61

April 22, photographs of site of Millmead.

July 1, correspondence with Dr. A. W. Rowe, Lyell Medallist, on Devon chalk and species of *verbascum*.

November 4, Guildford magistrates lose case against Gertrude Jekyll to demolish summer house at Millmead.

October 28, Mr. E. R. Squelch gardener at King Edward VII Sanatorium to Munstead for training.

1905

January 22, 'Bloody Sunday' massacre in St. Petersburg.

Rebellion in Russian forces: Battleship Potemkin: Tsarist concessions.

Treaty of Portsmouth (U.S.A.) ends Russo-Japanese War, after destruction of Russian fleet.

Marriage of Princess Margaret to Crown Prince Gustav Adolf of Sweden. "The Flower Princess" developed a garden at the summer palace of Solfiero, Hälsingborg, owing much to Gertrude Jekyll and Claude Monet.

Death of Henry George Moon (b 1857), artist.

Death of Frederick William Thomas Burbidge (b 1847), botanist.

Death of Simeon Solomon (b 1840), painter and draughtsman.

1906 62

May 11-22, to Lindisfarne Castle with Edwin Lutyens.

June 14, opening ceremony King Edward Sanatorium by King Edward VII.

July 19, photographs of Mr. F. Jackson, Tarn Moor, Hindhead.

Preparing book on *Flower Decoration in the House* for publication, based on articles in *The Garden*, 1881-2.

October 11, photograph of Albert and Fred Borall with giant gourds in a wheelbarrow.

1906

Prime Minister: Sir Henry Campbell-Bannerman (1836-1908), Liberal, till 1908 after 'landslide' majority in Britain.

General Strike in Russia.

San Francisco destroyed by earthquake.

Simplon tunnel opened for rail traffic.

First Labour Members of Parliament elected.

Movement for women's suffrage becomes active in Britain.

George Bernard Shaw *The Doctor's Dilemma*

Pablo Picasso (1881-1973) *Les Demoiselles d'Avignon*.

Paul Cèzanne (1839-1906) *Le Jardinier*.

Death of Henrik Ibsen (b 1828), Norwegian dramatist and poet.

Death of Hercules Brabazon Brabazon (b 1821).

1907 63

May 6, photographs of the Spring Garden, Munstead Wood.

August, visit to Lady Emily Lutyens, wife of Sir Edwin, at Rustington.

September 11, operation on her nose.

Preparing book on *Colour in the Flower Garden*.

Wood and Garden, translated into German and published by Julius Baedeker of Leipzig.

1907

New Zealand becomes a Dominion.

Lawrence Johnston acquires Hidcote.

Death of Sir Michael Foster (b 1836), Professor of Physiology, Cambridge, author, cultivated irises.

Death of Sir Thomas Hanbury, gardener and creator of botanic garden at Mortola, Liguria, Italy.

Death of Jacob Blumenthal (b 1829), pianist to Queen Victoria and host of weekly musical soirées.

1908 64

Children and Gardens published.

May 17, Jacques Blumenthal dies.

June 3, her niece Pamela Jekyll, marries Reginald McKenna, MP, First Lord of the Admiralty.

1908

Young Turk Revolution till 1909, led by Mustafa Kemal Ataturk (1881-1938).

Prime Minister: Herbert Henry Asquith (1852-1928), Liberal, till 1916.

Old age pensions introduced by David Lloyd George (1863-1945), Chancellor of the Exchequer.

Emmeline Pankhurst imprisoned for militant activities.

Death of George Nicholson, Kew gardener and Curator.

1909 65

March, bad attack of influenza.

May 19, Roger Fry, English artist and critic, visits Munstead Wood; Ellen Willmott visits Munstead Wood.

August 9, Edwin Lutyens at Munstead Wood: "breakfast at 9 (sausages, bacon, eggs, coffee), best tea at 11, lunch at 1 (beef suet pudding, stuffed tomatoes), bed 1.30-3.30, coffee, Tea 4.30, Dinner 7.30."

August 10, Gertrude Jekyll's poem *Oh! for a pea in purple pod.*

1909

Union of South Africa formed.

Robert Peary (1856-1920), American explorer, reaches North Pole.

Louis Blériot (1872-1936) makes first cross-channel flight.

Henry Ford (1863-1947) pioneers Model T chassis – beginnings of cheap motor cars.

Ellen Willmott *Warley Garden in Spring and Summer.*

Sir George Sitwell (1860-1943) *An Essay on the Making of Gardens.*

Arnold Schoenberg (1874-1951), Austro-Hungarian composer, *Erwartung.*

				1910	Death of Peter Barr, florist, specialising in narcissi, and author.
1910	66	May, to Bembridge, Isle of Wight.			Death of King Edward VII (b 1841).
		Mr. James Britten, Mr. E. A. Bowles and Mrs. Helen Allingham visit Munstead.			King George V (1865-1936) succeeds to throne.
		Suffers from colitis.			Labour Exchanges established in Britain.
		May 12-16, to Bembridge.			First Post-Impressionist Exhibition organised by Roger Fry (1866-1934).
		July 20, her niece Barbara Jekyll, marries Francis McLaren, MP (born 1886 and died on active service in 1917).			Ellen Willmott *Genus Rosa,* illustrated by Alfred Parsons.
		August 19, Roger Fry at Munstead Wood.			Richard Strauss (1864-1949) *Salome* first performance in London, based on Oscar Wilde's poem.
		Writes for *Country Life* about Ellen Willmott's garden at Warley Place.			Igor Stravinsky (1882-1971) *The Firebird.*
					Death of Florence Nightingale (b 1820), nurse, organiser of nursing in Crimean War, author.
					Death of Leo Tolstoy.

May, to Bembridge, Isle of Wight.

Mr. James Britten, Mr. E. A. Bowles and Mrs. Helen Allingham visit Munstead.

Suffers from colitis.

May 12-16, to Bembridge.

July 20, her niece Barbara Jekyll, marries Francis McLaren, MP (born 1886 and died on active service in 1917).

August 19, Roger Fry at Munstead Wood.

Writes for *Country Life* about Ellen Willmott's garden at Warley Place.

1910 Death of Peter Barr, florist, specialising in narcissi, and author.

Death of King Edward VII (b 1841).

King George V (1865-1936) succeeds to throne.

Labour Exchanges established in Britain.

First Post-Impressionist Exhibition organised by Roger Fry (1866-1934).

Ellen Willmott *Genus Rosa,* illustrated by Alfred Parsons.

Richard Strauss (1864-1949) *Salome* first performance in London, based on Oscar Wilde's poem.

Igor Stravinsky (1882-1971) *The Firebird.*

Death of Florence Nightingale (b 1820), nurse, organiser of nursing in Crimean War, author.

Death of Leo Tolstoy.

1911 67 Writes Preface for Wilhelm Miller's book, *The Charm of English Gardens* published by Hodder and Stoughton in New York.

February 22, Roger Fry at Munstead Wood.

September 15-22, to Looe, Cornwall. Thomas Veitch's nursery, Exeter.

November 15-16, Roger Fry at Munstead Wood.

Herbert becomes Chancellor and Secretary General to the Order of the Hospital of St. John of Jerusalem.

Walter publishes his book on Artur Schopenhauer.

1911 Great British rail strike.

Liverpool `Bloody Sunday' clashes between police and strikers.

British MPs paid for first time.

National Insurance Act.

Roald Amundson (1872-1928) reaches South Pole.

Reginald McKenna (1863-1943), First Lord of the Admiralty, exchanges cabinet places with Winston Churchill, Home Secretary.

William Robinson *Gravetye Manor.*

Max Beerbohm (1872-1956) *Zuleika Dobson.*

Sir Thomas Beecham (1879-1961) presents Diaghilev's Russian Ballet in London.

Death of Sir Joseph Dalton Hooker, Director of Kew and author.

1912 68 *Gardens for Small Country Houses* with Lawrence Weaver published by Country Life.

April, to Bosham.

April 15, the SS Titanic sank; memorial to one of its officers, Jack Phillips of Godalming, is designed with Thackeray Turner.

Herbert retires from Civil Servce, visits Walter in Jamaica and starts his researches into family history.

1912 China becomes a Republic under President Sun Yat Sen.

Outbreak of Balkan Wars.

Great British coal strike.

Last expedition of Robert Scott (1868-1912) reaches South Pole.

Second Post-Impressionist Exhibition includes works by Vanessa Bell (1879-1961).

Death of George Maw, author of *Monograph of the Genus Crocus,* plant collector, industrialist, chemist and geologist.

1913 69 June 16-23, to Bosham, Chichester.

August 19, agrees to write foreword to Mrs. Frances King's book, *The Garden Day by Day,* published in New York in 1928.

Creates Heath Garden at Munstead Wood.

1913 Treaty of Bucharest.

Henry James *A Small Boy and Others.*

Death of Alfred Russel Wallace (b 1823), animal geographer, wrote on natural selection, plant collector, author.

1914 70 May 1, describes Asquith's cabinet as "this wretched government" and refers to their "odious insurance tax". Her niece Pamela's husband, Reginald McKenna was Home Secretary in the government.

August 19, photograph of west end of south border with hydrangeas, dahlias and wisteria: last dated photograph.

Edward sells collection of Etruscan vases.

1914 June 28, assassination of Archduke Francis Ferdinand at Sarajevo.

August, Britain declares war against Germany and Austria – Hungary.

August 13, Japan declares war on Germany.

British protectorate over Egypt proclaimed.

December 29, First Zeppelin appears over British coast.

William Bean, foreman of the Arboretum at Kew, *Trees and Shrubs Hardy in the British Isles.*

Auguste Rodin (1840-1917) presents a collection of his bronzes to the British nation.

Christopher Nevinson (1889-1946) cosignator of the avant-garde artistic *Futurist Manifesto.*

Percy Wyndham Lewis (1882-1957), novelist, painter and critic, co-founder of Blast and Vorticist movement.

Gustav Holst *The Planets*

1915	71	May 11, exhibited *Lunaria biennis* Munstead Purple at the Floral Committee, Royal Horticultural Society.	**1915**	February, Dardanelles campaign.

1915 71 May 11, exhibited *Lunaria biennis* Munstead Purple at the Floral Committee, Royal Horticultural Society.

Wrote preface to Mrs. Frances King's book *The Well Considered Garden* published in New York by Charles Scribner's & Sons.

June 26, corresponds with Lady Ottoline Morrell (1873-1938), hostess at Garsington Manor, about pot pourri.

August 21, finishes work of planting and laying out paths on Hydon Heath for the National Trust as a memorial to Octavia Hill.

1916 72 May 31, gives collection of textiles to Victoria and Albert Museum, including two monks' habits, one of which had been made by her in 1895 for a model and based on an original from the Franciscan convent at Crawley.

July 18, Award of Merit from Floral Committee of the Royal Horticultural Society of *Lavandula spica* 'Barr's large-flowered Munstead Dwarf'.

Death of Frederick Eden.

1917 73 August 27, Lady Sackville (mother of Vita Sackville West) and Sir Edwin Lutyens visit Munstead.

December, designs and plans for the war cemeteries, Imperial War Graves Commission. Collaboration with Sir Edwin Lutyens and Sir Herbert Baker (1862-1946), English architect and old friend with whom she had corresponded about planting in South Africa.

Begins to keep hens.

1918 74 Publication of *Garden Ornament* by *Country Life*. Contributes pamphlet to Civic Arts Association, Burnley, on public parks and gardens.

1919 75 Temporary deafness and long illness.

May 16-30, with Kate Leslie to Charmouth.

Cenotaph design by Sir Edwin Lutyens.

1920 76 Making "trees for the Delhi model" for Sir Edwin Lutyens.

1915

February, Dardanelles campaign.

April, Gallipoli landings. Bernard Freyberg wins D.S.O. (and later won 3 bars).

Infantry battles in France and Germany.

Germans first used gas.

May, sinking of the 'Lusitania'.

Coalition government formed, under Asquith with Reginald McKenna as Chancellor of the Exchequer.

Anti-German riots in the East End of London 1915-1916.

Bertrand Russell removed from Cambridge fellowship for pacifist activities.

1916

February 21 – December 18, Battle of Verdun.

July 1 – November 18, Battle of Somme; Bernard Freyberg awarded V.C.

Kitchener drowned when 'Hampshire' struck mine.

December 16, Lloyd George forms War Cabinet; Prime Minister till 1922. Asquith and McKenna resign.

Sinn Fein rising in Ireland.

Death of Rev. Henry Nicholson Ellacombe, gardener at Bitton, Glos., and author.

Death of Edward Mawley, garden writer and rose expert.

1917

April 6, U.S.A. declared war on Germany.

March, Tsar abdicates.

June 2-8, Battle of Messines.

July 31 – November 6, 3rd Battle of Ypres.

September 15, Russia declared a Republic.

November 6, Passchendale captured by British.

November 7, Bolshevik Revolution leading to Civil War, under leadership of Vladimir Lenin (1870-1924).

November 20 – December 3, Battle of Cambrai.

King George V assumes name of 'Windsor' by Royal Proclamation.

Balfour Declaration offers a national home for the Jews in Palestine.

1918

General Ferdinand Foch (1851-1929) becomes Supreme Commander of the British, French and American Armies and dictates the terms of the Allied Victory.

November 9, the Kaiser escapes to Holland.

November 11, Armistice signed by Germany.

December 1, Proclamation of Kingdom of Serbs, Croats and Slovenes (Yugoslavia) in Belgrade.

Nancy Astor (1879-1964) becomes first woman Member of Parliament.

Logan Pearsall Smith (1865-1946) *Trivia*.

Lytton Strachey (1880-1932) *Eminent Victorians*.

Death of Sir Hubert Parry, English composer.

1919

January 18, Peace Conference, Paris.

June 19, German Fleet scuttled at Scapa Flow.

June 28, Treaty of Paris settles map of Europe

Glasgow 'Bloody Friday' – confrontation between police and strikers.

First flight across Atlantic by Alcock and Brown.

Reginald Farrer *English Rock Garden*.

Death of William Goldring, Kew gardener, garden designer and author.

1920

January, first meeting League of Nations.

August, Ottoman Empire broken up.

Prohibition in U.S.A.

Sat to William Nicholson (1872-1949), English painter.

Professor Georg Georgsen, the Danish landscape architect, and Göste Reuterswärd, the Swedish garden designer climb over the fence into Munstead Wood, are shown the garden by Albert Zumbach, have tea with Miss Jekyll and are required to climb out the way they came in.

Designs garden for Edward when he moves to Kent.

Degrees first open to women at Oxford University.

Death of Richard John Farrer, plant collector, gardener, author.

Death of Sir Edmund Giles Loder, created garden at Leonardslee, Sussex.

Death of Alfred William Parsons (b 1847), artist and garden designer.

| 1921 | 77 | January 6, receives book on James McNeill Whistler from William Nicholson. | 1921 | Mao Tse Tung (1893-1976) founds Chinese Communist Party. |

January 13, private view of William Nicholson's portrait, Grafton Gallery.

January 29, Nicholson portrait published in *Country Life*.

June, visit from Mrs. Nellie B. Allen, landscape gardener, New York.

Death of Edward Jekyll (brother, born in 1839).

Prime Minister: Andrew Bonar Law (1858-1923), Conservative, October till 1923.

Irish Free State set up by Peace Treaty with Britain.

Post War trade slump.

Unemployment over one million and remains at that figure until 1939.

Lytton Strachey *Queen Victoria*.

Birth of Prince Philip of Greece, future consort of Queen Elizabeth II (Duke of Edinburgh).

Death of George Paul, nurseryman, specialising in roses.

Death of Henry John Moreton (3rd Earl of Ducie) (b 1827).

| 1922 | 78 | Supervises laying of foundations for war memorial designed by Sir Edwin Lutyens in Busbridge churchyard. Christ's Hospital, Horsham, tree cutting. Hydon National Trust Committee in Godalming. | 1922 | October, Benito Mussolini's (1883-1945), 'March on Rome'; takes power in Italy. |

June 14, her niece, Barbara McLaren (nèe Jekyll) marries Bernard Freyberg, VC, DSO and bars (1889-1963).

Bernard Freyberg awarded Hon. LLD at The University of St. Andrews.

Irish Free State established.

| 1923 | 79 | Visits from Sir Henry and Lady Wood and Dame Ethel Smyth to Munstead Wood. | 1923 | Prime Minister: Stanley Baldwin (1866-1937), Conservative, till 1924. |

Wireless installed at Munstead Wood by Herbert Jekyll.

September 19-21, to Hayling Island.

October 10-17, to Bognor Regis.

Earthquake in Japan; huge damage in Tokyo.

Turkish Republic proclaimed: last Sultan deposed.

Winston Churchill *The World Crisis* (1923-29).

Wiliam Walton (1902-83) *Facade,* words by Edith Sitwell (1887-1964).

Marriage of Duke of York (b 1894, Prince Albert and later King George VI) to Lady Elizabeth Bowes-Lyon (b 1900).

| 1924 | 80 | Designs and makes models for the garden of The Queen's Dolls House. Writes a tiny booklet on her gardening recollections and experiences for the Library of the Dolls House. | 1924 | Prime Minister: Ramsay MacDonald, first Labour Government, January – November. |

April 8, donates to Victoria and Albert Museum for costume section a felt hat from Ravenna bought in 1870s: "it has been badly moth-eaten while in my careless possession, but has been in the oven and is now free".

Prime Minister: Stanley Baldwin, Conservative, till 1929

Death of Lenin; Joseph Stalin (1870-1953) consolidates his power.

George II of Greece deposed – Republic declared.

Death of James Britten.

| 1925 | 81 | August, sends chanterelles to Herbert Cowley, editor of *Gardening Illustrated*. | 1925 | Adolf Hitler (1889-1945) *Mein Kampf.* |

September 14, Herbert Cowley visits Munstead Wood.

November 17, gift of Trilliums from Mrs. Frances King.

Paul Hindenburg (1847-1934) elected German President, till 1934.

Summer Time Act made permanent.

Geoffrey Jellicoe and J. C. Shepherd *Italian Gardens and the Renaissance.*

Frank Brangwyn (1867-1956) *British Empire Panels.*

Death of Maria Theresa Earle (née Villiers), gardener and author.

| 1926 | 82 | Award of Merit for *Pulmonaria angustifolia azurea* 'Munstead Blue'. | 1926 | Chiang Kai-Shek (1887-1975) establishes Kuomintang Government in Nanking, China. |

General Strike in Britain.

B.B.C. granted charter as a public company; general

manager John Reith (1889-1971).

Ralph Vaughan Williams opera *Hugh the Drover*.

Birth of Princess Elizabeth (later Queen Elizabeth II).

Death of John T Bennett-Poë (b 1865).

Death of Claude Monet.

Death of Helen Allingham (b 1848).

1927	83	February 14, death of Leonie Blumenthal, leaving her a legacy of £500. Retirememt of Alfred Zumbach.	**1927**

Charles Lindbergh (1902-74) flies Atlantic alone in the *Spirit of St Louis*.

1928	84	June 1, correspondence with Dr. F. A. Hampton (Jason Hill) on scents. December, death of Carry Eden.	**1928**

Charles Kingsford-Smith (1897-1935) flies the Pacific.

German Airship with 60 persons crosses Atlantic.

The Women of Britain are enfranchised.

Death of Sir William Thiselton-Dyer, Director of Kew, author, plant collector.

1929	85	Notes that "skirts are getting longer again". October, to Aldwick, Bognor Regis. Death of Walter Jekyll. Awarded Veitchian Gold Medal from the Royal Horticultural Society. Dedication in Curtis's *Botanical Magazine* with a portrait. Massachusetts Horticultural Society awards her The George Robert White Medal of Honour. December 24, collaborates with Oliver Hill on Marylands, Hurtwood.	**1929**

American Slump and Wall Street crash hastens world-wide Depression.

Prime Minister: Ramsay MacDonald, Labour, till 1931

Graf Zeppelin makes numerous successful international flights.

Richard Byrd (1888-1957) flies over the South Pole.

Sir Thomas Beecham presents festival of Frederick Deliusí(1862-1934) music.

George Bernard Shaw *The Apple Cart*.

Sir Jacob Epstein (1880-1959) *Night and Day* sculpture for London Transport.

Death of Sir Robert Lorimer (b 1864), Scottish architect.

1930	86	Writes 43 articles for *Gardening Illustrated*.	**1930**

Mahatma Gandhi (1869-1948) launches civil disobediance movement in India.

Airship R 101 destroyed in France on first flight to India, 48 lives lost.

Sissinghurst acquired by Sir Harold Nicholson (1886-1968) and his wife Vita Sackville-West (1892-1962).

J. Maynard Keynes (1883-1946) *A Treatise on Money*.

Roger Fry *Henri Matisse*.

Winston Churchill *My Early Life*.

Birth of Princess Margaret.

Death of Samuel Arnott, horticultural writer.

Death of Ernest Henry Wilson, Kew gardener, collector of plants from China, author.

1931	87	June 16, Award of Merit from Floral Committee of the Royal Horticultural Society for *Lupinus polyphyllus* 'Munstead Blue'.	**1931**

Spain becomes a Republic.

Japanese occupation of Manchuria.

Great floods in China – Yellow River changes course.

Resignation of Labour Government and formation of coalition under Ramsay MacDonald, till 1935.

Gold Standard suspended.

Logan Pearsall Smith *Afterthoughts*.

Virginia Woolf (1882-1941) *The Waves*.

1932	88	September 29, death of Herbert Jekyll. October 4, Sir Edwin Lutyens visits: "Bumps self-possessed and herself very feeble. She was in her bedroom with a delicious dusk blue felt cap on her head". December 9, death of Gertrude Jekyll, soon after her 89th birthday.	**1932**

Hitler loses election, but appointed Chancellor (1933).

Franklin Delano Roosevelt (1882-1945) elected President of the U.S.A.

Kingdom of Saudi Arabia formed by Ibn Saud (1880-1953).

Ottawa Imperial Conference.

Sydney Harbour Bridge opened.

George Bernard Shaw *Too True to be Good*.

Bertrand Russell *Marriage and Morals*.

1933		August 8, Sir Edwin Lutyens reports that, "the garden at Munstead Wood has collapsed ... no Bumps and no longer the 11 Essential gardeners".	

References and notes

Chapter 1
Primrose Arnander

1. The Times, Saturday 10th December 1932. p.12 Col.a

2. Agnes Graham, (1860-1937), youngest daughter of William Graham (1817-1885) Liberal MP for Glasgow, art collector and patron of the Pre-Raphaelites.

3. Jekyll, Francis. 1934. Gertrude Jekyll: A Memoir. London, Jonathan Cape.

4. Jekyll, Herbert. Studies in Family History. Vols I; (II); III; Appendix. Bound manuscript. Private collection.

5. Paternal Grandmother: Anna Maria Sloane (1773-1808) (See footnote 26). Maternal Grandmother: Emily Poulett Thomson (1788-1855).

6. Jekyll, Thomas (1570-1653): antiquary. Dictionary of National Biography. The year of his death is given as 1653, instead of 1652, as given by Herbert Jekyll, op. cit.

7. Morant, Philip (1700-1770); historian of Essex. Dictionary of National Biography.

8. Smith, Logan Pearsall. 1933 Gertrude Jekyll. In "Reperusals and Re-collections". London, Constable & Co. Ltd. Chapter V. p.49-65, 1936.

9. Hill, Francis, born c. 1646; half-brother to Sir Joseph Jekyll. His second son, also called Francis became secretary to his uncle when he was Master of the Rolls, and his grandson, Joseph Hill (1733-1811) built the house, Wargrave Hill, which he later bequeathed to Joseph Jekyll MP.

10. Jekyll, Sir Joseph (1663-1738) Master of the Rolls. Dictionary of National Biography.

11. Somers, John (1651-1716) created Baron Somers of Evesham in 1697. Lord Chancellor of England. Dictionary of National Biography.

12. Jekyll, Herbert op. cit.

13. Jekyll, Thomas D. D. (1646-1698). Dictionary National Biography. There is a discrepancy between the dates given for his death by Dictionary of National Biography and Herbert Jekyll op. cit.

14. Clarke, Hannah (1690-1727). Her brother Thomas was the father of Mary Vassall (1748-1835), whose daughter Elizabeth married Lord Holland in 1797 and presided as the political hostess at Holland House.

15. Annals of King's Chapel, Boston p.244 (Herbert Jekyll op. cit.).

16. British Colonial Papers, Palfrey. Ref. IV 397 (H. J. op. cit.).

17. Probate Registry of the County of Middlesex, Mass. (H. J. op.cit.) No. 12528. Headed "Heirs of John Jekyll 1779. Stow"

18. From a pamphlet sent to Herbert Jekyll in 1928 entitled – "Jekyl Island, Some Historic Notes and Some Legends' collected by Charlotte Marshall Maurice. 'And A Brief Outline of the Early Days of the Jekyl Island Club' made by Charles Stewart Maurice".

19. 1748. The Treaty of Aix-la-Chapelle which brought to an end the War of Austrian Succession.

20. William Charles, 4th Earl of Albemarle (1772-1849) an intimate friend of Edward Jekyll. "Joseph Jekyll in a short memoir of his father says, 'From the Novel Distribution of the Prize Money I have heard him say he gained more by the Frieght of his friend Lord Albemarle's Treasure than by the Spoils of the Enemy. The Climate of the West Indies injured his Constitution. I heard Lord Keppel tell him on his Death Bed that their own habits of Abstemiousness from strong wines in those stations had been detrimental, and that Persons less temperate had preserved their Health'." Herbert Jekyll, op. cit.

21. Montagu, John (1718-1792). Fourth Earl of Sandwich. First Lord of Admiralty 1771. Dictionary of National Biography. He gave his name to the Sandwich Islands, and the sandwich, created when he called for beef between two slices of bread to sustain him during a 24 hour gambling session.

22. Herbert Jekyll. op.cit.

23. Joseph Jekyll (1753-1837) Master in Chancery 1815. Dictionary of National Biography

24. Petty, Sir William, first Marquis of Lansdowne (created 1784) and second Earl of Shelburne (1737-1805). First Lord of the Treasury 1782-3. Conceded Independence to the United States and made peace with France and Spain. His administration was overthrown by Fox and North, 1783. He lived at Bowood and had in his gift the pocket borough of Calne. Dictionary of National Biography.

25. Mirabeau (1749-1791). French revolutionary. At the meeting of the States General in 1789 he represented the Third Estate and became President of the National Assembly but died soon after. He was an admirer of the British constitution and an accomplished orator. Chambers Encyclopedia.

26. Letters to the Rt. Hon. Nathanial Bond M.P. (1754-1833) from Joseph Jekyll. Private collection.

26. Hans Sloane (1739-1824) MP, Col. of West Hants Militia, 1776; lived at South Stoneham, Hants. Secretary to his second cousin, Rt. Hon. Hans Stanley when he was Ambassador to the Empress of Russia. Hans Stanley died in 1800 and left his estate at Paultons to Hans Sloane after the death of the 2 surviving Stanley sisters, Lady Mendip and Mrs. D'Oyley. Lady Mendip died in 1802 and Hans Sloane took over the estate which was surrendered then by Mrs. D'Oyley. At her death in 1821 Hans Sloane and his family assumed the name and arms of Stanley and were known as Sloane Stanley thereafter.

28. 'The houses were all demolished in 1890 and the street ceased to exist, the site being occupied by the extension of the Admiralty'. Herbert Jekyll op.cit.

29. William Sloane Stanley (1782-1860) (Herbert Jekyll's great uncle) married in 1806 Lady Gertrude Howard (1783-1870) daughter of the 5th Earl of Carlisle.

30. Bourke, Algeman (ed.). 1894. Correspondence of Mr. Joseph Jekyll with his sister-in-law Lady Gertrude Sloane Stanley. 1818-1838. Preceded by some letters written to his father from France 1775.
London: John Murray. Mr. Bourke- the 3rd son of the 6th Earl of Mayo – was married to Lady Gertrude's great-granddaughter, Gwendoline Sloane Stanley.

31. Joseph Jekyll – a letter to Mrs Hill 6 Feb. 1824. Bound manuscript, private collection.

32. Julia Hammersley (1813-1895) third daughter of Charles Hammersley (1782-1862) of Cox's Bank and his wife Emily Poulett Thomson (1788-1855).

33. Anna Louisa Flint (1813-1865) – daughter of Sir Charles Flint, Resident Secretary of the Irish office, and Anna Maria Seton, 4th daughter of Daniel Seton, Governor of Surat. From an article by Emily Climenson who was the daughter of Anna Louisa Flint, widow of Joseph Jekyll. Climenson, Emily J. 1901. Jekylliana. The Gentleman's Magazine 291, 346-366.

34. Spencer Dudley Montagu, youngest son of the 4th Baron Rokeby.

35. Joseph Jekyll to Hugh Leycester 5 Aug. 1828. Joseph Jekyll's letters to Hugh Leycester, a life long friend are collected and bound in manuscript volume, private collection.

36. Joseph Jekyll to Lady Gertrude. 31 Aug 1833.

37. Smith, Logan Pearsall op. cit.

Chapter 2
Annabel Freyberg

1. Bourke, Algernon (ed.) 1894. Correspondence of Mr Joseph Jekyll with his sister-in-law, Lady Gertrude Sloane Stanley, 1818-1838. Preceded by some letters written to his father from France, 1775. London, John Murray. The quotations used here are from the manuscripts, and not the published version edited by The Hon. Algernon Bourke. Private Collection.

2. Ibid.

3. 27 July 1824, and ibid. p.145.

4. 24 October 1829 and ibid. p.199.

5. George (1762-1830), Prince Regent from 1788, succeeded his father as George IV in 1820. Stephen, L. and Lee, C. (eds.) The Dictionary of National Biography. Oxford University Press. Vol. VII, p.1071 passim.

6. 13 November 1830 and op. cit., p.251.

7. Jekyll, Herbert. Studies in Family History. Volume I. Manuscript. Private Collection.

8. 4 October 1836, op. cit., p.347.

9. Jekyll, F. 1934. Gertrude Jekyll: a memoir. London, Jonathan Cape.

10. Edward Bigge's nephew, Lord Stamfordham (private secretary to both Queen Victoria and George V, and childhood friend of Walter and Herbert Jekyll) sent this extract to Herbert in September 1928. The four Bigge brothers, Charles, Edward, John and Matthew, came from Linden near Stamfordham in Northumberland where Edward Jekyll and his brother, Joseph were frequent visitors.

11. Letter from Walter Jekyll in Jamaica to Mrs. Charles Hammond, 22 November 1917. Private Collection.

12. The quotations from Herbert and Walter Jekyll here and subsequently come from two books of written reminiscences in manuscript. The sources of the quotations are identified by the initials HJ or WJ in parenthesis.

13. See Chapter 1, note 9.

14. The verbena garden was redesigned for Col. Ricardo by Gertrude Jekyll in 1905.

15. Bound volume of letters from Edward Jekyll to Lady Duff Gordon. 1854. Private collection.

16. Ibid, 29 November 1854.

17. Ibid, 20 December 1854.

18. Ibid.

19. Ibid, 3 March 1855.

20. Ibid, 3 May 185.

21. Ibid, 6 July 1855.

22. Op. cit.

23. Mr., afterwards Sir Henry Layard, was known by the children as Mr. Bull.
Sir Austen Henry Layard (1817-1894) was renowned for his excavations of Nineveh under the patronage of Stratford Canning, later Viscount Stratford de Redcliffe. In fact from 1842 onwards he had excavated Nimrûd which he assumed erroneously was within the precincts of Nineveh. Dictionary of National Biography Supplement. 1901. Vol. 22. p.954 passim.

24. Op. cit.

25. John James Stevenson (1831-1908) was an architect in the offices of David Bryce in Edinburgh and George Gilbert Scott in London, where he met Norman Shaw, William Eden Nesfield, E.R. Robson, William Morris. He evolved a simple form of brick design sufficiently in sympathy with early eighteenth century architecture to become known as the 'Queen Anne' style. He designed and built for himself The Red House, Bayswater Hill (1871-3), now demolished. With William Morris, he became one of the original members of the Society for the Protection of Ancient Buildings.
Dictionary of National Biography. Supplement. 1 1901-1911. London, Smith, Elder and Co. p. 414
Girouard, M. 1977 Sweetness and Light: the 'Queen Anne' Movement 1860-1900. Oxford. Clarendon Press.

26. Jekyll, Edward. Tour in Ireland, 1849 July 19 – August 10. Private Collection.

27. Op. cit.

28. Anon. 1891. A garden in Venice. The Garden. 40 (1032), 191, 195.
Anon. 1891. Vine-covered walk in a Venetian Garden. The Garden 40 (1035), 259.
Eden, F. 1903. A Garden in Venice. London, Country Life. 135pp.
Wiel, A. 1900. A Garden in Venice. Country Life Illustrated. 8, 72-76.

29. Part of The Garden of Eden including a bothy was acquired by the Earl and Countess Munster and was described in 1965.
Kemp, C. 1965. The hidden gardens of Venice. In, Harling, R. (ed.) The Garden Book pp. 189-192. London, Condé Nast Publications Ltd.

30. Letter from Edward Jekyll to Lady Duff Gordon. op. cit. 19 January 1855.

31. Ibid, 25 June 1855.

32. Ibid, 6 July 1855.

33. Houffe, Simon. 1984 Gertrude Jekyll and Bedfordshire. Bedfordshire Magazine. pp.218-9.

34. Christie, Manson and Woods. Catalogue of ancient Greek vases, the property of Edward J. Jekyll. London, 6 July 1914.

35. Edward Jekyll to Lady Duff Gordon. op. cit. October 1854.

36. Ibid, November 1854.

37. Ibid, 25 April 1855.

38. A letter from Herbert Jekyll to Canon S. Reynolds Hole in 1871 was printed in The Garden. December 9, 1871, p.51.
"Knowing you to be pre-eminent as a horticulturist, I beg to bring to your notice a magnificent species of the Aloe Tribe (Agave telegraphica).
This highly ornamental plant flourishes best by the side of roads and on railway embankments, and I can strongly recommend it to your notice, feeling that it would succeed admirably at the edge of the high-road at the foot of your lawn, where it would be seen to great advantage from your drawing-room windows.
A philanthropic Government is actively employed in propagating this rare and deservedly-admired plant, and should you desire to have a few specimens, I am empowered to supply you with them at the expense of country, and to plant them in suitable situations.
The Agave telegraphica is native of Great Britain, but has been successfully acclimatized in all parts of the world. It succeeds equally in all soils, and remains in flower all the year round.
We have hitherto been unsuccessful in our endeavours to

raise if from seed, but a large stock is now at the Government nursery-gardens, and the plants sustain no injury from being moved at the full growth. Believe me, yours truly, "HERBERT JEKYLL, L.R.E."

39. The Souls, formed in the 1880s, were a coterie of well born intellectuals, including Arthur Balfour, George Wyndham, Harry Cust, Lord Curzon, Lady Desborough, Violet Manners, Laura and Margot Tennant.

40. Agnes Lowndes Jekyll DBE (1860-1937) She was a magistrate for Surrey since 1925, sat on the Guildford Bench and was on the panel of the Children's Court: she was created DBE in 1918 in recognition of her public works. She was Chairman of the St. John's Hospitals Supply Warehouse at Clerkenwell and for ten years was chairman of the visiting committee of the Borstal Institutions for Girls at Aylesbury. She was a Governor of Godalming Secondary Education County Council School. She was a keen lover of Master and Pre-Raphelite old paintings, and was skilled in needlework. A collection of the articles she wrote for The Times was edited by her and published as:
Jekyll, A. 1922. Kitchen Essays, with receipts and their occasions. London. T. Nelson and Sons; republished 1969 by Collins, with an introduction by her daughter Lady Freyberg. Obituary: The Times 47,595, p.16, col.b. Friday, 29 January 1937

41. Jekyll, W. 1904. The Bible Untrustworthy: a critical comparison of contradictory passages in the Scriptures with a view of treating their accuracy. London, Watts and Co.

42. Walter Jekyll translated Francesco Lamperti's text into English: Lamperti, F. 1884. The art of signing according to the ancient tradition and personal experience. Technical Rules etc. Translated by W. Jekyll, London, Ricordi. vit 67 pp.
Lamperti, F. 1883. L'arte del canto in ordine, alle tradizioni classiche ed a particolare esperienza. Norme tecniche, etc. Milano, p.71.

43. There is a family tradition that Robert Louis Stevenson's character, Dr Jekyll, in The Strange Case of Dr Jekyll and Mr Hyde is based on Walter, who was the same age as Stevenson. This book was written in 1885 but publication was delayed until 1886. Robert Louis Stevenson (1850-1894) moved to Bournemouth, where Walter Jekyll was living, in 1884. The Stevenson family lived at a lodging house overlooking the sea, called Wensleydale with "a gloriously sparkling view of the Needles and the Isle of Wight". Lloyd Osbourne, his stepson, described Robert Louis Stevenson at this time - "he was never afterwards so boyish, so light-hearted: it was the final flare-up of his departing youth". The family bought a house overlooking Alum Chine in west Bournemouth and changed the name from Seaview to Skerryvore, "in commemoration of the most difficult and beautiful of all the lighthouses erected by the family". There "he was a prisoner in his own house ... there could be no pretence that he was not an invalid and a very sick man".
Osbourne, Lloyd 1924, Stevenson at Thirty-seven. Preface to R.L. Stevenson The Strange Case of Dr. Jekyll and Mr. Hyde. Tusitalia edition. London, William Heinemann Ltd. vii-xviii.
Hennessy, John Pope 1994, Robert Louis Stevenson. London, Jonathan Cope.

44. Jekyll, W. 1907. Jamaican Song and Story: annancy stories, digging songs, ring tunes and dancing tunes collected and edited by W. Jekyll. London Folk-lore Society. pp. xxxviii + 288.

45. During his sister Gertrude's editorship of The Garden, and subsequently, he contributed a series of long articles on his garden in Jamaica:
1900. A Jamaica Garden the house and its surroundings. The Garden 58 (1500),125-7.
1900. A Jamaica Garden. The Scitamineae. The Garden 58 (1501), 141-2.

1900. A Jamaica Garden. The Garden 58 (1502), 161-2.
1900. A Jamaica Garden. The Garden 58 (1503), 181-2.
1900. A Jamaica Garden. The Garden 58 (1518), 447-9.
1901. A Jamaica Garden. The Garden 59 (1526), 108-9.
1901. In the Port Royal Mountains, Jamaica. The Garden 59 (1532), 223.
1901. A Jamaica Garden. The Garden 59 (1537), 314-5.
1901. A Jamaica Garden. The Garden 59 (1539), 344.
1901. A Jamaica Garden. The Garden 59 (1540), 372-3.
1901. A Jamaica Garden. The Garden 59 (1543), 437-8.
1902. A day in a Jamaica Garden. The Garden 62, 123-125.
1902. A day in a Jamaica Garden. The Garden 62, 137.
1902. A day in a Jamaica Garden. The Garden 62, 173.
1902. A day in a Jamaica Garden. The Garden 62, 193.

46. Walter Jekyll died on 17 February 1929 at Bower Hill. He is buried in Lucea churchyard. The inscription on his gravestone reads, "musician, gardener, philosopher, teacher and writer. He lived 34 years in this island of his adoption where he gave himself to the service of others and was greatly beloved by all who knew him". Venn, J.A. (compiler) Alumni Cantabrigiensis Part II, 1752 to 1900, p.559.

Chapter 3
Joan Edwards

1. The School of Art-Needlework was founded in 1872 with the object of raising the standard of contemporary embroidery and providing suitable employment for gentlewomen. According to a price list at the back of the handbook a linen cushion cover embroidered in the workroom with one of Gertrude Jekyll's periwinkle or iris patterns would have cost approximately £3 or, if traced ready for working by the customer, between 7s 6d and 12s 6d. The Princess of Wales was one of the Patrons and later commissioned work from Gertrude Jekyll; so also did Princess Louise, Marchioness of Lorne, the sculptress daughter of Queen Victoria, who was herself an embroiderer and drew patterns for a similar organisation, The Ladies' Work Society, of which she was the President.

2. Higgin, L. 1880. Handbook of Embroidery. London; Sampson Low, Marston, Searle and Rivington, xii + 106.

3. Ibid. Plate Nos 9 and 10, p.(79).

4. Jekyll, Francis. 1934. Gertrude Jekyll. A Memoir. London, Jonathan Cape, p.87.

5. Jekyll, G. 1927. Miss Jekyll and her flower garden. Gardening Illustrated 49 (2529), 531-4. Reprinted as 'About Myself. Some early reminiscences: a paper read to the Garden Club', pp. 10-16, in Francis Jekyll and G. C. Taylor (eds). 1937. A Gardener's Testament. A Selection of articles and notes by Gertrude Jekyll. London, Country Life. Reprint 1982, Woodbridge, Antique Collectors' Club.

6. Henry Cole (1808-82) was closely associated with the Prince Consort in planning the 1851 and 1862 Exhibitions. He was First Secretary of the Department of Practical Art which, in 1853, became the Department of Education and Science. He founded a number of educational institutions based upon his theory that the standard of British design could be raised by providing opportunities for students and the public to study the best work by previous generations of European and Oriental artists and craftsmen.

7. John Marshall (1818-1891) was Professor of Anatomy at University College and at the Royal Academy. In 1853, he gave the first course of lectures on anatomy to art students at Marlborough House – a course he repeated when the art schools were removed to South Kensington. In 1878 his book on Anatomy for Artists was published.

8. Jekyll, Francis. 1934. op cit. p.38.

9. Christopher Dresser, Ph.D., F.L.S. (1834-1904) studied botany at the University of Jena and art at the Central School of Design. He was interested in the history of design and the relationship between science and art. In 1860 he

became Professor of Botany at South Kensington Art School and the London Hospital Medical School. He was the founder of the Art Furniture Alliance and editor of the Furniture Gazette. His publications include The Development of Ornamental Art and a portfolio of patterns called Studies in Design.

10. Richard Redgrave, R.A. (1804-80) was one of the first artists to paint social subjects in contemporary dress, e.g. "The Seamstress", "The Poor Teacher" and "The Governess". He neglected his career as he felt impelled to devote his energies and influence to improving the standard of industrial art. He was First Keeper of paintings in South Kensington Museum, Inspector of the Queen's pictures, and co-author with his brother, Samuel, of A Century of Painting which is still regarded as a useful reference book.

11. Chevreul, Michel Eugene. 1837. De la loi du contraste simultanté des coleurs, et de l'assortiment des objects colorés, considéré d'aprés cette loi dans ses rapports avec la peinture, les tapisseries des Goblins . . . les tapis, la mosaique, etc. Translated by John Spanton, London 1857.

12. J. M. W. Turner's oil painting of "Clapham Common" measures 230 x 445 mm, and Gertrude Jekyll's copy is the same size. The painting was given to Sir Gilbert Frankland Lewis (1808-1883)

13. Sir Herbert's copies were shown beside Turner's original water colours in 1961 in an exhibition at the British Museum entitled "Forgeries and Deceptive Copies".

14. Described in Jekyll, Francis. 1934. op cit. pp.41-76.

15. Charles Newton, K.C.B. (1816-94) joined the staff of the British Museum in 1840. In 1852 he became Vice-Consul at Mitylene where he carried out excavations resulting in the acquisition by the Museum of a series of masterpieces of classical art. He was supported in this work by the British Ambassador at Constantinople, Lord Stratford de Redclyffe who, twenty years later, commissioned work from Gertrude Jekyll for his home at Frant, Sussex. In 1860 he was appointed Keeper of Greek and Roman Antiquities, British Museum, and subsequently Professor of Archaeology at University College, London.

16. Ann Mary Newton (1822-66) was the daughter of Joseph Severn the friend of John Keats. She became a popular portrait painter. She also made numerous witty, humorous sketches, 75 of which were exhibited as: "Caricatures of ourselves" at the Oxford Arts Club, London, in November 1922.

17. Joseph Jekyll (1754-1837), great nephew of Sir Joseph Jekyll (1662-1738), Master of the Rolls under George I. Joseph Jekyll's portrait was painted by Sir Thomas Lawrence, P.R.A. See also Francis Jekyll. 1934. op cit. p.20-21.

18. Jekyll, Francis. 1934. op cit. p.205.

19. These were five lengths of velvet ribbon, Italian, 18th century; an Algerian embroidered headdress, l8th-19th century; a child's embroidered cap, Italian or French, 18th century.

20. George Dunlop Leslie (1835-1921) was the son of Robert Leslie and friend of Constable. The letters that passed frequently between them are one of the great sources of information on Constable's life and character. George Leslie studied at the Royal Academy schools and painted landscapes with children, especially views of the Thames. In 1888 Our River was published.

21. Repoussé work is the technique of making raised patterns usually on silver and pewter.

22. Jekyll, Francis. 1934. op cit. p.87.

23. Alphonse Legros (1837-1911) was a French painter who settled in England, and in 1863 started teaching at South Kensington Art School; from 1876-92 he was Professor of Etching at the Slade School of Art.

24. Jekyll, Francis. 1934. op cit. p.88.

25. Jacques Blumenthal (1829-1908) was born in Austria and studied under Bocklet and Sechter in Vienna and Halévy in Paris. He settled in England in 1848 and became pianist to Queen Victoria. He composed and published piano pieces and songs of which "The Message" and "The Requital" are two examples. Leonie Blumenthal (?-1927) was "unusually gifted in all manner of minor arts" (The Times, Obituary of Gertrude Jekyll, 10th December 1932, p. 12, column 1), she and her husband entertained their large and gifted circle of friends not only at 43 Hyde Park Gate but also at Le Chalet, between Montreux and Les Avants.

26. The Times. Saturday, 10th December, 1932. p.12, column 1.

27. Hercules Brabazon (1821-1906) worked exclusively in watercolours on a small scale and whenever possible in the open air but did not exhibit anything until he was 71 when the quality of his work was instantly recognised.

28. Barbara Leigh-Smith (1827-91) was an artist and pioneer of further education for women and the enfranchisement of women. She was a cousin of Florence Nightingale. In 1857 she married Eugene Bodichon, a French surgeon, anthropologist and social reformer who lived in Algiers. "Scalands", the house she built on the family estate at Robertsbridge, Sussex, to the furnishing and decoration of which Gertrude Jekyll made a number of important contributions, was in the style of an old Sussex manor house with a latched door opening straight into the book-lined living room. She made an important collection of blue and white Algerian pottery.

29. Frederick Walker, A.R.A. (1840-75) was regarded as one of the most talented illustrators of the 1860s. He died young and was buried at Cookham-on-Thames where many of his landscapes were painted.

Editors' note : Joan Edwards gave the Museum of Garden History's Richardson Lecture in 1993, and subsequently published it. The lecture elaborates many of the statements made here, and the reader is referred to this publication:

Edwards, Joan. 1993. Gertrude Jekyll : Before the Boots, the Gardens and the Portrait. Dorking, Bayford Books.

Figure 3.2   Notes by Dorothea Nield on her embroidery of Gertrude Jekyll's Iris design.

Chapter 4
Fenja Gunn

1. The book appears to have been used initially for dried botanical specimens, mainly ferns, that Miss Jekyll was collecting and obtaining identifications in the 1880s. One caption reads "HARD FERN Allosorus crispus Newman p.103 Coll. Comm." The book was then reversed, so that these captions are now hidden.
Book size: 11" wide and 17$^1/_4$" deep.
Binding: Olive leather spine and matching fabric binding.
Number of pages: 88
Paper: Thin, cream coloured, slightly mottled. No watermarks.
End Papers: Cream, with embossed oval stamp on one end paper: "Andrews Bookseller Guildford."
Title of book: "Designs for Carving" in Miss Jekyll's handwriting on a cream rectangle of paper.

2. There are many drawings and designs in the workbook which confirm Miss Jekyll's love of working with fabric and embroidery. Her designs include ideas for stitch patterns, lace quilting and motifs for textiles. I have only briefly alluded to these as Joan Edwards has described these crafts in Chapter 3.

3. Gertrude Jekyll. Wood and Garden. Published by Longmans, Green & Co. 1899. Title page. Miss Jekyll describes herself as a 'working amateur'. Gertrude Jekyll. Home and Garden. Published by Longmans, Green & Co. 1900. Chapter XI p.163 'English workmen in general ... seem to have an idea that the amateur's practice may come into competition with their trade. Those who show this spirit can hardly know how hugely the compliment ... flatters the vanity of the amateur'.

4. See p.46.

5. See p.44 and Figure 3.1.

6. Owen Jones. Grammar of Ornament. Published by Day & Son in 1856. Vol I Proposition 6 p.4: 'Beauty of form is produced by lines growing out one from the other in gradual undulations'. This principle is described and demonstrated in diagram form on pp. 24 and 25 of Joan Edwards' Gertrude Jekyll. Before The Boots, The Gardens And The Portrait, the published text of the Richardson Lecture given at The Museum of Garden History in 1993.

7. See p.47.

8. See p.53.

9. Home and Garden. Chapter XI p.166.

10. In many ways this quartet of necklaces is the most exciting set of items in the book. Early doubts about their provenance have recently been largely dispelled by expert opinion at The Victoria and Albert Museum confirming that these pieces were in all probability designed by Gertrude Jekyll herself.

11. Home and Garden. Chapter XI p.170.

12. Ibid. pp.162, 163.

13. See p.51.

Chapter 5
Mavis Batey

1. Anon. 1851. The Art Journal Illustrated Catalogue of the Industries of All Nations. London. Facsimile. 1970. New York City, Bounty Books, Crown Publishers Inc.

2. Baker, Herbert. 1944. Architecture and Personalities. London, Country Life, p.16.

3. Jekyll, Gertrude. 1901. Orchards, Surrey. The residence of Mr William Chance. Country Life 10 (243), 272-9.

4. Jekyll, Gertrude. 1900. Wood and Garden. London, Longmans, Green & Co., p.4.

5. Batey, Mavis. 1974. Landscape with flowers. West Surrey – the background to Gertrude Jekyll's art. Garden History: The Journal of the Garden History Society 2 (2), 12-21.

6. First published as a pamphlet under the title Labour and pleasure versus labour and sorrow, 1880. Cund Bros., Birmingham. It was given the title The Beauty of Life and published in:
   Morris, William. 1882. Hopes and fears for Art. London, Ellis and White. Second Edition pp. 71-113. The Beauty of Life. Delivered before the Birmingham School of Art and School of Design (1880).
   Cole, G. D. H. (ed.). 1934. William Morris. Stories in prose, stories in verse, shorter poems, lecturs and essays. (Centenary Edition). London, Nonesuch Press, pp. 538-64.

7. Jekyll, Gertrude. 1904. Old West Surrey. London, Longmans, Green & Co., p.viii.

8. Ibid, p.287.

9. Jekyll, Gertrude. 1900. Home and Garden. London, Longmans, Green & Co., p. 10.

10. Ibidem, p. 2.

11. Morris, William. 1895. Gossip about an old house on the upper Thames. The Quest 4, 13. Birmingham, G. Napier & Co.

12. Letter from Robert Lorimer to R. S. Dods quoted in:
   Savage, Peter. 1980. Lorimer and the Edinburgh Craft Designers. Edinburgh, Paul Harris Publishing, p. 25.
   Anon. 1981. Lutyens. The work of the English architect Sir Edwin Lutyens (1869-1944). London, Arts Council of Great Britain, p.74.

13. Jekyll, Gertrude. 1900. Home and Garden. London, Longmans, Green & Co., p.18.

14. Robinson, William. 1896. The English Flower Garden. London, John Murray. 5th edition, p.8.

15. Jekyll, Gertrude. 1918. Garden Ornament. London, Country Life and George Newnes Ltd., p.xi.

16. Ruskin, John. 1873. Modern Painters, Volume 4, Part 5 "Of mountain beauty", Chapter 1, pp.9-26. Of the Turnerian Picturesque. In E. T. Cook and Alexander Wedderburn (eds) 1904. The Works of John Ruskin, Vol. 6, Library Edition, London, George Allen.

17. Massingham, Betty. 1966. Miss Jekyll. Portrait of a Great Gardener. London, Country Life Limited, p.50.

18. Letter by Edwin L. Lutyens to Lady Emily Lutyens, 9 April 1908. London, British Architectural Library. LuE/9/6/6 (ii-viii).

19. Chevreul, M. E. 1839. De la loi du contraste simultané des couleurs et de l'assortiment des objects colorés considérés d'aprés cette loi dans ses rapports avec peinture, les tapisseries.... Paris, Pitois-Leurault. Translated from the French by Charles Martel, 1854.
   The 1967 edition by Faber Birren omits the last chapter on the application of Chevreul's colour principles to the art of horticulture.

20. Jekyll, Gertrude. 1914. Colour Schemes for the Flower Garden. London, Country Life Ltd., 7th edition, p.99.

21. Ibid, p.80.

22. Massingham, Betty. 1978. Taste-makers in American gardening. Louisa King's work and ideas. Country Life 164 (4240), 1141-2.

23. King, Mrs. Francis. 1915. The Well-Considered Garden. New York, Charles Scribner's Sons, p.x.

24. King, Mrs. Francis. 1925. Chronicles of the Garden. New York, Charles Scribner's Sons, p.x.

Chapter 6
Paul Everson

Abbreviations:
   CAD – Computer-aided Drafting
   DoE – Department of the Environment
   IoAAS – Institute of Advanced Architectural Studies, York
   NMR – National Managements Record
   OS – Ordnance Survey
   RCHME – Royal Commission on the Historic Monuments of England

1. DoE 1986. List of Buildings of Special Architectural or Historic Interest. District of Waverley (Parishes of Bramley, Busbridge, Hambledon, Hascombe, Thursley, Witley and Wonersh).

2. Nairn, I. and Pevsner, N. 1971. The Buildings of England, Surrey. Harmondsworth, Penguin Books. pp.377-8 (Revised by B. Cherry).

3. Taylor, C. 1979. Total archaeology or studies in history of the landscape. pp.15-26 in A. Rogers and R. T. Rowley (eds.) Landscape and Documents (Standing Conference on Local History).

4. RCHME 1989. Annual Review 1988/9, pp.26-7.

5. RCHME 1992. Annual Report 1991/2, p.15.

6. Tankard, J. 1990. Annotated Catalog of Gertrude Jekyll's six photo-albums at the College of Environmental Design, Documents Collection, University of California, Berkeley. Unpublished typescript. vii+239.
   Tankard, J. and van Valkenburg, M.R. 1989. Gertrude Jekyll: A Vision of Garden and Wood. London. John Murray.
   van Valkenburgh, M.R. 1987. The flower gardens of Gertrude Jekyll and their twentieth century transformation. Cambridge, Mass., MIT. Design Quarterly, 137.
   van Valkenburgh, M.R. and Tankard, J.B. n.d. Gertrude Jekyll: A Vision of Garden and Wood. An exhibition sponsored by Bank of Boston. Exhibition Catalogue. Bank of Boston.

7. Taylor, C. 1991. Garden archaeology: an introduction. In A.E. Brown (ed.) Garden Archaeology. CBA Research Report no. 78, 1-5.

8. Everson, P. 1991. Field survey and garden earthworks. In A.E.

Brown (ed.). op.cit., 6-19.

9. Jekyll, G. and Weaver, L. 1912, A garden in West Surrey. pp. 36-45. In Jekyll, G. and Weaver, L. Gardens for Small Country Houses. London, Country Life.

10. Gradidge, R. 1980. Dream Houses. The Edwardian Ideal. London; Constable.

11. RCHME 1951. Dorset I. West, p.80.

12. RCHME 1970. Dorset II. South East, p.409.

13. Taylor, C. 1983. The Archaeology of Gardens, Princes Risborough, Shire Publications,

14. RCHME 1991. Change and Continuity. Rural settlement in North-West Lincolnshire, pp.175-7.

15. RCHME 1979. Northamptonshire Vol. II. Central Northamptonshire, pp.75-7.

16. SyRO. Surrey Record Office, Kingston-upon-Thames. Godalming Tithe IX Town tithing, and XI Upper Easthing tithing.

17. Jekyll, G. 1915. A self-sown wood. The Garden 79 (2252), 34.

18. English Heritage 1985. Register of Parks and Gardens of Special Historic Interest in England. Part 40, Surrey.

19. Jekyll, G. 1900. Wood and Garden. London, Longmans, Green and Co. p.48.

20. Travers Morgan. 1982. Royal Parks Historical Survey: Hampton Court and Bushy Park. 3 vols. For the Department of the Environment.

21. NMR. Unpublished archive plan and report deposited in the National Monuments Record.

Chapter 7
Martin Wood

1. Hussey, C. 1950. The life of Sir Edwin Lutyens. London, Country Life, p. 23. See also "Miss Jekyll", Country Life 15/9/1934 p.272.
Avray Tipping, H. 1932. Gertrude Jekyll: an appreciation. Country Life 72 (1874), 689.

2. Jekyll, F. 1934 Gertrude Jekyll; A Memoir London, Jonathan Cape.
Bramley Park was built for the Earl of Egremont of Petworth, who was a patron of J.M.W. Turner. The Earl used the house to break the journey to Petworth and to supervise his investment in the Wey and Arun Canal. The house was demolished in 1951.

3. Freyberg, Annabel. 1991. Review of Gertrude Jekyll by Sally Festing. World of Interiors. November 1991, pp.45-6.

4. H.M. Probate Registry, Somerset House, London. Will of Julia Jekyll.

5. James Cousins letter to author, 6 August 1992. The word Munstead was thought to be derived from the Anglo-Saxon "Munt", meaning a lofty hill, and "Stead", meaning a place. It is more likely, due to the connection to Windsor Great Park, that it is derived from the word "Mund", meaning protection or guardianship, in this case, of the King. See also Parker, E. 1935 Highways and Byways in Surrey London, Macmillan & Co. Second edition p.68.

6. Parker, E. op cit., p.69.

7. Courtesy of James Cousins. These maps are held in the Guildford Muniment Room of Surrey County Council.

8. Jekyll, G. and Weaver, L. 1912, Gardens for Small Country Houses. London, Country Life, p.68.

9. Held in the Documents Collection, of the College of Environmental Design, University of California, Berkeley, California, U.S.A.

10. See Joseph Spence (1699-1768) letter to Rev. Mr Wheeler of 1751 which is reprinted in Hunt, J.D. and Willis, P (eds). 1975. The Genius of the Place London, Elek, p.268 et seq.

11. Jekyll, G. 1928. The Way In. Gardening Illustrated 50 (2569), 347. 2 June 1928.

12. Harold Falkner (1875-1966) of Farnham was a gentleman architect and a regular visitor to Munstead Wood for more than 20 years. See Brown, J. 1978. Eric Falkner. The Surrey County Magazine 9 (6), 94-5 and 102.

13. Massingham, B. 1966 Miss Jekyll, Portrait of a Great Gardener. London Country Life. pp.69 & 70.

14. Jekyll, G. 1932. The Court and its Planting. Gardening Illustrated 54 (2799), 655. October 29, 1932.

15. Jekyll, G. and Weaver, L. op.cit. p.42.

16. Jekyll, G. 1899. Wood and Garden. London, Longmans. p.9.

17. Jekyll, G. 1928. The Nut Walk in Spring. Gardening Illustrated 50 (2568), 324. May 26, 1928.

18. Frank Young, from notes of conversation with author.

19. Jekyll, G. 1899. op.cit. p.11.

20. More detailed information on the planting in the Spring Garden can be found in:
Jekyll, G. 1908 Colour in the Flower Garden London. Country Life
Jekyll, G. 1930 The Spring Garden. Gardening Illustrated 52 (2677), 418. June 28, 1930.

21. Jekyll, G. 1899. op.cit. p.101.

22. Jekyll, G. 1899. op.cit. p.104.

23. Sigismunda, daughter of Siffredi, High Chancellor of Sicily, was betrothed to Count Tancred who succeeded Roger to become King of Sicily. However, Roger made it a condition for his succession that he marry Constantia thus uniting two rival lines and preventing war. Sigismunda, no doubt feeling betrayed, married Earl Osmond who challenged Tancred and was killed. When she ran to comfort her dying husband Tancred thrust his sword into her and killed her.
Jekyll, G. 1900. Home and Garden p.71.
In 1897, Lutyens wrote to his wife, "we sat cheek by jowl on the cenotaph to Sigismunda (the seat under the birch tree, so called on account of its monumental simplicity – do you remember?)"
In, Percy, C. & Ridley, J. (eds.) 1985. The Letters of Edwin Lutyens to his wife Lady Emily. London, Collins. p.48.

24. Hussey, C. 1950. op.cit. p.391.

25. Frank Young letter to author November 15, 1987.

26. Will of Julia Jekyll.

27. Jekyll, G. 1928. Heracleum mantegazzianum. Gardening Illustrated. 50 (2591), 657. October 13,1928. A photograph published in this article shows the flower stems of the Hogweed with one of her gardeners, Arthur Berry.

28. Jekyll, G. 1900. Home & Garden London, Longmans. p.164.

29. Jekyll, G. 1908. op.cit. p.33.

30. This strain of Lupin pre-dates the Russell strain raised by George Russell of York by more than thirty years. They were remarked on by Harold Falkner in Massingham, B., Miss Jekyll: portrait of a great gardener. London, Country Life. p.69.

31. Jekyll, G. 1927. The Yew Cat. Gardening Illustrated 49 (2536), 641. October 15, 1927.

32. The only known record of the Pansy garden is a watercolour by Thomas Hunn exhibited at the Christopher Wood Gallery, Belgravia, London, in May 1990.

33. Jekyll, G. The use of grey foliage with border plants. Country Life 40 (1031), 401-2. October 7, 1916. During the Great War a number of the borders were used for the cultivation of vegetables.

34. Jekyll, G. 1927. The Grey Garden, Gardening Illustrated 49 (2542), 738-9.

35. Judith B. Tankard, letter to author 17 October 1992. Mrs Tankard has made a detailed study of Miss Jekyll's photographs, cataloguing the six known albums at Berkeley and co-authoring with Michael van Valkenburgh a book "Gertrude Jekyll: A Vision of Garden and Wood" London,

(John Murray 1989).

In Lutyens' plan of May 1893 the wall behind the main flower border is shown, together with the summerhouse, pergola and spring garden. Reef Point Gardens, Collection of Designs by Gertrude Jekyll. File No. 1. Folder No. 1. Item 3. University of California Berkeley.

36. Jekyll, G. 1899. op.cit. p.212.

37. Colour in the Flower Garden op.cit. p.52. et seq.

38. A much more detailed examination of Turner's influence on Miss Jekyll can be found in the Antique Collectors Club reprint of Colour Schemes for the Flower Garden (1982) in a preface by Tom Turner. This is also mentioned in English Garden Design (Antique Collectors Club 1986) also by Tom Turner.

39. Jekyll, G. 1922. Colour Effects in the Late Summer Border. The Garden 86 (2647) 398. September 9, 1922. A number of similar effects are detailed in this article.

40. Jekyll, G. 1926. Pyrethrum uliginosum with Michaelmas Daisies. Gardening Illustrated 48 (2487) 671. November 6, 1926.

41. Jekyll, G. 1926. The late Michaelmas Daisies. Gardening Illustrated 48 (2491), 729. December 4, 1926. This article contains, as does the article of November 6, extensive details on the Aster varieties used.

42. Frank Young letter and sketch plan to author November 15, 1987.

43. Jekyll, G. 1919. Useful Plums. The Garden 83 (2465) 67. February 15, 1919. Plum varieties listed are; Early Prolific, Early Orleans, Victoria and Coe's Golden Drop.

44. Frank Young, notes of conversations with author.

45. Jekyll, G. 1917. Some good Gooseberries, The Garden 81 (2386), 321. (August 11, 1917). Miss Jekyll grew a large number of different varieties. These were; Red Champagne, Langley Green, Langley Gale, two bushes of Warrington, two of Early Sulphur, a row of Ironmonger and a few bushes of Whinham's Industry.

46. Letter to Munstead Wood Survey Working Group from Mr J. Albury, Fruit Advisor R.H.S. Garden Wisley 29 October 1992. See list in Chapter 6.

47. Frank Young notes of conversation with author. See also, Home & Garden op.cit. p.236 et seq.

48. Godalming Museum Library. Miss Jekyll's account books. Envelope 16. Notebook. Maroon card. 4" x 7". Title "Fulmer Court, HENS Jany 1916. HERBS".

49. Jekyll, G. 1924. A Cypress Hedge. Gardening Illustrated 46 (2363) 375. June 21, 1924.

50. Jekyll, G. 1927. Inchmury, a fine garden pink. Gardening Illustrated 49 (2522), 421. July 9, 1927.

51. Jekyll, G. 1930. Rose Zephyrine Drouhin. Gardening Illustrated 52 (2684), 541. August 16, 1930.

52. Jekyll, G. 1924. Borders round a house. Gardening Illustrated 46 (2343), 68. February 2, 1924 and, 1931 Hardy Vines on house walls. Gardening Illustrated 53(2734) p.481. (August 1, 1931)

53. Wood and Garden. op.cit p.146 & 147.

54. The Rhododendron 'Bianchi' was possibly raised by Maurice Young a well known nurseryman of Milford. It was from him that Miss Jekyll obtained her plants of this hybrid. According to Frederick Street, Rhododendron (Cassell, London 1965), Bianchi was an early form of Continental motor-car. He also notes that as late as 1950 'Bianchi' was the only true pink flowered Rhododendron he knew.

55. Jekyll, G. 1924. Rhododendrons. Gardening Illustrated 46 (2365), 400. July 5, 1924.

56. Colour in the Flower Garden op.cit. p.12.

57. Jekyll, F. 1934. op.cit. Foreword by Sir Edwin Lutyens. pp.7-9

58. Jekyll, G. 1924. A river of Daffodils. Gardening Illustrated 46 (2362), 363. June 14, 1924.

59. Colour for the Flower Garden (5th Edition) op.cit. p.7.

60. Jekyll, G. 1931. Native ferns in the garden – IV. Gardening Illustrated. 53 (2707), 61. January 24, 1931.

61. Wood & Garden. op.cit. p.95 & 142.

62. Frank Young notes of conversation with author.

63. Jekyll G. 1918. Hardy Azaleas. The Garden 82 (2458), 478. December 28, 1918. Notes on Azalea varieties can also be found in "Wall, Water and Woodland Gardening" 8th edition published in 1933.

In one of the notebooks at Godalming Museum (Envelope7) in a section entitled "Home - Azaleas and Heath Garden" are notes indicating how Miss Jekyll experimented with the plantings of azaleas. For example, "On right, opposite Cistus lusitanicus a soft orange, shift to Ferns by lilies & put in its place a pink"; "In front of the non-blooming occidentalis there is a small double rose colour A. it is on the right beyond Candlebury Gate. Clear a lot of R. lucida beyond this and behind Candlebury Gate"; "four azaleas of those ordered will be left for new clearing, probably not enough, the seedling ponticum from above might be added & more Daviesii. 9 were ordered from Ant. Warterer". The date of this description is not known but the other two entries in this notebook are 1899 and 1913 so this description may post-date 1913.

64. Jekyll, G. 1915. A young heath garden. Country Life 38 (978), 464. October 2, 1915. Further notes can be found, along with a sketch of planting detail in Wall, Water and Woodland Gardening. 8th edition published in 1933.

65. Lutyens Family Papers (LuE), Library of the Royal Institue of British Architects, London. LuE/20/4/3 (iii-). Letter from E.L.L. to Lady Emily Lutyens, 8 August 1933. In, Percy, C. & Ridley, J. 1985. op.cit. p.430.

66. Frank Young letter to author November 15, 1987. Frank Young (1907-1989) was born at 177 Brighton Road. He went to work for Sir Herbert Jekyll in 1925 and then moved to Miss Jekyll in 1926 or early 1927 after Authur Stacy had left following a row with Albert Zumbach. After Miss Jekyll died Lady Jekyll asked him to stay on but, as the future was uncertain, he left and worked for Colonel Bailey at Bowyers Court, Wisborough, Sussex. In 1949 he went to work for Mr J E Lowy at Husseys, Lower Foyle, Hampshire and remained there until Mr Lowy died in the early 1970s. I was introduced to Frank Young through the kindness of my friend Lady Clark in November 1986. The above information is by the courtesy of Mrs. V. Kenward, Frank Young's daughter.

67. Gertrude Jekyll: A Memoir. op.cit. p.121.

68. Frank Young letter to author November 15, 1987.

69. Frank Young notes of conversation with author.

70. Lutyens, Edwin 1934. Foreword. In, Jekyll, F. op.cit., pp.7-9.

Chapter 8
Michael Tooley

1. Earle, C.W. 1987. Pot-pourri from a Surrey garden. London, Smith Elder. p.250-1.

2. The Gardeners' Chronicle 23, 84 and 86, 17 January 1885.

3. It is known that Francis Jekyll continued to supply plants to Amy Barnes-Brand at Woodhouse Copse, Holmbury St. Mary, and subsequently at Burrows Farm, Shere. In 1937, he wrote to her, "as you are such an old and faithful customer of ours, I should like to supply you with what you ask for as far as possible, and I enclose a copy of the last edition of our catalogue". The last invoice for plants is dated 11 July 1941. Royal Horticultural Society, Lindley Library.

4. This nursery operated from 1929 until 1939, supplying plants to Vita Sackville-Wests's garden nearby at Sissinghurst. It was closed down at the outbreak of the Second World War but many of the plants were moved to the garden of West Lodge, Malton. Boyle, J. and Tooley, M. 1990. Charles Hervey Grey 1875-1955. The Northern Gardener 44(3), 14-15.

5. Jekyll, G. 1899. Wood and Garden. London, Longman. pp.192-3.
    Jekyll, G. 1908. Children and Gardens. London, Country Life. 1933 edition, p.63.

6. Alfred Savill and Sons. "Munstead Wood", Near Godalming, Surrey. Catalogue of Furniture Sale. Wednesday and Thursday 1st and 2nd September, 1948. 26pp. Lots 109, 192, 194, 195.
    Fiori, A. & Paoletti, G. 1896-1909 Flora analitica d'Italia. Padova.
    Fiori, A. & Paoletti, G. 1895-1904. Iconografia florae italicae, ossia flora italiana illustrata. Padova, Udine. Hegi, G. 1906. Illustrierte Flora von Mitel Europa, mit besonderer Berücksichtigung von Deutschland, Oesterreich und der Schweiz. München, J.F. Lehmann. 3 vols.

7. The Preservation of the Native Flora of Great Britain. The Gardeners' Chronicle 24, 51. 11 July 1885. The Times 31,491. 6 July 1885, p.7 col. b and p.9 cols d & e.

8. Editorial. The Gardeners' Chronicle 24, 48, 11 July 1885. The Times 31, 491. 6 July 1885. p.7 col. b.

9. The Garden 19 (489), 364, 2 April 1881: The Garden 19 (494), 485, 7 May 1881; The Garden 19 (496) 536, 21 May 1881.

10. The Gardeners' Chronicle 21, 154. 2 February 1884.

11. The Garden 21 (551), 414. 1882 10 June

12. Extracts from a collection of letters from Gertrude Jekyll to William Robinson. Quotation reproduced by kind permission of Mrs. Elizabeth Gilpin.

13. Jekyll, G. 1884. A handy tool for plant collection. The Garden 25 (641), 174. 1884 March 1.

14. Goldring, W. 1882. Munstead, Godalming. The Garden 22 (562), 191-193. 1882, August 26.

15. Anon. 1883. An autumn border at Munstead. The Garden 24 (618), 239. 1883, 22 September.
    J(ekyll), G. 1882. Colour in the flower garden. The Garden 22 (575), 470, 1882 November 25.

16. Noble, C. 1880. Lilium giganteum. The Gardeners' Chronicle 15, 22, 80, 85.

17. A.O. 1880. Lilium giganteum. The Gardeners' Chronicle 15, 148.

18. Jekyll, G. 1900. Wood and Garden. p.97.

19. Jekyll, G. 1889. Lilium giganteum. The Garden 35 (901), 165. 1889 February 23.

20. Dod, C.W. 1885. Plants in flower at Edge Hall. The Gardeners' Chronicle 24, 106. 1885, July 25.

21. Anon. 1884. Romneya coulteri. The Garden 26 (667) 400-401. 1884, November 8.

22. J(ekyll), G. 1886. Romneya coulteri. The Garden 29 (746), 207, 1886, March 6.

23. J(ekyll), G. 1885. Carpenteria california. The Garden 28 (713), 64. 1885 July 18.

24. Anon. 1887. Carpenteria california. The Garden. 31 (793), 100-101. 1887. January 29.

25. The Gardeners' Chronicle 3, 48-49. 1888, July 14. Journal of the Royal Horticultural Society 11. Extracts from the Proceedings xxvii. 1888, July 10.

26. See note 14. and Robinson, W. 1883. The English Flower Garden. London, John Murray. 1xix-1xx.

27. Letter from Miss Jekyll to Mr. Robinson 4 January 1883. Mrs. Elizabeth Gilpin.

28. Godalming Museum. Gertrude Jekyll's Account Books. Envelope 40. Miscellaneous notes from 1911 to 1928, including Notes on Recent Numbers, Late flowering roses, Plants in nursery, Garden notes Country Life 1923, and Lower nursery roses in nursery August 1928.

29. University of California, Berkeley, Reef Point Gardens Collection of Designs by Gertrude Jekyll. File No. X, Folder No. 224, Item No. 3.

30. Royal Horticultural Society. Lindley Library. Jekyll/Barnes-Brand correspondence. Letter 1. 20 September 1926; Letter 37, 29 March 1932.

31. Borough of Godalming. Minutes of the Proceedings of the Council and Reports of the various committees 1969-1970. 1969, July 7. Minute 204, pp. 130-131. "Mrs. Terence Turner, Priory Orchard, Station Approach, Godalming – A notebook and 2 small sketches belonging to Gertrude Jekyll to join the set of her notebooks which had been presented to the Museum at an earlier date".
    Mrs. J. Charman and I have read the Minutes of the Proceedings of the Council, and of the Library Committee and the General Purposes Committee from 1932 until 1969, but have been unable to find any reference to the set of notebooks referred to in the 1969 minute.
    The notebooks vary in size, but most measure about $4^{1}/_{2}$" x $7^{1}/_{4}$". The covers are limp maroon, blue or green card and the books comprise sheets with steel staples, and ruled as cashbooks.

32. There are six sources for the commissions upon which Miss Jekyll worked:
    1. Jekyll, F. 1934. Garden Plans. In, Jekyll, F. Gertrude Jekyll : a memoir. London, Jonathan Cape. 1938 Re-issue. pp.208-233. Index of Garden Plans. 241-245.
    2. Streatfield, D. n.d. Card Index arranged alphabetically by house name and owner's name and chronologically. University of California Berkeley, College of Environmental Design.
    3. Massingham, B. n.d. [Description of items in each folder, organised as the Reef Point Gardens Collection of Designs by Gertrude Jekyll at Bar Harbour, Maine].
    4. Tankard, J. n.d. [The Massingham Catalogue with 12 introductory pages listing the contents of the 17 reels of microfilms, and an alphabetical list of the commissions on microfilm]. From #1032 (File No. I. Folder No. 1) to #1258 (File No. X. Folder No. 226).
    5. Tankard, J. B. 1990. Annotated Catalog of Gertrude Jekyll's Six Photo Albums at the College of Environmental Design, University of California, Berkeley. vii+240.
    6. Godalming Museum, Godalming. 37 account books (Envelopes 3 to 39 and 41) and a book containing a list of Plans 1920-1929 (Envelope 2).

33. Godalming Museum. Miss G. Jekyll's Account Books. Envelope 27. Highmount 1909, 1910.

34. V.N. Gauntlett and Co. Ltd., Japanese Nurseries, Chiddingfold, Surrey [Catalogue] No. 97, 400pp. c. 1910. Godalming Museum, Godalming, Surrey.

35. Account book for Holy Island, 1910. 1911. Envelope 29. Miss Jekyll's Account Books. Godalming Museum, Godalming, Surrey. Account book for Durbins, 1911. Envelope. 29 Miss Jekyll's Account Books, Godalming Museum, Godalming, Surrey. Account book for Hatchlands, 1914. Envelope 21. Miss Jekyll's Account Books. Godalming Museum, Godalming, Surrey.

36. University of California, Berkeley. College of Environmental Design, Documents' Collection. File No. X, Folder 224. Miscellaneous Folder. Unnumbered item.

37. Jekyll, F. 1934. Gertrude Jekyll: a memoir. London, Jonathan Cape, p.187.

38. The Sanatorium was a personal project of King Edward VII. The foundation stone was laid on 3 November 1903 and the opening ceremony was on 14 June 1906. The building, setting and garden were remarkable. They were described by a reporter for The Times in the following way: the building was constructed of "dark red brick, relieved by dark blue lines and white stone facings: the roofs, which are steep pitched, are of red handmade tiles. This great red building rearing its head and stretching out its long arms on the slope of a hill against the green background of trees produces a curious effect, which is heightened by the brilliant green shutters attached to the ranges of the windows, making green

on red and red on green ....The whole place is embedded in woods, chiefly pine and oak, yet it is not at all shut in. The noble open prospect to the south gives all the sense of air, space and freedom that such a place should have. ....The gardens have been laid out by Miss Jekyll, with the fine art of simplicity: but as there is at present hardly a blade of grass in them the effect is not so agreeable as it ought to be, and it will be in time, no doubt." (The Times 38,045. 13 June 1906, p.6. col.d.). By 1909 the effectiveness of Miss Jekyll's plantings could be seen and were described in detail with eight photographs and a plan in an article in Country Life (Anon. 1909. Wall-gardening at the King's Sanatorium. Country Life. 26 (672), 701-704, 705).

39. Godalming Museum. Miss G. Jekyll's Account Books. Envelope 28.

40. Correspondence from Miss Jekyll to Mr. Atkinson, Clerk of Works. Quotations by kind permission of Mrs. K. Goatcher.

41. Her visit to the castle on Holy Island was from 11 to 22 May 1906, and has been described in Tooley, R and M. 1990. Lindisfarne Castle: the Garden. The National Trust. Whilst she was there Hercules Brabazon died and from Holy Island Castle she wrote, "Nobody has helped me more than Mr. Brabazon to understand and enjoy the beauty of colour and of many matters concerning the fine arts...." (Massingham, B. 1966, Miss Jekyll: portrait of a great gardener. London. Country Life. p.107).

42. The three sources for this list are:- a. note 32,1: b. note 32, 6; c. note 32, 4.

43. Hastings, M.A. and Tooley, M.J. 1984. Bibliography of Gertrude Jekyll's published works. In, M.J. Tooley (ed.) Gertrude Jekyll: artist, gardener, craftswoman. Witton-le-Wear, Michaelmas Books. pp.137-151.

44. King's College Library, Cambridge. Fry papers. Section XIV. Diaries and Memo Pads. Diaries 1909, 1910, 1911.

45. King's College Library, Cambridge. Fry papers. Section IV. Family correspondence 2 letters by Roger Fry to his father Sir Edward Fry. No. 803, 8 April 1908.

46. Plan and description from Mrs. Pamela Diamand (neé Fry) 21 July 1979. Frances Spedding reports that Miss Jekyll visited Durbins on several occasions and that the garden was divided into six levels by her, with a vegetable garden on the lowest level. p.116 in Spalding, F. 1980. Roger Fry: Art and Life. St. Albans, Granada Publishing. However, Denys Sutton describes four terraces. Sutton, D. 1972. Letters of Roger Fry. 2 volumes., p.31. London. Chatto & Windus.

47. Rose Sidgwick was a graduate of Somerville College, University of Oxford, and was appointed Lecturer in History at the University of Birmingham. She joined Margery Fry who was the First Warden of University House, Birmingham, a hostel for women undergraduates in the University. She died of influenza in New York in 1918 whilst a member of the British Universities Mission to the U.S.A. Jones, E.H. 1966. Margery Fry: the essential amateur. London. Oxford University Press.

48. Letter from Rose Sidgwick to Margery Fry. 26 June 1913. Mrs. Pamela Diamand.

49. Letter from Pamela Fry to Agnes Fry. 9 June 1917. Mrs. Pamela Diamand.

50. Godalming Museum. Miss G. Jekyll's Account Books. Envelope 25. Renishaw.

51. The plan for the Long or Green Alley is in Tooley, M. and R. 1982. The gardens of Gertrude Jekyll in Northern England. Witton-le-Wear, Michaelmas Books. p.17.

52. Sitwell, Osbert. 1948. Great Morning, being the third volume of Left-Hand, Right-Hand! An autobiography. London, Macmillan and Co. Ltd., pp. 59-60. Reproduced by kind permission of Mr. Frank Magro.

53. Godalming Museum. Miss G. Jekyll's Account Books. Envelope 24. Amersfort, Berkhamsted [pp.1-13]; Hydon Ridge [pp.28-35]

54. Jekyll, G. 1900. Home and Garden. London, Longmans, Green and Co. Preface, p.viii.

55. Royal Horticultural Society, Lindley Library. Jekyll/Barnes-Brand correspondence. On an envelope in the collection addressed to Mrs. Amy M. B. Barnes-Brand, Madgehole Farm, Shamley Green, Nr. Guildford, Surrey and date marked 28 January 1952. In Mrs. Barnes-Brand's hand written on the envelope, "Valuable keep with care. Letters from Miss Gertrude Jekyll. Letters to me."

56. Leslie, G.D. 1888. Our River: personal reminiscences of an artist's life on the River Thames. London, Bradbury, Agnew and Co. p.35.

Chapter 9
Michael Tooley

1. Prance, G.T. 1991. Rates of loss of biological diversity: a global view. In, I.F Spellerberg, F.B.Goldsmith and M.G.Morris (eds.) The scientific management of temperate communities for conservation. Oxford, Blackwell. pp.27-44.

2. Simmons, J. 1987. Is it too late? A personal view of conservation in botanic gardens. Professional Horticulture 1(1), 10-16.

3. Pattison, G.A. 1989. The National Council for the Conservation of Plants and Gardens. Professional Horticulture 3, 124-127.

4. Brickell, C. and Sharman, F. 1986. The vanishing garden : a conservation guide to garden plants. London, John Murray, in association with The Royal Horticultural Society.

5. Jekyll, G. 1928. Garden plants of seventy years ago. The New Flora and Silva 1(1), 4-8.

6. J(ekyll), G. 1884. Notes from Capri. The Garden 25(635), 33. 19 January 1884.

7. Royal Botanic Gardens, Kew. Inward Books 1878-1883 p.537. 1883, December 27. Entry 534.

8. Royal Botanic Gardens, Kew. Inward Books 1878-1883 p.500, 1883, August 11. Entry 352; p.512, 1883 September 24. Entry 412. Inward Books 1909-38 : Decorative Department 1917, December 1. p.100.

9. Jekyll, G. 1879 Wood and Garden. London, Longmans. p.193.

10. Jekyll, G. 1900. Home and Garden. London, Longmans. p.272.

11. Stafleu, F.A. and Cowan, R.S. 1979. Taxonomic literature: a selective guide to botanical publications and collections with dates, commentaries and types. 2 volumes. Utrecht, Bohn, Scheltema and Holkema. The Hague, Dr. W Junk b.v.

12. Jekyll, F. 1934. Gertrude Jekyll: a memoir. London. Jonathan Cape. p.145 and 147.

13. Royal Horticultural Society. Index to Journal and Proceedings 1838-1935 and List of Awards 1859-1935. [ed. F.J. Chittenden]. London, Royal Horticultural Society.

14. Anon. n.d. Some of the best hardy plants for border, shrubbery and rock garden grown by Miss Jekyll, Munstead Wood, Godalming. 15pp.

15. Antirrhinum 'My special strain' 1911 Letter from Miss Jekyll to Mr. Ernest de Taeye 9 March 1911. Renishaw Estate Office, Eckington. Jekyll, G. Colour schemes for the flower garden. London, Country Life. Seventh edition. pp. 57, 69 & 89. Jekyll, G. 1901. Wall and Water gardens. London, Country Life. p.33. Jekyll, G. 1888. A fine white snapdragon. The Garden 34 (880), 293. 29 September 1888. Jekyll, G. 1902. Nursery gardens: China Asters and Antirrhinums. The Garden 62 (1610), 218-9. 27 September 1902. Jekyll, G. 1918. Pink snapdragons. The Garden 82 (2412), 70. 9 February 1918.

16. Aquilegia "Munstead White". 1884 Anon. 1881. [The white single garden Columbine]. The Garden 19 (449), 589-590. 11 June 1881. Anon. 1884. A white columbine. The Garden 25 (653), 445. 24 May 1884.
W.B.H. 1887. Munstead white columbine. The Garden 31

(812), 526. 11 June 1887.

Tallack, J.C. 1890. Aquilegia: Munstead White. The Garden 37 (970), 573. 21 June 1890.

M. 1891. [White Aquilegias]. Journal of Horticulture and Cottage Gardener 23 (575), 6. 2 July 1891.

Barr & Sons. 1898. Barr's Seed Guide. London. p.38. no.439.

Irving, W. 1901. The Aquilegia Family. The Garden 59 (1529), 167-169.

Anon. 1914. Aquilegia Trial, 1914. Journal of the Royal Horticultural Society 40, 272-275.

Anon. 1928. Aquilegias tried at Wisley, 1927. Journal of the Royal Horticultural Society 53, 161-164. Tipping, H. Avray. 1933. The Garden of To-day. London, Martin Hopkinson. p.201.

17. Aster 'Peperharow' and Aster 'Munstead Purple'. 1882, 1916. Wolley Dod, C. 1882. Aster Archer Hind and Asters in general. Gardeners' Chronicle 18 758. 9 December 1882.

Jekyll, G. 1910. Michaelmas Daisies. Country Life 28 (722), 659-60. 5 November 1910.

Jekyll, G. 1914. Flower borders in September. In Colour Schemes for the flower garden. Seventh edition. London, Country Life pp.87-91.

18. Campanula persicifolia 'Chauderon'. 1883
Jekyll, G. 1883. Campanula persicifolia. The Garden 24 (617), 219. 15 September 1883.

Anon. 1883. An autumn border at Munstead. The Garden 24 (618), 239. 22 September 1883.

Anon. n.d. Some of the best hardy plants for border, shrubbery and rock garden grown by Miss Jekyll, Munstead Wood, Godalming. p.2

Beck, T. 1993. A house of great delight. In, Gertrude Jekyll 1843-1932: a celebration. London, Museum of Gardening History. pp.16-19.

Correvon, H. 1901. The Genus Campanula. The Garden 59 (1535), 276-7. 20 April 1901.

19. Cardamine pratensis flore-pleno 'Miss Jekyll' 1896
Wolley Dod, C. 1881. Double Ladies' Smock. The Gardeners' Chronicle 15, 638 14 May 1881. Jekyll, G. 1900. Home and Garden. London, Longmans 102-3. Photograph opposite p.103. Jekyll, G. 1901. Wall and Water Gardens. London, Country Life. p.35.

Jekyll, G. 1911. Bog gardens. Country Life 29 (751), 740-1.

Jekyll, G. 1923. Waterside planting. Country Life 53 (1377), 713.

Jekyll, G. 1928. Double Cuckoo Flower (Cardamine pratense fl. pl.) Gardening Illustrated 50 (2573), 408.

Proceedings of the Royal Horticultural Society 1896. p.lxxxii. Bound in with the Journal 20. 1896-7.

The Gardeners' Chronicle 19, 592. 1896.

The Garden 49 (1277), 352. 1896, May 9.

Tankard, Judith B. 1990. Annotated Catalog of Gertrude Jekyll's Six Photo-albums. Album Three 1886-1888. Photograph 688[missing] Double Cuckoo Flower.

20. Cheiranthus mutabilis (syn. semperflorens) 'Munstead' 1916
Jekyll, G. 1900. A garden of wall flowers. In, G. Jekyll. Home and Garden. London, Longmans. pp.32-38.

Jekyll, G. 1922. Wallflowers in the spring garden. The Garden 86 (2636), 246. 27 May 1922.

Jekyll, G. 1929. Old-fashioned flowers. In E. T. Ellis (ed.) Black's Gardening Dictionary. London, A. & C. Black Ltd. Second Edition, pp.692-696.

Barr and Sons. 1916. Barr's Hardy Perennials. London. p.8.

21. Chrysanthemum maximum 'Munstead'. 1898
Jekyll, G. 1920. Chrysanthemum maximum. The Garden 84 (2548), 467. Barr & Son. 1898. Barr's Hardy Perennials and Alpines. p.14.

Correspondence between Miss Jekyll and Lady Ridley, Blagdon, 17 & 23 October 1929. See also, Tooley, M. and R. 1982. The gardens of Gertrude Jekyll in Northern England.

Witton-le-Wear, Michaelmas Books, Blagdon, pp. 28-40.

22. Digitalis 'Munstead White'. 1887
Jekyll, G. 1887. White foxgloves. The Garden 32 (820), 103. 6 August 1887.

Jekyll, G. 1899. Wood and Garden. London, Longmans. opp. p.150 and p.270.

Jekyll, G. 1914. Colour Schemes for the Flower Garden. London, Country Life. p.43 & p.46.

Jekyll, G. 1918. White Foxgloves. The Garden 82 (2443), 346-7.

Jekyll, G. 1919. White Foxgloves. The Garden 83 (2467), 92.

Jekyll, G. 1920. White Foxgloves. The Garden 84 (2539), 361.

Jekyll, G. 1927. Foxglove Munstead White. Gardening Illustrated 49, (2525), 469.

Jekyll, G. 1932. White Foxgloves in woodland. Gardening Illustrated 54 (2757), 20.

Jekyll, G. 1932. White Foxgloves. Gardening Illustrated 54 (2794), 582.

23. Helianthus 'Munstead Primrose'. 1898.
Jekyll, G. 1924. Some problems of the flower border. Gardening Illustrated 16 August 1924.

Barr and Sons Ltd. 1898. Barr's Seed Guide. London.

Barr and Sons Ltd. 1899. Barr's Seed Guide. London, p.56. No 1096.

24. Helleborus orientalis 'Gertrude Jekyll'. 1884
Jekyll, G. 1923. Lent Hellebores. Country Life 10 March 1923.

Barr and Son Ltd. 1884. Descriptive autumn catalogue of bulbs and plants for all seasons. London. p.35. No. 1512.

Barr and Son Ltd. 1888. Barr's Daffodils. London. p.26.

Barr and Sons. 1916. Barr's Hardy Border Perennials. London. p.12.

25. Lavandula spica 'Munstead'. 1916.
Jekyll, G. 1900. Plants for poor soils. In, G. Jekyll Home and Garden. London, Longmans, pp.184, 185-7.

Jekyll, G. 1914. [A dwarf kind of Lavender]. The flower border in July. In G. Jekyll. Colour schemes for the flower garden. London. Country Life. Seventh edition. pp.66-7.

Jekyll, G. 1926. Dwarf lavender. Gardening Illustrated 48 (2480), 569.

Journal of the Royal Horticultural Society 42. 1916-17. Proceedings clxviii Floral Committee 18 July 1916.

Journal of the Royal Horticultural Society 87 136. 1962.

Journal of the Royal Horticultural Society 89 1964. Extracts of Proceedings 53.

Barr and Sons. 1916. Barr's Hardy Perennials. London, p.2.

26. Lunaria annua 'Munstead Purple'.
Jekyll, G. 1908. Children and Gardens, London, Country Life.

Jekyll, G. 1924. Some desirable annuals. The Garden 88 (2724), 58-9.

Carters 1933. The Blue Book of Gardening. Catalogue 1933. p.115. No. 7541.

Journal of the Royal Horticultural Society 41 1915. Extracts of Proceedings cxvii

27. Lupinus polyphyllus 'Munstead Blue' and 'Munstead White'. 1929
Jekyll, G. 1929. Lupin Munstead strain. Gardening Illustrated 51 (2627), 477.

Jekyll, G. and Weaver, L. 1912. Gardens for Small Country Houses. London Country Life.

Jenkins, E. H. 1913. The Hardy Flower Book. London, Country Life.

Falkner, H. n.d. [Munstead Wood]. In, B. Massingham Gertrude Jekyll: portrait of a great gardener. London, Country Life. pp.68-9.

W. H. Simpson & Sons. 1930. Autumn Catalogue. Birmingham. p.20.

W. H. Simpson & Sons. 1938. General Catalogue. Birmingham. p.56.

Anon. 1931. Perennial Lupins tried at Wisley, 1929-1930. Journal of the Royal Horticultural Society 56, 115-120.

28. Narcissus 'Gertrude Jekyll' 1882.

Burbidge, F. W. 1882. New daffodils. The Gardeners' Chronicle 17, 472. 8 April 1882.

Burbidge, F. W. 1883. A new daffodil (Gertrude Jekyll). The Garden 23 (582) 31.

Burbidge, F. W. & Barr, P. 1884. Ye Narcissus or Daffodyl Flowre, and hys Roots, with hys historie and culture, ec, ec. London, Peter Barr & Son.

Moore, T. & Barr, P. 1884. Nomenclature of Narcissus. The Gardeners' Chronicle 21, 607-8.

Tooley, M. J. 1984. [Narcissus Gertrude Jekyll]. In, Tooley, M. J. (ed.). Gertrude Jekyll: artist, gardener, craftswoman. Witton-le-Wear, Michaelmas Books. p.158.

29. Nigella 'Miss Jekyll'. 1900.

Jekyll, G. 1900. Wood and Garden. London, Longmans. p.251.

Jekyll, G. 1908. Children and Gardens. London, Country Life. 1933 edition, p. 41 and opposite pp.42 & 43.

R. D. 1884. Nigella damascena. The Gardeners' Chronicle 22, 248. 23 August 1884.

Journal of the Royal Horticultural Society 36, 1910, p.202 & 706.

Tipping, H. Avray. 1933. The Garden of Today. London, Martin Hopkinson. p. 109.

Carters. 1933. The Blue Book of Gardening. 1933 Catalogue. London. p.130, catalogue nos. 7731, 7732 and 7733. Photograph of 'Miss Jekyll, Blue'.

30. Paeonia decora 'Gertrude Jekyll'. 1898

Jekyll, G. 1900. May – The Paeony Garden. In, Wood and Garden. London, Longmans, pp.72-76.

Stern, F. C. 1946. A study of the genus Paeonia. London, The Royal Horticultural Society 37. Paeonia peregrina. pp.97-98.

Barr and Sons. 1898. Barr's Hardy Perennials and Alpines. London. p.48.

Barr and Sons. 1899. Barr's Seed Guide 1899. London, Barr & Son. p.66.

31. Papaver nudicaule 'Munstead Poppies' and 'Munstead White'. 1884.

Anon. 1882. [Papaver alpinum]. The Garden 21 (552), 417. 17 June 1882.

Anon. 1884. Iceland Poppies. The Garden 26 (659), 13. 5 July 1882.

G. 1884. The Iceland Poppy (Papaver nudicaule) Plate 464. Drawn at Munstead July 20. The Garden 26 (676), 380-381. 1 November 1884.

Jekyll, G. 1924. Poppies. Country Life 56 (1439), 174-5. 2 August 1924.

Robinson, W. 1883. Two mountain flowers (Papaver alpinum and Anthemis aizoon). Plate 410. The Garden 24 (622), 342-3. 20 October 1883.

Hartland, W. B. 1887. Iceland Poppy: Munstead White. The Garden 31 (812), 527. 11 June 1887.

W. 1887. White iceland poppy. The Garden 31 (812), 526. 11 June 1887.

Barr and Son, formerly Barr and Sugden 1884. Descriptive spring catalogue of choice seeds for flower and kitchen garden. London. p.33, No. 2010.

Barr and Sons. 1899. Barr's Seed Guide. London. p.67, No. 1450.

32. Papaver somniferum 'Munstead Cream Pink'. 1917

Jekyll, G. 1924. Poppies. Country Life 56 (1439), 174-5. 2 August 1924.

Jekyll, G. 1932. Cream pink poppy. Gardening Illustrated 54 (2791), 537.

Anon. 1918-1919. Annual Poppies at Wisley, 1917. Journal of the Royal Horticultural Society 43, 485.

Anon. 1928. Annual Poppies at Wisley, 1927. Journal of the Royal Horticultural Society 53, 335.

Wilks, W. 1889. The Shirley Poppy: its history. The Gardeners' Chronicle 5, 308, 309.

Carters. 1933. The Blue Book of Gardening. 1933 Catalogue. London. p.149. Catalogue no. 8196.

33. Primula cortusoides Jekyllae 1885

H. W. W. 1881. Primula cortusoides. The Gardeners' Chronicle 15, 150-1. 1881, 29 January 1881.

D(ewar), D. 1885. A new Primula (P. cortusoides Jekyllae). The Garden 28, 266. 12 September 1885.

Dewar, D. 1886. Synonymic List of the Species and forms of the Genus Primula. Journal of the Royal Horticultural Society 7, 275-295. p.278.

34. Primula 'Munstead Bunch' 1886 and 'Munstead White'. 1890

A. D. 1885. Yellow Primroses. The Garden 28 (725), 374-5. Plate 513. 10 October 1885

A. D. 1891. Single white primroses. The Garden 39 (1015), 419.

A. D. 1898. Hardy Primroses. The Garden 54, 142-3. Plate 1184.

Anon. 1881. [Primroses]. The Garden 19 (495), 489. 14 May, 1881.

Anon. 1885. [Royal Horticultural Society 14 April 1885]. The Gardeners' Chronicle 23, 514.

Anon. 1886. The Primula and Auricula Show. April 20 and 21. The Garden 29 (753), 383. 24 April 1886.

Anon. 1891. Floral Committee. Extracts from the Proceedings of the Royal Horticultural Society. xlvi. In, Journal of the Royal Horticultural Society 13, 1891.

Anon. 1892. A useful white primrose. The Garden 41 (1063), 297. 2 April, 1892. Engraving of Primrose Munstead White.

Anon. 1901. Bunch Primrose Sultan. The Garden 59 (1541), 395. 1 June, 1901. Illustration by H. G. Moon.

Anon. 1901. New and Rare Plants. The Garden 59 (1539), 362. 18 May, 1901.

Arnott, S. 1891. Hardy flower notes. Journal of Horticulture and Cottage Gardener 22 (566), 337-8. 30 April, 1891.

Arnott, S. 1899. Primrose Munstead Early White. The Garden 55 (1423) 124. 25 February 1899.

Jekyll, G. 1890. A useful white Primrose. The Garden 37 (964), 448.

Jekyll, G. 1899. The Primrose Garden. In, G. Jekyll. Wood and Garden. London, Longmans. pp.216-220.

Jekyll, G. 1903. The Bunch Primroses. Country Life 13 (330), 574.

Jekyll, G. 1923. Munstead Bunch Primroses. The Garden 87 (2688), 256-7.

Jekyll, G. 1923. Bunch Primroses. Country Life 54 (1395), 418-9.

Jekyll, G. n.d. In a primrose wood. In, F. Jekyll and G. C. Taylor (eds). 1937. A Gardener's Testament. London, Country Life. 1982 edition, Woodbridge, Antique Collectors Club, pp.321–322.

Sinclair, J. & S. 1985. Primrose Seeds by Barnhaven. Catalogue 8/85. Brigsteer, Cumbria. 38pp.

Carters. 1933. The Blue Book of Gardening. Catalogue 1933. London. p.159. Catalogue no. 8162.

35. Pulmonaria angustifolia azurea 'Munstead Blue'. 1919

Chittenden, F. J. 1936. The Award of Garden Merit. 198 Pulmonaria azurea AGM August 8 1926. Journal of the Royal Horticultural Society 61, 255-6.

Jekyll, G 1919. Pulmonaria azurea. The Garden 83 (2482), 274.

Thomas, G. S. 1966. The Modern Florilegium. Windlesham, Sunningdale Nurseries p.47.

Vaughan, M. 1935. Spring Notes from a woodland garden. My Garden 4 (15) 373-377.

36. Rose 'Gertrude Jekyll'. 1986
Austin, D. 1988. The Heritage of the Rose. Woodbridge, Antique Collectors' Club. Revised 1990. p.192.

37. Sedum telephium 'Munstead Red'. 1916
Jekyll, G. 1914. Bedding plants. In, G. Jekyll, Colour Schemes for the Flower Garden. London, Country Life. Seventh edition. pp.83-5.
Praeger, R. Lloyd. 1920-1921. An account of the Genus Sedum as found in cultivation. Journal of the Royal Horticultural Society 46, 1-314.
Chittenden, F. J. (ed.) 1951. The Royal Horticultural Society Dictionary of Gardening. Oxford, Clarendon Press.

38. Vinca minor 'Gertrude Jekyll'. 1885
Anon. 1881. Vinca acutiloba – white periwinkle. The Garden 20, December 17 1881.
Jekyll, G. 1885. The lesser periwinkles. The Garden 28 (701), 359. 25 April, 1885.
Jekyll, G. 1900. Home and Garden London, Longmans. p.33.

39. Viola 'Jackanapes'. 1888
Anon. 1898-9. Report on Violas at Chiswick, 1898. Journal of the Royal Horticultural Society 22, 375.
Anon. 1899-1900. Floral Committee 11 July 1899. Proceedings of the Royal Horticultural Society. In Journal of the Royal Horticultural Society 23, p.cxxxi.
Anon. 1913. Violas at Wisley, 1913. Journal of the Royal Horticultural Society 39, 387.
Anon. 1922. Violas at Wisley, 1922. Journal of the Royal Horticultural Society 48, 128 & 129.
Brickell, C. and Sharman, F. 1986. The Vanishing Garden: a conservation guide to garden plants. London, John Murray and The Royal Horticultural Society. p.12 & 227. Plate 77.

40. Tooley, M. J. 1994. Lost legacies. Plants improved and bred by Miss Jekyll. The Horticulturalist: Journal of the Institute of Horticulture 3 (3), 9-12.

Chapter 10
Richard Bisgrove

1. Jekyll, G. 1899. Wood and Garden. London, Longmans, Green, p.219.

2. Hussey, C. 1953. The Life of Sir Edwin Lutyens. London, Country Life.

3. Copyright has since been reinstated in accordance with European Union legislation, and Miss Jekyll's publications are back in copyright until AD2003.

4. See, for example, Massingham, Betty. 1966. Gertrude Jekyll: portrait of a great gardener. London, Country Life.

5. Wood and Garden, p.192.

6. Ibid., p.104-5.

7. Ibid., p.14.

8. Ibid., p.120.

9. Ibid., p.251.

10. Ibid., p.216.

11. Ibid., p.89-90.

12. Jekyll, G. 1901. Home and Garden. London, Longmans, Green, p.271-3.

13. Wood and Garden, p.13.

14. Ibid., p.52-3.

15. Ibid., p.85.

16. Ibid., p.137.

17. Ibid., p.139.

18. Home and Garden, p.128-135.

19. Wood and Garden, p.17.

20. Ibid., p.97. A longer and amusing account of the lily planting, used to reprimand a visitor who attributed the success of the lilies to luck, occurs on pp.142-3.

21. See, for example, Home and Garden, p. 3 and Chapter XXII "Things Worth Doing".

22. Wood and Garden, p.81-2.

23. Home and Garden, p.278.

24. Ibid., p.25.

25. Wood and Garden, p.4.

26. Home and Garden, p 26-7.

27. Wood and Garden, p.46-7.

28. Ibid., p.21-2.

29. Ibid., p.26-31.

30. Ibid., p.8-9.

31. Ibid., p.7.

32. Ibid., p.5-6

33. The Reef Point collection of Miss Jekyll's Drawings includes over 2,000 plans for some 250 gardens. 50 plans are published and analysed for their plant associations in Bisgove, R. Gardens of Gertrude Jekyll (Frances Lincoln 1992)

34. Jekyll, G. 1925. Colour Schemes for the Flower Garden. 6th edn. London, Country Life, p.4.

35. Home and Garden, p.75-6.

36. Colour Schemes, p.110.

37. Wood and Garden, p.51.

38. Ibid., p.109.

39. Ibid., p.56

40. Ibid., p.56-7.

41. Ibid., p.57.

42. See Hermann, L. Turner Phaideon 1986 pl.133. Original in the Cleveland Museum of Art, Ohio (J. Tankard personal communication)

43. Ibid., p.129.

44. Ibid., p.52.

45. Ibid., p.95.

46. Ibid., p.113.

47. Ibid., p.220.

48. Home and Garden, p.17.

49. Ibid., p.18-20.

50. Wood and Garden, p.28.

51. Ibid., p.154-6.

52. Ibid., p.158-60.

53. Ibid., p.171.

54. Ibid., p.157.

55. Home and Garden, p.58.

56. Wood and Garden, p.60.

57. Colour Schemes, p.18.

58. Simonds, J. O. 1961. Landscape architecture. The shaping of man's natural environment. London, Iliffe Books.

59. Home and Garden, p.141-2.

60. Wood and Garden, p.185-7.

61. Colour Schemes, p.134-5 and facing illustration.

Chapter 11
Heather Angel

1. Jekyll, G. 1901. Home and Garden. London. Longmans, Green & Co., pp.24-25.

2. Ibid., p. 278.

3. Lutyens, Sir Edwin. 1934. Foreword in Gertrude Jekyll: A Memoir by Francis Jekyll. London. Jonathan Cape. p.9.

4. Jekyll, Gertrude. 1908. Children and Gardens. London. Country Life and George Newnes Ltd., p.50.

5. Tankard, Judith B. and Michael R. Van Valkenburgh. 1988. Gertrude Jekyll: A Vision of Garden and Wood. London. John Murray. p.148.
The photograph albums were part of a bequest made by Beatrix Farrand to the University of California, Berkeley in

1955, and are part of the Reef Point Collection.

6. Ibid. p.5-6.

7. Tankard, Judith B. 1990. Annotated Catalog of Gertrude Jekyll's six photo-albums at College of Environmental Design Documents Collection, University of California, Berkeley.

8. Tankard, Judith B. and Van Valkenburgh, Michael R. 1988. op. cit. p.148

9. Jekyll, Francis. 1934. Gertrude Jekyll: A Memoir. London. Jonathan Cape, p115-6

10. Julia Margaret Cameron (née Pattle) was famous for her portrait photographs and her 'volcanic energy and extravagent generosity.' She made photographic portraits of Charles Darwin, Robert Browning, Alfred Lord Tennyson (1809-1892) and the Queen's pianist Jacques Blumenthal (1829-1908). Of the latter, Lady Emily Tennyson wrote on 25 April 1867, "Mrs Cameron has made some magnificent photographs, clear and smooth, as well as picturesque. Ally (Alfred Tennyson, the Poet Laureate) says no Titian is so fine as that of Blumenthal. He is a little man, and as usual with her little men, comes out a grand one." This was written from farringford, the Tennysons' house on the Isle of Wight. An adjoining property, 'The Briary', had been bought by G.F. Watts and Mr. and Mrs., Henry Prinsep, who were related to the Jekylls. Mrs. Prinsep was Sarah Monckton Pattle and Julia's sister. Another visitor to the Tennysons' summer home at Farringford was James Henry Mangles, who grew and bred Rhododendrons at Valewood in the River Wey Valley about a mile from the Tennysons' summer house at Aldworth. It was at Harry Mangles' home that Edwin Lutyens first met Gertrude Jekyll.
    Knies, E.A. (ed.) 1984. Tennyson at Aldworth: the diary of James Henry Mangles, Athens, Ohio. Ohio University Press.
    Hoge , James O. 1981. Lady Tennysons' Journal, Charlottesville, University Press of Virginia.

11. Schaaf, Larry J. (text). 1985. Sun Gardens: Victorian Photograms by Anna Atkins. New York. Aperture. 104 pp.

12. Ibid. p.8.

13. Talbot, W.H. Fox. 1844. The Pencil of Nature. London. Longman Brown, Green and Longmans.

14. Tankard, Judith B. 1990. op. cit.

15. "Flower-Spray of Carpenteria Californica.... from a photograph taken at Munstead in June," by G.J., West Surrey, The Garden, Vol. 28 (18 July 1885), p.64.

16. Garden Competition, The Garden, Vol. 28 (17 October 1885). p.395

17. Lutyens, Sir Edwin. 1934. op. cit.

18. Jekyll, Gertrude, 1908. op. cit. Between pp. 100-101

19. Personal communication, Michael Pritchard, FRPS

20. Jekyll, G. 1899. 3rd edition. Wood and Garden. London, Longmans Green & Co., preface, p.v.

21. Ibid., preface, p.v.

22. Ibid., opposite p.27. The snowstorm of December 26 and 27 was quite exceptional, and has been described by Baldwin Latham of Croydon. The snow began to fall at 6.00 pm on 26 December and ceased at 4.20 am on 27 December. The average snow depth was 15 inches. The snow was wet, dense and heavy and was "driven by a fierce easterly gale, so that it adhered very tenaciously to all objects with which it came in contact." He continued, "Great destruction of trees and evergreens has occurred in my garden and in the neighbourhood owing to the combined force of the gale and the weight of the snow." In, Symons's Monthly Meteorological Magazine 21 (252), 173-4. 1886.

23. Ibid., p.28.

24. Salmon, C.E. 1931. The Flora of Surrey. London. G. Bell & Sons Ltd. p.653

25. Jekyll, Gertrude. 1899. op. cit., opposite p.40.

26. Ibid., opposite p.61.

27. Ibid., opposite p.55 below.

28. Tankard, Judith B. and Michael R. Van Valkenburgh. 1988. Gertrude Jekyll: A Vision of Garden and Wood. London. John Murray. Plate 51, p.95.

29. Jekyll, Gertrude. 1908. op. cit., opposite p.98.

30. Ibid., between pp.98-99.

31. Ibid., opposite p.91. Dorothea Strachey was Lytton Strachey's sister, and married Simon Bussy in 1903.

32. Ibid., opposite p.105.

33. Personal communication, Kate Rouse, Assistant Curator, The Royal Photographic Society.

34. Jekyll, Gertrude. 1899. op. cit. p.100.

35. Tankard, Judith B. and Van Valkenburgh, Michael R. 1988. op.cit. Plate 16, p.59.

36. Jekyll, G. 1904. Old West Surrey – Some Notes and Memoirs. London, Longman Green & Co. pp.320.

37. Tankard, Judith B. and Michael R. Van Valkenburgh. 1988. Gertrude Jekyll: A Vision of Garden and Wood. London. John Murray. Plate 59, p.104.

38. Ibid., p.5.

39. Jekyll, G., Wall, Water and Woodland Gardens. London, Country Life, preface. p.vi

40. Angel, Heather, 1988. Photography as a tool in garden design. The Photographic Journal. September 1988.

41. Gertrude Jekyll used photographs for the following garden commissions, amongst others: Chart Cottage (1911), Fairhill (1911), Warren Hurst (1913), Little Aston (1914), Holywell Court (1918), Marks Dane (1919), Tunworth Down (1919), Girton College (1920), Chownes Mead (1920), Oaklands (1921), Drayton Wood (1921), Watlington Park (1922), South African War Memorial (1923), The Old Lighthouse (1923), Burnt Axon (1925), Greenwich, Conn. USA (1924), Old Glebe House, USA (1926), Stonepitts (1926), Ickwell House (1926), Plumpton Place (1928), The Court, St. Fagans (1928), Blagdon (1928).

42. Jekyll, G., Wall, Water and Woodland Gardens. London, Country Life, preface. p.vii.

43. Tooley, Michael and Rosanna. 1982. The gardens of Gertrude Jekyll in Northern England. Witton-le-Wear, Michaelmas Books, p.28.

44. I am indebted to Lord Ridley for kindly allowing me access to the album containing his mother's photographs and the correspondence between his mother and Gertrude Jekyll. See also, Fleming, Laurence and Gore, Alan. 1979. The English Garden London, Michael Joseph. pp. 223, 224, 225.

45. Tooley, Michael and Rosanna. 1982. op. cit. p.34.

46. Amery, Colin. Colourful Miss Jekyll, in Country Life, 17 May 1984. pp. 1378-9.
    Two of the autochromes of the Iris and Lupine Garden, heavily retouched, were published as frontispieces in Gardens for Small Country Houses by Gertrude Jekyll and Lawrence Weaver, and in The Hardy Flower Book by E. H. Jenkins. The latter was published in 1913, and it is possible that the autochromes were taken by one of the photographers at Country Life in the summer of 1911.

47. Jekyll, Gertrude. 1899. op. cit. Opposite p.27.

48. Jekyll, Gertrude. 1908. op. cit. Opposite p.105.

Chapter 12

Susan Schnare and Rudy J. Favretti

1. Gertrude Jekyll was fortunate in her first publisher, Longmans; Wood and Garden and Home and Garden were published simultaneously in London and New York in 1899 and 1900. All the books she wrote for Country Life were published by Charles Scribner's Sons in New York.

2. King, Mrs Francis. 1925. Chronicles of the Garden. New York. p.39.

3. op. cit., pp.98–9.

4. Lawrence, Elizabeth, 1964, Introduction in Jekyll, Gertrude. On Gardening. New York. p.17.

5. Jekyll, Francis. 1934. Gertrude Jekyll: A Memoir. Northampton, Mass. pp.223, 230,232.

6. In 1910 or 1911, Gertrude Jekyll wrote a preface for Wilhelm Miller's book, the Charm of English Gardens in which she expressed the opinion that, "it would seem most fitting that a national style of gardening for America should develop on 'Colonial' lines. The old homes of the eighteenth century are full of dignity and simple charm, because the taste of the time was singularly pure and sincere, moving in one direction only, that of a temperate and subdued classicity." Miller, Wilhelm 1911. The Charm of English Gardens. London, Hodder and Stoughton.
Wilhelm Miller was an author and horticulturalist, who edited the fourth edition in 1906 of the Cyclopedia of American Horticulture jointly with Liberty Hyde Bailey.

7. Betty Massingham, personal letter, 12 November 1979.

8. Ibid.

9. Gertrude Jekyll was very aware of these problems. "A true enthusiasm for horticulture is rapidly growing among Americans. Those who have travelled.... seek to beautify their homes by means of one of the forms or ways that they have seen in Italy and England.... They are willing to spend lavishly, but in their haste they think to acclimatize by means of direct imitation, whereas it were wiser first to observe closely, to assimilate at leisure and then to reproduce the spirit of what has been seen and desired by methods better suited to home conditions. An English garden, and, still less, and Italian garden, cannot be exactly imitated in the greater part of the vast area of the United States. ....having studied what is best in the older gardens and seen how the best effects come of unaffected restraint and use of simple means, the wise way will be to find and use the best of the native equivalent plants and not to use too many in any one composition." In, Miller, W.1911. op.cit.

10. Massingham, Betty. 1966. Miss Jekyll. London. Country Life. p.70.

11. Ibid., p.135.

12. Page, Russell. 1962. The Education of a Gardener. London. William Collins. p.93.

13. Mrs Grace Groesbeck to Miss Gertrude Jekyll, 6 December (1914), File 5, Folder 120, Documents Collection, College of Environmental Design, University of California, Berkeley.

14. Mr George Davis, interview held in Perintown, Ohio, November 1980.

15. Betteman, Iphigene. 1960. 'Elmhurst', Historical and Philosophical Society of Ohio Bulletin. pp.201–17.

16. Mr John W. Warrington, personal letter, 5 March 1980.

17. 'Centennial History of Cincinnati', from the Files of the Cincinnati Post.

18. Will of Grace Groesbeck, Clermont County Probate Court, Batavia, Ohio.

19. 'Mrs Groesbeck Rites', Clermont (County, Ohio) Sun, 1957.

20. Mr George Davis.

21. Mrs Adams, interview held in Ohio, November 1980.

22. Mr Edward Hudson to Miss Gertrude Jekyll, 25 July 1924, File 9, Folder 191, Documents Collection, College of Environmental Design, University of California, Berkeley.

23. Mrs Stanley Resor, interview held February 1980.

24. Notes and Plans, File 9, Folder 191, Documents Collection, College of Environmental Design, University of California, Berkeley.

25. Mrs Helen Resor to Miss Gertrude Jekyll, 3 September 1924, File 9, Folder 191, Documents Collection, College of Environmental Design, University of California, Berkeley.

26. Miss Gertrude Jekyll to Mrs Helen Resor, 28 September 1925, File 9, Folder 191, Documents Collection, College of Environmental Design, University of California, Berkeley.

27. Ibid.

28. Ibid.

29. Miss Gertrude Jekyll to Mrs Helen Resor, 15 September 1924, File 9, Folder 191, Documents Collection, College of Environmental Design, University of California, Berkeley.

30. Mrs Edward Duble, personal letter, 18 April 1980.

31. Mrs Edward Duble, personal letter, 29 February 1980.

32. Mrs Margaret O. Holt, personal letter, 17 February 1980.

33. Mr George Yarwood, personal letter, 14 January 1980.

34. Mrs Edward Duble, personal letter, 29 February 1980.

35. Crews, Richard E. 1978. The Glebe House. p.15.

36. Ibid.

37. Mary Baker, interview held November 1979, Woodbury, Connecticut.

38. John H. Grant, 'Annie Burr Jennings: A Tribute', In Memoriam.

39. 'Text of Miss Annie Burr Jennings' Will, Filed for Probate', Bridgeport (Connecticut) Post, I August 1939.

40. Farrington, E. I. (ed.). 1938. Gardener's Travel Book. Boston, Massachusetts Horticultural Society.

41. Miss Annie Burr Jennings to Miss Gertrude Jekyll, 8 November 1926, File 9, Folder 196, Documents Collection, College of Environmental Design, University of California, Berkeley.

42. Mrs Margaret. Holt, personal letter, 17 February 1980.

43. Seabury Society, Minutes of Meetings of the Glebe House Committee, Meeting of 28 June 1927.

44. Miss Gertrude Jekyll to Miss Annie Burr Jennings, 6 December 1926, File 9, Folder 196, Documents Collection, College of Environmental Design, University of California, Berkeley.

45. Eleanor Tyrrell to Miss Gertrude Jekyll, 25 March 1927, File 9, Folder 196, Documents Collection, College of Environmental Design, University of California, Berkeley.

46. Seabury Society, Minutes.

47. Ibid.

47. Jekyll, Francis. 1934. op. cit. pp.I69–70.

49. Miss Gertrude Jekyll to Annie Burr Jennings, 5 May 1927, File 9, Folder 196, Documents Collection, College of Environmental Design, University of California, Berkeley.

50. Miss Gertrude Jekyll to Miss Annie Burr Jennings, 6 December 1926, File 9, Folder 196, Documents Collection, College of Environmental Design, University of California, Berkeley.

Chapter 13
June Swann

1. Jekyll, G. 1900. The Workshop. p.108-121, in G. Jekyll, Home and Garden. London, Longmans, Green & Co. p. 109.

2. A sample of the mud taken in 1982 by M.J. Tooley, was examined for its pollen and spore content by Mrs. J. Huntley, who recorded the following taxa: Betula (birch), Alnus (alder), Corylus (hazel), Compositae subfamily Tubuliflorae (includes daisies), Gramineae (grass), moss spores and fungal spores.

3. Jekyll, G. 1900. Life in the Hut. p 289-296, in G. Jekyll, Home and Garden. London, Longmans, Green & Co. p293.

4. Steen, M. 1943. William Nicholson, London, Collins. p.140

5. The Tate Gallery, London. Catalogue Documentation, 5548. Miss Jekyll's Gardening Boots. Inscr. "Nicholson 1920" b.l. and 'For E.L. . . . W.N.' t.r.. Oil on plywood, 12¼" x 15¾" (32.5cm x 40cm), including red painted border approximately ¼" (0.75cm) wide.

6. Letter from W. Nicholson to Lady Jekyll. Quoted in Jekyll, F. 1934. Gertrude Jekyll, a memoir. London, Jonathan Cape.

pp.188-9.

7. Lutyens, M. 1980. Edwin Lutyens. London, John Murray. p.26.

8. See also discussion in Tooley, M.J. 1984. A record of the Gertrude Jekyll Exhibition [December 1982] p.111-132, in Tooley, M.J. ed. Gertrude Jekyll: artist, gardener, craftswoman. Witton-le-Wear, Michaelmas Books. pp.129-30.

9. In a letter to William Robinson dated 5 February 1883 Miss Jekyll wrote, "Your French boots have come and I send them up today – marking the parcel Boots outside for fear your people in your possible absence might think they were Flowers Perishable and put them in water – though they would stand it better than some other kind – Don't be frightened at their new pale complexion - a few greasings and wettings will cure that. I hope they will be right though I see the heels are a good $\frac{1}{8}$" higher than you ordered – the pattern shoe and a box of grease are enclosed with them." Reproduced by permission of Mrs. Elizabeth Gilpin.

Index

PLANT INDEX
Illustrations shown in **Bold Type**